THE POLITICS OF REVENGE

SADDAM HUSSEIN

The Politics of Revenge

SAÏD K. ABURISH

BLOOMSBURY

First published 2000
This paperback edition published 2001

Copyright © 2000 by Saïd K. Aburish

The moral right of the author has been asserted

Picture Credits

Gamma; page 1 *bottom*, 2 *bottom*
Popperfoto: page 5 *top*, 6 *bottom*, 8 *bottom*
Sygma: page 3 *bottom*, 4 *top*, 5 *bottom*, 6 *top*, 7 *top & bottom*
Topham Picturepoint: page 2 *top*, 3 *top*, 4 *bottom*

Every reasonable effort has been made to ascertain and acknowledge the
ownership of copyrighted photographs and illustrations included in this volume.
Any errors that have inadvertently occurred will be corrected in subsequent
editions provided notification is sent to the publisher.

Bloomsbury Publishing Plc, 38 Soho Square, London W1V 5DF

A CIP catalogue record for this book is available from the British Library

ISBN 0 7475 4903 6

10 9 8 7 6 5 4 3 2

Typeset by Hewer Text Ltd, Edinburgh
Printed in Great Britain by Clays Ltd, St Ives Plc

CONTENTS

THE MIDDLE EAST

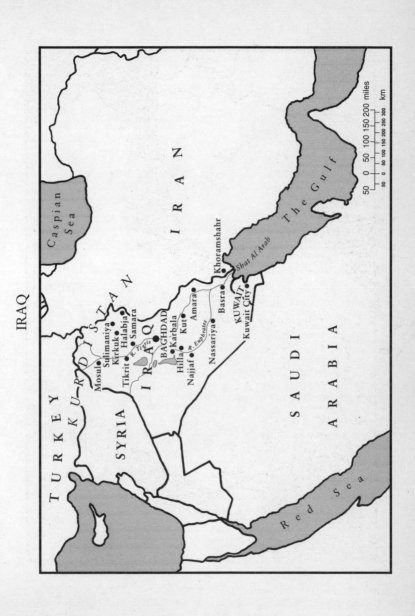

IRAQ

1

Cruel Ancestry

Much of what the press and biographers have written about Saddam's life is true. But it represents a one-sided story since it is limited to reports of his actions; no attempt is made to explain the background to his emergence on the world stage and to locate him in Arab and twentieth-century history. Judged absolutely and in comparison with those of his Arab contemporaries, his achievements are substantial, and some of them will outlive the current deafening noise surrounding his reputation. The possibility that he will occupy a place of honour in Arab history and condemnation elsewhere has to be understood in the context of the history of Iraq, its geopolitical position, its covetous neighbours and the major powers which believe Iraqi oil is so significant that they cannot leave the country alone.

Saddam's role and reputation must be weighed along with the unfulfilled desires of the Iraqi people, and their justified historical belief that they have been denied the right to realize the potential of their land and earn it a place among modern nations. In other words, Saddam as an individual may be unique, even demonic, but he is also a true son of Iraq. Even his use of violence to achieve his aims is not a strictly personal characteristic, but rather an unattractive trait of the Iraqi people reinforced by their history.

Thousands of years ago Mesopotamia ('the land between the rivers'), as it was known by the Greeks, was one of the great cradles of civilization. Its strategic importance on the overland route between Europe and Asia, combined with the agricultural potential of the rich fertile expanse between the Tigris and the Euphrates in an otherwise arid region, meant that it was constantly fought over.

Ancient Mesopotamia is associated with dozens of kingdoms and empires: Sumerian, Akkadian, Babylonian, Hittite, Hurrian, Kassite, Elamite, Assyrian and, in more recent centuries, Arab, Persian and Ottoman. Whilst some of these entities expanded, then contracted and often disappeared of their own accord, most of them replaced each other violently, through conquest or rebellion or a combination of both.

In the fourth century BC, Alexander the Great captured Babylon and cut a swathe through the region on his eastward journey of conquest. In the eighth century AD, by then already known as Iraq, it was conquered by Arab Muslims who established the Abbasid caliphate and built the legendary Baghdad. But even this flourishing empire, with its libraries, scientific achievements and poetry, was anchored in violence: more than eighty of its ninety-two caliphs were murdered as a result of feuds over succession, corruption or palace intrigues. In the thirteenth century, in an orgy of slaughter and looting, the Mongol hordes ransacked Baghdad and destroyed the great libraries, the cultural inheritance of the Abbasids. During the seventeenth and eighteenth centuries both the Persians and the Ottoman Turks tried to establish dominance over Iraq and turned it into a battleground; eventually the Turks incorporated the territory into the Ottoman Empire. From the late nineteenth century the British sought to control Iraq to safeguard their route to India. After the First World War and the defeat of the Turks, Britain occupied Iraq and briefly administered it as a mandate territory. What followed was a monarchy of Britain's creation.

The violence and cruelty which accompanied every change in the governance of the country throughout its history occasionally took novel forms which left an indelible imprint on the local population. Two examples stand out. Upon entering the city of Najjaf in 694 AD, the Muslim conqueror Al Hajjaj Bin Yusuf Al Thaqafi described the Iraqis as people of 'schism and hypocrisy' and declared, 'I see heads ripe for cutting and verily I am the man to do it'.[1] When in 1258 Hulagu, the grandson of Genghis Khan, laid siege to Baghdad, he bombarded the fortified inner city to rubble and ordered the breaking of the dykes on the Tigris, thus drowning most of the population.[2] It therefore comes as no surprise that, on hearing of the killing in 1958 of the British-backed royal family, the Hashemite descendants of Mohammed, the Orientalist Freya Stark wrote, 'Even the massacre of the prophet's family is no novelty on that soil.'[3]

Leaving human violence aside, the natural environment itself has been no kinder to Iraq. Floods, earthquakes, plague, famine and the wretchedness of a land where the temperature can fluctuate by 40 degrees Centigrade within a single day have contributed to the emergence of an indigenous personality at war with nature and the rule of man. Every conqueror left people and aspects of their culture behind, and the depopulation of the original inhabitants through natural disasters, civil strife and war allowed the new arrivals to create a greater impression than would normally have been the case. The influence of the Mongols who remained after their conquest, for instance, was considerable because two-thirds of the original population had been massacred. By the twentieth century the country contained a rich ethnic and religious mix of Arabs, Kurds, Turkomans, Persians, Chaldeans, Yezedis, Sabaens and Jews, along with smaller groups of Afghans, Azeris and Hindis. Even in the 1920s, 44 per cent of the members of the chamber of commerce were Jewish. In the words of the celebrated journalists, John Bulloch and Harvey Morris, Iraq remains the least Arab of the Arab countries.[4]

The turbulent history, harsh environment and multi-stranded culture of Iraq have produced a complex and unique conglomerate which lacks the ingredients for creating a homogeneous country and a commitment to the idea of a national community. Modern Iraq is a fractured society in which numerous clusters, tribes, ethnic and religious groups pay genuine tribute to the idea of a nation state, but one which accords paramountcy to their particular tribal, ethnic or religious background.

The schism between Sunni and Shia Muslims typifies the problem. This religious split began in AD 680 over the nature of the prophet's succession, and grew under Persian and then Ottoman Turkish rule. The Persians promoted their Shia co-religionists, while Sunni Turkey supported its own. Each group mistreated the others when in power and denied them their rights, and the cleavage eventually assumed a socio-economic nature – since Turkish supremacy lasted longer than Persian it gave the Sunnis an educational and wealth advantage over the Shias which still remains. Today, most Sunni Muslims are Arab nationalists who want union or closer relations with the rest of the Arabs, whilst many Shias work towards closer ties with Iran. Thus conflicts between narrow loyalty and the larger dream of nationhood are constant, and lie behind the incoherence and habitual disorder which racks the country.

Saddam Hussein is not the first, nor is he likely to be the last, dictator of Iraq. When such a neurotic individual superimposes himself on this arena of discord, we are confronted with a ruler suffering from a patterned defect. In Saddam's case there is a morbid, dangerous preoccupation with creating a whole out of the disparate parts. I call it a patterned defect because most Iraqis suffer from it. Given the opportunity, each of them would pursue Saddam's aim of creating a unified, strong Iraq in his own way.

However, despite the cultural mélange, the character of Iraq is basically Arab. This is because the Arabs, who ruled the country for six centuries, had a religion which produced a developed culture. Their predominance was reinforced by the movement into Iraq of tribes from the Arabian peninsula. The Arabness of Iraq has been part of the search for a unifying national identity. Saddam's commitment to meld what exists on the ground under the umbrella of Arab culture was tried by many leaders before him, though in a less deliberate and brutal manner. This is why there have been many occasions when being Arab was subordinated to being Iraqi, when the latter was considered to be more of a unifying umbrella, even under Saddam Hussein.

The arrival of the British during the First World War, and their subsequent occupation of the country, compounded the legacy of the Persians and Ottoman Turks. Discovering that imposing direct rule on Iraq was unaffordable, the British sided with the more educated minority Sunnis (then, as now, around 20 per cent of the population) and used them to perpetuate the inequality that the Turks had created. (Former Iraqi cabinet member Abdel Karim Al Ozrie claims that the extensive Iraqi diplomatic service did not have one Shia ambassador until 1956.) But those who laid the foundations of modern Iraq during the past two centuries also left a lasting impression on the land which went beyond building an unsound political structure. To this day Iraqi Arabic is replete with non-Arabic words, mostly Turkish and Persian but some introduced more recently. *Fasanjoon*, an Iranian dish, has been claimed by many Iraqis as their own. The word for 'good' is not Arabic but the Turkish equivalent, *khosh*. Lack of good manners is described in a phrase which also recalls the days of Ottoman Turkey, *adab sis*. And even a whorehouse is a *kharakhanah*, for it was the Turks who introduced these establishments to Baghdad and other cities. The Iraqis use the English 'glass' instead of its Arabic equivalents, *cass* or *kubaya*, and the upper classes say 'countryside' instead of *rif*.

Nevertheless, despite being the offspring of its tortured historical search for identity, Iraq does have a distinct social and economic character. This came into being in the mid-nineteenth century,[5] when the Turks introduced the *tanzimat* (the concept of organization through codifying the law) and tried to turn the country into a functioning territory within the Ottoman Empire. Contrary to the claims of Orientalists, which the press adopt too readily, the country as a geographical unit was always united by the two rivers and, except for a relatively brief period towards the end of Ottoman Turkish rule, authority under them was centred in Baghdad.[6] The legend which claims that Iraq is a country stitched together by the British from three *villayats* or provinces, Baghdad, Mosul and Basra, is shallow. Turkey created these *villayats* by decentralizing from Baghdad for a brief time before the First World War. The historian Malik Mufti refutes the claim without hesitation by stating that 'Iraq [as created by Britain] was not an entirely artificial concept'.[7]

What victorious Britain did produce after the First World War was an Iraqi government which controlled the same territory that Saddam Hussein governs today. It confirmed those borders in 1926, five years after it had established the Iraqi monarchy and imported an Arab king, Faisal I, to deputize for it while investing real authority in the British High Commissioner. It is true that the boundaries of modern Iraq were drawn in response to Western interests,[8] in accordance first with the 1916 Sykes–Picot Agreement, which divided the Middle Eastern spoils of the First World War between Britain and France, and later in recognition of the British desire to control the city of Mosul and its oil. But the core of Iraq as a place with a people was already in existence under the Ottoman Empire and even earlier.

The British and the new monarchy worsened the historical problems which had always bedevilled the country. The imported king had never been to Iraq before the British appointed him.[9] He belonged to the minority Sunni sect and, above all, he ruled without governing.[10] Faisal himself accepted the paramountcy of the High Commissioner and admitted that he was no more than 'an instrument of British policy';[11] the Orientalist Gertrude Bell, one of the people behind Faisal, wrote to her father on 8 July 1921 to complain about how tiring 'making kings' was. The opinion of the majority Shias was totally ignored. To support Faisal, the British took the easy way out and elevated to positions of power Sunnis who had served as officers under Turkey.

In 1920, just before the plans for imposing the monarchy were finalized, the Shias rose up against the infidel British and their plans. Because most Iraqis wanted to be independent and free, the rebellion eventually spread to include those Sunnis outside the small, elite circle whom the British were promoting. Both Muslim sects turned against the *franji*, the European usurper, and the result was some two thousand British casualties including 453 dead. The strength of the uprising caused the British to resort to two elements of warfare which have been copied by Saddam in more recent times: they employed their air force against civilians and they used gas.[12] The Christianity of the British, the lateness of their conquest, their lack of sensitivity to local conditions (which included dependence on a minority) and their willingness to resort to force and chemical warfare administered a shock to the country's social system from which it has never recovered.[13] It was the British conquest of Iraq which set the stage for what is happening today.

Along with ignoring the Shias the British allowed the promise to grant the Kurds independence, which had been included in the 1920 Treaty of Sèvres, to lapse. Iraq as represented by the Shias, the Kurds and those Sunnis, mostly from the lower classes to which Saddam's tribe belonged, who sought independence – in total, nearly 70 per cent of the population – was now resolutely anti-British. As a result the conquerors were forced into ever heavier reliance on the Sunni aristocrats, who were allowed to control the government. There were also some Shia tribal leaders who succumbed to the enticement of land grants, former officers in the Turkish Army who were made generals and ministers and were also given land, Jews, who got special protection, and the Assyrians and other minorities who were employed in the new administration.

Operating with a shackled king who proved more astute than they had anticipated and who lamented the absence of social cohesion in his country,[14] the British later added to the explosive situation by supporting the tribes to undermine him and by creating a special force of Christian levies to use selectively to protect their interests and oil installations. They opened a direct line of communication with the leaders of the abandoned Kurds and used them intermittently to support and undermine the central government. In fact, they dealt directly with the small ethnic and religious segments of Iraq and the leadership of the Kurds and Shias without deferring to the Sunni government that they had created – among other things, they stipulated that the Minister of Finance be a Jew.

Just as the long-term history of Iraq contained and nurtured violence, the British, following short-sighted policies similar to those employed by Iraq's ancient conquerors, contributed measurably to the ethnic, religious and social divisions which beset the country. Because the average Iraqi was beyond their reach, British policies precluded the creation of a democracy and included looking the other way while supporters of Britain, even some prime ministers, murdered and imprisoned popular politicians in the tradition of the centuries-old Iraqi reliance on violence to express political opinion. The Kurds, among others, resorted to the gun to try to attain their national aspirations, and the Shias sought Iranian support to undermine the government.

That violence continues to be part and parcel of the Iraqi personality is no accident. The monarchical system, which governed Iraq until 1958 and which the 1921 Peace Conference in Cairo designed, was unsound and contained the seeds of its eventual destruction. The historian H. V. F. Winstone cites the words of Gertrude Bell, a participant in the Peace Conference, to demonstrate how little attention was paid to the long-term effects of what was being discussed and planned. Her recollections of a conversation among three of the conference delegates went like this:

First statesman: The country will be badly governed.
Second statesman: Why should it not be badly governed?
Third statesman: It ought to be badly governed.[15]

There is no reason to suppose that they did not have Iraq in mind.

Although King Faisal was put on the throne of a country which was expected to be badly governed, he still tried his utmost to improve the situation and undertook moves, including recognition of Shia rights, to bridge the gap between his realm's diverse components. Against British resistance, he devoted a great deal of time and effort to creating a strong army to give his country pride and to serve as a nucleus for integrating its people. Interestingly, his attempts at enfranchising all segments of the population included encouraging the Tikritis, Saddam's poor and ignored relations, to enter the armed forces. King Faisal died in 1933 before he fully realized his dream and was succeeded by his incompetent and hot-headed son, Ghazi. Instead of using the Army to unite the country, by placing it above politics, Ghazi made it another instrument of division. In 1936 the semi-literate Ghazi colluded with General Bakr Sidqi and staged a coup, which ushered in a whole age of coups. The Army became a faction, a participant in the endemic violence, and politicians tried to control it and manipulate its composition.

Saddam Hussein was born about the time of Ghazi's suspicious death in 1939. He was the product of a poor childhood which produced bitter experiences that he has never forgotten or overcome. In many ways he is very much like all the rulers of Iraq since King Faisal I, but for his highly individualistic utter lack of psychological or sociological restraints. Saddam too has tried to unify Iraq through a strong army and, inventively, the use of the country's diverse past. However, his lack of restraint is imported: he has modelled himself after and adopted the ways of Joseph Stalin and merged them with his tribal instincts. This synthesis of Bedouin guile and Communist method, a unique combination, is what confuses both his friends and his adversaries. Because of regional and international factors which had nothing to do with the fate of the people of Iraq, Saddam has been courted, supported and eventually opposed by the West. This too has allowed him space to operate which other Iraqi dictators did not have. Whether or not Saddam would have managed to create a strong, independent Iraq had the West left him alone will be addressed through the telling of his life story. Whether the Iraq that Saddam sought to create was what the Iraqi people wanted is another vital component of this biography.

2

The Shadow of Al Zuhour Palace

Although he has been on television on a semi-regular basis since the early 1990s and tens of thousands of news articles have been written about him, an air of mystery and confusion continues to surround the life, actions and importance of Iraq's President. In fact, it is becoming increasingly difficult to separate the exaggerations and inventions about Saddam Hussein from the truth, even when the facts are against him. This covers everything from how his name is pronounced to his place and date of birth and, more importantly, to why he has joined Hitler and Stalin as one of the most hated political personalities of the twentieth century.

To the average Iraqi, the natural arbiter of how Iraqi names should be pronounced, he is Isdam, and not Saddam as his name is written or Suddam as it is pronounced – certainly not Sa-dam as George Bush embarrassingly insisted on calling him. It is an uncommon Arabic name, a cross between 'clasher', 'confronter' and 'collider'. A collision between two cars is an *istidam*, and an unexpected event with serious, mostly unhappy, results is a *sadmah*. A person who causes a *sadmah* is Saddam.

His name tells us a great deal about Saddam's background: it is not only old-fashioned but implies a lack of social standing. The Sunni aristocracy of Iraq has always been inclined towards gentler names, many of which were adopted and Arabized during the rule of Ottoman Turkey. Middle-class Sunnis emulate their social superiors and shun connotations of violence. Most Shia names have religious associations, whilst the Kurds and other minorities follow their own traditions. Only the lower classes of Sunni society, nomadic Bedouin tribes and their settled kin use names that suggest strength and violence. This implied low social background is supported by other family names. Although his father had a regular name, Hussein, his mother was called Subha, his three surviving half-brothers Barazan, Sabawi and Watban, and his dead brother Idham. They too are unusual, and most Iraqis I have questioned allude to their archaic nature and profess ignorance of their origin. Subha is a name remembered by most people in an old song, *Ya Subha hatti al siniya*, which depicts the bearer of the name as a maidservant – it was banned by the government of Iraq years ago. Among the boys, only Sabawi stands for something; loosely translated, it means 'lionlike'. The other two names have no meaning.

There is no dispute as to Saddam's place of birth, although one version of his name has blurred the details. He was born a hundred miles north of Baghdad in the small Sunni Muslim village of Al Awja, just east of the historic but impoverished town of Tikrit, the former Roman fort town of Meonia and the birthplace of Saladin. (Saladin, a major figure during the Crusades, was a Kurd; the area neighbours Iraqi Kurdistan and there is a large Kurdish element in the local population.) The meaning of Al Awja seems to have escaped chroniclers of Saddam's life. Literally, it means 'crooked'. During the 1930s, when Saddam was born, most Iraqis dispensed with family names and called themselves after their fathers and the towns where they were born. Had Saddam linked his name to Al Awja, he would have become Saddam Hussein Al Awja, 'the crooked collider or clasher, son of Hussein'. Mercifully, he dispensed with this association and, until the 1970s, called himself Saddam Hussein Al Tikriti, after the larger nearby town. This elevation by association resembled Stalin's claim that he hailed from the Georgian capital, Tbilisi, and not from the tiny unknown town of Gori.

According to Saddam he was born on 28 April 1937. In 1980 this date was made a public holiday, an occasion for mass celebrations and several days of non-stop television coverage – a sponsored renewal of the fealty of the people to their leader. But the Iraqi writer Dr Hamid Al Bayati casts serious doubt on this assertion and has produced a birth certificate dated 1 July 1939.[1] Many Iraqis interviewed by me admit the possibility that Saddam's actual date of birth may differ from the recorded one. Inhabitants of backward villages such as Al Awja very often failed to register births until much later, if at all. But that would make people appear younger, and therefore offers no explanation for the discrepancy in Saddam's case.

The more likely reasons for changing his date of birth are social and political. It could have been done when he married his first wife and first cousin on his mother's side, Sajida Khairallah Tulfah. Sajida was born in 1937, and Saddam could have changed or invented the official record of his birth to conceal his marriage to an older woman, in Arab society an unusual event which is still frowned on. Alternatively, the alteration could have been made later when Saddam was a contender for his country's leadership; an older candidate would have had a better chance of winning. Although supposedly a modern party confusedly modelled after nationalist and socialist movements in Europe, the Ba'ath and its leaders still subscribed to the cultural precepts of the Middle East. Marrying someone older and coming ahead of one's elders in a political movement violated the over-riding codes of tribalism.

It would be in character for Saddam to try to overcome the hurdle of being too young to lead. But whether born in 1937 or 1939, he was at most thirty-two years old in 1969 when he became head of his country's dreaded security apparatus, the Ba'ath Party's Deputy Secretary General and Iraq's Vice President and heir apparent. A remarkable achievement anywhere, it was even more so in traditionalist Iraq.

His exact date of birth aside, Saddam was born to Subha Tulfah Al Musallat and one Hussein Al Majid, already absent and presumed dead at the time of Saddam's birth. His mother, known from pictures and by reputation, lived in Tikrit until her death in 1982. Her tomb there is a huge shrine built on Saddam's orders at Iraqi government expense to celebrate the hallowed resting-place of the Mother of Militants, the revered mother of the President and of his three half-brothers, all of whom were rewarded with high office after Saddam became President in 1979. But little is known about Hussein Al Majid's life or where he is buried. One story asserts that he died of natural causes months before Saddam's birth, another claims that bandits killed him, and a third alleges that he disappeared to escape the awesome, domineering Subha.

The most unlikely theory to explain the absence of Hussein at Saddam's birth, one advanced by some of his Iraqi opponents, is that Subha was the local whore and Saddam was a bastard. The story was carried during the Gulf War by popular Western news-papers thirsty for anything that would demonize and undermine the enemy. Not only is there no evidence to support this cruel allegation, but villages such as Al Awja were too small to have whores or whorehouses. In any case, the social make-up of the community precluded such things (the villagers, in particular the religious people, would have prevented it because it affected their reputation and beliefs), and Subha had relations whose Arab sense of honour would have led them to kill her if she had indulged in such pursuits.

Nevertheless, there is evidence to support the idea that Subha was a forceful woman who overshadowed her weak husbands. In villages and towns of settled Bedouins such as Al Awja and Tikrit the status of women was usually lower than that of their counter-parts among nomadic tribes – they were kept isolated and ordered to be silent. But Subha talked to men who were not close relations, wandered around unaccompanied and refused to keep herself under lock and key. Within her family she participated in meetings which were normally the exclusive domain of men. Even her clothing showed a measure of independence: although she wore the traditional all-enveloping *abba* it had unusually wide sleeves which showed part of her arms, and this was considered a sign of lack of modesty. What might have been nothing more than strength of character and outspokenness in a society where women were customarily docile might have earned her an undeserved reputation.

An attempt was made to settle the issue of who Hussein was in 1995, when the Iraqi magazine *Aleph Ba* published the first picture of him. However, most Iraqis dismissed it as a fraud.[2] What prompted the attempt to reinvent Hussein is unknown and curious, particularly in view of Saddam's silence on the subject for most of his life, even when talking to friendly biographers. This, however, should not imply that there is any truth in the stories about Subha and Hussein's non-existence. Members of the Al Majid clan accepted Saddam as the son of the mysterious Hussein and as a clan member from the start, well before he became important and a source of benefit to his relations. The true story is probably a simple one: Hussein had obviously never amounted to much in life and, though the less said about him the better, *Aleph Ba* was involved in a misguided rehabilitation attempt.

The anti-Saddam writer Dr Hamid Al Bayati, mentioned earlier, has devoted considerable time to unearthing uncomplimentary aspects of Saddam's life, but admits that Hussein existed and states that one of his jobs was as a servant in the household of Tewfiq Al Sweidi, a former Prime Minister of Iraq under the monarchy.[3] Salah Omar Al Ali, a civilized, urbane Tikriti, one-time colleague of Saddam as Minister of Information and member of the Revolutionary Command Council of the Ba'ath Party in the 1960s and 1970s, knows Saddam and the history of his family well. He accepts that Hussein existed, but refuses to point to a specific job. He settles for: 'He wasn't anything. No member of that family ever achieved much until . . .'[4] Ali speculates about the possibility of Hussein's death in a violent accident: 'After all, the people of Al Awja were so violent, their visits to Tikrit prompted many merchants to shut their shops.'

Again, the similarity between Saddam and Stalin is striking. Stalin had a strong-willed servant mother whom he revered and with whom he corresponded, but his father was a drunken cobbler who died young and about whom little was said.

In fact, except for a few families such as the Alis who owned enough land to attain respectable middle-class status, there was very little to achieve in Al Awja, Tikrit and their surroundings. It is a particularly poor part of Iraq, similar to the badlands in a Western movie. Most of the land belonged to the state, and it was not productive enough to interest the large landowners from the cities. The district of Tikrit was known only for its watermelons and the skin boats called *kalaks* which carried them down the Tigris to Baghdad. Disease was rampant, in particular malaria, bilharzia and tapeworm. Most people suffered from one or more of these endemic maladies, which affected their strength and ability to work. While there are no records on the subject, life expectancy was very short.

The people of Tikrit and its surrounding area belonged to the Albu Nasser, also known as Bejat, a minor tribe of settled Sunni Muslims. They were known as a difficult lot of people, cunning and secretive, whose poverty drove most of them to pervert the Bedouins' legendary qualities of being warlike and fearless into dishonesty, theft and violence.[5] The Iraqi Kurd writer Kamran Karadaghi states that the Tikritis' favourite saying was *iqtulu waqta' khabarou* meaning 'Kill him and end his news' – the

concept of 'news' had always been important in traditional nomadic Arab society, and the Tikritis and their kin lived up to this
reputation and were known for eliminating their enemies for the
smallest of reasons.[6] It is little surprise that some people think
Hussein was murdered for some inappropriate reason and that the
whole thing was hushed up.

The tribal bonds which held the Albu Nasser together were
strengthened by intermarriage. Subha and Hussein were second
cousins. When Saddam was born, she followed tradition and ceded
the honour of naming him to his paternal uncle Hassan (not to be
confused with her next husband),[7] and this was another confirmation that Saddam's father existed. Unable to cope on her own after
Hussein's disappearance she soon married again, this time to Hajj
Hassan Ibrahim, another cousin of both herself and her first
husband. Among the many reasons given for this particular marriage was the fact that cousins did not have to pay a dowry, and by
the sound of things Hassan was too poor to afford one. Many
claim that Subha had another brief marriage between Hussein and
Hassan,[8] but there is little to substantiate this claim. Nor did her
final marriage, after Hassan's death, produce any children or leave
an impact. What matters is Saddam's life in the household of Subha
and Hassan the Liar, as the people of Al Awja called Saddam's
stepfather,[9] partly because of his unjustified adoption of the
honorific title of *hajj*, meaning one who has made the pilgrimage
to Mecca.

That Hassan Ibrahim did very little work is established beyond
doubt, and, like his wife, he was illiterate. Not a single history of
Iraq or Saddam associates his stepfather with any gainful employ-
ment or praiseworthy activity. Subha and Hassan belonged to the
poorer fringes of an already poor tribe. An Arab family's financial
status can be assessed by analysing the way they dress when posing
for a photographer, to the lower classes always a special occasion
for which they don their best clothes, and by the size and config-
uration of their houses, in which they invest most of what they
have. There are a number of pictures of Subha and Hassan, both
together and individually. Typical of her class, she was a hefty
woman in her formless, ground-length black *abba*, and on occasions she has prayer beads in her hands. It is easy to see where
Saddam got his big head; in the pictures hers is wrapped in a black

band which comes down to the middle of her forehead. She has Bedouin tattoos of small circles on her chin, cheeks and forehead, and her grim stare betrays her unease with the formality of picture-taking. The only photograph which shows a relaxed Subha is one taken after her son became President, in which she is grabbing Saddam to embrace him while he is bending to accommodate her expression of affection. Everything else in the pictures, particularly the tattoos, confirms her as a settled Bedouin.

In another picture Subha is accompanied by Hassan Ibrahim wearing Arab headdress, sporting a Bedouin goatee which covers the centre of his chin and carrying a sword. He is wearing thick-lensed glasses and a frown. The sword is borne proudly but awkwardly, obviously a prop for the picture occasion. The rest of his native Arab dress is of poor quality. In fact, everything about the couple suggests poverty and belonging to the lower echelons of tribal life. In yet another picture Hassan is carrying a shotgun, once again evidence that he attached importance to being armed as a sign of manliness.

Subha and Hassan's family shared their mudbrick dwelling with their animals, in all likelihood nothing more than a donkey and two or three sheep. Saddam himself told his loyalist biographer Amir Iskandar that he 'lived in a simple house'.[10] That is an understatement. Pictures of the family home appear in many books but they are not clear. Much more interestingly I saw them hanging in the offices of some Iraqi officials, including that of Minister of Information Latif Nassif Jassem, in the late 1970s and early 1980s, when Saddam emphasized his humble origins to endow his regime with a populist aura and closeness to the people. (This is probably the only instance in modern times that an Arab leader has celebrated his humble origins to endear himself to his people.) The house appeared to be a one-room affair similar to many in Al Awja. The room would have been occupied by Subha, Hassan, Saddam and his brothers, while the animals inhabited the shed attached to it. There was no lavatory, running water, electricity, kitchen or anything which we normally associate with the term 'house'. Those who lived in such huts were known as the people who ate with all five (*ili baklyu bi al khamsah*), because they had no utensils and ate rice-based, largely meatless food with their hands from a communal pot. The whole family slept on the mud floor in cramped, unhygienic conditions.

In Middle Eastern society this way of living produced a particular type of child. Because of lack of space the young spent most of their time outside in the narrow, dirty, dung-filled alleys of their villages and towns. They formed gangs, stole from farmers and each other, and conducted feuds and clan wars which often lasted for years. To their poverty they added the qualities of being tough, courageous and vicious at an early age. Many of them never attended school but became farmers or shepherds or escaped to the cities to become servants, labourers and occasionally taxi drivers. This was the fate which awaited Saddam, and these were the elements which formed his early personality.

He told his biographer Amir Iskandar that he was never young, that he was a melancholy child who shunned the company of others.[11] But he described the same alley conditions which left him introspective and friendless as endowing him with 'patience, endurance, tenacity and self-reliance'. Saddam also admitted that his birth 'was not a joyful occasion and that no roses or aromatic plants bedecked his cradle'. To judge the truth of these statements they must be put into the context of the social conditions of the time.

The fact that Saddam had no father mattered, as did Hassan the Liar's addiction to the local coffee house, an institution known to the Iraqis as the *muntada al rijal* or men's club. In reality it was a focus for the idle and useless macho members of any community, the *jilifs* (rough ones) who sent their children out to tend sheep or plant seeds while they regaled each other with stories of honour and heroism. Decent men of means avoided coffee houses. Yet, speaking of his early childhood after he became President of Iraq, Saddam say that being fatherless left no bitterness in him. But biographers Karsh and Rautsi contradict this and say that the absence of a father made other children mock him,[12] which made him introspective and unhappy. Karsh and Rautsi's account is the more likely one and young Arabs do mock fatherless children, because fathers are the source of protection against outsiders, even relations. In Islamic tradition a fatherless child is *yateem al ab*, or an orphan on his father's side. The holy Koran nobly commands people not to 'distress orphans', but this dictate is very seldom obeyed. Moreover, the very explicitness of the Koranic command suggests that members of Muslim society in general were inclined to be unkind to orphans, particularly on their father's side, and to look down upon them.

For Saddam, the agony of derision began with his stepfather. That Hassan Ibrahim beat him with a stick is probably true – people of his ilk did so frequently – but since it is a common occurrence its significance should not be exaggerated. Hassan also appears to have wanted to get rid of his stepson. The *Sunday Times* and other sources[13] claim that Hassan the Liar often shouted: 'I don't want him, the son of a dog.' This too is not unusual among lower-class Arabs, and there is not much to calling people 'son of a dog'. Although misunderstood by Western writers, to most Arabs it is a minor term of abuse. Still, the combination of being fatherless, of suffering general hardship and mistreatment, and of having to tolerate the harsh words and ways of Hassan the Liar must have left an imprint on Saddam's psyche. While it does not constitute solid proof, the absence of any mention of Hassan the Liar in Iskandar's and Matar's pro-Saddam biographies, and in the ghost-written, thinly disguised autobiographical work of his early life (*The Long Days* by Abdel Amir Mua'la), does indicate a wish to erase Hassan Ibrahim's memory from his mind.

On the other hand, the works which ignore Hassan make much of the nobility of Subha. After he became President, Saddam made a point of telling anyone who asked him that he visited his mother 'as often as possible'. It goes further, and Iskandar's mention of young Saddam being 'melancholy, lonely and never young',[14] written with Saddam's approval, comes very close to revealing an inner anger.

So Saddam became what the Arabs call an *ibn aziqa*, or Son of the Alleys – someone who lacks domesticity and manners. There are stories of him stealing chickens and eggs to feed his family, others of him selling watermelon on the train which stopped in Tikrit on its way from Mosul to Baghdad. Yet other tales recount his use of an iron bar to kill stray dogs, and of becoming a noted *shaqi*, or tough, at an early age. There is not a shred of evidence, however, to suggest that he led a children's gang or represented anything special. Except for the shame of admitting that he felt the absence of a father, what Saddam told his biographers could have been the experiences of any *ibn aziqa* forced into this way of life through poverty. Judged by when this statement was made, in the early 1980s, Saddam's admissions make a great deal of sense. The reflections on his character were circumstantial and not of Saddam's own making. As a result, they endeared him to many Iraqis who had grown up in similar conditions.

Why should Saddam hide anything when his childhood was typical? His family knew where he spent his time and probably knew about his activities, even approved of them. Where else would a child of his age go with raw eggs or a live chicken? In contrast to this picture, biographer Iskandar has Saddam telling us how much he loved the family's white horse and how he was so severely affected by its death that his right arm became semi-paralysed.[15] True or not, the roles of chicken thief and horse lover are not mutually exclusive. A friendless boy left to fend for himself could have been pushed to steal, and the same child could have developed affection for an animal. Saddam's later life shows a clear fondness for horses and legends of knighthood; he seizes every opportunity to ride a white horse, and perhaps it all started with preferring the company of a horse to that of his family. Saddam's recollections as told to Iskandar and Matar demonstrate his flair for telling stories which appeal to people both politically and in human terms.

Toughing it with the neighbourhood street gangs did not occupy all of Saddam's time. Hassan the Liar followed tradition and put his stepson out to work at the age of six as a farmhand and shepherd, something that children of his age did if they were not sent to school. Saddam went to the fields barefoot since his family could not afford to buy him shoes. In fact, the boy was 'ashamed of his appearance and jealous of others'.[16] Whatever shame the young Saddam felt, his unhappy relationship with his stepfather, the birth of stepbrothers who, according to Arab custom, took precedence over him within the Hassan household, and a growing sense of isolation and loneliness drove him towards identifying a model for himself outside his immediate surroundings. Saddam's hero was his maternal uncle Khairallah Tulfah, a former second lieutenant in the Iraqi Army who had become a schoolteacher. He was modern enough to wear Western clothes and later became Saddam's father-in-law, adviser, an honorary general in the Iraqi Army, Mayor of Baghdad and a considerable source of influence on his nephew's early personal and political life.

Saddam left home to live with his maternal uncle in 1947. The uncertainty about Saddam's date of birth has led some chroniclers of his life to claim that this took place when he was ten years old, while others state that he was only eight.[17] Khairallah was then teaching at a school in Al Shawish, another village near Tikrit. He had been cashiered and imprisoned for five years for participation in the 1941 Rashid Ali Rebellion, when a group of nationalist army officers rose against the pro-British government of Iraq and briefly established a pro-Nazi regime. This very important fact and its influence on Iraq, Khairallah and Saddam will be discussed in more detail later, after examining the motives and nature of Saddam's unusual move.

Biographer Fuad Matar describes Saddam's leaving home and going to live with the Khairallah Tulfahs as his first rebellion.[18] He attributes the whole dramatic episode to the fact that Saddam wanted to emulate his cousin Adnan, Khairallah's son (later a trusted aide who became Chief of Staff of the Army and Minister of Defence). Though a year younger than Saddam, Adnan was attending school and could read and write. He made a point of demonstrating his superior capabilities whenever he met his cousin, and the young *yateem al ab* is supposed to have been jealous and determined to become Adnan's equal. Matar claims that Saddam ran into some relations while 'escaping' from Hassan's hovel to Khairallah's house in the middle of the night, and that these people sympathized with his plans, gave him a gun to protect himself during the short trip and paid his bus or taxi fare. The same story was repeated in Iraqi newspapers without reference to a bus or taxi ride, emphasizing Saddam's love of education by explaining how he made the dangerous trip barefoot. Regardless of which story one believes, both of them reveal determination and persistence – two qualities Saddam possesses to this day.

Except for wishing to be as advanced as his cousin – illiterate children are usually jealous of literate ones – the rest of the story sounds like an attempt to create a myth. The names of the relations who supposedly sponsored Saddam's trip are not given and the business of giving a child a gun sounds absurd, even in Tikriti terms. Besides, the whole thing could not have taken place without the approval of the dominant figure in the family, Subha. Because she could have brought Saddam back home, and yet did not do so, it is safe to assume that she was behind his escape. Very close to her brother and proud of him, she must have tired of the constant feuding between her son and husband and seen the move as a solution to the problem. Also, in view of the fact that she later took pride in the schooling of her other children, there is no reason to suppose that she was not sympathetic with Saddam's ambition.

Saddam himself entered school at the age of eight or ten, the final reward for his perseverance. The fact that this illiterate boy was so much older than the children being taught alongside him, and probably the butt of their cruelty, must have been traumatic for him. Indeed there are unverified stories that he fought with many of them and that some suffered the consequences of their mockery later in life, when Saddam had become important. Whether these are true or not, everybody accepts that Saddam, though not studious, was endowed with an unusual memory, perhaps a photographic one, and that he never forgot a slight or an insult (or, indeed, a kindness, as later stories will testify). Still, an Iraqi politician who was once close to him insists that this period of suffering produced a sense of inadequacy in Saddam, that being hungry, shoeless and later behind in school did give rise to serious complexes which were revealed in his later behaviour. This opinion is shared by the few people who knew him in his early teens. The one thing which is accepted even by his most committed enemies is that Saddam was an exceptionally intelligent child, a fast learner who was calculating and methodical from the start.

The two surviving pictures from that period show a boy with a round face, flat hair, large ears, small but piercing eyes and, in line with his circumstances, a most unhappy expression. There was nothing resembling a sparkle in him, but that was to change in a few years. Pictures taken at the age of fourteen or fifteen introduce a handsome, more relaxed and happy young man with an attractive smile and a twinkle in his eye. Some of them show him taking delight in donning traditional Arab dress and flirting with the camera.

Here it is important to point out that the political turmoil consuming Iraq during this period appears to have had no direct effect on Saddam's immediate or extended family. Iraq was in a state of upheaval concentrated in Baghdad, Basra and Mosul, and the political movements and parties of the time ignored such backwoods places as Tikrit. The ruling elite was very unpopular and governments rose and fell with frequency though without providing solutions acceptable to the Iraqi people, who wanted total change and the elimination of British influence. But the absence of organized political entities beyond the main cities limited the feeble attempts at reform. Had political activity reached Tikrit, Khairallah would have been in the thick of events.

In December 1947 a government headed by Saleh Jaber, the first Shia Prime Minister in the history of modern Iraq, negotiated with Britain to draw up the Portsmouth Treaty, intended to replace the agreement which had been in existence since 1930. It was colonialism in disguise; the new treaty granted the British most of the rights contained in the old one. The resultant riots lasted for weeks and led to scores of dead and hundreds of wounded until Jaber resigned and the treaty was annulled.

In May 1948 the British ended their mandate in Palestine, and the newly declared State of Israel started seizing land that had belonged to Arab settlers for centuries. The Iraqi Army joined those of other Arab countries and went to Palestine to fight the Israelis, but gave a dismal performance. This was attributed by many Iraqis to the government, which they accused of conspiring with the British to give Palestine to the Jews. These two developments; the willingness of the ruling elite to sign a treaty with Britain which maintained Iraq as a tributary country, and the Army's performance in Palestine, led to what the Iraqis called the *wathba*, a street-level uprising which lasted for weeks and came close to paralyzing the government. The elite's hold on power was loosening. Iraqis such as Khairallah, bitter over their conditions and sympathetic to anything which undermined the established order, began to see a change in their fortunes. But at this point they had nothing other than words to push things forward.

Some time in the early 1950s Khairallah moved to Baghdad to teach at a school there and Saddam, by then a member of his uncle's family, went with him. They lived in Al Kharkh, a lower middle-class suburb full of new arrivals in the city, and Saddam attended the local school. Al Kharkh was a mixed neighbourhood of poor Sunnis and Shias, a fact that has been ignored by previous biographers. Because Al Awja and Tikrit were totally Sunni, it is safe to assume that his new home represented Saddam's first contact with Shias.

Disenfranchised lower-class people are inclined to resent other groups who share their status without uniting against the source of their problems, and the Tikritis manifested greater prejudice towards the Shias than most. Khairallah in particular did not like them, and this feeling must have transmitted itself to his young ward. To people like Khairallah the Shias were not true Arabs but kin to their Persian co-religionists, and they were willing to use all possible means to keep the Shias down and prevent them controlling Iraq through sheer force of numbers. Because more than half the population was Shia, this meant that the principle of a democratic Iraq was unacceptable to lower-class Sunnis.

There is evidence that Saddam undertook menial jobs to earn money while at school. Mu'in Nunu states that he worked as assistant to a driver.[19] This amounted to working in a parking lot touting for would-be passengers to share a taxi to a certain destination; he would call out something like 'To Ana! One more passenger to Ana and we're leaving' The pay was a tiny proportion of the driver's takings and depended on his generosity. A former member of the Ba'ath Party says that Saddam also sold cigarettes on the street, carrying a tray and shouting out the names of the brands he was hawking.[20] Another former Ba'athist insists that Saddam worked in coffee houses and had to resist the advances of the many Iraqis who fancied young boys.

Life was still difficult, but what mattered most to Saddam was that he was at last going to school. And there was one more important point to remember about that period. Khairallah's household included his pretty daughter Sajida, by then herself a teenager and later to be the first wife of her first cousin.

To Saddam, the way out was to follow in the footsteps of his uncle and become an army officer or a teacher. In the 1920s King Faisal I had set up a system whereby poor young men with a low level of education were provided with funding to complete the course of studies required to enter military college. Saddam took the entrance examination in 1953 or 1954, but failed. The family felt he had been turned down because of Khairallah's political past and his own participation in the 1952 riots called the *intifada*. Because his uncle was against all the pro-British governments, young Saddam had joined the riots without considering the consequences. Now his rejection left him with yet another complex. When he became Vice President of Iraq in the early 1970s he compensated for this snub and made himself an honorary general. After becoming President in 1979 he eventually elevated himself to field marshal and Commander-in-Chief of the armed forces. His desire to become an officer was similar to Stalin's, who too envied the officer class and took revenge on them by making himself a field marshal and placing them under his direct command.

There was more to life in the household of Khairallah Tulfah than living on the edge of poverty; there was anger and bitterness too. Khairallah had never forgotten or forgiven his dismissal from the Army and his imprisonment. He blamed his consequent lack of position and social status on the British and the pro-British government of Iraq, and spoke of both with venom constantly. In the words of historian William L. Cleveland, Khairallah and many others like him suffered from 'lingering anti-British hostility'.[21] Because of Khairallah's reputation for personal violence people took to calling him behind his back Sharallah, or 'the violence of Allah'; his real name means 'the bounty of Allah'.[22] Ideologically, there is little difference between the hundreds of Khairallahs of the 1940s and the young men who eventually joined the Ba'ath Party.

More importantly in terms of Saddam's future life, Khairallah was seeing a great deal of certain Tikriti army officers, in particular one Ahmad Hassan Al Bakr – the opposite of Khairallah, he was a teacher turned army officer. A first cousin of Khairallah's on his mother's side and a nationalist officer in the Iraqi Army who had somehow escaped his cousin's fate in 1941, Bakr eventually participated in the coup which overthrew the Iraqi monarchy in 1958, and in the coups which followed it. He assumed absolute power over Iraq in 1968 and, accepting Khairallah's advice, adopted Saddam and made him his second-in-command and heir apparent. According to someone who knew both Khairallah and Bakr well, the former was a firm believer in the use of relations instead of party members or ideologues to run a government. 'Blood is thicker than ideology', he is supposed to have told Bakr when he prevailed on him to depend on someone as young and inexperienced as Saddam.

The gatherings of Tikriti officers at Khairallah's home are worth noting. The only one who had made it into national politics in the 1920s and 1930s, Mawloud Mukhlis, had been close to the King and, capitalizing on Faisal's liberal policies, had backed many of his fellow townsmen to enter the Army. Because this opportunity had considerably more potential than the traditional jobs available to them, many Tikritis readily accepted Mukhlis's patronage and became soldiers and officers. In relation to the size of Tikrit, there were more Tikritis in the Army than from any other town. And Tikritis had a number of things in common: a background of poverty; a belief that the British and the regent who was behind Khairallah's dismissal, and the governing elite, were evil; jealousy and ill intent towards the Sunni upper classes, who were insensitive to their plight; and a historical lack of trust of the Shias.

Saddam took in all of Khairallah's fulminations, Bakr's more measured condemnations and the opinions of other Tikritis and merged them with the inner anger engendered by his lack of a father, unhappy early home life and failure to enter military college. He started forming a political position. To his biographer Iskandar, Saddam said that his uncle spoke of 'resistance and struggle',[23] naturally against the elite which made up the Iraqi government and their British sponsors. Talking about the same subject to biographer Fuad Matar, Saddam gave Khairallah's angry declarations an ideological hue and said that 'his uncle spoke in nationalist but not in Communist terms'.[24] Whatever the words used by Khairallah and his fellow Tikritis – and Saddam has always been a past master at altering his recollections to fit the political atmosphere of the moment – the Baghdad household in which Saddam grew up in the late 1940s and early 1950s drove him towards a preoccupation with politics and away from his studies and other pursuits. The thoughts and ideas to which Saddam was exposed in the Khairallah household were particularly those of the disenfranchised Iraqis of the Sunni persuasion.

Saddam identified with the most wretched of a historically wretched land, the poor within the Sunni minority, perhaps no more than half of the Sunnis who were in any case a mere 20 per cent of the population. Nowadays the poor Sunnis from Tikrit, Ana, Dour and Samara, with a smaller group from Mosul and others like them, run the country under Saddam. They are bound together by common background and prejudices and identify with Saddam against the elite Sunnis who ran the country under the monarchy and the British, while rejecting the Shias completely.

The Shias, also historically disenfranchised, differed. Since they formed the majority of the population, their original exclusion from power was a political and not a sociological act – both their rich and their poor were relegated. They continue to have a genuine political grievance against the Iraqi government as an institution.

Under the monarchy, their anger was directed against the Sunni establishment. Under Saddam, the same anger is directed against Sunnis whose claim to power does not even include superior education and background. Being governed by lower-class Sunnis reduces the Shias' status even further and represents a diminution of the original, unjustified denial of their political rights.

To understand Saddam completely, one needs to go beyond the beliefs and teachings of Khairallah and his kindred spirits and to examine the period of Saddam's birth and the years immediately before. If poverty and denial of an education created Saddam, then we need to know what was behind them, or what people thought was behind them, and what that produced when combined with the endemic violence of the Tikritis. These formative elements of Saddam Hussein's life must be considered within the context of the overall social and political atmosphere of the country.

Many of Iraq's historical problems – divisions between Sunni and Shia, Arab and Kurd, not to mention occasional troubles with the small Christian minority – have already been mentioned, as has Britain's contribution to their continuance. Excluding the Shias from government and reneging on their promises to the Kurds were mistakes that the British never tried to correct. On a lower scale, the tribes opposed the government and each other; there were conflicts between Bedouins and townsmen; cities competed with one another and resisted the central government, and even neighbourhoods within cities fought each other because of local rivalries or because their populations belonged to different religious or ethnic groups. These divisions were occasionally used by the British and by pro-British politicians to keep the country weak and dependent on them. From the time of the creation of the country in 1921 most Iraqis blamed the British, the monarchy and the Sunni elite for their problems, even those of which they were not guilty.

This is one of the reasons that ethnic, religious and tribal divisions did not interfere with the emergence of a national will: the communal problems were attributed and subordinated to the larger issue of a common enemy. The Iraqi national will surfaced during all major confrontations between the people and the central government, expressing itself as a common desire to improve the people's standard of living, as a wish to reclaim once-Iraqi Kuwait and to incorporate it in the mother country, and in the wide support for the Palestinian people against Jewish plans to create a Zionist state in their country. Of course, the Iraqis also wanted to exercise greater control over their natural wealth, specifically to realize greater income from the work of the British-run Iraqi Petroleum Company (IPC). To the average Iraqi the pro-British establishment was nothing but a collection of traitors used by the British, who had targeted Iraq as the most promising Arab country, to keep its people backward and poor.

These problems amounted to an explosive mixture of internal, regional and international conflicts. To contain the results of these cross-currents, under British supervision internal alliances between the monarchy and ruling elite were formed, undone and remade on a regular basis. However, because the various combinations which resulted produced no fundamental solutions to the country's problems and the triangular alliance resisted change and remained intact, the majority of the Iraqis still had little or no say about happenings within their country. Democratic reform mechanisms were not available to the people or were denied them, and the Iraqi people once again had no option but to express themselves through violence. History was repeating itself.

This background makes clear that superimposing the violent politics of Iraq on the inherent and acquired personal traits of Saddam is the key to understanding his life and Iraq's destiny. Every single one of the conflicts which I have mentioned mattered to the Iraqi people. Uncle Khairallah preoccupied himself with these problems as if they were his very own, and so did young Saddam. This strong focus on politics is often difficult for outsiders to understand, but people in unstable regions such as the Middle East follow politics the way people in the West follow sports and stories about the rich and famous.

Despite his popular appeal, King Ghazi was the catalyst which made every single problem facing his country worse. As already mentioned, he came to the throne in 1933 at the age of twenty-one. Although naive, only semi-literate, homosexual in a country which frowns on it, and tactless to the point of discourtesy, he was to upset the political balance of Iraq through changing the role of the monarchy. Under his father, Faisal I, the monarchy had deputized for the British while occasionally arguing with them over mostly minor issues. Since 1921 the British had used the king as a symbol of the country's unity, and the monarchy as an institution capable of gathering Iraq's diversity under a British-made crown. The Sunni monarchy depended on the Sunni establishment, protected British air routes to India, tolerated IPC's monopoly of Iraq's oil (in 1928 the British had promised the country a 20 per cent participation in the oil concession, but never kept their promise), rigged elections to keep its supporters in power, and acted as a deputy sheriff for Britain within the Middle East. It is worth emphasizing that once Britain realized the extent of Iraq's oil reserves the need to manipulate the government was reinforced; at the same time no effort was made to ease the economic plight of the people by sharing this wealth. In fact, even the laws which governed the ownership of land under the British favoured rich landowners over poor peasants, and were not as advanced as those which had existed under Ottoman Turkish rule. (The figures differ, but under Britain between 1 and 3 per cent of the population were allowed to own 55 per cent of all farmland.) And the British monopoly of Iraqi trade was total: a £1500 investment by Imperial Chemical Industries (ICI), for instance, grew to £1.5 million in a few years.[25]

All this began to fall apart after the unexpected death of Faisal and the accession of Ghazi. The young king was totally anti-British and instinctively populist. Acting without any design, but with some naive admiration of Kemal Ataturk, the modernizer of neighbouring Turkey, he came close to undoing the style of government set up by the British in 1921. He would not cooperate with pro-British politicians, opposed the policies of IPC and showed an unusual responsiveness to the demands of the people. The idea of resisting British hegemony and creating a modern nationalist government made Ghazi very popular and elevated him to the status of a hero.

Ghazi's radical views formed at an early age. He was born in 1912 in the Hijaz, now part of Saudi Arabia, to descendants of the prophet, the noble House of Hashem. His grandfather, Hussein I, had allied himself with the British against Turkey during the First World War in return for British promises to make him King of the Arabs. Those promises were never fulfilled and Ghazi grew up resenting the British for humiliating his grandfather. A one-year stay at Harrow School in 1928 and a briefer stint at the Royal Military Academy at Sandhurst were unsuccessful. He blamed his dismal academic performance on the British and the experience made him neurotic and unreliable.

Ghazi eventually graduated from Iraq's military college, still an academic under-achiever but with a flair for horsemanship and a mechanical aptitude. In 1932, while his father was on a visit to Europe, a serious rebellion broke out against the central government. The insurgents were Christian Assyrians, a mere 5 per cent of the population, and the affair was probably inspired by the British.[26] Ghazi and others thought the latter were trying either to undermine Iraq because more and more politicians were demanding greater freedom and expressing resentment over Britain's suffocating hegemony, or to weaken him and force him into toeing a line more accommodating to Britain. The British plans, if that is what they were, backfired. In his father's absence the crown prince unleashed the Iraqi Army and Air Force on the Assyrians, defeated them and became the embodiment of a nationalist hero capable of undermining British plans.

Although everything he did was divisive, Ghazi became a unifier – not one holding his country together in accordance with British designs, but one who integrated his country's conflicting components into a popular desire for a totally united and independent Iraq capable of leading the rest of the Arabs towards another period of glory. To his people, the anti-British policies he pursued were enough to overcome his shortcomings.

The following year this hero-prince replaced his conservative, dependably pro-British father. Instead of being remote and above politics Ghazi revelled in the love of his subjects, enjoyed his reputation as a military conqueror, wore uniform as frequently as possible and spent considerable time with anti-British army officers. Not for the first time in its long history, Iraq became a battleground where independent nationalist forces struggled with an alliance composed of a minority of local leaders supported by outside powers. On one side was a semi-literate king who, though loved by his people and Army and capable of expressing their supreme political ambition, had no programme or plan of action, not even wise advisers. On the other side stood the British and their cabal of hand-picked politicians who had run Iraq since it fell into their hands, together with most members of Ghazi's own family, in particular his first cousin Abdul Ilah.

In 1934–5 Ghazi put down several tribal rebellions in central Iraq which were aimed at weakening his government; these were inspired by the pro-British politicians, if not by the British them-selves. In 1936 Ghazi helped the upstart General Bakr Sidqi, who had led the Iraqi Army against the rebellious Assyrians and tribes-men, to stage a bloody coup which prompted many seasoned pro-British politicians to flee the country. Though the reasons behind the coup were unclear and its buffoon of a leader was assassinated in suspicious circumstances the following year, Ghazi's standing with the Iraqi Army and people continued to grow. Even his mistakes, including the major one of politicizing the Army, were subordinated to the popular fact that he was anti-British.

In 1937, using his mechanical talents but without much thought to the consequences, King Ghazi established his own broadcasting station in the royal palace of Al Zuhour; it was known to the Iraqis as Radio Qasr Al Zuhour. Using army officers and himself dou-bling as a broadcaster, he created a propaganda vehicle committed to the Arab cause[27] and spread his anti-British message throughout the Middle East. His broadcasts became popular in those Arab countries which could receive them – Syria, Jordan, Palestine and Kuwait – and he became the most celebrated Arab of his day: ten out of fourteen members of Kuwait's Legislative Council voted for union with Iraq under Ghazi. A simple, uneducated king using modern communications was upsetting British plans in the Middle East – perhaps because they had no popular support behind them.

When Ghazi responded to his growing reputation and began to advocate the annexation of Kuwait and the provision of direct help to the Palestinians against the Jewish settlers, Britain's cries of foul became undiplomatically shrill. The British Ambassador to Iraq, Maurice Patterson, demanded that the Al Zuhour radio station be shut,[28] but on occasions the King refused to see him. R. A. Butler, a member of the British cabinet, told Iraqi politician and former Prime Minister Tewfiq Al Sweidi that 'the king was playing with fire'.[29] Even official communications between the British Embassy and London were relatively explicit on the subject of containing or removing the King.[30]

The pro-British politicians who had escaped Iraq after the Sidqi coup but returned after his assassination (for which no one was ever tried), were even more determined to rid their country of the popular King than were their British masters. Sabah Said, the unintelligent son of Nuri Said, fourteen times Iraqi Prime Minister, wanted Ghazi killed.[31] Nuri Said himself, along with most other politicians, was keen to create a regency council to run the country in Ghazi's place,[32] while others hoped to get Ghazi's uncle Zeid to replace him. But Ghazi's first cousin and brother-in-law, Prince Abdul Ilah, totally pro-British and undoubtedly the most unpopular ruler in the turbulent history of Iraq, was more to the taste of the British and the local kingmakers. Unlike the retiring Zeid, Abdul Ilah was a bitter, twisted man who would not shy from conspiring to remove or assassinate a cousin. Rumours of coups, assassinations and changes in government and the Army's command were endless, and involved some of the most important figures in the country. Khairallah and his fellow Tikriti officers belonged to the activist pro-Ghazi elements in the armed forces.

Late on 3 April 1939 Ghazi, driving his car in the company of two members of the palace staff, had an accident; he died in the early hours of the following day. But was it really an accident, or was the popular King killed? All the evidence suggests the latter. The car was supposed to have hit a telephone pole but looked undamaged, and there were no signs that the King, as his enemies claimed, had been driving at high speed. The fatal wound in the back of Ghazi's head could not have resulted from an accident involving the front of the car. According to the Iraqi artist and writer Nuha Al Radi her great-uncle Dr Saeb Shawkat, entrusted with examining the King before his burial, refused to sign the death certificate.[33] The then Minister of the Interior, Saeb's brother Naji Shawkat, spoke of having to cover up a murder. All attempts at conducting a post mortem examination were refused by the pro-British politicians who immediately took over the running of the country. Abdul Ilah, who became regent because Ghazi's son was only four years old, wanted the whole affair closed as soon as possible. The King's companions in the car, Eid bin Said and Ali bin Abdallah, were never seen again. Even the first judge entrusted with conducting the investigation of the accident was dismissed by the government for wanting to do the job thoroughly. The message from the British Embassy to the Foreign Office on the day of Ghazi's death, 4 April 1939, is missing from the files. The following day the *Guardian* newspaper stated that 'Ghazi's death solved a problem for the British who were thinking of removing him.'[34]

King Ghazi's death had far-reaching consequences which haunt Iraq and the rest of the Middle East to this day. The crowds which followed his cortege asked for vengeance and singled out the pro-British Nuri Said with shouts of 'Thou shalt answer for the blood of Ghazi!' The historian Hanna Batatu, even with the benefit of hindsight, offers a sober but equally damning judgement: 'The death of Ghazi ruined the crown.'[35] Certainly the monarchy lost all credibility because his death proved that the British would never accept anything except 'their' king or regent. The people of Iraq wanted the opposite, a king who would be more than a figurehead symbol of unity and would unite their country through expressing their desires. They wanted a king who would close their divisions, heal their social wounds and become a magnet for all the Arabs of the Middle East. They thought that his articulation of their grievances would eliminate British hegemony over Iraq and other Arab countries and end Britain's control of Iraq's oil wealth.

The old-line politicians on whom Britain depended were so tainted by the regicide that they never recovered their ascendancy. Abdul Ilah, like his popular cousin a homosexual, suffered crude insults which Ghazi had escaped: the Iraqis described him as someone who drags on his back (*bejur 'ala dahru* – the ultimate Iraqi pejorative). The Iraqi Army, having lost its hero, was more politicized than ever before. Turmoil bred more turmoil, and neither the British nor their friends made sensible moves to placate the people. Instead, the self-centred politicians began to court army cliques as a way of attaining power. The Army was no longer an instrument in the hands of a popular king, and its worth was bid up and down by power-seekers nearly on a daily basis. Amazingly, the British did nothing to contain the situation.

Early in 1941, a group of army colonels who resented the policies of their creator, Nuri Said, struck out on their own to continue what Ghazi had started. After considerable vacillation the four, Kamil Shabib, Mohammed Salman, Fahmi Said and Saluhheddine Sabbagh, known to the Iraqis as the Golden Square, adopted a pro-Nazi stance and supported a government headed by Rashid Ali Al Keilani, after whom it was named the Rashid Ali Rebellion. The colonels fell under the influence of the Mufti of Palestine, then a refugee in Iraq who wanted to ally the Arabs with Germany, which was at war with Britain. With British assistance the unpopular regent, Abdul Ilah, fled the country in the company of various politicians.

The British refused to accept the new government, launched a military campaign against it on 19 May and had taken complete control of Iraq by the 30th. As in 1991, the Iraqi Army performed badly, in this case despite German and Italian offers of help. Rashid Ali and the Mufti escaped to Germany, but the colonels were executed, three immediately and one when Turkey repatriated him after the Second World War. Supported by British bayonets, Abdul Ilah was back to oversee the executions and carry out what he called a 'purification' campaign: 324 army officers including Khairallah were cashiered.[36] Although he always exaggerated the level of his involvement, Khairallah was not a prime mover in these events and was punished merely for belonging to the group.

Although it was an extension of past developments and did no more than complete what began with Ghazi's death, the Rashid Ali Rebellion was one of the most significant developments in the history of modern Iraq.[37] It provided irrefutable proof that the crown of Iraq was controlled by outsiders, a creation of the British conquerors[38] who overlooked the criminal behaviour of their supporters, perhaps even when it involved killing a king. Indeed, what followed the Rebellion amounted to a reoccupation of Iraq by the British until 1946;[39] eight of the seventeen years between the Rebellion and the overthrow of the monarchy in 1958 were administered under martial law. The inherent instability of the country gathered momentum and became chronic. This is the background which makes Khairallah's dismissal and imprisonment one of the most formative political acts which shaped the life of Saddam Hussein.

Saddam and his generation were the product of the machinations which eliminated the rightful occupant of Qasr Al Zuhour and of the legacy of the Rashid Ali Rebellion. He grew up obsessed with avenging the deaths of Ghazi and the colonels of the Golden Square. The Iraqis felt that the regent and the pro-British politicians had stabbed them in the back, and their hatred of this group was so pronounced and so close to the surface that strong man Nuri Said, perennial Prime Minister of the country, always carried a sidearm to protect himself.

Kids like Saddam continued to sing 'Lahat ro'os al hirabi' or 'The tips of spears have appeared', the banned anthem of the

Futuwa, the paramilitary youth organization modelled on the Hitler Youth which came to life under the banner of Ghazi in the 1930s. They believed in the teachings of Sati' Al Husri, an educator who emulated the Germans and wanted Iraq to unite the Arabs the way Prussia had united the Germans. A whole generation of Iraqis revelled in being called the Prussians of the Middle East and tried to live up to this claim. Schoolchildren, often the element who best reflect emerging public opinion, responded to most acts of the reimposed pro-British government by rioting and chanting anti-British slogans. Ghazi and the colonels were mourned in songs and poems which were distributed secretly.

The treaty signed in December 1947 at Portsmouth was a feeble attempt at change. Among its most unacceptable aspects was the retention of two RAF bases, Habaniya and Sin Al Thibban. Its signing provoked riots and the security forces and Army were then ordered to open fire on unarmed demonstrators, which turned the situation into a confrontation between the people and the triangular alliance. In the end, because the people kept rioting despite heavy casualties, the treaty failed. On analysis, it was a half-hearted effort which made the internal situation of the country worse.

The Army's invasion of Palestine in 1948 in support of their fellow Arabs against the Israelis was another move to placate the people, but it backfired. The Iraqi people have always believed in their Army and in the notion of being the Prussians of the Middle East, and its defeat was blamed on political decisions rather than military incompetence. There were stories that it was sent into battle without ammunition and other necessities, in this case essentially true, that it failed to coordinate with the rest of the Arab armies and that it refused to go to the aid of the Egyptians when they came under Israeli attack. Khairallah and Saddam shared the popular reaction to the treaty and to the defeat in Palestine.

By the early 1950s, young Saddam was a regular participant in anti-government demonstrations. After Gamal Abdel Nasser overthrew the government of Egypt in 1952 and began promoting Arab unity, Saddam was among the students who invoked his name during the frequent riots against the rulers of Iraq. His pursuit of formal education appeared to be at an end and whatever Khairallah had instilled in him was being amplified, expanded or occasionally changed in accordance with the teachings of the Egyptian leader. His Tikriti instincts had not left him and, unlike other students, he began carrying a gun. To his fellow semi-professional agitators he became known as *a bu mussaddess*, or He of the Gun.[40] His new status appealed to him and he found life as a tough on the edge of politics more to his liking. He began to devote his life to it while making a marginal living from odd jobs.

As if to provide the restive population with more reasons to oppose it, in 1955 the Iraqi government joined the Baghdad Pact, an anti-Communist alliance which also included Turkey, Iran and Pakistan. It was another act of self-preservation which backfired. Aimed against the USSR and Nasser, the alliance ensured the continuation of anti-government disturbances and provided Saddam with the only known outlet for his energies. In 1956 matters deteriorated when Iraqis exploded with anger against their government for its implicit support of the British, French and Israeli invasion of Egypt during the Suez Crisis. Once again there were dozens of dead and wounded.

Saddam now became a student leader of anti-government demonstrations. A sign of worse things to come, he relied on alley boys and criminal elements and talked them into joining the student protesters. He set up roving gangs of thugs who specialized in beating up their opponents, including shopkeepers who refused to shut their businesses in protest at government policy. The acceptance of his behaviour by fellow student leaders confirmed the Iraqis' national love of toughness and disdain for compassion.[41]

Later in 1956 he is alleged to have been peripherally involved in a plot to overthrow the government.[42] Anti-Saddam political groups, understandably not a reliable source of information, dismiss this story. But there is reason to believe that it was true: it was retold later during some trials of people who knew him at the time. However, there are no grounds for believing that it stood any chance of success or that it was anything more than one of many badly organized plots involving students and junior army officers.

At the same time Saddam began to keep the company of a more organized group of students who belonged to the Ba'ath, a political party founded in Syria in the 1940s. Its programme called for Arab unity, and the party had branches in several other Arab countries. Most Ba'ath members were university students and intellectuals and they came from the upper middle classes. Here again, Saddam's situation was similar to Stalin's among the Communist revolutionaries of the early twentieth century: both men's backgrounds and limited education made them stand out as oddities. Furthermore, neither Stalin nor Saddam had the benefit of being 'big city revolutionaries', those who knew their establishment opponents because of the common background. But he watched them, learned from them and showed respect for them, while compensating for his absence of qualifications and intellectual powers, through physical activity, toughness and hard work. But developing these talents was not enough to make him a fully fledged member of this privileged group. Contrary to the self-serving statements that he made to biographer Fuad Matar[43] and others, he did not become a member of the party until 1959, when he was in Damascus. Until then, the tightly structured membership system of the party had limited him to the position of 'supporter', essentially a sub-member who still needed to prove himself. This explains why his occasional arrests never led to his being imprisoned, as were some of his colleagues. Even the police thought he was too junior to worry about.

There is a non-political story about Saddam during this period, late 1956 or early 1957, which merits examination. Those who tell it claim that he killed a cousin after the man insulted his uncle Khairallah. But investigations have uncovered nothing to support this allegation. It is not that Saddam was incapable of murder, or that insulting Khairallah was not enough provocation for Tikriti blood to be spilled and Tikriti behaviour to assert itself. It is simply a matter of an unknown victim and a lack of details, both of the original insult and of where and how the murder was committed. Either the tale is a complete fabrication or it has been confused with another with which I will deal later. Moreover, in 1956 and 1957 Saddam was promoting his own image as a tough guy, and he could have started the rumour himself to claim a dubious honour which would embellish his personal credentials.

Early in 1958, the divisions among the Arabs assumed concrete forms. Nasser had survived Suez and come out of it with his stature enhanced. Through his ability to stand up to the West he became the most popular Arab leader of the century, commanding loyalty on street level throughout the Arab world, Iraq included. Syria, politically adrift and in need of an anchor, was anxious to unite with Egypt. Though reluctant to accept the Syrian offer, Nasser's advocacy of Arab unity forced him to do so and to set up the United Arab Republic (UAR). The pull of Arab unity was so strong that the Iraqi government responded by creating the Arab Union with Jordan. The UAR was backed by the USSR and had wide popular appeal among all Arabs, while the Arab Union had Western support and depended on the old elite which had run Iraq since the end of the First World War.

On 14 July 1958, after innumerable attempts and false starts during the previous three years, the Iraqi Army finally overthrew the monarchy. It was the natural culmination of everything which had happened since 1921. An army created to hold the country together was the only organization capable of toppling the government and it did, with bloody relish. The Iraqi Army had suffered three humiliations which it never forgot: the assassination of King Ghazi, the execution of the Golden Square and the defeat in Palestine. When it rose to avenge its honour the officers who led it could trace their lineage to these three events, which explains why their move met with no resistance. Not a single Iraqi Army unit tried to protect the monarchy, the instability of whose thirty-seven years of existence was reflected in an astonishing fifty-eight cabinets during that period.[44]

The army rebels, a committee of 'Free Officers', as they called themselves, headed by Brigadier Abdel Karim Kassem and Colonel Abdel Salam Aref, stormed the palace of Qasr Al Rihab with the intention of massacring the entire royal family. To pre-empt any possibility of the monarchy being restored they made sure of murdering King Faisal II, Ghazi's son, towards whom the people felt affection because of his father. Killing a son to avenge a father's assassination was an ironic act of Shakespearean dimensions.

Saddam was among those who greeted the coup with undisguised joy. To him and his fellow Ba'athists, and to many Iraqi believers in Arab unity, it was meant to unite Iraq with the UAR, and the shouting in the streets of Baghdad was in support of Nasser rather than the unknown leaders of the coup. But things did not go according to the Ba'athists' hopes; soon Brigadier Kassem adopted an Iraq-first policy and became a serious opponent of the Egyptian leader, his pan-Arab plans and his supporters. This was the beginning of a new phase for Iraq and the rest of the Middle East.

It also marked a new beginning for the fatherless lad from Tikrit. Ghazi, the Golden Square and Khairallah's imprisonment had been avenged. But failure to act on the issues which the forebears of the 1958 coup had represented, including annexing Kuwait and liberating Palestine, guaranteed that more turmoil was on the way.

3

A Gun for Hire

The 14 July 1958 coup and its far-reaching consequences are as vital to understanding Saddam as his very early days in Tikrit. It changed the established order in a fundamental way, and affected the daily life of every Iraqi citizen. A mere hour after Radio Baghdad had announced the end of the monarchy well over a million people were celebrating in the streets, and killing and looting were among the ways in which they expressed their joy. Even children recalled the words of Al Hajjaj and recited stories of Iraqi violence. The modern Arab world had never known anything like it.

The only person to escape being murdered at the Qasr Al Rihab was the wife of regent Abdul Ilah, whom the rebels left for dead in the middle of the pile of royal corpses. In their only act of respect, the Army took the body of the twenty-three-year-old King to a secret burial place. That of his uncle, the hated Abdul Ilah, was claimed by the mob. After being dragged through the streets for hours it was dismembered in a most gruesome way, and the remains were hanged in front of the Ministry of Defence as a public spectacle. For two days it dangled from the same spot where in 1941 Abdul Ilah had brutally exhibited the dead bodies of the members of the Golden Square. The Iraqi Army and people were getting their revenge.

At first Prime Minister Nuri Said managed to avoid being captured by the Army and self-appointed vigilantes, but after two days the people finally caught up with him. Dressed as a woman, he feebly tried to face them with a pistol. They killed him, ran their cars back and forth over his body, buried him, then disinterred him and tore what remained into a small scraps. His fingers and other parts of his body were paraded by people in the matter of a football trophy, and there were reports that some people drank his blood and ate his flesh. The Baghdad Hotel, a symbol of the affluent elite, was attacked by angry mobs. Its residents, including Jordanian ministers who were in Baghdad to finalize the setting up of the Arab Union, were herded into trucks and many of them were killed, some after being beaten up savagely. Bands of young men attacked the wealthy neighbourhoods of Baghdad, Basra, Mosul, Kirkuk and other towns and cities. The number of people summarily killed will never be known, but thousands were arrested, including dozens of army officers loyal to the monarchy.

The coup's leaders, Kassem and Aref, were not directly responsible for the behaviour of the crowds, but their first official acts betrayed a closeness between their own attitude and what the people were doing, and they did nothing to stop the violence. Among the earliest announcements of the Committee of Free Officers was the creation of a Communist-style People's Court to try the enemies of the people. Although he later moved to other duties, Colonel Ahmad Hassan Al Bakr, Saddam's eventual mentor, was among those appointed to this court. The Orientalist and Iraq specialist Freya Stark lamented, 'It [the coup which created the revolution] unleashed the savagery for which Iraq in her long history has been notorious'.[1] As during the 1920 rebellion and other anti-monarchist and anti-British upheavals, there was no distinguishing between Iraqi Sunnis and Shias: their hatred of the *ancien régime* made them one.

In comparison with other countries, the scale of the brutality in Iraq was unique. Syria, the Arab country closest to Iraq in its social composition, had suffered several coups in the early 1950s, but nothing as extreme as the events that followed the 1958 Iraqi coup ever took place there. In 1949 the Syrian Army did kill President Husni Zaim and his Prime Minister, but it was merely a matter of colonels settling scores among themselves and there was no mob behind the Army. Nasser's 1952 coup in Egypt was a relatively peaceful affair: King Farouq was sent into exile on a yacht, the pashas who had helped him ruin Egypt lost their land but were not molested, a number of Egyptian army officers were dismissed and a handful of them put on trial. In Iraq, the crowds recalled every single shred of hatred in the violent history of a violent land.

The revolution unleashed by the 1958 coup affected not only Iraq but the whole of the Middle East, and even had repercussions throughout the rest of the world. Within Iraq, the people became a restless rabble. Saddam claims that he was among them, probably with some of his young thugs. They chanted the name of the symbol of Arab unity, Gamal Abdel Nasser of Egypt: 'We're your soldiers, Gamal', was the slogan of the day, ignoring the fact that all his life Nasser abhorred violence.[2] But it was the totality of the death of the old social order which turned the coup into a revolution. The monarchy was no more. The Sunni elite which had run the country under it had lost its raison d'etre, and the Army emerged as the guardians of a government run along populist-leftist lines which included promises to enact land reform and support the workers and peasants. In fear of their lives, the British Ambassador, Sir Michael Wright, and his wife took refuge outside their official residence. To the Iraqis Lady Wright was the uncrowned queen of their country, and forcing her to hide to save her life was a symbol of victory as significant as the pile of royal bodies.[3]

Brigadier Abdel Karim Kassem came from a poor background, but the rest of the Free Officers who had been instrumental in carrying out the coup were from middle-class families. Kassem had a Shia Kurdish mother but the others were Sunni, which reflected the composition of the officer corps. Their backgrounds aside, what all the officers advocated was radical. It expressed the feeling of the common people, who had felt the oppression of the triangular alliance of the British, the monarchy and the Sunni elite and to a lesser degree some rich Shias whose support had been bought with land grants.

The revolutionary nature of the coup affected all the surrounding countries. Iran and Turkey, which under the monarchy had been Iraq's allies in the Baghdad Pact, found themselves undermined by an unfriendly government in their backyard. Israel, which had always seen Iraq's military potential as a danger to its security, was confronted by a new regime made up of officers who had fought in Palestine and which therefore took a much harder line against Israel than the monarchy, which had preoccupied itself with the perceived Communist threat. Jordan, Iraq's partner in the Arab Union, was left in a precarious position and everyone expected it to fall to pro-Nasser elements.

The immediate problem was Arab unity,[4] which the West had always opposed. The prospect of Iraq joining Syria and Egypt in the UAR was real, and so was the threat that the call for Arab unity might snowball and give rise to a Nasser-led country big enough and strong enough to swallow the rest of the Arab countries. This posed a direct threat to Western interests in Saudi Arabia and the rest of the oil-producing sheikhdoms. And a UAR which included Iraq might achieve military parity with Israel and endanger Turkey and Iran.

The international situation was an ominous extension of the regional one. The coup had caught the West napping, but the threats it generated, particularly to its oil interests, had to be met. The Free Officers had expected Nasser to back them against possible outside attempts to stop them and he did, unambiguously threatening that, 'Any aggression against Iraq is one against the UAR.'[5] But although the USSR was behind Nasser, the West hurried to serve notice that it would not allow the revolution to spread. American marines landed in Lebanon to help pro-West President Camille Chamoun, already fighting insurgents loyal to Nasser. British marines landed in Jordan to prop up King Hussein's shaky regime. The prospect of a march against the new rulers of Iraq and a confrontation with Nasser which would drag in the USSR loomed large. The international press was full of articles on the way Nasser's control of Middle Eastern oil would affect the global power game.

Statesmen from countries not directly involved in the developing confrontation trekked to Baghdad to determine the nature of the new regime and how best to calm the situation. Among them was former Canadian Foreign Minister Paul Martin. His meeting with Iraq's new leader, Kassem, left him in a state of shock. When the Canadian complained about the violent nature of what had happened, his host produced a picture of himself waving to a crowd of hundreds of thousands. 'Do you think they're all wrong, your excellency?' he inquired.[6]

But what mattered more – indeed, it was a most important turning point in the history of the Middle East – was a secret meeting which had already taken place between Kassem and the

British Ambassador, Sir Michael Wright. According to Hani Fkaiki, a former Ba'athist leader and minister and supporter of Arab unity, it took place twenty-four hours after the coup.[7] This assertion, and what the two discussed, is supported by prominent Iraqi politician Abdel Sattar Douri, two former Iraqi officers who spoke on a non-attribution basis, and a member of Saddam Hussein's present government who too opted to remain unnamed. Though there is minor disagreement on this point, the meeting, which was held at Kassem's request, is supposed to have lasted for over five hours. During this time Kassem made certain assurances to Wright regarding the nature of the coup and he was to follow this up with action which supported his intentions.

According to all my informants, Kassem assured Wright that the Iraqi coup was a strictly internal affair and that he had no intention of joining the UAR. Furthermore, the new leader guaranteed the continued flow of Iraqi oil to the world market. He asserted that the West had nothing to fear and that there was no need to use the forces which had landed in Lebanon and Jordan and were equipped to march on Baghdad.[8] Kassem's words thus saved Iraq from a Western military attack.

On 16 July Kassem proved his point by refusing to allow Nasser, who had flown to Moscow to consult with Khrushchev about the developing crisis, to land in Baghdad on his way back to Cairo.[9] Had the Egyptian president been allowed to do so, Kassem's hand would have been forced and Iraqi–UAR unity would have been declared immediately. This would have reduced the unknown Kassem to a follower of Nasser, the idol of the rampaging crowds. Kassem's later behaviour, too, displayed a friendly attitude towards Britain and a British wish to accommodate him. Moreover, his eventual open opposition to Nasser supports the allegations of Fkaiki and the rest.

This is the atmosphere within which Saddam and his fellow Ba'athists operated. Their initial support of Kassem assumed that he was leading Iraq into an Arab union, and they had no idea of what was happening behind the scenes (Fkaiki only discovered it years later). Kassem had included a number of pro-Nasser Arab nationalists in his cabinet, including the young leader of the Ba'ath, Shia Fuad Al Rikabi. His partner in the leadership of the coup, Aref, was a fervent believer in Arab unity and wanted Iraq to join the UAR immediately. Most Iraqis were with the small Ba'ath Party and Aref, but Kassem favoured an independent, inward-looking Iraq.

The differences of opinion between Kassem and most of the Free Officers surfaced before the end of 1958. Iraq was divided and threatened with civil war. Bereft of popular support, Kassem depended on a highly organized Communist party and a handful of officers who wanted an independent country. The other side, pro-UAR, included the Ba'ath and many able officers but was led by the impetuous Aref. Veteran Iraqi politician Sidiq Shanshall spoke of the country being contested by two people, one of whom 'was half crazy and the other half sane'.[10] As it happened, Kassem, aided by the utter ineptness of Aref, came out ahead. Rikabi resigned from the cabinet in protest. Aref was exiled, then tried for attempting to overthrow the government, imprisoned and finally pardoned. The rest of the officers, suddenly leaderless, retired to conspire against the new government. Saddam's joy, along with that of millions of other Iraqis, turned to anger. But, because something resembling gang warfare was taking place in the country, this time his services were truly needed.

From October 1958 the Ba'ath began using Saddam's gang of petty criminals to counter the activities of the Popular Resistance, one of the organizations set up by Kassem to deal with the opposition. A government-sponsored, Communist-led militia which tried to impose a reign of terror, the Popular Resistance represented the first attempt by an Iraqi government to institutionalize paramilitary organizations and use them for oppression. Its members adopted the slogans of '*Maku za'im ila Karim*', or 'There is no leader except Karim', meaning Abdel Karim Kassem, and '*Al za'im al awhad*', 'The sole leader'. The Ba'athists, meanwhile, were committed to 'One Arab nation with an eternal message' and 'Unity, liberty and socialism'.

With government approval the Popular Resistance built road blocks and inspected cars, molested pedestrians and entered houses without search warrants. Unable to confront them directly, the Ba'athists and other Arab nationalist groups resorted to hit-and-run tactics. They obtained a printing press, and began distributing leaflets against Kassem. Saddam was involved in both activities. Nowadays even former Ba'athists are unwilling to credit Saddam with any success, but there is little doubt that he was effective and better prepared for gang warfare than the more educated, urbane party members. He managed the odd ambush against members of the Popular Resistance and his group killed and wounded some of them. He also visited schools and universities to urge students to do more. It was his small group who at night distributed the illegal leaflets and pamphlets containing calls for revolution against Kassem which could earn their writers and distributors long prison terms or even summary execution. But government support for the pro-Communist force gave it the upper hand. Saddam was arrested and roughed up a number of times, but he was still not important enough to be kept in prison. Even his fellow Ba'athists still thought of him as mere muscle and did not make him a full member. he remained on the fringes as a 'supporter'.

Eventually there was an incident which landed him in jail for six months from November 1958. As with so many other events in Saddam's life, both supporters and detractors admit that it was a mixture of the political and the personal. His arrest followed the murder of a Tikriti whose name Saddam's chroniclers cannot agree on. He has been called Sa'adoun Alousi, Sa'adoun Nasiri, Sa'adoun Tikriti and Hajji Sa'adoun. The last name is the one that former Ba'ath leader Salah Omar Al Ali uses, and because he knows more about Tikriti names than the others I shall follow his example.

Hajji Sa'adoun, like Saddam's uncle Khairallah, was a schoolteacher in the Al Kharkh district of Baghdad. But unlike Khairallah and Saddam, he was a supporter of the Kassem regime. Professional jealousy between him and Khairallah was exacerbated by these differences in political outlook, which became an issue when the two ran for the same council seat in Tikrit. Khairallah lost, and soon afterwards was fired from his job too. That he blamed Sa'adoun for his misfortune is established, but whether Saddam later killed the man while the latter was visiting relatives in Tikrit is impossible to prove.

Fuad Matar claims that the man who was killed in Tikrit was a policeman.[11] Others deny this but do not rule out the possibility that Sa'adoun had been a police informer. Unwilling to give Saddam the benefit of innocence until proven guilty, all Western biographers and writers insist that he killed the man. But this is far from clear-cut. Saddam and Khairallah were arrested and tried for the murder, but eventually released for lack of proof. These events took place under a government which frowned on their political inclinations, viewed the murder of a supporter seriously and hence was disinclined to afford them leniency. But why would Saddam mention the incident to biographer Matar and state that the dead man was with Kassem's police? It implies an admission and a justification at the same time

Whatever the facts, Saddam's and Khairallah's imprisonment by the Kassem regime enhanced their political reputation within Arab nationalist and Ba'ath circles. Hani Fkaiki, already a leading Ba'athist and in prison for opposition to the government, was in the Sardi prison when Saddam and Khairallah were confined there. He told me that the two kept to themselves, and confirmed this in his memoirs.[12] This too is strange: had the murder been political Saddam typically would have taken pride in having committed it. Perhaps there was a murder and it was more personal than political, or perhaps there was no murder at all. Whatever the truth, Saddam's newly enhanced reputation was to play a major part in his future.

On 6 March 1959 the Peace Partisans, another Communist-front organization beholden to Kassem, held a national convention in Mosul. Hundreds of thousands of Communists and sympathizers descended on the city from all parts of Iraq. Objecting to their unruly presence and their mistreatment of the citizens of Mosul, the local army commander, Colonel Abdel Wahab Al Shawaf, ordered his troops to restore order and personally disposed of the leader of the conference, a Communist lawyer named Kamil Al Kazanji. What followed was a free-for-all which involved every segment of the population, the clearest demonstration ever recorded of the divisions racking Iraq. According to historian Hanna Batatu:

> For four days and nights Kurds and Yezidis stood against Arabs; Assyrian and Aramian Christians against Arab Muslims; the Arab tribe of Albu Mutaiwit against the Arab tribe of Shamar; the Kurdish tribe of Gargariyyah against Arab Albu Mutaiwit; the peasants of Mosul country against their landlords; the soldiers of the Fifth Brigade against their officers; the periphery of Mosul against its centre; the plebeians of the Arab quarter of al Makkawi and Wadi Hajjar against the Arab aristocrats of the

Arab quarter of al Dawwasah; and within the quarter of Bab al
Baid, the family of al Rajabou against its traditional rivals the
Aghawat . . .[13]

What became known as the Mosul Rebellion left behind a trail
of blood which still haunts the soul of Iraq. The pro-Kassem
elements, including the Communists, triumphed. Dead was the
pro-Nasser leader of the rebellion, most of the army officers who
supported him and a good number of Arab nationalists and
Ba'athists. As a young news correspondent of twenty-three, I
witnessed hundreds of dead and wounded being brought to the
Syrian city of Kamishly, the nearest major outpost, because the
medical facilities in Mosul could not cope with the huge number of
casualties.[14]

A large number of the original Free Officers were arrested and
put on trial as traitors to Iraq and the regime. The small but
organized Ba'ath Party moved into the breach. Of all the pro-
Nasser forces calling for unity with the UAR, it was the one group
which, in terms of organization, came out of the Mosul Rebellion
relatively intact. In April the Ba'athists, with UAR connivance,
decided to assassinate Kassem. Rikabi, the leader of the Ba'ath
Party, initiated the move, but the real orders came from the Syrian
branch of Nasser's UAR. (Whether Nasser himself knew about it
cannot be confirmed.) Young Ba'athists including a friend of
Saddam's, Abdel Karim Shaikhally, went to Damascus for special
training by Nasser's police.[15] They returned to Iraq to carry out
their plan in August.

According to Saddam a Ba'athist messenger, Ahmad Taha Al
Azuri, came from Baghdad to Tikrit to invite him to participate.
The messenger had a very simple question for him: 'Are you ready
to kill Kassem?'[16] Saddam's fictionalized biography *The Long
Days*, in which he calls himself Mohammed Hussein Saqr, tells
a slightly different version which implies that Saddam was ordered
to take part, and its ghost writer speaks of Saddam being summoned to Baghdad for 'an important assignment'.[17] The knowledgeable former Ba'athist Salah Omar Al Ali describes both
versions of the story as 'nonsense – he was made part of the plans
to assassinate Kassem last-minute, in place of one Shaker Hleiwait.
They needed a gunman.' Once again the details are immaterial in
terms of the outcome, and Saddam Hussein participated in an

attempt to assassinate General Abdel Karim Kassem on 7 October 1959

Saddam is proud of this part of his life. In July 1982 he escorted *Time* magazine senior editor Murray Gart and correspondent Dean Brelis to the spot where he tried to kill his country's leader, and described the whole thing with considerable glee. The audio tape of Saddam talking the journalists through the event is in my possession.

Kassem was in the habit of driving through Al Rashid Street, Baghdad's main thoroughfare, during the afternoon without adequate protection. Saddam's role in the seven-man assassination team was a secondary one: he was supposed to provide cover to enable his companions to escape after they had killed the leader as his car drove past. But that day Kassem was a few minutes late, so that by the time his car eventually appeared the conspirators had succumbed to nerves and everyone started shooting at the same time. Saddam has always admitted this, and spoken of difficulty controlling 'his emotions'.

Kassem was hit in the arm and shoulder and seriously wounded, and his driver was killed. But the lack of organization showed and members of the hit squad directed their fire against each other. One of them, Abdel Wahab Ghoreiri, was killed. Saddam suffered a wound in his leg. Many claim that the failure of the plan was down to Saddam and that the others had followed instructions. He is also accused of responsibility for Ghoreiri's death.[18] But again it is a difficult accusation to prove, particularly in view of the participants' silence on the subject. What is definitely true is that Ghoreiri was left behind. Although the rest managed to escape, through identifying Ghoreiri the authorities knew who his fellow conspirators were.

There was no follow-up to the assassination attempt – no one tried to capitalize on it and attempt a take over of the government. Saddam himself laments this openly, calls the whole operation 'elementary'[19] and admits that each of the participants went a different way because they had assumed that they would be successful and would not need places to hide. He has used this event as an example with such frequency and emphasized the need for preparation so often (it appears in the works of all his loyalist biographers) that it is safe to accept it as one of the factors which turned him into a methodical organizer, one of his greatest attributes to this day. But however lacking in organization, the plot represented the beginning of the legend which thrust Saddam into Iraqi politics in an open and irreversible way.

Saddam's basking in the glory of his revelations to *Time*'s Gart and Brelis was in character. In *The Long Days* he inflated his role in the attempted assassination of Kassem, reinventing it as a heroic act which demanded extraordinary physical and spiritual strength, the superhuman qualities which naturally made him Iraq's undisputed leader. However, recording this in a book was not enough for Saddam and in 1983, four years after he became President, *The Long Days* was made into a six-hour television series. To guarantee its success he used me, then a consultant to his Ministry of Information, to hire the well-known director Terence Young to edit the film and ensure that it was of the highest quality.[20] The man who played the part of Saddam was his relative Saddam Kamel, who eventually defected from the regime and suffered the consequences. Because Saddam believes in eradicating all traces of such people, all copies of the film have since been withdrawn from sale.

According to Saddam's record in *The Long Days*, his wound was so serious that he could hardly walk. He and a friend used a razor blade to extract a bullet from his calf and thus saved his life.[21] This is an exaggeration of serious proportions. Dr Tahseen Mua'la, a former Ba'athist and now an opponent of Saddam living outside London, treated Saddam at the time. His story goes as follows: 'I was summoned by Iyyad Said Thabet, the leader of the group, to treat Samir Al Najjar, who was seriously wounded. They called me because I belonged to the party. I did treat Najjar, and then they told me there was another young man who had a superficial wound and I did treat him, and that was Saddam Hussein. All this is a matter of record. It came out when I was arrested and tried in front of a Kassem court for aiding and abetting the would-be assassins.'[22] Indeed, the story recalled by dozens of Iraqis who remember what followed that assassination attempt supports Dr Mua'la's version of events.

Further examination of this incident reveals other characteristics of Saddam which are with him to this day. He not only learned the need to plan and organize through experience in the streets and by analyzing the failure of the attempt on Kassem's life, he simultaneously and instinctively developed an appreciation of the value of propaganda. In fact, all of *The Long Days* is nothing but a dramatization of much simpler facts. The rest of Saddam's story tells how, after the bullet was removed, he escaped to the only place he knew, Tikrit. But of course the security police was after him, so after two days he left Tikrit and headed towards Syria. In the process he crossed the Euphrates with his clothes stacked on his head to keep them dry, spent nights with Bedouin tribes after appealing to their sense of honour, bought a horse, and finally dressed in Bedouin garb to cover another leg of the journey, all of which took seven days. Supposedly he arrived in Syria to a hero's welcome.[23]

Saddam did escape to Tikrit, probably in pain, and the security forces were indeed after him. He did cross the Syrian desert, and it is likely that he did so with great difficulty. Later he was received at the Syrian border town of Abu Kamal by members of the Ba'ath Party already in exile in that country. Moreover, his wound had become inflamed during the journey and he was now in even greater pain.[24] All of it was heroic, if somewhat different from Saddam's version. My interviews in 1995 with Hani Fkaiki and Abdel Sattar Douri, both of whom were in Syria at the time of Saddam's arrival, reveal that he received considerable sympathy because of his wound but little attention as a political activist. He was a minor figure, and among the refugees greater notice was taken of more important Ba'athists such as Abdel Karim Shaikhally, another of the would-be assassins.

Because Saddam was only twenty or twenty-two years old, what to do with him was a problem. While recovering he participated in the various meetings of Iraqi exiles and Syrian Ba'athists, but he had little to say. Eventually the authorities in Syria, the junior member of Nasser's UAR, decided to send all such young Iraqis, about five hundred of them, to Cairo to continue their education.[25] The organizer of this plan was Abdel Majid Farid, later a special adviser to president Nasser in charge of Iraqi exiles in Egypt.[26] Saddam and Shaikhally did not object to the move, and it was left to older, more seasoned Ba'athists to conduct the campaign against Kassem from Damascus. However, Saddam did achieve something during his three-month stay in Damascus. It was then that he met Michel Aflaq, the Christian Syrian co-founder of the Ba'ath and its spiritual leader. Aflaq took a shine to the silent Saddam, honoured him by making him a full member of the Ba'ath party, and retained a good impression of him and his capabilities.[27] Old Ba'athists explain this in terms of the wily Aflaq recognizing Saddam's toughness and the prospect of using him as a *sanad* – a backer-up in time of trouble, in particular someone who frightens others.

In Cairo Saddam entered Qasr Al Nil high school in the Dokki district, where he lived. From 1959 until his graduation in 1961 he lived the life of a political exile with the usual preoccupation with events in his own country, and was totally dependent on the small salary provided by the UAR government. There is nothing to indicate that he changed his ways and became a good student. Naturally his version of how he used his time is slightly different from the truth: he told his biographer Iskandar that he 'emulated Nasser and played chess and . . . was not distracted by night life and read a great deal'.[28] But this is a modest exaggeration, and his assertion that he devoted time to reading is supported by others who knew him later – though he appears to have paid special attention to studying the lives of great men, Stalin included. On leaving Qasr Al Nil he enrolled at Cairo University to study law, but his political interests came first and, after doing very little work, he eventually dropped out.

Within Iraq, there were the show trials of the other participants in the attempt on Kassem's life and of the Free Officers whom Kassem accused of sympathizing with the Mosul Rebellion and an equally ugly subsidiary one which took place in Kirkuk in July 1959. Both groups were making their mark in the People's Court. The army officers on trial, led by the founder of the Free Officers, Colonel Rifa'at Hajj Sirri, behaved impeccably. The taunts of Kassem's foul-mouthed first cousin Colonel Fadhil Abbas Al Mahdawi, in charge of the court, did not move them. I covered their trial as a twenty-four-year-old reporter, and was moved to the point of weeping. They accused Kassem of betraying the purpose of the 1958 revolution, Arab unity, refused to apologize for their actions and faced the firing squads like men of honour. But however strong an impression the officers left on the psyche of an Arab world glued to their radios for the latest news from the People's Court in Iraq, it was Saddam's fellow conspirators who changed the direction of Middle East politics.

There is little doubt that putting the Ba'athist conspirators on trial backfired. In court, the handsome, perfectly turned out Iyyad Said Thabet was a study in courage. He stated that, to him, killing Kassem was a duty because he deviated from Arab nationalism and promoted an Iraqi identity supported by the Communist Party. Arabism came ahead of all else. Salim Issa Zeibak, another participant in the assassination attempt, pointed an accusing finger at Mahdawi and spoke with stunning clarity about 'not expecting mercy from this court and its chairman'. His readiness to die for the cause of Arab unity was elevating, even to non-believers. (I heard Selim's words on radio in Beirut in the company of his father, who responded, 'That's my boy! That's how I brought him up.') Yusra Said Thabet, Iyyad's sister and a fellow conspirator, shouted down the chairman of the court with slogans of commitment and defiance which made Arab womanhood proud. Altogether, the Ba'athists on trial did more to guarantee a future role for their party in Iraq than all the planning of Aflaq, the UAR and the Iraqi exiles. It was the Ba'ath party's finest hour. There were fifty-seven members of the party and other Arab nationalist groups, including officers, on trial, and seventeen of them were executed. Saddam was sentenced to death *in absentia* but, having opted to leave the country rather than face trial, he did not share in the party's hour of glory.

Iraq's relations with the rest of the world in 1959 and 1960 reflected and influenced what was happening internally. There was a strange convergence between British and USSR policy regarding the country. The British supported Kassem because they thought the Arab nationalists, including the Ba'athists, who were calling for unity with Nasser were the real danger to British and Western interests rather than the Communists. They followed their policy of opposing Arab unity and Nasser, despite reports by their ambassador, Lord (Humphrey) Trevelyan, that after the assassination attempt Kassem went 'a bit crazy . . . into a very peculiar state of mind'.[29] The USSR was under an obligation to support the local Communists, the most organized and effective in the whole Middle East, and found Kassem easier to deal with than the independent-minded Nasser. The United States, as usual, saw Communism as the greater danger and American diplomats and spies began referring to 1959 as the Year of the Bear, meaning the year of Communist dominance. A split between Britain and the USA and an implicit US–Nasser alliance aimed at stopping the Communists from taking over Iraq took place. Naturally, the Ba'athists followed Nasser.

It is ironic that none of those who were tried over the attempt to assassinate Kassem ever attained leadership position in Iraq. As with many political movements throughout history, the leadership of the Ba'ath was inherited by the careful survivors and planners rather than the front-line activists, the people of commitment. Saddam belonged to the latter group, preferring the confining and dispiriting life of an exile to imprisonment and trial within Iraq. In Cairo he spent a lot of time in political debate in a more cosmopolitan atmosphere then that of Baghdad, drinking tea in the Indiana and Triumph cafés and thinking about his future. He wrote to his family regularly.

This period produced a story which is difficult to reconcile or associate with the Saddam we read about in the Western Press today. His loneliness appears to have driven him to spend a lot of time with the doorman of the building where he lived. Nasser aide Abdel Majid Farid claims that the man was kind to Saddam, and that his behaviour left an lasting impression on the solitary young man which the latter never forgot. Saddam sent the doorman presents on a regular basis until the 1991 Gulf War. But the company of the generous Egyptian was not enough, and Saddam's tribal and political ties showed in two developments in 1961 and 1962.

In June 1961, Kassem followed in the political footsteps of King Ghazi and claimed Kuwait as a province of Iraq. This was aimed at countering British plans to offer independence to the Emirate, which had been a British protectorate since the implementation of the Sykes–Picot Agreement after the First World War. Saddam, the committed believer in Arab unity, rushed to the local post office and wired Kassem a telegram of support.[30] An Iraqi–British confrontation developed and Kassem, advised by a very able economist, Mohammed Hadid, enacted legislation (Law 80) to reclaimed all Iraqi land not actively being explored for oil by the Iraqi Petroleum Company, IPC. This British-led consortium had a concession to prospect for, extract, price and sell the oil of Iraq for a period of seventy years. Saddam sent Kassem another telegram of support. With Kuwait threatened and the IPC concession in jeopardy, the British policy towards the Iraqi dictator began to change. The Arab countries, as divided as ever, supported Kuwaiti independence and set a military force to protect the Emirate against Kassem. It was an Arab solution and Saddam looked upon it as an act of betrayal against Iraq and its legitimate claim.

In early 1962, the Egyptian-exiled Saddam took time off politics and celebrated his intended marriage to his cousin Sajida (still in Iraq) by giving a big party for his fellow exiles. Shaikhally acted simultaneously as party organizer and guest of honour. This somewhat distant arrangement was possible because in Islam it represented just the *kitb al kitab* or official aspect of the marriage, which becomes valid only after it is consummated. It was an act which reflected the Bedouin background of Saddam and his relations, who had agreed to the marriage through correspondence. Although Saddam had written to Sajida, what mattered was that his uncle Khairallah had promised her to him as a wife since they were young. This was Saddam's subscription to the tribal custom which the Bedouin call *'attayat ab*, or a father's gift. The only non-Bedouin element was that Saddam sent a wedding ring.

Saddam followed his betrothal celebration by visiting various parts of Egypt. Pictures taken in Alexandria and Luxor show a tall, slim, very handsome young man. Mostly tieless, he obviously paid great attention to his clothes and looked neat and well groomed. But this did little to relieve his moroseness and, though he liked Egypt, he had few Egyptian friends. He redoubled his Ba'ath Party activity and devoted most of his time to it. The Ba'ath branch in Cairo dealt with Iraq, the Gaza Strip, the Sudan and North Africa, and Saddam showed genuine interest in the problems of the other Arab countries through reading and listening to his colleagues. The local activists, mostly students, soon elected him as a member of the command of this branch, but it is not clear whether his elevation was acceptable to the overall party leadership in Damascus or an unauthorized honorarium. But whatever his party position, what mattered most at this time was how the Egyptian police were treating him.

Countries which host political exiles inevitably try to control them, and this was true of the way the Egyptians treated Saddam and his Iraqi colleagues. That the Egyptians kept an eye on him and searched his small apartment during his absence is undoubtedly true[31] and, judged by the way it is reported in *The Long Days*, it definitely disturbed him. But what was behind it? There was reason for Egyptian intelligence to suspect the Ba'athists because Syria had seceded from the UAR in 1961 and the Ba'ath leadership in Damascus, Aflaq included, had backed the break. There were also stories of a personal nature which implied that the Egyptians were looking for weapons because Saddam had threatened some of his opponents with physical violence. Much more importantly, there was reason to believe that the restless young rebel was in touch with the local station of the CIA in an effort to forge an alliance with the Americans against the Communist-leaning Kassem. CIA director Allen Dulles had already declared in 1959 that 'Iraq was the most dangerous spot on earth.'[32]

It is my belief that it was contacts between Saddam and the CIA that led Egyptian security to hound him. The new position of the Ba'ath party towards Egypt and Nasser did change his status as a political refugee, but Saddam and his group opposed the break-up of the UAR and the Egyptian authorities knew it. Their contacts with the anti-Egyptian Ba'ath in Syria were practically severed, and Egyptian security knew this as well. However, the accusations of violence to the extent of committing murder while in Cairo do not hold, and are at best exaggerations.

Among anti-Saddam writers, Al Bayati states that Saddam was arrested for killing an Egyptian by throwing him out of the window of his apartment.[33] Mu'in Nunu claims that the murder took place in 1960 and confirms that the victim was Egyptian.[34] But Abdel Majid Farid, one of Nasser's closest associates and the man who was in charge of Iraqi exiles, describes these allegations as 'nonsensical'. In fact, it is impossible to believe that the Egyptian authorities would have overlooked the murder of one of their citizens by a lowly member of the Ba'ath party. (There is another allegation that he killed an Iraqi in Cairo in early 1963,[35] and this too is dismissed by people who should know.) All this aside, the Egyptians were capable of disarming Saddam without resorting to the methods they employed. However, according to *The Long Days* Saddam was detained briefly in Cairo for threatening people who spied on him, by the sound of it Iraqis who were close to the Egyptian security apparatus.[36]

On the other hand, there is evidence of Saddam's frequent visits to the US Embassy in Cairo.[37] In early 1961, before the break-up of the UAR, the contacts of Iraqi exiles with the Americans in Cairo were sanctioned by the Iraqi section of Egyptian intelligence,[38] under the direction of Taher Yahya. Hassan Al Said refers to Egyptian security document D/16829 dated 19 June 1961 to confirm these contacts.[39] But while the contacts obviously took place and Iraqis involved in the politics of the period confirm them, the question is why Saddam was of interest to the Americans (and the Egyptians who, after encouraging them, eventually frowned on the contracts). Were the Americans desperate enough to use a junior member of the Ba'ath Party?

The answer is yes. The Americans were so determined to overthrow Kassem that they opened their doors to everyone in sight. I myself was witness to similar American activities in Beirut, and remember being aghast at the way young Iraqi exiles spoke of their connections with the CIA openly and embarrassingly. An Iraqi by the name of Khayat used to tell everyone that he had the number of Allen Dulles's direct telephone line – just in case. later, I discovered that the fool was indeed a CIA agent.

In fact what Saddam was doing can be explained in terms of two things. First, he did not think that cooperating with the CIA represented treason. Arabs are believers in the old maxim that the enemy of my enemy is my friend, and the USA was Kassem's enemy. This was an act of convenience, and there is no reason to assume that money was a factor. Secondly, Arab political cooperation tends to be of a temporary nature, an act of accommodation rather than an alliance. It was Nuri Said of Iraq, probably making the only utterance for which he will be remembered, who stated that 'you cannot buy an Arab but you can rent one'.[40] There was a mutuality of interest which the Americans made use of and they rented Saddam to work for them, as they were to do after he became President of Iraq. And the Egyptians, who had initiated the contact, kept an eye on him and searched his apartment when he was not there as a way of keeping on top of the situation.

The Ba'ath–CIA conspiracy against Kassem was considerably more extensive than intermittent American contacts with Saddam Hussein. The plans to overthrow the Iraqi leader, led by William Lakeland who was stationed at the Baghdad embassy as an attaché, represented one of the most elaborate CIA operations in the history of the Middle East. To guarantee success, the Americans had to have several things in place. The cooperation with minor Ba'athists in Cairo was part of a bigger picture of Ba'ath–CIA complicity.[41] The cooperation was the work of James Critchfield, a specialist in Communist infiltration brought to the Middle East to deal with the danger of a Communist take over in Iraq. However, there is nothing to link Critchfield with what followed the initial contacts. The efforts in Cairo were subsidiary ones and the CIA was in simultaneous contact with important elements of the Ba'ath party in Damascus and Beirut. Despite protests against this alliance by Ba'athist Syrian government member Jamal Attassi, the Iraqi Ba'athists insisted that Kassem could not be overthrown without American help. There were other contacts with Christian Ba'athists in Lebanon. Furthermore, the CIA had secured a promise of cooperation from Nasser which, because of the nature of covert activities, still did not mean that keeping an eye on Saddam and others was not necessary.

Kassem was not without friends and the Yugoslavs, among others, told him of the plot to overthrow him. Colonel Saleh Mahdi Ammash, a Ba'athist officer in the Iraqi Army who was among the conspirators, was arrested in January 1963, along with a number of colleagues including a Shia firebrand by the name of Ali Saleh Al Sa'adi who led the party's civilian wing. There is reason to believe that Kassem's interrogators obtained confessions from some of them regarding the impending coup. Even Kassem's former Foreign Minister Hazem Jawad states unequivocally, 'We knew of the CIA–Ba'ath contacts'.[42] Why Kassem did not act to intercept a coup which involved the CIA, Ba'athists in exile, Ba'athist officers within his Army, Nasser's intelligence service and even members of the *ancien régime* under the monarchy remains a mystery. Perhaps, as his later behaviour suggests, he did not believe it would succeed.

Whatever the reason, Iraq Army units started their move against Kassem on 8 February 1963. They were led by General Ahmad Hassan Al Bakr, Khairallah and Saddam's Tikriti relation. Bakr had been imprisoned by Kassem in 1959, but was never tried and had joined the Ba'ath party while in detention. His quiet and determined ways and his high rank had assured him prominence among fellow Ba'athist officers arrested by Kassem and he became their leader, later identified as the leader of the military wing of the party. Communications between the civilian and military wings were relatively easy and they were able to coordinate their anti-Kassem move without much interference from the government.

By Middle Eastern conspiracy standards, the 1963 coup was not a well-organized affair. The date had been pushed forward to 8 February because Ammash and some fellow conspirators had been arrested and the troops under the command of the rebels were only a small part of the armed forces. Most Army units were reluctant to join the Ba'athist move. The rebels had a few planes and just eight tanks, most of which broke down on their way to attack Kassem's redoubt in the Ministry of Defence. Still, for two days rebel units and four Hawker Hunter Aircraft led by Wing Commander Munther Al Windawi pounded Kassem's compound while his loyalists resisted. To his lasting honour, Kassem refused to arm the tens of thousands of Communists, peasants and workers who had trekked to his headquarters to offer to defend him, while the Ba'athists did arm and use their civilians in a support capacity. When he eventually surrendered after two days of savage fighting which resulted in hundreds of dead and wounded, it was to save the country from further bloodshed. After his request to keep his sidearm and to be tried openly were refused, he no longer answered the questions of his captors. Rejecting a blindfold, he died like a gentleman officer, shouting: 'Long live the Iraqi people!'[43] In hindsight, because of his work for the poor, his austere ways and the first-ever recognition of Kurdish rights in Iraq which he had announced upon seizing power in 1958, Kassem retains more of the affection of the Iraqi people than any leader this century.

What followed the overthrow of the only Arab regime which came to power this century without outside help was sinister. First, there was a campaign to eliminate Communists, socialists, Peace Partisans and other Kassem supporters. Then there was the Western reaction to the coup. And thirdly there was the short-lived government, mostly Ba'athist, which followed it and which led to the emergence of the Ba'ath and Saddam Hussein as a power in Iraq. Arab writers and others from Britain, the USA, France and elsewhere, among them Mohammed Heikal, Patrick Seale, Marion and Peter Sluglett, Heather Deegan and Kassem's former Minister of Information Ismael Aref, have mentioned the elimination campaign without providing details. The details confirm the existence of a violent Iraqi national personality and Western connivance against Iraq which wrecked all chances of establishing a sensible government there, at the time and for the foreseeable future.

Most of the elimination campaign was carried out by the National Guard, the name given by the rebels to the Ba'athist and Arab nationalist civilians who fought alongside the Army to topple Kassem. The idea for this organization came from Senior Ba'athist Ali Saleh Al Sa'adi during the party's years in the wilderness. Its primary target was members of the Popular Resistance, whom the Ba'athists had cynically dubbed 'The Red God'. These were leftist Kassem supporters who, unlike the Ba'athists, were devoted to Iraqi instead of Arab causes. But the national Guard's brief was to annihilate all the opposition, and by August its numbers had risen from five thousand to twenty thousand. It was placed under the command of the bloodthirsty Munther Al Windawi, the man who had led the aerial attack on Kassem's headquarters and was now given the role of 'protecting the revolution'. The number of Communists and leftists eliminated is a matter of dispute; writers' estimates vary from seven hundred to thirty-five thousand. Many were disposed of on an individual basis – a knock on the door followed by a hail of bullets; others died under torture or in groups of up to thirty at a time. After considerable research I have compiled a list of over eight hundred names, but the real figure is undoubtedly considerably higher.

Those killed included people who represented the backbone of Iraqi society – lawyers, doctors, academics and students – as well as workers, women and children. The elimination campaign lasted several months, and members of the National Guard and their operatives used lists provided by the CIA.[44] Seven out of thirteen members of the Central Committee of the Communist party were killed, but so were people who had ceased to have any connection with the Communists and their supporters. Hani Fkaiki told me that during this period no fewer than fifty-five Communist cells were raided, and that most raids resulted in shoot-outs with many dead and wounded.

The murders of people who had left the Communist Party reveals something about the origin of the CIA lists. Their primary source was one William McHale, a CIA agent operating under the cover of *Time* magazine correspondent and the brother of Don McHale, then a senior CIA officer in Washington. McHale obtained his names in Beirut from an ex-security officer under the monarchy, a former deputy of Bahjat Attiyah, the monarchist security supreme who was hanged in 1958, and the information was out of date.[45] But McHale, though he provided the longest list, was not alone, and a senior Egyptian intelligence officer, Christian Ba'athists in Lebanon, Saddam's small group in Cairo and other individuals and groups contributed to this shameful exercise. As often happens on such occasions, some people were killed as a result of personal vendettas.

Casting all diplomatic precedents to the wind, the United States contacted the anti-Kassem rebels hours after the coup, well before its outcome became a certainty, and promised them recognition.[46] James Akins, the former US Ambassador to Saudi Arabia but then an attaché at the US Embassy in Baghdad, told Robert Kaplan, 'On account of the coup we enjoyed better relations with Iraq.'[47] Some time later Ali Saleh Al Sa'adi, who became Minister of the Interior and Deputy Prime Minister in the regime which replaced Kassem, offered the unequivocal, 'We came to power on a CIA train.'[48] It was a Ba'ath–CIA coup, but the Americans, in addition to saving Iraq from a pro-Communist regime, wanted something in return.

According to Hani Fkaiki, a major participant in the affair, the Iraqis gave William Lakeland, assistant military attaché at the Baghdad Embassy and a CIA operative who had been in Cairo when Nasser overthrew King Farouq in 1952, Russian-built Mig-21s, T-54 tanks and Sam missiles for the United States to assess their effectiveness.

In April 1963 the Americans flew in much-needed arms from Turkey and Iran to the northern Iraqi city of Kirkuk, which enabled the new government to fight the Kurds in that region. Up until then the Americans had been supporting the Kurds against Kassem in a rebellion which had begun in 1961.[49] The American stab in the Kurdish back went further and, in an open act of betrayal which was to set a precedent, they openly advised the Kurdish leader Jallal Talabani to end the rebellion.[50] The Kurds as usual deserved better, particularly since they had been informed of the coup against Kassem and given in their tacit cooperation.

To Dr Ahmad Chalabi, now chairman of the leading opposition group, the Iraqi National Congress, commercial benefits followed the military ones and were just as important. The American companies Parsons, Bechtel and Mobil, among others, were given contracts and concessions. Robert Anderson, a former Treasury Secretary under Eisenhower and then a CIA trouble shooter who operated a CIA-front corporation called Interser – whose board of directors was made up of CIA operatives with the exception of Jack McCrane – became the lead in Iraqi–American commercial relations.[51] The cooperation between William Lakeland and Ammash and other officers was open and total. In fact, while Nasser had to a small measure cooperated in the coup, he advised Ali Saleh Al Sa'adi to be careful of Lakeland and the CIA. Lakeland had been one of Nasser's contacts when he overthrew King Farouq in 1952.

Once again, Saddam had reason to rejoice. The coup's primary aim was the restoration of his country's Arab identity in place of what Kassem had stood for, its narrower Iraqi one. Moreover, this was not only a Ba'athist coup but one led by Ahmad Hassan Al Bakr, by whom Saddam had long ago been adopted. But Bakr had ceded the nominal position of leadership to Abdel Salam Aref, Kassem's partner in the 1958 anti-monarchist rebellion, who too was committed to Arab unity. The better-known Aref, whose presence broadened the support for the coup within the Army, became President and Bakr accepted the premiership. They merged their forces into the National Council for Revolutionary Command. Like the rest of the party Saddam accepted that the Ba'ath, at best numbering around three thousand, was in no position to rule by itself. But the Ba'ath expected Aref to be only a figurehead president.

Saddam himself watched the coup unfold for about two weeks and then headed back to Baghdad via Damascus. In the Syrian capital he has a reunion with Ba'ath leader Michel Aflaq at which their relationship was renewed and strengthened. Saddam returned to Baghdad with an earful of instructions, the exact content of which remains a mystery but which gave him a sense of power. In March the Army staged a Ba'athist coup in Syria and Aflaq's position as head of the Syrian regional command (covering the country of Syria) and the Ba'ath National Command (the one that controlled the party throughout the Arab world) was enhanced. This added to the stature of his protégé, enabling Saddam to move ahead of more important members of the party without opposition.

It was Bakr, probably after consultation with Khairallah, who prevailed on Aref to appoint Saddam to membership of the president's Bureau.[52] This vague title allowed him to roam without control. But from day one he showed interest in organizing the Ba'athist rabble, including the National Guard;[53] paying back the Communists for their past misdeeds against the Ba'ath and fellow Arab nationalists; and controlling small organizations the importance of which eluded others. Both Hani Fkaiki and Salah Omar Al Ali state that he visited detention camps to supervise the 'punishment' of the Communists. Fkaiki names the Muthaqafeen and Fellaheen (educated and peasant) camps as receiving special attention from Saddam. Geoff Simons supports this, but claims that Saddam personally tortured prisoners in Qasr Al Nihaya, 'The Palace of the End',[54] Abdul Ilah's former residence which, as the name suggests, had been turned into a massive prison from which no one returned.

The words of eye witnesses Fkaiki and Al Ali cannot be refuted; Saddam was definitely involved in torture. However, it is impossible to determine the nature of his involvement and the exaggerations of Iraqi opposition groups have not been helpful. There is no verification that Saddam personally killed people or ordered their bodies to be dissolved in bathtubs of acid, as some have alleged. This technical detail aside, little doubt exists that he sanctioned killings. The possibility of direct personal involvement is revealed by his own words in *The Long Days*: 'We must kill those who conspire against us.' And, as would become one of his trademarks in the future, he paid special attention to the ad hoc security apparatus, the Bureau of Special Investigation which decided who should be charged with crimes against the people. To Iraqi Kurdish journalist Kamran Karadaghi, that was when Saddam started using Stalinist maxims openly, above all, 'If there is a person then there is a problem; if there is no person then there is no problem.'

The other political activity which preoccupied Saddam on his return home was to organize the civilian cells of the party on a selective basis, a serious step beyond his organizing of young toughs. He established contacts with the bureaus which dealt with the *fellaheen* (peasants), devoted considerable time to increasing the overall civilian membership of the party and visited Damascus twice to see Aflaq.

In personal terms, he finalized what had begun in Cairo and married Sajida. Their wedding picture, with the two sitting next to each other in an obvious state of happiness, has been reproduced in innumerable books and articles, and the two were a very attractive couple by any standard. Unlike Saddam's mother, Sajida, with her light skin and pleasing oval face, was committed to Western dress. She wasted no time in becoming pregnant.

It took the Ba'athists a mere three months to start an ideological struggle. Sa'adi's civilian branch of the party was distinctly left of centre. The military branch, headed by Bakr, consisted of right-wing elements and centrists backed by Aflaq in Damascus, who visited Baghdad immediately after the coup and on other occasions. Although party meetings regularly produced a majority against them, Saddam stuck with the anti-leftists and threatened their opponents with a fiery speech at a meeting in Damascus in May 1963. The Ba'athists feuded over everything, from the nature of land reform to the speed with which Iraq should seek union with Syria and Egypt. Though the UAR experiment had failed, there was an attempt at three-way union which Nasser rejected and a proposed union between Iraq and Syria which came to nothing. Among their major and more significant points of difference were their policies regarding Kuwait. The leftists were for continuing Kassem's and Iraq's traditional attempts to claim it, while the pragmatist right recognized Kuwait as an independent country in return for a package of financial aid provided by the frightened Kuwaitis, but steadfastly refused to demarcate the border between the two countries.[55]

This split in the party provides the first solid proof of Saddam's violent inclinations and the way he applied them to his political opponents. More than once he tried to ingratiate himself with Aflaq and Bakr by offering to kill Ali Saleh Al Sa'adi and Taleb Shabib, another leftist Ba'ath civilian leader.[56] His bosses turned him down, but noted his willingness to resort to similar action in the future. In early November 1963, the tension between the two branches of the Ba'ath reached a climax. During a meeting of the party's command, Saddam, waving a gun and accompanied by a group of armed followers, entered the meeting hall and arrested Sa'adi and his group, who, under duress, were immediately put on a plane to Madrid.

The in-fighting had left the party divided and weak, which presented an opportunity for President Aref to act. Resenting the Ba'ath's arrogant ways and the attempt to relegate him to a figurehead, on 18 November he used Army units loyal to him to stage a coup within the February coup. Reclaiming power from the Ba'athists, he invested it in himself. Bakr was appointed Vice President for a brief time, then dismissed and put under house arrest along with Brigadier Abdel Karim Nasrat, another Tikriti officer. A warrant was issued for Saddam's arrest. Aref followed this by dissolving the National Guard, a highly popular move because its bloody ways had alienated most Iraqis. Later, the Aref government released a White Book which recorded the criminal acts of the National Guard including the elimination campaign, saddled the Ba'ath with responsibility for them and absolved Aref. Simultaneously, he created a new Army-based special force, the Republican Guard. Subsequent accusations that Saddam was the creator of this notorious organization are misplaced, although he did expand it and made it an army within the regular Army. The nucleus of this force was the 20th Infantry Brigade which Aref turned into an elite unit,[57] ironically, to protect himself against the Ba'ath.

By the beginning of 1964 Saddam was on the run again, but by this time he had established a name for himself. In April he secretly went to Damascus to attend another national (pan-Arab) Ba'ath conference; this too was rent by disagreement between the various factions trying to decide the future of the party. He spoke often and forcefully, voicing opinions reflected by those of Aflaq, by then an opponent of Nasser with a different approach to Arab unity. Towards the end of the conference, the usual meeting of minds between Aflaq, the Christian ideologue head of the party, and his *sanad* (heavy-duty 'muscle') produced a decision to create a temporary Ba'ath party Regional Command in Iraq. Naturally Aflaq appointed Saddam to the new command. He was still only twenty-five or twenty-seven years old.

On his return to Iraq Saddam and a small group devoted themselves to organizing an underground party. The Aref secret police were not very effective and it was not difficult to operate from hiding. Hundreds of Ba'athists were involved, and Saddam managed both to maintain contact with Bakr and to consult Khairallah while the latter was under house arrest in Tikrit. Politics was the only pursuit which he regarded as more important than reading, and as in Cairo he read for several hours a day. But two efforts occupied more of his time: organizing a party apparatus to deal with the peasants, and taking charge of the party's contacts with the military in Baghdad and elsewhere. However, Saddam the man of action would not settle for organizing without acting. Despairing of mounting an Army-based move against Aref and the leaders of the November coup, he initiated plans to assassinate Aref. He conspired with the president's chief of guards, a certain Lieutenant Naji Majid, to enter the National Assembly during a cabinet meeting and carry out his intended task.[58] Unfortunately for him, Majid was transferred at the last minute and the plan had to be aborted. A while later he and Abdel Karim Shaikhally, his friend from the days when they had attempted to kill Kassem, hatched a plan to attack the Presidential Palace on 5 September with home-made bombs made with TNT which they had acquired on the open market.[59] But the plot was discovered the day before and they were apprehended at Shaikhally's house. According to his biographer Iskandar, Saddam's reaction to the member of the security force who tried to arrest him backed by machine guns was a cool, 'My dear fellow, what's this about? Machine guns? Is there no government?'[60]

While there are serious questions to be answered about this incident and the exact date of his arrest, a number of vital events took place during this period which have been consistently mis-reported by historians and biographers. My extensive research, which included over a hundred interviews, allows me to clarify them and set the record straight. Saddam did refuse an order from Aflaq to get out of Iraq and go to Syria.[61] He did manage to make recordings against the Aref regime which were smuggled to Syria and broadcast over Radio Damascus. But, above all, at that time Saddam had nothing to do with the Ba'ath's security apparatus, Jihaz Hunein, which, according to most books written about Saddam and Iraq, was the KGB-like organization which he eventually used to attain power.

Originally set up to guarantee discipline amongst party members and thus the excesses that followed the 1963 coup, it has been mistakenly referred to by many writers as Jihaz Haneen or Instrument of Yearning. They attribute the strange name to cynicism on Saddam's part, asserting that he wanted to give this apparatus a friendly name to make it acceptable to the people. In fact it is Jihaz Hunein and not Haneen, and it is named after the battle of Hunein in the early days of Islam, at which the prophet and his companions prevailed over a far superior force. The man who headed this organization until the Ba'ath seizure of power in 1968 was none other than Salah Omar Al Ali.[62] As will be explained later, it was only after the Ba'ath came to power that Saddam assumed responsibility for the security apparatus which by then had a different name and a different function. It is now clear that Saddam did not use this organization to help the Ba'ath take over the country but became involved in it well after that event.

According to Saddam, his days in prison were difficult ones. Iskandar, Matar and *The Long Days* record him saying that he was kept in solitary confinement for a long time. His refusal to cooperate with the authorities earned him special attention, and at one point he was made to sit on a chair for seven days. Furthermore, he was kept in the Public Security Building under the eye of its director, Abdel Qader Al Janabi. During this period he is supposed to have been summoned to a meeting with Prime Minister Taher Yahya, who unsuccessfully tried to prevail on him to cooperate with the Aref regime. Saddam is supposed to have refused a number of chances to escape to avoid jeopardizing the situation of comrades who would have stayed behind.

Whether any of this is true remains unknown. The only witness to events at the time, Abdel Karim Shaikhally, Saddam's prison companion, equal in the party command and the one he called 'my twin', was killed by Saddam in 1972. What is established is that Sajida visited him regularly and always took him books to read, that unlike the Ba'ath the Aref regime treated its prisoners fairly and that recognition of his talents followed him behind bars. In 1965, Aflaq made Bakr Secretary General of the Iraqi Branch of the Ba'ath Party and Saddam was elevated to Deputy Secretary General. This was the beginning of three-way consultations, occasionally using Sajida as messenger, which culminated in a decision that Saddam should escape. According to Saddam, Sajida often carried messages wrapped in the clothing of their son Udday, then a few months old.

Developments within the Ba'ath party and in Iraq in 1966 were to determine what followed. On 23 February, the left wing of the Ba'ath party in Syria staged a successful coup and ousted Aflaq and his fellow founder Salah Bitar from the National Command, which controlled Iraq as well. In April Aref died in a helicopter crash and was replaced by his feckless brother, General Abdel Rahman Aref. The need for Saddam to be out of prison superseded all previous considerations. On 23 July, after twenty months in jail, Saddam escaped while being transferred between prisons. He, Shaikhally and another inmate bribed the drivers of the prison van to stop at the Gondole Café in Abu Nawas Street and escaped to a waiting car while their guards pretended to be eating. The whole episode reveals a certain level of laxity among those in power.

The government of Abdel Rahman Aref, corrupt and unable to establish a popular base to replace what had died with Abdel Salam Aref, put out feelers to the Ba'ath and other groups and tried to establish a coalition national salvation government. The Ba'ath turned them down. For reasons which will be explained shortly, the party thought everything was going their way. In this they were right.

About two months latter, the leftist National Command of the Ba'ath Party located in Damascus ousted Bakr and Saddam from the Regional Command in charge of Iraq. The two Tikritis refused to go and instead set up their own Iraqi Command, following it with a new national Command which competed with the one in Damascus and purported to speak for the party throughout the Arab world. Though ostensibly in hiding, they managed to operate relatively openly and to establish contacts with the Arab Revolutionary Movement, in particular the Deputy Chief of Army intelligence, Colonel Abdel Razaq Al Nayyef, the Commander of the Republican Guard, Colonel Ibrahim Al Daoud, and the Commander of the special Presidential Guard, Colonel Sa'adoun Gheidan. Saddam the pragmatist had a hand in establishing the new alliance whose sole purpose was the overthrow of the government.

4

Playing Stalin to Bakr's Lenin

Often it is more important to speak of what precedes and follows a coup, its causes and what determines its success or failure, than to describe the event itself. The Iraq which existed at the time of the 1968 coup, a revolutionary republic looking for direction, differed considerably from the pro-West monarchy which was overthrown in 1958. The structure and sources of power had changed and, unlike the 1958 revolution, the 1968 seizure of power contained unmistakable signs of what might follow which were generally ignored both inside and outside Iraq.

It was Saddam Hussein, a rising Ba'athist star of twenty-nine or thirty-one, who expressed the prospects awaiting the country and who, after three decades of control and against huge odds, continues to fashion what emerged and will remain a subject of debate for centuries. According to three participants in the coup, who now belong to different factions of the Iraqi opposition and spoke to me separately and off the record, Saddam never tried to disguise his dream. In party meetings and in meetings between the Ba'athists and some of their supporters he was remembered for repeating the same refrain: 'When we take over the government I'll turn this country into a Stalinist state.' The people who told me this story were officers in the Iraqi Army; two generals, one of whom became ambassador to an Arab country; and a former Commander of the Presidential Guard. Along with everyone else, at the time they did not take young Saddam's statement seriously.

The coup itself was a classic blend of inevitable historical forces and the will of an intelligent, single-minded and complex indivi-dual. The subsequent transformation of Iraq both refutes and supports the notion that individuals shape history as well as the opposing idea that historical forces create leaders. Inadvertently, Saddam may have changed the study of history.

The problems facing Iraq immediately before the coup were a combination of old issues reshaped by the changes brought about by the Kassem government. The Kurds still wanted a Kurdistan to express their interests, within Iraq or independent from it. For the first time in the modern history of Iraq, the Shias were expressing their grievances in an organized way through their religious leadership. The country was conducting a war with the IPC oil consortium and the governments behind it, and jeopardizing its primary source of income in the name of oil nationalism. The issue of whether Iraq should unite with a big Arab country under Nasser, or follow policies which emphasized a separate Iraqi identity while accepting the country's Arabness, had not been resolved to the satisfaction of advocates of either policy. Kuwait loomed as a national dream on which all Iraqis agreed, but remained unattainable.

President General Abdel Rahman Aref was a weak individual and his government was incapable of addressing any of these major issues. Of course, the Cold War was still on and Iraq's desire and ability to tackle them was of interest to the major powers. Oil, the country's strategic position and the Arab–Israeli conflict precluded allowing the Iraqis to solve their own problems.

After a brief hiatus and another attempt at solving their problem after the overthrow of Kassem, the Kurds had risen again late in 1963. In 1964 President Abdel Salam Aref, the most staunchly anti-Kurd leader in the modern history of the country, had used napalm and chemical weapons against them. But even in the face of this onslaught the Kurds could not keep a united front. In 1966 Jallal Talabani had broken away and created what became the Patriotic Union of Kurdistan (PUK), an educated, less tribal grouping. But the traditionalist Mulla Mustapha Al Barzani still commanded greater support, either personally or operating under the umbrella of the Kurdish Democratic Party. He could never decide whether he wanted an independent Kurdistan or an autonomous Kurdish region within Iraq.[1] Essentially he was after personal supremacy[2] and he sided with whoever provided him with support, on occasions even relying on help fro the Iraqi central government against his compatriots.

Though they had a better deal than their fellow Kurds in Turkey or Iran,[3] most Iraqi Kurds followed Mulla Mustapha's confused policies. The degree of inconsistency in what he sought is attested to by his dependence on help from outside powers which included the USA, USSR, Israel and Iran. Obviously, he did not subscribe to a specific ideology and on occasions he could not differentiate between the self-serving support he got from outsiders and real Kurdish interest.

Ever since the 1920s, negotiations between the Kurds and the central government in Baghdad had always broken down over the extent of independence which they sought, together with their wish to control the oil-rich city of Kirkuk and to have their own militia. Even the 1966 government of civilian Abdel Rahman Al Bazzaz, a thinking moderate who was totally committed to granting the Kurds equal rights (which had been accepted for the first time by Kassem in 1958), failed to settle the Kurdish problem because of opposition from the anti-autonomy elements in the government and the Kurdish leadership. In faraway Cairo, Nasser had seen the damage that Kurdish rebellions inflicted on Iraq and the Arabs, and sympathized with the Kurds to the extent of supporting their declared wish to become an autonomous region of Iraq with guaranteed ethnic rights.[4]

The crux of the Kurdish problem is not difficult to understand: all Iraqi governments feared that granting the Kurds some rights would eventually lead to the creation of an independent Kurdistan. Simultaneously, the Kurds themselves suffered the consequences of 'a clumsy, provincial and untutored' leadership[5] whose behaviour contributed more to this notion than it did to improving the lot of the Kurdish people. In fact, some sensible offers to the Kurds were rejected because their leaders feared for their positions.

In reality, the problem of the Shias in Iraq has always represented a greater danger to the survival of the Iraqi nation state than that of the Kurds. Iraq could survive a Kurdish secession but not a Shia one, which would remove more than half the population. However, in the Shias' case the most external assistance they could count on was sympathy from Iran. They were always committed to a united Iraq and, except for brief periods of Iranian hegemony over Iraq, had suffered discrimination all the way back to the days of the Abbasid Empire over a thousand years ago. The Shia exclusion from power which the British had inherited from the Ottoman Empire had been perpetuated until Kassem showed a willingness to grant them greater acceptance than they had enjoyed before. And although they were involved in the political parties of the 1940s, 1950s and 1960s, and eventually in the emergence of the Ba'ath and Communist parties as competitors for control of the country, they appeared unable to assume power and behaved as if they suffered from an inferiority complex which stopped them from exercising it. In fact, when it came to positions in the Army or government the Kurds were well ahead of the Shias.

In 1957, a year before the overthrow of the monarchy, the Shias finally set up a religion-based party, Al Dawa Al Islamiya. It grew slowly and in the late 1960s came under the control of Mohammed Bakr Al Sadr, a firebrand cleric, man of learning and inspiring speaker. The party's programme was and remains ostensibly democratic: it calls for the holding of free elections that would empower the majority of the people. But the vague call for the establishment of an Islamic republic created doubts regarding their ultimate aim. During the 1960s, under both Kassem and the Aref brothers, the Shias' grievance against their overall situation, though utterly justified, centred on a specific act which was a manifestation of Iraq's wish to become a modern state.

Among Kassem's many laudable acts was the appointment of the first woman minister in the Arab world, the Communist Dr Naziha Al Duleimi. He followed that by adopting the Personal Status Law, a civil law which superseded the Koranic dicta on the status of women in Muslim society in matters such as divorce and inheritance. The Arefs, though Sunnis, were religious and viewed the law with misgivings, abandoning some of its elements. However this did not satisfy Sadr and his fellow Shia, Sayyed Muhsin Al Hakim, who insisted on total repeal of the law. In 1968, the emergence of the Shias under the banner of an organized political movement was hampered by argument with the government over this single issue.

The more basic question of whether the Shias owed their allegiance to religion more than to the Iraqi state, as Hassan Alawi alleges,[6] had been exacerbated by the unexpected arrival in Iraq of Ayatollah Khomeini in 1964. Khomeini, although an Iranian exile running away from the Shah and a potential competitor to Sadr and Hakim in the religious arena, supported a more militant religious attitude. There is no doubt that his presence in Iraq contributed to a worsening of relations between the Iraqi Shias and their central government and undermined their traditional commitment to Iraq. After Khomeini gained control of Iran in 1979, his uncompromising attitude was a major cause of the Iran–Iraq War.

The third problem facing the government of Abdel Rahman Aref was his country's relations with the IPC consortium. Kassem had started the ball rolling in 1960, by hosting the first-ever OPEC (Organization of Petroleum Exporting Countries) meeting, which no one else was willing to do or capable of achieving. He reconfirmed his commitment to a nationalist oil policy in 1961 by wresting control of 99.5 per cent of the land of Iraq from IPC, which had deliberately refused to prospect for oil in this territory. This had kept the level of Iraqi oil production down, even under the pro-British monarchy. In 1964 the first Aref, Abdel Salam, created the Iraqi National Oil Company (INOC). Both Arefs tried to market some of the country's oil under their control through this entity, a major move which threatened the position of the oil companies throughout the Middle East. The oil companies fought back. They tried to stop the Iraqis through legal means, by suing purchasers, and by using their power in the market place. Among other things, they would not supply oil to countries which dealt directly with the Iraqi government.

Iraq's oil potential is today probably the greatest in the Middle East, with reserves of somewhere between 260 and 320 billion barrels.[7] The country is ultimately capable of producing 11 million barrels of oil a day. Moreover, it is the cheapest oil in the whole world to extract. In the 1960s, it cost 6 cents a barrel compared with 8 cents for Saudi oil.[8] The realization of the country's oil potential had been hampered by the nature of the consortium which made up IPC: five of the seven international oil companies – BP (British Petroleum), Shell, Esso, Mobil and Compagnie Francaise des Petroles (CFP), together with Gulbenkian (Mr 5 per cent) which was run by BP. Operating through this consortium, formed in 1928, did not suit BP, which had the loudest voice among the members because it managed the consortium and Britain controlled Iraq. BP already owned most of the oil of Iran and Kuwait. Lifting Iraqi oil would mean sharing the benefits with the other members of the consortium, whereas the profit from developing Iranian and Kuwaiti oil production went only to BP. To stop other members of the consortium lifting more Iraqi oil, BP drew up the regulations of IPC in such a way that any member needing more oil had to pay extra, and to commit itself to a five-year production schedule. In other words, if Mobil needed more than its share of what IPC was producing then it had to take that extra share, and pay more for it, over five years. In a market which fluctuates over much shorter periods of time this was an impossibility – a fall in demand would create a short-term build-up of oil reserves that could not be accommodated.[9]

I will deal with the problem between the Iraqi governments and the oil companies throughout this book, but in 1968 it consisted largely of Iraq wanting the French consortium ERAP and the USSR to help develop and market its oil. What both Arefs wanted included the entry of the USSR as a full participant in the Middle East oil stakes. Since the early twentieth century Western governments have supported their oil companies, and in this case both Britain and the USA opposed Iraq's plans to increase its oil production. So the IPC consortium and the international marketers of oil succeeded in limiting Iraqi success and setting a precedent.

The other problem confronting the pre-1968 coup regime concerned the nature of their relationship with the rest of the Arab world, in particular the Palestinians, Nasser and Kuwait. Ostensibly committed to Arab unity, both Arefs welcomed Nasser's rebuffs of their proposals to consolidate their hold on Iraq. Nasser had feared failure as had happened after the creation of the UAR, and demanded guarantees of success. The Arefs, though they had used the Nasser veto to establish themselves at the helm of the Iraqi government, could never create a cohesive movement behind them. They still paid tribute to Nasser as the leading Arab of his times and adopted some of his socialist schemes within Iraq, but by 1968 the prospects of real unity had receded, though not that of a common Arab front representing a unity of purpose. The defeat of the Arabs by Israel in 1967 was the final nail in the Aref coffin. It exposed the type of inter-Arab cooperation that both Arefs had advocated as a failure, especially in terms of support for the Palestinians.

Lastly, there was the perennial problem of Kuwait. The recognition of Kuwait by Iraq which had followed the 1963 coup was halfhearted, and Kuwait had to bribe the Iraqis to obtain it anyway. However, because all Iraqis, regardless of political persuasion, believed that Kuwait belonged to them, no Iraqi government ever accepted the demarcation of the border between the two countries and the problem was never finally settled. According to Adnan Pachachi, former Iraqi Foreign Minister and UN Ambassador under the Arefs, 'We simply wouldn't finalize the border problem, though they wanted to do it. They kept raising the problem and we kept changing the subject – to their dismay.'[10]

With a measure of justification, the writer Hassan Al Said cites the reputable French newspaper *Le Monde* and says that 'The change [in Iraq] was not for internal reasons only.'[11] Iraqi opposition leader Ahmad Chalabi describes the 1968 coup as the second stage of CIA–Ba'ath cooperation.[12] The urbane Adnan Pachachi uses measured words to describe what might have happened: 'I don't know of outside involvement, but perhaps it happened. The regime of Prime Minister Taher Yahya was pro-Nasser and un-popular with the West. It would make sense.'[13] The eminent historian Hanna Batatu quotes President Abdel Rahman Aref as speaking of the involvement of 'non-Iraqi hands'. The background to all these statements is considerable.

Before the coup there were two issues of commercial/political concern to the CIA, oil and sulphur. The Iraqi National Oil Company (INOC) had granted an oil concession to the French company ERAP in 1966 and had invited the Russians to develop the huge North Rumeillah field (because it straddles the Iraqi–Kuwaiti border it was one of the causes of the invasion of Kuwait by Iraq in 1990). INOC was achieving modest success selling oil from smaller fields, and ERAP and the Russians recognized the potential of the deals with Iraq and were working towards becoming a regional factor in the oil industry. Simultaneously, the price of sulphur on the international market had gone up and made its mining in the region of Mishaaq in northern Iraq economically viable. The Aref government wanted to give this concession to the French.

To the Americans, the loss of Iraqi oil and sulphur meant the loss of Iraq. Although there were rumours of British plans for a paratroop drop to control the oil fields and put an end to the ERAP and USSR concessions and the Iraqi government's independent oil policy, in reality it was the Americans who were shaping the West's policy towards Iraq. So it fell to them to stop Aref's Iraq before its actions set a precedent for the rest of the oil producers. The Americans began by putting out feelers to Iraqi ambassador Nasser Al Hani in Beirut.[14] One of the people trying to gain the concessions for the Americans was Beirut-based Paul Parker, an

American banker and Treasury agent known to me. He extended his contacts to one Lutfi Obeidi, an Iraqi lawyer and politico with many friends within the Ba'ath party, and, to give his efforts an acceptable commercial cover, made a tentative agreement with shipping tycoon Carl Ludwig to transport the oil. The second American entrusted with fixing the overall crisis initiated by these moves was former Secretary of the Treasury Robert Anderson. He travelled to Baghdad several times with open-ended offers for the oil and purchase offers from Pan American Sulphur Co. and Gulf Sulphur Co.

Anderson's efforts were so open and occasionally crude that in 1967 demonstrations took place in Baghdad, with marchers shouting: 'Go back home, Anderson!' But Anderson would not give up, and he and Parker started courting people both inside and outside the government. Aref himself accused intelligence chief Nayyef of having been in the service of the oil interests.[15] But the more important connection, according to Ahmad Chalabi, came out of the meeting between Anderson and Bakr, which was arranged by Parker and Obeidi one year before the coup and at which oil and sulphur were discussed. These contacts followed what happened in 1966, when Saddam wrote a letter to the US Consulate in Basra asking for their help in overthrowing the government.[16] Certainly the announcement of the dismissal of Nayyef explicitly accused him of involvement with outsiders, and surely the Ba'ath did not discover this in the two weeks between 17 and 30 July 1968 but must have known about it already. Years later, in his memoirs, Nayyef himself supported the allegation of the CIA involvement when he clearly stated '. . . for the 1968 coup you must look to Washington'.[17] The question is not whether the CIA was involved, for America welcomed this coup as well; the question is how involved it was and with whom. What is almost certain is that the arrangement with the CIA was reached in 1967, before the Arab–Israeli War, and that the outcome of the war created a pervasive anti-American feeling which made it difficult for the Iraqis to fulfil its terms.

By Iraqi standards of violence, the 1968 coup was a non-event. The recruitment by the Ba'ath conspirators of Colonels Nayyef, Daoud and Gheidan of the Arab Revolutionary Movement left President Abdel Rahman Aref virtually defenceless. Nayyef was the most important, with a power base of fifty or sixty army officers who accepted him as their leader. Still, the Ba'athists wanted to take no chances where credit for the coup was concerned, and Saddam insisted that some of them should join the Army units on their way to the palace. He put on the military uniform of a lieutenant and rode on a tank, as did several other Ba'athists including his half-brother Barazan and Salah Omar Al Ali. With help from Gheidan's Presidential Guards they moved into the compound at 2 a.m. on 17 July. After disarming a handful of soldiers who had not been included in the instructions to accommodate the conspirators they entered the palace to confront Aref. The atmosphere in Baghdad had strongly suggested that something of this nature was on the way – the American-born wife of the present opposition leader Saleh Jaber woke up saying, 'They are at it again.'[18]

It was a totally bloodless coup and Saddam's later claims, accepted by journalists and historians as they are, need to be corrected. He has said that he learned how to fire the gun of a tank during some sort of assault, and the role of his favourite half-brother Barazan has been deliberately inflated.[19] According to a participant in the events, two rounds were fired by tanks after a false report that Aref was going to resist. Beyond that there was enough confused rifle and machine gun fire to wake people up, but no real fighting took place.

It was left to General Hardan Al Tikriti, a member of the military wing of the Ba'ath Party and one of the conspirators, to ask Aref to resign. After a few words of protest Aref agreed to leave for London to join his ailing wife, but only after and he and his deposer had had a cup of tea together.[20]

Aref's uneventful departure was followed by the usual announcement of a new government and pronouncements regarding national aspirations, the Arab cause and the liberation of Palestine. The National Council for Revolutionary Command was dissolved and replaced by something similar, the Revolutionary Command Council (RCC) with Bakr as its chairman. Prior to the coup, the Ba'ath had openly challenged the government and organized public demonstrations in which Bakr had personally participated. Aref had offered him a position in the government which, still wanting a Ba'ath-controlled administration, he had refused. This is why almost all Iraqis dismissed the event, because they had assumed the Aref government was too feckless to continue in office. Most people's greatest fear was that the Communists might replace it. This was true of the Shias in particular, because their religious leadership had issued a *fatwa* against Communism in 1960, when Kassem had depended on the Communist party to fend off Nasser's followers. When people discovered it was a Ba'athist takeover they uttered a sigh of relief and went about their daily lives. No demonstrations or celebrations accompanied the downfall of Aref, just the Ba'athist slogans of 'Unity, freedom and socialism' and 'One Arab nation with an eternal mission'.

Saddam, though Deputy Secretary General of the Ba'ath Party, did not figure in the new government appointments or as a member of the RCC. Bakr's appointment as president was expected, but the premiership went to a non-Ba'athist, Nayyef. Daoud became Minister of Defence and Nasser Al Hani, until then Ambassador to Lebanon, was promoted to Foreign Minister. In fact, only six out of twenty-four members of the cabinet were Ba'athists. The second most important Ba'athist was General Hardan Al Tikriti, who became Chief of Staff of the Army; he was followed by General Saleh Mahdi Ammash, an ally of the Tikritis, who became Minister of the Interior. Though conflicting explanations have been offered, Saddam's age and the need to satisfy the non-Ba'athist participants in the coup by offering them positions were behind his temporary exclusion from government.

Saddam the tireless worker and methodical organizer was nevertheless not out of the picture. Having decided to dissolve Jihaz Hunein, the Ba'ath party internal security apparatus, the new government decided to create an expanded security service in addition to the one which had existed under all governments, Al Amn Al 'Am, or General Security. The bad reputation that the Ba'athists had earned when the National Guard carried out the elimination campaign in 1963 led them to give the new organization an insipid name, the Office of General Relations. But fearing that involvement in a security system might tarnish their personal image and standing within the party, none of the new leaders wanted to assume responsibility for it. None except Saddam, that is, who accepted the role in what amounted to an act of sacrifice. It was an oversight on the part of the Ba'athists which was to cost many of them and Iraq dearly. Saddam, alone or with family help, still retains direct control of the country's security system.

Saddam had set his eyes on adding more government departments to his personal control, but that had to wait until the Ba'ath completed and consolidated its hold on power. Meanwhile, he carried out another remarkable act which his colleagues foolishly overlooked. He occupied an office right next to that of the President and had direct access to him all the time. According to Saddam's Egyptian biographer Amir Iskandar, on 30 August, a mere fourteen days after Aref's forced resignation, Saddam single-handedly engineered the removal of the Prime Minister and Minister of Defence. Daoud had been sent to Jordan to inspect Iraqi troops stationed there since the 1967 war with Israel and Saddam handled Nayyef personally.

Gun in hand, he is supposed to have marched into Bakr's office while the latter was having lunch with Nayyef, told the Prime Minister that he was under arrest, berated him harshly for intruding on 'a revolution for which the Ba'ath had paid in blood' and hustled him into a car bound for the airport where a plane was waiting. Nayyef pleaded for his life and his four children while Saddam at his side ordered him to salute back when they passed through road blocks, to prevent any rescue attempt by loyal troops who would obey his orders. With his hand ready to grab the gun hidden under his jacket Saddam sent Nayyef off to Morocco, though his days as ambassador there were to be brief.[21]

Once again I am forced to address myself to what Saddam has told his loyalist biographers, because the scarcity of original sources led other writers to accept their word as the truth and this is what the world now believes. This story too was the work of Saddam the supreme embellisher of historical facts. According to Salah Omar Al Ali, who was there when Nayyef was arrested, the decision to remove Nayyef and Daoud and entice Gheidan into supporting the action of the Ba'athists was taken before 17 July and it was a collective decision. In the words of Al Ali,

Nayyef was a very clever and ambitious man and though we needed him to get rid of Aref we knew we couldn't live with him. What Saddam did on 30 July had been planned before 17 July and had our agreement. The rest of his story is basically true. Nayyef was having lunch with Bakr at the palace and he did plead for his life and Saddam promised him that no harm would befall him if he behaved himself and did not try to resist. And yes, Saddam ordered him into a car and after showing him that he was carrying a gun saw to it that Nayyef behaved normally when passing the guards around the presidential palace because some of them were indeed loyal to Nayyef. Then Saddam took him to the airport and sent him off to Morocco, instead of to Beirut or Algeria as Nayyef had asked.[22]

Salah Omar Al Ali, a man whose care with words is obvious to an interviewer, said that Saddam would have killed Nayyef had the latter not obeyed him. Others corroborate his story including the last part. Iskandar's story is essentially correct, except for the very important fact of who ordered Nayyef's removal and confirmed the Ba'ath in power. It was not Saddam.

Just hours after this dramatic episode, Bakr made a speech to the people announcing 'the completion' of the revolution and accusing Nayyef of conspiring with foreign companies and powers against the interests of Iraq. In it Bakr, at Saddam's suggestion, made himself his own Prime Minister and Commander-in-Chief of the armed forces. Bakr's delivery of the speech is recorded on film which contains one of the most dramatic visual images of Saddam ever seen. He is standing behind his relation carrying a sub-machine gun across his chest, the way soldiers from Communist countries did during parades. The Leninist father figure, Bakr, was being guarded by the one member of the party who had no problems with using violence to achieve his aims.

The same speech condemning Nayyef and announcing his banishment as Ambassador to Morocco, a typical Stalinist move, contained a decree dismissing Daoud, who was in Jordan inspecting Iraqi troops who had been stationed there since the 1967 war with Israel. Hearing this on the radio, Daoud arranged to go to Saudi Arabia to live; he remains there, divorced from Iraqi politics, to this day. Foreign Minister Hani was also dismissed, but allowed to go home unmolested because he was not a military man and did not represent a threat. But this was only a brief reprieve, for in November 1968 he was kidnapped from his house by four unknowns, murdered and his body dumped in the River Tigris. According to most sources the assassins were Ba'athists belonging to the new security service, the Office of General Relations, who were under instructions to eliminate all potential sources of opposition to the new regime.[23] As with so many of these cases, the evidence is circumstantial and it is impossible to verify or refute this allegation in a satisfactory legal way.

It was at this point that Saddam, very much like Stalin, started expanding his role and gathering as many departments under him as possible. When he assumed responsibility for the security apparatus he was already in charge of the *fellaheen* (peasants') office. But soon enough he added education and propaganda to his portfolio. According to a former member of the Iraqi government who spoke on non-attribution basis, Saddam told Bakr, 'Give me authority and I will give you a party capable of ruling this country.' Another former officer of the Iraqi Army, who also spoke on condition of anonymity because he still has a family in Iraq, reconfirms that it was Khairallah who was responsible for the sudden rise in Saddam's authority. Bakr had made Khairallah provincial governor of the Baghdad *villayat*, an important position which allowed him to continue to see the president on a regular basis. Khairallah is supposed to have repeatedly told Bakr, 'You're among the very few of our leaders who've had more than one chance – use it. Saddam is your son. Depend on him. You need the family to protect you, not an army or a party. Armies and parties change direction in this country.'

Because he recognized Saddam's skills and needed him, Bakr, born in 1914 and hence old enough to be Saddam's father, accepted the offer in an open and obvious way which was noticed by other members of the RCC. Remarkably, it was then that the Iraqi Ba'athists invited Aflaq, living in self-imposed exile in Brazil, to return to Iraq to lead them against their leftist competitors who were running the other Ba'ath party from Syria. With this, the split into an Iraqi and a Syrian Ba'ath was complete. Originally based on an ideological division between left and right, it eventually became a personality clash between Syrian and Iraqi leaders. Aflaq's *gada'*, tough guy, finally lived up to his mentor's expectations.

That Saddam was growing in importance and becoming a power behind the 'father leader' and the 'spiritual leader', as the Ba'athists called Bakr and Aflaq respectively, was undoubtedly true. Unfortunately other members of the leadership, the Iraqi counterparts of the Communist leaders eliminated by Stalin such as Kamanev and Bukharin, still did not take Saddam or what he was doing as seriously as they should have. One of the reasons for being dismissive was his lack of official position, and another was his age. Furthermore, attaining power through Stalinist methods backed by Arab tribal loyalties was something that no one else had considered.

Lebanese biographer Fuad Matar states that Saddam secretly became Bakr's second-in-command and deputy head of the RCC immediately after the dismissal of Nayyef, but admits that there was no official announcement to that effect without explaining why.[24] Except for the traditional Arab attachment of importance to age as a measure of wisdom, there is no answer to this short-lived mystery. Saddam officially assumed his position as Under Secretary General of the Revolutionary Command Council in January 1969, just a few months later, and with that came the title of Vice President. This is when Saddam proudly coined for himself the title of *sayyed al na'ib*, or Mr Deputy, so it is most unlikely that someone so enamoured with status would have kept a promotion secret as Matar suggests.

Very much like Stalin, Mr Deputy Saddam was now working fourteen to sixteen hours a day. Control of the Army was to come later, but for the time being the twin approach of controlling the security service and the party though using his family was enough. He paid little attention to his three young children, though the girl was the apple of his eye – his second son, Qussay, had been born in 1966 and Raghid, his first daughter in 1967. Saddam's analytical, conspiratorial mind was on something else: the CIA and its real and imagined conspiracies.

Because the problems facing the new Ba'athist regime were so great and even the most optimistic expectations of what Saddam and others were doing would have taken a long time to realize, the situation which had originally led to the demise of the Aref regime started to deteriorate. The Ba'athists began to fear that their rule might not last as long as had their first grasp of power in 1963. Above all, the country was facing a financial crisis. As always during internal crises, relief could be achieved through the Stalinist method of diverting people's attention to external threats. To Saddam and company that danger came mainly from the CIA, the same people who had helped install them in power in 1963 and had in all likelihood contributed to their success against Aref.

In 1968, it was Saddam the master tactician who decided to resort to the classic ploy to get greater support for the government. It began on 9 October with accusations that the Shias had been plotting against the regime because they were receiving instructions from Radio Ahwaz, a propaganda organ located in Iran and sponsored by the Shah. When this did not get people sufficiently worked up, it was time to turn around the widely suspected CIA connection and attack the Agency by transferring the responsibility for contacts with it to others. Cleverly relying on the anti-American atmosphere which followed by 1967 Arab defeat, Saddam decided his way out would be via the CIA and Zionist conspiracies against the regime. This is not to suppose that the latter was not true – Israel had had spy rings in Iraq going back to the 1940s, and some operatives of Mossad, the Israeli secret service, were Iraqi Jews – but the major CIA conspiracy of November 1968 which was supposed to be headed by Colonel Midhat Hajj Sirri was definitely a fabrication.

Colonel Hajj Sirri had been exiled in Syria but returned to Iraq after the 1963 coup. The brother of Rifa'at, the founder of the Free Officers who was executed by Kassem, and a one-time aspirant to Iraqi leadership, Midhat had become Mayor of Baghdad under the Arefs. A totally honest and popular man, and a potential magnet for non-Ba'athists and opposition parties including what remained of the pro-Nasser army officers, he represented a problem for Saddam. This is when the Ba'athists looked into his background methodically and used it to try him and eventually to execute him.

During his stay in Syria he had befriended me and I introduced him to my father, *Time* magazine correspondent Abu Saïd Aburish. The two saw a great deal of each other in Beirut. According to my father, 'We talked about everything under the sun, including the political situation in Iraq, but he was the most loyal of Arabs and utterly committed to his country.'[25] The Ba'ath had nothing against Sirri but, determined to remove him, arrested him and accused him of being a CIA agent, which was treason. Sirri was subjected to endless interrogation and some torture, but steadfastly refused to admit to having a CIA connection, either directly or through Abu Saïd Aburish. Finally, in an act which was to repeat itself hideously in the future, the interrogators threatened to rape female members of his family. To protect his honour Sirri succumbed, admitted spying for the CIA and implicated his friend. In a final act of humiliation he was forced to appear on Baghdad television to repeat his confession. His honour intact, he was sentenced to death and hanged a short while later.

A colleague of his in Syria who spoke without wishing to be identified described what happens as follows: 'The CIA–Ba'ath connection was a loose one, unlike 1963. Midhat was so popular within the Army he represented a threat to an obviously insecure regime. So why not kill two birds with one stone – eliminate him and gain benefit from accusing the CIA? He was the most decent of men. Nobody believed them – nobody does to this day.' It was not only that Midhat was popular, but disposing of him marked the end of what remained of the 1958 Free Officers, the original revolutionaries who had paved the way for the Ba'ath to assume power. And wasn't it Bill McHale of *Time* who had helped them in 1963? To the Ba'athists, accusing another *Time* correspondent of spying came naturally.

The response to the supposed Zionist plot, which coincided with the CIA one, began in December 1968. Over thirty people, including sixteen Jews, mostly from the city of Basra, were accused of spying for Israel. Their guilt or innocence was predetermined by the way the case was handled. From day one the man in charge of propaganda, Saddam Hussein, was determined to turn this into a huge show. He filled newspapers, magazines, radio and television with news of the trial. According to all the media, Iraq was threatened because it was blessed with an exceptional leadership committed to the Arab cause. The Communist Party, the Ba'ath's on-off enemy, called for clemency but there was none of it: the accused had no chance. In January 1969 fourteen of them, including nine Jews, were sentenced to death.

If the act itself was criminal because the trial was not conducted fairly, then what followed might almost be called state-sponsored pornography. The dead were left hanging in Liberation Square for over a day. Radio Baghdad urged the faithful to witness for themselves 'what happens to enemies of the revolution'. Hundreds of thousands obeyed the call, and Bakr and Saddam made visits to the scene to be cheered by their people. Although Midhat Hajj Sirri's trial and execution had generated little attention, the hanging of the rest became an international incident. The whole world protested, but the regime still got away with it: foreign powers still had their eyes on oil, sulphur and other interests.

The Stalinist use of the threat of external dangers to the revolution was indiscriminate and included the Communists. In February 1969 the government imprisoned and then put on trial Aziz Al Hajj, leader of one of the two wings of the Communist party. It was obvious to anyone present at the trial that Hajj had been tortured beyond endurance. The broken man admitted to a Communist conspiracy and implicated many members of his party and their supporters. The government wasted no time in putting them on trial and twenty were sentenced to death, after suffering in the torture chambers of the Palace of the End.

The first round of 'cleansing', therefore, had included Arab nationalists, the CIA, Zionists and Communists, and for Saddam the time had now come to devote his energies to building the structure of the party and dealing with internal issues. He indulged in a number of actions which increased his popularity in the country, then targeted specific groups which represented source of danger to the Ba'ath as a whole and to the combined leadership of Bakr and Saddam in particular. And because Saddam was the innovator with an unerring sense of what pleased people, Bakr listened to him and accepted his recommendations.

Among Saddam's first popular acts was the freeing of thousands of detainees who had been imprisoned by the regimes of the Arefs and even some who had been sentenced to long terms under Kassem. He accompanied this action with a statement to the effect that 'the law is supreme' and that detaining people without due process of law would never happen again. The total number released is unknown but must have been substantial. In Nukrut Salman prison in southern Iraq, for instance, the number of detainees released was 1500. Another popular act was the reinstatement of more than ten thousand employees[26] laid off by the government because of the financial pressure which resulted from the IPC's punitive decision to reduce its production of Iraqi oil. Saddam did not stop there, but assumed the status of a patron who appointed people to positions within the party and the government. Nothing was too minor to engage his attention.

In the internal political arena, with Bakr's backing, Saddam took charge of relations with the Kurds and the Shias. The Kurds under the traditionalist Mulla Mustapha Al Barzani, head of the Kurdish Democratic Party, had been in touch with the Ba'athists[27] and extended friendship to them all along. But Saddam preferred the ways of the more forward-looking Jallal Talabani, which eventually backfired. Saddam also put out friendly feelers towards the Shias and promised them a vague subordination of the Personal Status Law to the Sharia religious courts. His efforts towards the Kurds were reasonably successful: a promise of negotiations towards granting them their rights succeeded. But the situation of the Shias differed, and their suspicion of the regime showed in their insistence on having their demands met and occasional refusal to meet with members of the government.

The attempts to placate outsiders did not divert Saddam from undertaking one of the most massive organizations of a dictatorial political party in modern times. In this he was assisted by a loyalist group which included his old friend Abdel Karim Shaikhally, his half-brother Barazan, party members Taha Yassin Ramadan, Izzat Douri, Sa'adoun Shaker, Salah Ma'aza, Mohammed Mahjoub and other trusted followers. The Ba'athist Party already had an elaborate structure with cells, divisions, sections, branches, regional command and ultimately a national command throughout the Arab world. In terms of membership there were supporters, partisans (grade one and grade two), candidates and full members.[28] After membership people rose to head cells, divisions and sections, and from there to membership of the regional command and eventually the national command.

Saddam expanded the recruitment base and expedited the process of climbing the ladder. He sent party members to every village and town in the country and pinpointed certain neighbourhoods within cities. The process of becoming a member was simplified, and with membership came jobs and other benefits. Large numbers of promising recruits were sent for indoctrination to the *madrasaat al 'idad al hizbi* or Party Preparation School.[29] The Shias in particular were targeted and the effort expended paid off: there were soon more Shia than Sunni members. Some of them were pleased to receive attention from a party which had on past occasions neglected them.

However, Saddam still paid special attention to people from a reliable background – those who hailed from Tikrit, Ana, Samara, Haditha and Mosul, and other Sunnis who shared his original lowly social status. In terms of advancement within party ranks, they took precedence over their fellow Shias. Despite the presence of party founder and philosopher Alfaq, this period witnessed the transformation of the Ba'athists from an organization of middle-class intellectuals to a tribal-based party, the bulk of whose membership had little education but greater commitment to the regime. This is why Saddam's order that all party members should spy on each other to detect any act of deviation was accepted without protest. It was this, among other activities, which justified the adoption of the rabble-pleasing slogan 'Nothing is ahead of the party'.

The next target for Saddam was the Army, the only organization capable of overthrowing the new regime and which had once rejected him as an officer candidate, saddling him with additional complexes and changing the course of his life. He also wanted to control the Army because he had recognized that Generals Hardan Al Tikriti and Saleh Mahdi Ammash, both Ba'athists of high standing with followings in the Army and a direct line to Bakr, were his competitors. With encouragement from Saddam, Bakr eventually turned against them, perceived them as a threat to his own control of the military and gave his protégé a free hand to deal with the situation. Lenin and Stalin had acted in the same way in the 1920s.

Initially, Saddam used the various real and imaginary threats to the regime to set up the Popular Army, a mass paramilitary organization with more members and greater power than its Popular Resistance and National Guard predecessors. Naturally it came under his personal control. Professional soldiers viewed it with considerable misgivings and said so, but Saddam persevered because an armed militia was a natural counterweight to the regular Army, even if less efficient. This was followed by another daring move which undermined the structure of the armed forces; he created a system of party commissars to be attached to the Army on all levels[30] and made them responsible to the civilian command of the party under him. Tikriti and Ammash began to show signs of restlessness and protested to Bakr. When the latter failed to listen to them, battle was joined between Saddam and the two Army commanders.

Bakr was aware of what was happening around him – in fact he was party to every decision. He had accepted Khairallah's advice blindly: Saddam was his adopted son of whom he was visibly proud. Even the trial on trumped up charges of the highly respected former premier Abdel Rahman Al Bazzaz and his sentencing to fifteen years' imprisonment elicited no protest from Bakr.

Although a fatherly figure to whom people attributed some wisdom, Bakr was not a particularly intelligent man and, contrary to common belief, he did not object to violence either in principle or in terms of how it was applied. With Saddam aiming at a monopoly on power, Bakr busied himself with making sure that all his retainers were family. His driver, cook, doorman, servants, bodyguards and accountant all came from Tikrit.[31] The naturally irreverent Iraqi people responded by adopting a satirical song written by Ahmad Al Challachi and originally broadcast on Radio Ahwaz (run by the Iraqi opposition in Iran) which lamented their lack of links to Tikrit; every time someone could not afford to pay a bill he attributed his lack of funds to the same cause. But with everything in Saddam's hands and the Tikritis in ascendance, it became impossible to finalize without violence the programmes which he had started. What followed exceeded the actions of Kassem's Popular Resistance and showed them, in comparison, in a good light.

In the late 1960s Bakr was in his mid-fifties and happy being a father figure. His unassailable position afforded him total protection, which in turn allowed him to leave the management of most problems to Saddam. Aflaq was in Baghdad, but merely offering philosophical blessings which interested no one. Only Saddam knew the reality of the looming threats to the regime, and in 1970 everything that he and the Ba'ath Party stood for was put to the test.

He began the year in character, fearlessly trying to tackle the major problems of the Kurds, Shia and oil. Because the Kurds had turned to the USSR for help and the latter had accommodated them, Saddam's first overseas trip was to Moscow to discuss the Kurdish problem. Finding the USSR's Premier Alexei Kosygin dead set against any plans to renew a military campaign against the Kurds, Saddam returned home and offered them an olive branch. 'If the Kurdish problem is handled exclusively militarily', he said, 'then we will all lose.'[32] It was Saddam at his very best: his statement was aimed at placating the Kurds and pleasing all sides. After that he initiated negotiations with Dr Mahmoud Othman, the able leader whom all Kurdish factions wisely accepted as their representative. To Othman, 'The negotiations were long, detailed and friendly and Saddam knew his subject and was brilliant.'[33] Both Saddam and Othman were determined to reach a solution, and on paper they did.

The 11 March 1970 Manifesto between the Iraqi government and the Kurds remains a landmark, and a point of reference which will influence any future solution to this problem. According to both the published and secret articles of the agreement, Othman, a seasoned negotiator, got what he wanted. The principle of autonomy was accepted and there were provisions for sharing the country's wealth, the teaching of Kurdish as a second language, the creation of Kurdish security forces and a rejection of interference by outside powers in Kurdish affairs. More importantly, the agreement contained articles guaranteeing the principle of democracy, including the holding of elections in Kurdistan. How the democratic principle was going to be applied to Kurdistan when it was not accepted by the central government for the rest of the country was not explained.

To Christine Moss Helms, Saddam 'granted the Kurds more concessions than ever before'.[34] Helms's reference is to the Manifesto, the appointment of five Kurdish members to the cabinet and probably to the fact that Saddam had managed to keep Kurdish leader Mulla Mustapha Barzani quiet by paying him a personal subsidy – monies which, through being distributed to others within his tribal network, would help maintain his primacy. All this was true, but what was happening was the forerunner of what we see today between the Palestinians and the Israelis: the absence of goodwill nullifies most agreements before the ink is dry. The implementation of the 1970 agreement was to take place over five years, but Saddam was not going to wait until the Kurds became democratic and then allow such notions to infect the rest of Iraq. He intended to undermine the Kurds, and his actions would determine the shape of many aspects of the agreement deferred to a later date.

He began with an attempt to change the ethnic make-up of the ever-contested city of Kirkuk to guarantee its eventual control by Arabs. Curiously, though both Arabs and Kurds claimed the city, the majority of its inhabitants were neither Kurds nor Arabs but Turkomans. A mere month after the agreement was signed, Saddam began to Arabize the city. Using offices of the central government he not only encouraged Arabs to move there but offered them financial assistance to do so. Barzani started doing the same thing and urged Kurds to live in Kirkuk. Slowly both sides started to ignore the provisions of the agreement, including the payment of subsidies to the Kurds for the building of schools, hospitals and other elements of modern infrastructure. The agreement was un-ravelling. And above all, Barzani had given up on the USSR and made things up with the West after a long period of estrange-ment,[35] so he rightly thought that he could depend on the help of Iran and Israel against Saddam. In other words Saddam was determined to control Kirkuk and its oil, an understandable breach of faith, but Barzani was turning away from the agreement because as usual he could not decide what he wanted and paid more attention to outside voices than to the realities in Iraq. The whole thing fell apart, above all because of the insecurity of the central government over what the implementation of the agreement might breed. By the end of 1970 the Kurds, with backing from Iran, Israel and the United States, were in rebellion again.

As for the Shias, their leadership, unable and unwilling to negotiate in the manner of the Kurds, had consistently demanded the repeal of the Personal Status Law and greater Shia representa-tion in the government. They rightly pointed out that in 1969, Tikritis represented over 60 per cent of the membership of the Revolutionary Command Council. Simultaneously, the govern-ment began identifying them as a greater danger than the Kurds to its security. The Shia opposition to the regime had become open very early, soon after the Ba'athist takeover. Although Mohammed Bakr Al Sadr was behind the Shias' new-found strength, at that point Saddam felt Sayyed Muhsin Al Hakim, a Shia religious leader of equivalent standing to Khomeini, and his sons Mohammed Bakr and Mahdi represented more of a threat. This reflected his tribal instincts – he saw a family cluster as more dangerous than Sadr by himself.

On 4 April 1969 Saddam had enacted the first anti-Dawa Party laws and restricted the activities of its members. In addition, over a number of years he arrested and later hanged seventeen sons and grandsons of Sayyed Muhsin Al Hakim. After the government accused him on national television of committing treason by being an Iranian agent, and produced witnesses, Mahid, one of Sayyed's sons, fled to the United Arab Emirates and from there to London where he continued to work against the Ba'ath. As will be detailed in Chapter 5, another son, Mohammed, managed to flee to Iran years later and settled there to use it as a propaganda base. According to Sahib Al Hakim, a member of the family who now lives in London and works as a human rights activist, there was no such thing as cooperation with Iran against the regime. It was Aflaq who advised Saddam to deal with the Hakim family after his eyes had been opened to their popularity and hence power, which represented a threat. Returning to Baghdad from a trip abroad, Aflaq was stunned at the number of people at the airport waiting to greet Sayyed Muhsin Al Hakim, who too was returning from a journey outside the country. Aflaq is supposed to have told Saddam to hit the Dawa before it was too late.[36]

The situation on the international and Arab fronts was not much better. The 1969 hangings had tarnished the reputation of the regime, and whatever expectations the West had of a change of policy regarding oil had not materialized and were unlikely to do so. Despite the mysterious and suspicious killing of Iraqi Communist party leader Mohammed Khadi, relations with the USSR continued to improve and negotiations towards concluding an arms deal were in progress. But more importantly, it was the Ba'ath's Arab policy which influenced the West's and the USSR's attitude towards the Ba'athists.

According to Abdel Majid Farid, 'Bakr had no intention whatsoever of ceding Iraq to Nasser in a union.'[37] In other words, despite all the slogans and the ideological commitment, the Ba'ath put Arab unity on the back burner to the extent of hounding pro-Nasser army officers and cashiering most of them. This pleased both superpowers, who always opposed Arab unity and thought it easier to manipulate individual Arab countries than united ones. The man behind this relegation of one of the basic tenets of the Ba'ath was Aflaq, who, embittered by the treatment he had received from Nasser during the union of Egypt and Syria in the UAR, was dead set against cooperating with him. This became policy during a conference of the Ba'ath party, which was beholden to Iraq. However, instead of admitting that they enjoyed exercising power, the Ba'ath attributed their disaffection to Nasser's acceptance of Secretary of State William Rogers' plan to settle the Arab–Israeli problem on the basis of UN resolution 242, the original document advocating a land-for-peace solution. Nasser had accepted the Rogers Plan, while the Ba'ath had rejected it and tried to assume the role of defender of Palestinian rights.

In September 1970 events in Jordan, where the PLO (Palestine

Liberation Organization) was based for convenience in infiltrating Israel, were to expose the flawed nature of Ba'ath support for the Palestinians. What became known as Black September, a bloody confrontation between the PLO and King Hussein broke out. The Palestinians came under attack from Hussein's much stronger forces, with their implicit American and Israeli backing. Fifteen thousand Iraqi troops had been stationed in Jordan since the 1967 Arab–Israeli War, and these were the Palestinians major potential source of help. Everybody expected them to weigh in on the Palestinian side, but the Iraqi forces did nothing. There were heated arguments within the Iraqi leadership for and against affording the Palestinians support, and many stories are told about this. According to writer and analyst Patrick Seale, Bakr himself told Arafat some time later, 'It was my decision not to support the Palestinians.'[38] The Ba'athists had feared that helping the Palestinians might turn Western support for King Hussein into an attack on their own country. Where Saddam stood on this issue remains unknown, but his preoccupation with consolidating the Ba'athist position in Iraq without outside entanglements would suggest that he was against coming to the aid of the PLO.

Whatever Saddam's position, the Black September crisis produced two results which were helpful to him. First, an exhausted Nasser who had tried to settle the conflict between Jordan and the Palestinians died from a massive heart attack on 28 September. With Nasser gone, the pressure of whether to adopt a policy calling for union with Egypt or to join a pact aimed at giving priority to confronting Israel was gone. The Iraqi Ba'ath gained breathing space to follow their inward-looking policies. Secondly, Saddam blamed the Iraqi Army's inactivity during the Black September crisis on others and used it to advantage. He had been conducting a campaign to infiltrate and control the Army. Early in 1970 twenty-nine officers and several civilians were executed for trying to overthrow the regime.[39] Later, an Iran-based plot against the regime was uncovered. Among those implicated were former intelligence chief and Prime Minister Abdel Razaq Al Nayyef, who had moved to Iran for this purpose, General Abdel Ghani Al Rawi and Sa'ad Saleh Jaber, son of a former prime minister. The Iraqi army officers who were supposed to carry out the actual coup turned out to be two agents of Saddam's, Colonels Fadhil Al Nasi and Mohammed Ali Said.[40]

The combination of Army unreliability and failure to help the Palestinians gave Saddam his chance to move against the Army's leadership. The arrest and trial of mostly junior officers he placed in the hands of Nazim Kazzar, the man he had installed as head of the security services. Kazzar, an ambitious killer about whom more later, had no compunction about undermining his country's armed forces. On 15 October Saddam's chief competitor at that point, Minister of Defence General Hardan Al Tikriti, was fired from his post and sent as ambassador to Algeria. He was replaced by a reliable native of Tikrit, General Hamid Shehab. To avoid entanglement in Iraqi affairs, the Algerians refused to accept Tikriti, however. So, by nature an activist, he moved to Kuwait to conspire against Saddam. It was there that Iraqi government agents, behaving like KGB assassins in the 1930s, gunned him down in May 1971. Tikriti's killing was followed by that of a General Mahdi Saleh Samarai in Beirut. Only Ammash remained in the way.

Saddam's internal programmes, which he controlled directly, were moving forward, and his attempt to expand the ranks of the party was a huge success. While the figures available are suspect, the count of members and supporters was reportedly increased to as many as four hundred thousand. Imposing the party on the country, establishing party cells in the tiniest of villages, was accompanied by penetration of the Army to such an extent that officers were afraid to talk to each other or trust even their closest colleagues.[41] Saddam decreed that the Ba'ath was the only party to which the armed forces could belong; membership of others was punishable by death. Simultaneously he provided the Popular Army with greater support and began to use it, as always intended, as a counterweight to the regular armed forces. By the mid-1970s it was a major factor in controlling the country.

Other moves, in the civilian sector, were nothing short of remarkable. Operating through loyalists within the Ministry of Agriculture, Saddam introduced an admirable land reform programme.[42] Trade unions loyal to the party were allowed to function and, although unable to question the overall government policy, they did address themselves effectively to the issues of workers' conditions and pay. An extensive social security system was introduced, and steps were taken towards improving health care. Saddam always paid special attention to women and now he amended the Personal Status Law yet again, this time to protect them against polygamy. Moreover, the doors were opened for women to enter certain professions, including the armed forces and particularly the Popular Army. Everything Saddam did had a social and socialist basis to it, but he was remarkably clever at introducing elements which took local conditions and Arab and Iraqi culture into consideration. To Haim Berber, Saddam gave Marxism 'a local Arab meaning'.[43] In fact, it was more effective than that implies. The combination worked, and Saddam became both recognized for his toughness and loved for his thoughtfulness towards the poor and disenfranchised.

All internal, national, regional and international developments aside, Saddam the person was changing. The journalist Kamran Karadaghi says that this was the period when 'Saddam became a model for the people around him in his dress. He had no background in it, but he dressed impeccably and the party faithful copied him.'[44] While true overall, Karadaghi's comments ignored the special attention that Saddam paid to shoes, a psychological legacy from his barefoot Tikriti childhood. This was also the period which revealed his flair for propaganda, both self-serving and state-serving. He had already taken pains to publicize the fact that his wife Sajida was working as a teacher as well as looking after her ever-increasing family (a fourth child, their second daughter Rana, had been born in 1969), and this appealed to the people. Pictures of Saddam the family man now began to appear in the newspapers, most showing him playing with one of his daughters. He and his family looked genuinely happy and represented a model for the country. But his unerring sense of the proper made him order the press to place his pictures below those of Bakr and Aflaq.

Realizing that such tools were effective, Saddam began to have his pictures taken with other children, visiting factories and with peasants. His penchant for creating an image for himself was followed by efforts to create an ideological background. Saddam started using the services of Aziz Mohammed Jassem, a prolific ghost writer who served him until his unexplained disappearance in 1991. Saddam was never short of opinions, which he expressed through Jassem's words. Synthetic as all this was, his ability to superimpose imported ideology on local conditions was nothing short of brilliant. Unlike past leaders of Iraq, Saddam had an elemental desire to speak to the people. From early 1970 Jassem began to produce articles, books and tracts about everything from family life to how local socialism should be based on Iraq's history. Later Saddam turned to radio and television as vehicles to carry his message to the people. Much of the programming was attributed to him. Baghdad television and radio praising Saddam sounded like their counterparts in Muslim countries broadcasting recitals of the Koran.

It is important to remember that Saddam demonstrated a greater understanding of ordinary people than any leader in the history of Iraq, even Kassem, who had failed to grasp people's antipathy to Communism. The following story illustrates his talents perfectly. A brother of Sheikh Khmayes of the important Obeid tribe in the Tikrit region was rumoured to have been killed by one of Saddam's brothers. According to the sheikh, the murderer was not apprehended because of his relationship to the leader. He made clear that he was out to avenge the death of his brother and kill Saddam himself. When he heard this, Saddam wisely decided against acting precipitately and causing a blood feud or tribal uprising. Instead, under the auspices of Bakr he set up a meeting to deny his family's involvement in the murder. When the sheikh would not accept Bakr's peace offer Saddam dipped his bread in yoghurt, Bedouin-style, and said, 'Sheikh, I think it is in your interest to solve this matter amicably. You cannot reach me while I am in office. I am too important and too well-protected. Should, Allah forbid, our regime be overthrown, then you will have to wait in line to get to me. Thousands are ahead of you in wanting to kill Saddam Hussein.' His argument was Bedouin in style and highly intelligent – and it worked. It serves as an example of Saddam's ability to talk to people in their own language rather than talking down to them as previous rulers of the country had done.

Another aspect of Saddam's cleverness was the way he deferred to his seniors, Aflaq and Bakr. He took care not to be photographed with either man with his jacket unbuttoned, and always stood half a step behind them. He would not speak until they had finished speaking or asked him for his opinion. Saddam told his biographer Fuad Matar that he had never entered the office of the father-leader, Bakr, without being announced, even when the latter summoned him for meetings. To Saddam 'This [politeness] is not a sign of weakness, it is a sign of strength.' And naturally enough he attributed his behaviour to subscription to Arab tradition and customs.[45] This is undoubtedly true and is attested to by people who knew him, including the reliable Salah Omar Al Ali. They also speak of how polite he could be in dealing with people in general.

Given this background, it is important to address another phoney story about Saddam. The *Observer* newspaper of 28 September 1980 and other publications and books have alleged that Saddam Hussein went to Baghdad University some time after the Ba'athist takeover and demanded a law degree. This is nonsense. In the Middle East things are simply not done like that. That Saddam wanted a law degree is probably true, for in his youth he had started studying for one, but he did not have to enter the university wielding a gun to obtain one now. All he had to do was drop a hint to the head of the university and the degree was his.

Unlike Saddam's origins and early activities, his performance after the Ba'ath assumed power is not shrouded in mystery. Amir Iskandar, though he always exaggerated Saddam's achievements, was right about one thing: Saddam was 'the engineer of the revolution',[46] certainly the man who made things happen. The historian Fouad Ajami uses Saddam's performance during this period to explain the man's character and attainments. To him, 'Saddam emerged from populist Arab nationalism.'[47] Noting Saddam's success at hoodwinking his colleagues and gaining popularity with the people, Hazem Jawad, Ba'athist Foreign Minister in the 1963 government, states, 'Our people are builders of dictators.'[48] But, as we shall see later, perhaps it was Michel Aflaq who knew his reliable *gada'* or tough guy better than most and he expressed his success at running Iraq succinctly: 'You are what people need.'

However much on target these statements are, there is something about the man which remains a mystery. When Naim Tawina, a Jew was imprisoned as a Zionist spy in 1971, he assumed he would be sent to the gallows. But luck was with him. Saddam was visiting the prison when Tawina was being interrogated in a corner and saw him. 'Don't touch that man!' Saddam screamed at the interrogator. Tawina was reprieved and eventually made it to Israel where, leafing through a magazine which carried a picture of the young Saddam Hussein, he realized why he had been spared. He remembered the same young man selling cigarettes in the streets of Baghdad; whenever he bought a packet Tawina had always tipped him.[49] This and the story about the Egyptian doorman offer a picture of a humanitarian Saddam which is difficult to reconcile with the rest of what is known about him. Intelligent, effective, methodical and polite he was and is, but there is violence in the man on both personal and institutional levels. Perhaps, just perhaps, he had read about how Stalin believed that terror is the way to a great society and subordinated his inner, more humane feelings to that. By the end of 1970, Saddam's monopoly on power in Iraq was complete.[50] Instability and inefficiency were receding,[51] but more terror and attempts at building a modern society were on the way.

5

Seeking Heaven

Saddam's twin approach to the consolidation of Ba'athist power continued until the end of 1973. First, enemies were neutralized, be they individuals, ethnic or religious groups or political parties. Simultaneously, ambitious social and economic programmes were pursued at breakneck speed. Aflaq continued to issue his homilies about Islam being the basis of Ba'ath philosophy, along with direct ideological attacks against Baghdad's leftist competitors, the Damascus Ba'ath. Bakr, secure in Mr Deputy's ability to control the country, was enjoying the majesty of office and ignoring the rumblings beneath him. His behaviour resembled that of Field Marshal Hindenburg, the elder statesman who paved the way for Hitler's assumption of total power in Germany in the thirties.

For Saddam, completing his individual elimination campaign was a necessity. His next target was Shia Fuad Al Rikabi, one-time Secretary General of the party in Iraq and organizer of the attempt on Kassem's life in 1959. Although no one considered him a danger, Rikabi had resigned his membership of the party and become a follower of Nasser. Soon after the 1968 coup he was imprisoned as a precautionary measure. But when several Ba'athists recalled his past record and asked for his release, towards the end of 1970 he was mysteriously stabbed in his prison cell and left to bleed to death. The assassin was never apprehended. According to many sources, the regime was determined to make an example of Rikabi to frighten pro-Nasser Iraqis.

Now it was the turn of Saleh Mahdi Ammash. Following General Hardan Al Tikriti's dismissal, in an attempt to placate the Army, Ammash had been elevated to Vice President in addition to being Minster of the Interior. But on 28 September 1971, while attending an Arab league meeting in Morocco, Ammash was dismissed from all his positions. Except for the ineffectual Sa'adoun Gheidan, he was the last major military figure standing between Saddam and the creation of an ideological army controlled by the party to replace the professional one.

The reduction of the Army to a branch of the civilian wing of the Ba'ath Party, which he controlled, was Saddam's idea. Considering its similarity to what happened in the Soviet Union in the 1930s, the idea probably took shape in his mind as he was reading biographies of Stalin. Until then, the military wing of the Ba'ath had been independent, led by Bakr, and had acted as a counterweight to the civilian branch. But the President and Commander-in-Chief accepted the move and the implied supremacy of his Mr Deputy without protest. The only thing Bakr did was to intervene with the RCC to spare the life of Ammash, and Mr Deputy, as astute as ever, went along with the wishes of the father-leader. Ammash was demoted to Ambassador in Stockholm, then Moscow and finally Helsinki. He died in Finland in 1975, in mysterious circumstances.

On the same day that Ammash was dismissed from his major posts in Baghdad, Abdel Karim Shaikhally was relieved of his post as Foreign Minister and given the lesser role of Ambassador to the United Nations. Shaikhally had been Saddam's closest friend, one of the young Ba'athists who tried to kill Kassem in 1959 and Saddam's fellow exile in Damascus and Cairo. People spoke of them as inseparable twins. However Shaikhally, an educated ideologue, had advocated the abandonment of the inter-Ba'ath feud and rapprochement with the Syrian Ba'ath. Moreover, he showed signs of rejecting Saddam's sole control of all government departments. His ambassadorial appointment was tantamount to exile, since he could not influence events from New York. Shaikhally eventually returned to Baghdad in his retirement, only to be shot to death in 1982 after visiting the post office to pay his electricity bill.[1]

One day after acting against Ammash and Shaikhally, on 29 September, a more elaborate government-sponsored attempt to kill Mulla Mustapha Al Barzani was organized by security chief Nazim Kazzar.[2] The Kurdish leader was at his mountain redoubt, a cave near Sulimaniya in northern Iraq, discussing Iraqi–Kurdish relations with a delegation representing Saddam. Suddenly the heavy native costume worn by the delegate who was sitting next to him exploded, killing the wearer instantly and wounding Barzani slightly. Ahmad Chalabi, leader of the opposition Iraqi National Congress, insists that 'it was a remote control explosion. They were getting into sophisticated stuff at this point.'[3] Obviously they had no compunction about killing the innocent wearer of the garment. Any chance of resurrecting the March 1970 Manifesto between Barzani and the government evaporated with the dust of the explosion.

Early in 1972, Saddam reached even higher. Shia agitation followed the exile and imprisonment of some members of the Hakim family, and their supporters persisted. In a most daring move he sent the Army to the Shia holy city of Najjaf and arrested Mohammed Bakr Al Sadr, who had become sole leader of the Shias after the death of Sayyed Muhsin Al Hakim in 1970. Sadr had proved implacable in his opposition to the regime and unresponsive to the government's appeals to tone down his fiery anti-Ba'ath sermons. Among the reasons for the failure to negotiate a truce was the two sides' inability to agree on where the meeting should be held. According to Shia exile Sahib Al Hakim, Saddam responded to an invitation from Sadr to visit him in Najjaf by saying that he feared for his life, and asked the latter to visit Baghdad instead. Sadr's terse reply was, 'If you're afraid to visit Najjaf then what do I say about visiting Baghdad?'[4] In a rare instance of over-ruling Saddam, Bakr ordered Sadr's release after a brief period of incarceration. But, without a change of position on either side, the problems between them soon resurrected themselves.

In mid-1972 Sajida Hussein gave birth to Hala, their third daughter and fifth child. Pictures of the family appeared in the newspapers and everyone looked happy and content. Aflaq and Bakr sent flowers and offered their congratulations, and this too was publicized. In personal and political terms everybody thought Saddam occupied an unassailable position – except Saddam. he had emasculated the Army, then he took control of it, and eliminated most of his competitors. The Ba'ath Party was increasing in numbers and his loyalists within it were running the country. But he still had no solution to the problems posed by the Communist party, the Kurds and the Shias. He then put the maxim of

'People with full bellies don's make revolutions'[5] into effect. Convinced that providing every Iraqi with economic incentives would overcome all political opposition to his policies, he decided that his only salvation lay in nationalizing the IPC oil consortium. It was the surest way of generating greater national income, a way of circumventing and undermining the opposition.

For Saddam, wresting control of his country's oil from IPC was a natural consequence of what he had started. Beginning in 1971, he used his position as the country's 'manager' to assume responsibility for negotiations with the oil consortium and to chair the Follow-up Committee on Oil Affairs and Implementation of Agreements. To a former official of the Iraqi National Oil Company, 'It was the best thing that happened to the country. I hate the man and I am a member of the opposition and don't want my name to be mentioned, but it was timely and he was brilliant.' My informant went on to tell me how the Iraqi oil experts had scoffed when they heard that Saddam had grabbed the 'oil portfolio', but how 'utterly staggered we were by how much he knew after the first meeting'. Saddam had read a massive amount about the problems between IPC and the Iraqi government and, endowed as he was with a photographic memory and exceptional intelligence, had managed to memorize most of it. More importantly, he had a solid appreciation of conditions within the oil market and knew that the demand-supply situation favoured the producers.

The major issue with IPC originated in the consortium's slowing down of Iraqi oil production in favour of that of other countries. This had been complicated by what Kassem and the Arefs had done – the enactment of Law 80 and the formation of INOC – and by the problems arising from the pressures imposed by members of the consortium and other major players in the oil market to stop Iraq selling oil from the fields it controlled. Of course, the governments behind the oil majors supported them. Saddam's response to the IPC position was very simple: he showed readiness to use their expertise to extract and sell Iraqi oil, but had no intention of allowing them to control the volume of oil being pumped and how much to charge for it. Other Arab members of OPEC were negotiating the purchase of 25 per cent of the consortia producing their oil, but without interfering with production or pricing. Saddam's position was therefore revolutionary and threatened both producers and concessionaires. The arrogance of the IPC negotiators helped him, for their counter-offers bordered on the perfunctory; and, having never felt secure in its ability to please the Iraqis after the enactment of Kassem's Law 80, IPC added insult to injury by reducing its production from the Iraqi oil fields even further. For Saddam, this was the moment to put his secret plan into action.

In February 1972, Saddam visited the USSR for the second time. Determined to please his hosts, he had previously put out feelers to the Iraqi Communist party to join the government and had for some time refrained from undertaking military offensives against the Kurds. When Soviet Premier Alexei Kosygin reciprocated Saddam's visit and came to Iraq to witness the first shipments from the Rumeillah oil field, which had been nationalized by Kassem and developed with Soviet help, the two countries decided to take things further. On 9 April they signed a fifteen-year Friendship and Cooperation Treaty. In early May the Ba'ath invited two members of the Communist party, Amir Abdallah and Nakman Talabani, to join the government. On the 13th, with conditions in the oil market tightening further in favour of the suppliers, and after consulting with President Bakr,[6] Saddam gave IPC's chairman Mr Stockwell, two weeks to accept the Iraqi government's terms.[7] Judged by the dismissive reaction, it is safe to assume that the threat was not taken seriously.

On 1 June the Iraqi government went ahead and nationalized IPC (Law 69). To Saddam this meant: 'Our wealth has returned to us.'[8] Nevertheless, his ability to combine daring with caution, the trademark of the Tikritis, led him to exclude the Basra Oil Company (BOC). It was the sister company of IPC and part of the consortium, but Saddam was hedging his bets. He wanted BOC to continue to produce oil and generate enough income to protect himself against failure, resultant bankruptcy and the loss of government. Meanwhile, he asked the Iraqi people to live on half their salaries.

Radio Baghdad began beaming the revolutionary message of 'Arab Oil for the Arabs'. The people were ecstatic and Saddam named 1 June 1972 'Victory Day'. In view of the feelings of their own people, and because Saddam had cleverly sought their support through OAPEC (the Organization of Arab Oil Producing and Exporting Countries), the Arab oil producers had no option but to back Iraq. Years later – and there is agreement on this among all the Iraqi oil experts whom I have interviewed – Saddam told his biographer Matar that 'not a single oil expert supported my decision'.[9] In fact even the Communist party had not demanded nationalization, because it had feared consequences such as the West withholding spare parts. This would have crippled INOC and lead to the stoppage of Iraqi oil production.[10] But acting with caution came naturally to Saddam, and before he moved he had protected Iraq against spare parts shortages by signing contracts for their supply from the USSR, Italy, Brazil and other countries.

An eye witness account of the way Saddam implemented his strategic decision has been supplied by Iraqi lawyer Sabah Mukhtar, then a junior official of INOC. He told me how Saddam personally handled every detail of the nationalization in a vintage performance which perfectly demonstrated how methodical and organized he was.[11] On the afternoon of 31 May all INOC employees were summoned to company headquarters and asked to stay there until further notice. In the early evening each was allowed to telephone his family to explain that he would be staying at work overnight. Around midnight, Saddam appeared in person and informed the staff of the decision to nationalize IPC. He spoke quietly and with self-confidence, telling them which offices to occupy, how to advise IPC staff of what had happened and which files to read to update themselves; he also directed them to treat yesterday's enemy with the greatest of courtesy.

It was un-Arab, a piece of organizational magic which appealed to the listeners, and it worked. There was not a single incident to mar the takeover and it was Saddam himself who later advised Mr Stockwell of the Iraqi decision. He did this with the utmost politeness and expressed a wish for the two sides to settle their differences amicably. The directive to his new officials, the people promoted the night before, was very clear: 'Do not stop production [of oil] under any circumstance.'[12]

In late June, Saddam travelled to France to visit President Georges Pompidou. Until then, the French had been moderately angered by the nationalization but slightly more open to Iraqi suggestions for making a settlement than were their fellow members of the consortium. Saddam dangled the prospect of cooperation with the French oil companies in exploring for and extracting oil from Iraqi fields other than those allocated to the USSR, and concluded a minor arms deal to prove to the French President that his country was not solely dependent for its military hardware on the USSR.

The other IPC members were less happy. The *Washington Post* of 7 June accused the USSR of being behind the nationalization, and it was right; it was the USSR which broke the Western oil monopoly as part of a regional policy aimed at neutralizing the West. French support came after the fact and was partially aimed at giving France a chance to balance the picture through becoming Iraq's primary contact in the Western camp. In February 1973, the issue of the legality of the nationalization decree and IPC's counter-claim was settled and Iraq's takeover of the Basra Oil Company began to be finalized slowly, just in case. Iraq began to exploit oil fields such as Majnoon, Nahr Omar, West Quama, Zubeir and Tawiya which had been hitherto ignored by the consortium. Majnoon and Nahr Omar alone were estimated to be capable of producing 850,000 and 400,000 barrels respectively per day. Simultaneously, because of conditions within the oil market, Iraq had no problem finding buyers, which included the USSR, France, Spain, Brazil, the German Democratic Republic and Hungary.

The USSR's help during this period continued to influence politics within Iraq. On 17 June of the following year, 1973, after lengthy negotiations the Ba'ath and the Communist Party cemented and extended the latter's participation in the government by forming the Patriotic National Front. President Bakr and Communist leader Aziz Mohammed signed a National Action Charter which made Iraq appear democratic and strengthened the Ba'ath's hand in dealing with other opposition groups. It was a masterstroke for the Ba'ath which undermined everybody except the Communist party, and the USSR soon showed its pleasure by requesting Mulla Mustapha Al Barzani and his Kurds to limit their anti-Ba'ath activities.

Bakr received as much credit from the nationalization of IPC as Saddam did. Mr Deputy never passed up an opportunity to emphasize the value of the father-leaders wise counsel and, as so often, more was attributed to Bakr's wisdom than was justified. Praising Bakr was part and parcel of everything Saddam did, an extension of his behaviour towards his protector and relation during the early consolidation period. This pleased and reassured the old man and made him more dependent on his protégé. Very soon after the formation of the National Patriotic Front Saddam deliberately sought to extend Bakr's involvement in attempts to guarantee the success of the oil nationalization. On his Deputy's prompting, the often ailing and relatively inactive Bakr went to Poland to discuss stepping up trade and political cooperation. Oil was the leading topic. As was Saddam's wont, he was trying to include yet another country in the list of those which brought Iraqi oil and sold INOC spare parts. Multi-sourcing everything to guard against possible disruption of supplies and over dependence on individual countries was later to become a habit, and Saddam also adopted it in his arms-buying programme.

Bakr's unaccustomed absence in Poland was used by his and Saddam's opponents to undertake the most serious attempt ever to overthrow the Ba'ath regime.[13] The President was scheduled to return to Baghdad from Warsaw on 30 June. There was a strong ceremonial military presence at the airport to greet him, and a group of conspirators had placed a number of their followers among the honour guard with instructions to shoot Bakr on his arrival. They were operating under orders from the head of the security services, which had been placed under the umbrella of the Office of National Security. Saddam had been the first head of this organization, and the chief conspirator was his hand-picked replacement and protégé Nazim Kazzar. The plan called for the security forces, then comprising the *mukhabarat* (the successor organization to the General Relation Apparatus) and general security, to follow up Bakr's assassination by occupying the radio and television stations and declaring the end of 'the Tikriti regime', especially Saddam and his father-in-law Khairallah.

Kazzar had set the ball rolling by arresting the two people apart from Saddam who were capable of stopping him, Army Chief of Staff and Minister of Defence General Hamid Shehab and Minister of the Interior Sa'adoun Gheidan, now the sole survivors of the non-Ba'athists involved in the 1968 coup. Kazzar held his two hostages in the cellar of the general security building. Quite by chance, Bakr's plane was four hours late. Kazzar, at the airport to 'greet' the President, decided the delay was deliberate. Thinking that the regime had discovered the existence of his plot, he cancelled the order to assassinate Bakr and hurried back to his headquarters to face Shehab and Gheidan. Some of the would-be hit-men fled and others secretly switched sides. Soon afterwards,

Baghdad television showed pictures of the arrival of the President with his respectful Mr Deputy meeting him.

Kazzar should have known better than to try to save himself and implicate others, but he wasted precious time by making one futile telephone call before fleeing towards Iran. Saddam took control of the situation after hearing about the arrest of the generals from their staff, and characteristically wasted no time in responding. Kazzar's convoy of official cars was chased by helicopter gun ships which attacked it and in the process killed General Shehab and wounded Gheidan. Kazzar was captured and brought back to Baghdad to face trial. On 7 July, a revolutionary court headed by Izzat Douri, Deputy Chairman of the Revolutionary Command Council, found him guilty and sentenced him to death. Seven security officers and thirteen army officers received the same sentence, and the executions were carried out the following day. Once again there were reports that tribal instincts prevailed and that some of the people executed had been merely relatives of conspirators and did not have the benefit of a trial. The only defendant whose death sentence was not carried out was one of Saddam's oldest Ba'athist friends, Abdel Khaliq Samarai. Unhappily for him, he had been on the receiving end of Kazzar's unsuccessful telephone call from the security headquarters. In an uncharacteristic act of kindness, Samarai was saved by the intercession of Michel Aflaq.

The Kazzar plot differs from others in significant ways other than having come close to succeeding. Kazzar was a Shia and resented the exclusive Sunni control of the government.[14] His anti-Tikriti feelings had led him to threaten to 'wipe Tikrit off the map'. Such an expression of resentment emanating from within the security system was surprising since that was Saddam's original power base, the apparatus which he had created and used to control the rest of the government. The imprisonment of Samarai amounted to a fortuitous neutralization of a Saddam competitor[15] and party ideologue whose opinions were in conflict with Mr Deputy's pragmatism. To Iraqi academic Faleh Abdel Jabbar, the Kazzar affair forced Saddam to emulate Bakr. He too now began to depend more on family members, including his half-brothers, than on the party, though without giving anyone enough power to threaten his own status. Khairallah created the idea of family dominance; Bakr acted on it and ceded everything to Saddam;

the latter eventually expanded it to include members of the Al Majid and Ibrahim families and other Tikritis.

While the plot marked the end of opposition to Saddam from the original members of the civilian branch of the Ba'ath, he then cleverly used it to his advantage. His street wisdom had told him that people were unhappy with much of the violence and human rights abuses perpetrated by the two branches of the Office of National Security. Saddam saw this as an opportunity to saddle others with the consequences of the policy he had instigated and blamed all previous unpopular acts of the security departments on Kazzar. In accordance with Saddam's Stalinist methods, overnight his erstwhile follower and protégé became a stranger and a traitor to the revolution. But he also took precautionary steps. Iraqi businessman Ghazi Al Ayyash claims that this was the time when Saddam proceeded to build more radio and television stations to protect himself against conspirators who might occupy the central one and use it in any future coup attempt. Ayyash remembers Saddam saying, 'They [the would-be conspirators] should know that occupying one radio or television station is not enough.'

Many questions regarding the Kazzar conspiracy will never be answered. They include the number of people involved, the kind of government the conspirators wanted to form, and whether the conspiracy was aimed against the Ba'ath party or was an example of one faction of it rising against another. And, of course, there is always the question of the involvement of outside powers. But these issues did not occupy the minds of the Iraqis for long. What started to make a huge impact on their lives and thinking were the benefits of the oil nationalization which were already evident, and which signalled that better times were on the way.

Saddam's instincts had been right. Controlling the country's oil proved to be an economic and psychological success, and the government propaganda machine used the rise in the standard of living to generate a sense of national unity and pride. But it was the October War of 1973 which turned this success into an unqualified strategic victory. The War against Israel was the result of Egyptian–Syrian planning, respectively the work of Presidents Anwar Sadat and Hafez Al Assad. Neither country trusted the Iraqi Ba'ath and Saddam was kept in the dark.

Iraq had continued to show signs of being inward-looking and had shunned Arab involvements and withdrawn its troops from Jordan soon after Black September in 1970. But in 1973 Iraq could not afford not to join the fighting. The surprise attack on Israel by Egypt and Syria started on 6 October and initially met with considerable success. Three days after the outbreak of hostilities the Iraqis sent thirty thousand troops, including a whole armoured division, to reinforce the Syrians battling it out with the Israelis on the Golan Heights. But because the Iraqi Army had no tank transporters, the armour units had to get to Syria on their own tracks, involving a drive of more than two days. As a result the crews went into battle dead-tired, and in an Israeli attack they lost nearly a hundred tanks and suffered heavy casualties. The war slowly ground to a halt by 26 October. Bitter at having been excluded from the decision to start the war and at the acceptance of UN Security Council resolution 333 to end it, Saddam complained about having to rely on radio news to discover what was happening and withdrew his forces from Syria immediately the fighting stopped.

What made the 1973 war different from previous ones was the use of the oil weapon – the accompanying Arab oil embargo initiated by Saudi Arabia and the Gulf States. Again, Iraq was excluded from the secret pre-war discussions. In response Saddam, with Bakr's backing, angrily adopted a position which challenged the rest of the Arabs. He refused to join the embargo except on the sale of oil to the USA and the Netherlands, who had been too vociferous in their support for Israel. Instead, he demanded a total severance of economic relations with the West. But an economic war against the West was something that the rest of the Arabs, including Egypt and Syria, refused to contemplate. The oil embargo lasted until March 1974. In the meantime, Saddam was free to follow an independent oil policy beneficial to his country while accusing the other Arab nations of being Western lackeys. Iraq capitalized on the shortage that the embargo created by producing more oil than ever before.[16] In 1974, Iraqi oil income rose to $5.7 billion from a pitiful $575 in 1972.[17]

It was this enormous increase in national income which offered Saddam his opportunity to change Iraq beyond recognition. The improved economic conditions meant that the threats to the Ba'ath regime were under control, though still underpinned by a massive security service. This gave Saddam his chance to implement the next stage of his strategic plan. He began by using Iraq's wealth to initiate one of the largest economic development programmes ever undertaken by a third world country. Simultaneously, he started an ambitious arms programme which went beyond purchasing military hardware and included extensive plans to build an arms industry. He was not only living up to the maxim of people with full bellies not making revolutions; creating one of the strongest armies in the Middle East was always part of his thinking.

As managing director of the consulting firm Growth International (GI), and later as chairman of its successor, Aburish, James and Associates, I participated in both these undertakings over a period of five years. In 1974 Beirut-based Arab Resources Management (ARM), run by an old school friend, Dr Ramzi A. Dalloul, was advising Iraq in both fields, first through dealing with the Minister of Planning and Deputy Prime Minister, Adnan Hamdani, and later by working with Saddam directly. ARM reached an agreement with GI to be their European procurement arm – to help them locate major companies to work in Iraq under the rules and regulations of the Iraqi government. Much of this chapter, and of Chapter 6 which deals exclusively with the arms programme, is therefore based on personal experience unavailable to others.

Unsurprisingly, because Saddam never overlooked even the smallest of details, the first request forwarded to GI by ARM was to find a firm to supply three thousand tank carriers to avoid a repeat of the Iraqi experience in Syria.[18] The second reveals a great deal about its true source, Saddam. Dalloul had received from Saddam and Hamdani a memorandum consisting of a single question: whether the 'best companies in the world' were working in Iraq. The two men knew perfectly well that they were not, but wanted a detailed answer because they felt it would tell them how foreign corporations viewed their country.

In response, I prepared a lengthy document which said, in brief, that major Western corporations were reluctant to work in Iraq. The reasons I listed included bureaucratic snarl-ups, constant changes in the Iraqi government's priorities, and the subordination of business to politics by awarding contracts to companies from friendly countries when those from politically unacceptable countries were more qualified to do the work. According to Dalloul, Saddam accepted all the points except the last. He told Dalloul that everybody favoured their friends and that Iraq had an obligation to trade with countries such as Yugoslavia. After making clear that this point was not negotiable, Saddam asked Dalloul to entice qualified Western corporations to help him achieve his plans. According to Saddam, there was enough business to go around.

Working closely with Hamdani and his able deputy, Salah Shaikhally, Dalloul began to inundate me and GI with requests which reflected Iraq's needs. Saddam wanted contractors to undertake housing projects, companies to build sugar-refining plants which would use sugar beet and dates, industrial concerns to mine phosphates from the huge deposits at Akashat and sulphur from the north, corporations to construct brick-making factories, others with experience in land reclamation projects, companies to start up dairy and egg farms, and ones with expertise in building railways, and fertilizer and other chemical plants. It was a wish list of staggering proportions – but then the price of oil kept rising. Saddam knew his country contained 10 per cent of the world's known reserves and he was determined to use it to join the twentieth century with a bang.

The civilian companies which I introduced to Iraq were well-known ones such as Morrison Knudson, ITT, and International Systems and Controls from the USA; George Wimpey, GKN, Taylor Woodrow and Booker McConnell from the UK; and others from Sweden, Denmark, France, West Germany, Canada, Poland, Ireland, Spain and Portugal. Because of the variety of what was needed and the speed with which Saddam wanted the projects completed, the Iraqis were accommodating to a degree which impressed the companies' representatives who visited them. But mistakes were made, including amusing ones. The Poles were asked to produce sugar from refining plants using dates, but some of them had never seen the fruit and most had no experience in the field. The Danes could not understand why Saddam wanted his dairy farms to be huge because this would increase the risk of disease spreading and make the farms difficult to manage – and they had no experience of the Iraqi climate. Because Saddam is a natural believer in grandiose schemes, convincing him that smaller dairy farms would be more productive and easier to manage was difficult, as was having to tell him that Australians and Americans were better qualified to deal with the conditions of his country.

There was a lot of duplicated effort, but the Iraqi technocrats were very competent – well ahead of their counterparts in the rest of the Arab world – and many of them showed the zeal of true believers in the future of their country. This created a good image in western corporate circles, which enhanced their reputation and made our efforts easier. And Saddam's preoccupations differed from those of the government of Saudi Arabia and the other Gulf states: in Iraq's case, importing luxury goods and wasteful consumer spending were not part of the chief planner's thinking.

It was to change later, but at the time Saddam was creating social forces while other Arab rulers were building palaces. Dalloul never tired of telling me how committed Saddam was to the 'transfer of technology', 'bridging the technological gap' and 'borrowing expertise'. Interestingly, Dalloul himself operated with a similar sense of commitment. Although a capitalist who enjoyed making money, he was essentially an ideologue-middleman who perceived what he was doing as a way of serving the Arabs and contributing to their advancement. In fact, as with the arms programme, we derived a particular satisfaction from being the instruments of Saddam's schemes. We felt he was seeking heaven for the Iraqi people. Unfortunately for some elements of the population, they would have to go through hell too.

During this period, which lasted until the very late seventies, absolutely nothing escaped Saddam's attention. He was determined to manufacture as much as possible locally, including storm windows and factories to make sandals. Nor did the corruption that goes hand-in-hand with doing business in most Arab countries escape his scrutiny. In 1975 and 1976 he enacted Laws 8 and 52, which made receiving bribes and commissions by Iraqi citizens punishable by death – and according to Kamran Karadaghi, Saddam never made idle threats.[19] To live up to his reputation as an enforcer of the letter of the law, in 1978 Saddam made an example of two deputy ministers. They were executed for taking bribes,[20] and their fate was publicized as a warning to others both within and outside the government.

In fact, what Saddam had in mind went beyond having the funds to build factories and plants. At the same time sophisticated plans were put in hand to create a human infrastructure to accommodate the building programme. First, realizing that his ambitions outstripped the public sector's ability to cope with them, Saddam began encouraging the private sector and facilitated its growth by creating agricultural, industrial and real estate banks. It was impossible to assess the size of an on-going effort, but by 1977 the private sector represented no less than 25 per cent of the economic output of the country, perhaps as much as three times its size in 1970. This did not, however, stop him from ordering private companies to pay the minimum wage which public companies were obliged to pay. To satisfy the needs of both the public and private sectors Saddam began building schools, including vocational ones, and sending more people for training to Europe and the United States. The building of hospitals and clinics was not far behind. Looking further into the future, he instigated a population expansion programme and offered families a government subsidy of $2500 for each child they produced. According to a statement made by Dalloul, 'Saddam thinks the country needs more people – millions more.'

Saddam was changing Iraq and he knew it. Not only did he initiate massive undertakings such as the Zubeir fertilizer, steel and chemical complex at an estimated cost of $45 billion,[21] he ensured that the pipelines which carried oil from all parts of the country were interconnected, with reverse flow mechanisms, which meant that he could use terminals in Syria, his own port of Basra and eventually Turkey, according to circumstances. This magnificent technical achievement also removed at a stroke Iraq's dependence on a single outlet – another example of the duplicative/protective factor. Nor did Saddam forget the everyday needs of his people: he built markets which improved the quality of basic commodities and brought electric power to four thousand villages.[22] But things were not just left there. To Saddam electricity had to be used in an immediate and beneficial way, so he set up a massive nationwide distribution of free refrigerators and television sets. Interestingly, in an attempt to calm his continuing confrontation with their religious leadership, he made the people of the Shia south come first – after all, there was a special need to have them listen to his message.

My recollections of Saddam's largesse during this period prompted me to inquire from one of the leading members of the Dawa party in London, Dr Heidar Abbas, whether this had any effect on the thinking of the average Shia. His answer was a guarded yes – it worked without solving the basic problem of the Shias' wish to have a share in government.[23] The economic programme was more than an expression of Saddam's belief in the docility of people with full bellies. According to a leading Iraqi scholar, Saddam borrowed an idea from London's Scotland Yard and started talking of 'a silk thread' between the government and the common man. Nor did Saddam ignore the Kurds after the failure of the 1970 Manifesto. I shall return to the political element of this later, but in strictly economic terms, in 1974 Saddam allocated to Kurdistan $3 billion, to be spent in ways similar to what he was doing in the south.[24]

There are three other aspects to this period in which I was only marginally involved but which deserve to be described in some detail because of their far-reaching implications. Continuing his economic development efforts, Saddam paid special attention to realizing his country's agricultural potential. He also made unprecedented attempts to eradicate illiteracy throughout Iraq. Finally, it was at this point that Saddam decided to add to his internal policies by reintroducing Iraq to the Arab arena. He started courting the Palestinians and sending them financial help. He also paid special attention to political and trade relations with other Arab governments. No one had yet thought of him as a leader of the Arab world and he did not try to impose any of his ideas on them. If anything, it was the superhuman energy of the man which should have alerted them.[25]

There is no better way to demonstrate Saddam's efforts in the agricultural field than to quote extensively from a document written by Michael Hamers, an Anglo-Dutch expert who worked in Iraq for several years as the manager of the Irish company JMJ. That Saddam was determined to mechanize agriculture[26] and reclaim land is known, but, as Hamers' document proves, it was the urgency of his plans, his flexibility and ability to motivate others which made all the difference in the world. What follows is an abbreviated version of Hamers' important report but essentially in his own words:

Irrigation is a necessity in a land of limited rainfall and very high summer temperatures with extremely high evaporation, and this is why water from the two rivers has been used since antiquity. With the use of the rivers' water, a problem arises, one which has been with us for centuries. Both rivers originate in the Caucasus, which, being relatively new mountain structures, contain a high proportion of soluble salts in the surface rock.

Given the rate of evaporation, it is inevitable that continuous irrigation will result in a build-up of salinity in the ground water, leading to sterility of the soil. In the past large landowners were content with modest crop returns, and the use of crop rotation allowed for the use of winter rains which washed away the salt into the two rivers and the sea. With modifications, this system prevailed from Babylonian times through Ottoman times and continued later. Nevertheless, over the centuries, salination turned much of the granary of the world into desert.

The distribution of land after the 1958 Kassem revolution produced small plots of land which meant cropping was increased and so was the use of water. This meant a higher level of salinity which precluded plant life. More land turned to desert and salt crusts were in evidence. The plan to give peasants land was in danger of self-destructing.

The Ba'ath party came to power in Iraq at a time when the deterioration of the land had reached alarming proportions. The Ministry of Irrigation was instructed to deal with the problem as a priority, but limited funds were not enough to implement plans to deal with the problem, though the technology to deal with it was available in the US, the Netherlands and other advanced countries.

Things changed after 1972 and the nationalization of the oil company by Vice President Saddam Hussein. The 1973 oil embargo and the increase in the price of oil increased Iraq's income substantially. Saddam Hussein, himself of peasant stock, related to this problem more than other leaders. Much of the additional income of the country was applied to land reclamation. In all this, Saddam Hussein was very much the moving power, because of genuine concern and because it strengthened his power base with the rural population.

In the mid-1970s a start was made in the south of the country, the Dujailah-Nassiriya area, to control the flow of irrigation water and the use of a subsoil drain network. It was a successful effort led by the British Company Marples Ridgway and set the standard for all future work of its kind.

With Turkey and Syria using more of the water of the two rivers the salinity problem was getting worse and more work was needed. The solution to this was provided by the Vice President who decided on the specific plan to be adopted. He [Saddam Hussein] wanted to reclaim 3 million hectares of land.

A flooding of the Tharthar depression, a lake of 2000 square kilometres, was a controversial part of the plan. A major canal was to divert saline water into it when the rivers where high and then to use mildly saline water when they were low. Saddam Hussein's hand was behind this. [*Author's note*: This proves that the plans to drain the marshes, now considered inhumane by anti-Saddam forces, were afoot in the 1970s, in cooperation with Western companies. In fact this undertaking started under the monarchy in the 1950s, and I shall discuss it more fully later.]

Until 1978, projects of reclaiming 5000 to 25,000 hectares were granted to contractors from East and West Europe and the Far East and things moved fairly smoothly. Gradually, as the oil income decreased, it became clear that the headlong pace of these projects could not be maintained. Of course, there were other projects in Kurdistan and other areas. It was an ambitious development aimed at re-creating the world's granary.

While Hamers' document deals with the development aspect of realizing the country's agricultural potential, it says very little about the nature of the rural communities that Saddam wanted to create. Initially he was enamoured with the idea of collectiviza-tion,[27] but switched back to individual farming and cooperatives when the Iraqi people showed signs of rejecting the Communist model. This complete about-turn was typical of Saddam's populist eclecticism. Having decided that collective farms were unpopular and somewhat unsuccessful, he immediately reduced their number and began to encourage the public sector.[28] His justification for this and other situations was a new Saddamism. Everything was subordinated to 'Our way is an Arab way', a maxim that Saddam originally invented to justify not being socialist or capitalist.[29] Saddam's 'Arab way' led him to start reducing the number of collective farms in 1975, and by 1982 they had all but disappeared.

The second task which engaged Saddam's mind, reflecting his background and its psychological wounds, was his commitment to education. His school building programme started soon after 1973, but that was not enough for him. He wanted a totally literate country, and he wanted it overnight. It was another strike for equality and against those who had become privileged through the exclusivity of education.

As usual, Saddam used a combination of encouragement and threat. He began in 1977 by declaring a Day of Knowledge as the start of his eradication of illiteracy programme. Then he issued a decree in which he described the undertaking as the Comprehensive National Campaign for Compulsory Education, and called on all illiterate men and women between the ages of fifteen and forty-five to learn to read and write. Of course, the threat was the prison term which awaited those who disobeyed Saddam's decree. In eighteen months the number of teachers and bureaucrats assigned to this effort had reached 62,000, backed by educational experts from the Arab world and other countries. Three-quarters of a million people were enrolled in the programme.[30] UNESCO was so impressed that it gave Saddam the Kropeska Award[31] for promoting its campaign to wipe out illiteracy world wide. UNESCO also studied the way things were being done in Iraq to make them a model for similar efforts in other parts of the world. By 1982, no fewer than 2 million Iraqis would have gone through the eradication of illiteracy programme.

Visiting Iraq when all this was in full swing, I was amazed at the amount of time allocated to this plank of Saddam's policy in the press and on the radio and television. Television in particular was used extensively to promote the overall programme and as an instrument of education. It was not just a case of Saddam deciding to pursue a personal ambition – as always, he saw fit to turn his ideas into a national preoccupation. In the words of Iraqi businessman Dia Al Falaki, 'He put the whole state apparatus to work for the eradication of illiteracy programme.'[32] Even men who spent their time in coffee houses talked about the programme, in a jokey way though without belittling it. They simply referred to the more ignorant among them by ironic new nicknames. 'How is Plato?' they would address someone who had just mastered the alphabet. And good-heartedly, some of them would ask the newly educated to compose poetry for them.

Three times the number of girls were now attending school. Even Kanan Makiya, the Iraqi author of *Republic of Fear* and *Cruelty and Silence* and probably Saddam's severest critic in the international arena, admits that this period produced a change in the status of women. In Saddam's mind, elevating women was the same as making people literate, and the two programmes were aimed at raising the general level of the population's skills. Because of the labour shortage women had joined the work force in 1974, but now they were allowed into areas hitherto closed to them. Makiya asserts that the number of women teachers rose to 46 per cent of the total, and that they accounted for 29 per cent of the doctors, 70 per cent of the pharmacists and 46 per cent of the dentists.[33] Makiya also acknowledged that in 1977 women were for the first time admitted into the armed forces.[34] Many of the more zealous recruits were assigned to the more ideological Popular Army. But it did not stop there: even the armed forces academy was opened to them, and some women became pilots in the country's air force.[35]

One must remember that this took place at a time when women in Saudi Arabia could not walk the streets unaccompanied by male members of their family, and they are still not allowed to do so. In Iraq in 1970, 34 per cent of all females were going to school, but by 1980 the figure had risen to 95 per cent.[36] To this day, Saddam is more popular with Iraqi women than he is with men.

In Stalin's USSR and Saddam's Iraq, consolidation of power and internal economic planning took precedence over ideological commitment to the outside world. For many years the USSR ignored Communist parties in the rest of the world, and until 1974 Saddam placed strictly Iraqi considerations ahead of the mildest call for Arab unity of any form. Except for the on-going quarrel with the leftist Ba'ath in Syria, the focus of Iraqi attention was on domestic affairs. As Iraqi behaviour during Black September proved, even Palestine did not change this attitude. But success on the internal front eventually signalled a partial Iraqi return to the wider Arab field. However, except for a gesture towards Yasser Arafat and the PLO which had little chance of success, the readoption of Arabism mostly took the form of rejecting the budding attempts of other Arab countries to accept UN resolutions.

Some time during this period, and despite Bakr's personal contempt for Arafat,[37] the Iraqis invited the chairman of the PLO to join the Iraqi cabinet as Minister of Palestine Affairs and promised him considerable financial support. Arafat turned them down because accepting meant becoming more beholden to

Iraq than to other Arab countries, and he want to be all things to all Arabs. Saddam's angry reaction, and the reasons for it included Arafat's pursuit of Egypt and Sadat, produced an Iraqi attempt to play spoiler. He began to support Arafat's competitors within the PLO and to form new Palestinian groups. The most impressive of the pro-Iraqi organizations was the Palestine Liberation Front, a militant lot which opposed the acceptance of UN resolutions and dependence on the moderate Arab states.

In 1974, Iraq's support for the anti-Arafat forces took a more serious turn and Saddam closed the Baghdad offices of Fatah, the group within the PLO which Arafat had created.[38] When that failed to stop Arafat's implicit acceptance of UN resolutions and make him follow a pro-Iraqi policy, Saddam struck back by supporting the terrorist Abu Nidal, a former Fatah member who had turned against Arafat. Throughout 1976 and 1977 an Iraq–PLO war was waged throughout Europe and the Middle East.[39] The PLO's representative in London, Said Hammami, a leading advocate of dialogue with Israel, was assassinated in 1978 and his killing was followed by those of Izz Eddine Qalaq in France and Ali Yassin in Kuwait. This inter-Arab conflict continued until the Sadat Camp David initiative in 1978.

Late in 1978, Iraq convened an Arab summit conference without Egypt to form the Steadfast Front against the peace moves. Although Iraq eventually gave up the project, it led to the end of the war with the PLO. When PLO disaffection with Syria made it move closer to Iraq, Saddam saw the opportunity of an alliance with the PLO to undermine the Syrian Ba'ath and its leadership. To him Syria was the constant Arab enemy, and he never overlooked a chance to capitalize on anything that might harm his Ba'athist opponents in Damascus.

Activity elsewhere on the inter-Arab front was gentler in nature, not openly political and more effective. The huge economic expansion of 1974–5 led to manpower shortages which the Iraqis filled by importing labour from Egypt, Jordan, Morocco, Somalia and other Arab countries, and by the outbreak of the war with Iran in 1980 the number of Egyptian workers in Iraq had grown to 1.5 million. Saddam's policy allowed Arab workers entry without visas, provided them with health insurance and social security coverage, and took some of them into the security services and armed forces. Nothing of the sort had ever happened before, and

Saddam's actions represented concrete steps towards Arab oneness which superseded all the ideological rhetoric of the past. And nothing like it has happened since.

This was a deliberate, studied and somewhat covert policy to promote Iraqi leadership of the Arabs. 'Unity must come gradually', Saddam told his biographer Amir Iskandar.[40] Trying to benefit from the reputation of the most popular Arab leader this century, he paid tribute by stating, 'I was influenced by Nasser.'[41] In fact he was more action-oriented than Nasser, and Saddam only called the Egyptian's achievements in the field of unity the 'Nasser experiment'. He followed the programme to import Arab labour by other constructive steps. The National Fund for External Development (NFDE) was[42] an economic organization aimed at aiding other Arab countries. Its budget, though estimated at $800 million in 1977, was never published but it sponsored a range of activities from technical help to small farms in Somalia to exploring for minerals in Mauritania.

Perhaps the most novel, daring and potentially significant of Saddam's moves towards the Arab world was a scheme to import Arab farmers from Morocco and Egypt to help with his ambitious agricultural programme. It was not a case of importing individual workers: Saddam set his mind on moving whole villages with everyone and everything in them, and settling them in Iraq's rich farming regions. An example of this was the Egyptian village of Kholsa.[43] The purpose of his plan went beyond increasing the farming population and realizing the agricultural potential of the country; because the Egyptians and Moroccans were Sunni Muslims their numbers could have shifted the religious balance in the Iraqi population and helped him against the Shias. To Ahmad Allawi, a knowledgeable spokesperson for the opposition group the Iraqi National Congress, 'Saddam was always nicer to the rest of the Arabs than to the Iraqis.'[44] What Allawi meant was that the Arabs experienced Saddam's generosity without suffering the cruelty of his internal security apparatus. But the programme in any case came to an end with the Iran–Iraq War, which made it unaffordable and forced the imported villagers to return home. The whole experiment was thus relegated to what-might-have-been.

Without making overt political moves to lead the Arabs, Saddam was becoming a hero to the Arab masses. Everybody in the Arab world spoke of Iraqi generosity, and conversations that I had with

Egyptian workers in Baghdad were full of praise for the 'hero-brother' and the 'Arab knight'. Saddam coupled this approach, which endeared him to the average Arab, with steps to improve his relations with Arab governments. As pragmatic as ever, he set ideology aside and began referring to his southern neighbours as 'our Kuwait brothers' and speaking of 'the friendly relations' which bound Kuwait and Iraq.[45] He settled the border question which had existed with Saudi Arabia since the late 1920s by dividing the neutral zone separating the two countries between them; this gave satisfaction to the Saudis. Of course, he went beyond pleasing and appeasing pro-West countries and paid special attention to poor members of the league of Arab States; South Yemen and Somalia received more of his aid money than the rest. Interestingly, except for a standard $50,000 bribe to each visiting African leader, which most of them accepted, and perfunctory support for Muslim Pakistan against India, Saddam's aid to the rest of the world consisted of building mosques in Africa, South America and Europe.

Having made up with the PLO, Saddam's only problem in the Arab world remained Syria. The Ba'athists there tried to impose their will on the Palestinians. In 1976, Saddam actually moved Iraqi troops to the Syrian border in an attempt to pressure Syria into calling an end to its attacks on the Palestinians in Lebanon. The bitterness between the two sides, with each claiming guardianship over the Ba'ath and Arab thinking, precluded one of them from allowing the other to be successful enough to control the Palestinian cause, or any other.

Saddam's relations with the rest of the world were equally pragmatic. If there was a common thread to them, it was his belief that the dominance of the two superpowers would eventually be undermined by the emergence of a third force. In this regard Saddam was not as clear as he was on other issues. He visited Yugoslavia in 1976 and got to know Tito, and in 1978 he attended a non-aligned nations conference in Havana where be befriended Castro. (Interestingly, he refused to disembark in London during his return to Baghdad from Havana.) Visits to Turkey, and the usual junkets to France and the USSR, followed. With Egyptian President Sadat showing clear signs of pursuing peace with Israel, Saddam was slowly assuming the role of Nasser in the international arena. But, unlike the late Egyptian leader, he did not believe that the non-aligned nations were the counterweight to the predominance of the USSR and USA. He spoke of this country's relations with France as being special because 'France will play a basic role in unifying Europe',[46] and implied that a united Europe was the third force. The possibility of China being the third force he never totally accepted. Among other things, he thought it was too far behind in mastering technology.

However shallow this part of his thinking was, the one thing from which he never deviated was that the Arabs should have a position within the world and that it should be totally independent. To Fuad Matar he explained the friendship treaty with the USSR in terms of it 'not limiting us or making us followers', and followed that with 'Mohammed came before Marx.'[47] He firmly believed that an independent Arab position could influence the foreign policies of the USSR and the USA, and he was explicit in calling for Arab rejection of outsiders and their ideology. He went further and described the French, Russians and Americans as foreigners who did not understand the Arabs.[48] This elementary approach, which ultimately led to disaster in Kuwait, was the result of a lack of education which betrayed an inability to cope with totally new situations that required sound judgement more than instinct. The inadequacy showed itself in a piece of advice he gave premier Mujaib Rahman of Bangladesh when the latter visited Baghdad: 'You can't occupy the middle ground – that's one way of losing both sides.'[49] On many occasions the old conspirator betrayed a fear of outside powers making a Salvador Allende out of him – he was concerned that they might want to remove him in the way they did the Chilean leader in 1973. Saddam rejected the middle ground and believed in becoming strong enough to influence the major powers. How all these contradictory statements were subordinated to Saddam's need to become an influential power through acquiring an arms industry will be detailed in Chapter 6.

Saddam's assumption of the role of political philosopher as represented by his words in the biographies by Matar and Iskandar – and accepting his words is not the same as accepting his claims regarding his early days – fills with dismay a knowledgeable reader who is able to compare them with his concrete achievements within Iraq and the Arab world. His political philosophy did indeed expose his uneducated side, but this is something he had no way of understanding and there was no one near him who could fill the gap and escape the consequences. But Saddam the eclectic pragmatist persisted, and it was in 1975 that he carried out a stroke of genius which influenced his situation both inside and outside Iraq. In June that year, during an OPEC meeting in Algiers, Saddam reached an agreement with the Shah of Iran to settle the festering problem of navigation in the Shat Al Arab, the sixty-mile body of water formed by of the confluence of the Tigris and the Euphrates before they flow into the Gulf.

Sovereignty over this body of water which separates Iraq and Iran was given to Iraq in 1932 after many decades of disputes and resolutions under Ottoman Turkey, which also favoured Iraq. Iran had never accepted the agreement which ceded control of the Shat Al Arab to Iraq, and felt entitled to control half of the waterway. Because Iraq refused to renegotiate the primacy it was given in 1932, and for years charged tolls on Iranian ships navigating the waterway, there were a number of occasions when this problem came close to war. The feelings between the two countries had been exacerbated by the Iranian occupation in 1971 of two small islands in the Gulf which the Arabs thought belonged to them, together with some old border demarcation issues with its neighbour. In 1973 Iran not only declared the navigation agreement null and void, but with CIA help it provided Mulla Mustapha Al Barzani and his rebel Kurds with financial and military assistance to undermine Baghdad and weaken it as an ally of the USSR.

In 1974 and early 1975 the Kurdish rebellion claimed sixty thousand civilian and military casualties. The Iraqi Army proved totally incapable of administering a total defeat on the Kurds, great mountain fighters and improvisers that they were. Saddam could not afford for this internal rebellion to continue, so during the 1975 OPEC meeting he used the good offices of Algerian President Houari Boumedienne to meet the Shah and settle their problems. The new agreement stipulated that sovereignty over the Shat Al Arab should follow the Thalweg line, the deepest point of the water. Small adjustments satisfactory to both sides were made to settle the disputes along the two countries' 800-mile border. The issue of the two Gulf islands occupied by Iran in 1971 was ignored.

Above all, Iran undertook to stop helping the Kurds and to prevent help from other sources reaching them from Iranian territory. The Kurdish rebellion collapsed overnight. Saddam could claim another victory. Because the USA was Iran's partner in affording the Kurds assistance Barzani gave up and bitterly accused both of stabbing the Kurds in the back. He went to the USA and died there from natural causes in 1979. But the American disowning of the Kurds because of a perceived shift in Iraqi orientation away from the USSR was to set a precedent which would be followed in 1991.

I have deliberately left to the end the internal political developments which accompanied Saddam's success in the economic field, inter-Arab relations and the international arena, because these elements had a direct bearing on politics within Iraq. What happened in the internal economic and political fields and in terms of Iraq's Arab and international positions affected Saddam in a most fundamental and negative way.

The Kurdish problem, which Saddam temporarily solved by reaching the 1975 agreement with Iran, would not go away. Saddam had preceded the agreement by beginning to implement some articles of the 1970 Manifesto which had unravelled because of lack of goodwill on both sides. Tiring of Barzani's ways, in March 1974 he had given the Kurds two weeks to accept or reject his government's offer. Barzani had turned him down. Earlier, in June 1973, Barzani had angered Saddam by telling the *Washington Post* that Kirkuk's oil belonged to the Kurds and making plain his inability to compromise on that stance.[50] As well as being a major factor in reaching the 1975 agreement with the Shah, this had strengthened Saddam's position in the eyes of the rest of the Iraqis and justified harsh anti-Kurdish action now.

In 1976–7 Saddam started to move Kurds from their mountains in the north to other parts of the country, mainly the south. Initially, this uprooting of people accustomed to a centuries-old way of life was done on a small scale and went unnoticed. He followed with deliberate attempts to support other ethnic populations living in the Kurds' traditional homeland, by trying to move Arabs to the area and by creating a 10–15-mile-deep exclusion zone along Iraq's borders with Iran. He paid special attention to the Assyrians, Chaldeans and Turkomans, accepted their languages as official ones within Iraq and tried to turn them into a counterweight to the Kurds. Meanwhile, he attempted to entice dissident Kurds to join his government. And finally he created a government-sponsored Kurdish militia, the Jash or mules, paid them handsomely and used them to fight their fellow Kurds who wanted autonomy. He did not stop spending money to improve the lot of the Kurds, but did so grudgingly while trying to surround them and add to their disenfranchisement. For a while the problem of the Kurds died down, but nothing of a fundamental nature had been solved.

It was the problem of the Shias which showed signs of growing and threatening the Ba'ath's and Saddam's control of the country. In December 1974, during a period of successful economic development, Saddam executed five Shia clerics.[51] Shia clashes with security forces became routine. Sadr was imprisoned during that year but on his release the Shia leader resumed his activities. In February 1977 he, Alla Eddine Hakim and Mohammed Bakr Hakim (Sayyed Muhsin Al Hakim's remaining sons in Iraq) led a huge demonstration in the Shia holy city of Najjaf on the occasion of Ashura, the remembrance of the martyrdom of Al Hussein, son of Imam Ali. The security forces took no chances and there was a bloody confrontation. Eight more clerics were arrested, tried by a revolutionary court and executed. More than two thousand Shias were imprisoned, and Saddam expelled two hundred thousand to Iran[52] on the pretext that they were non-Iraqis. He followed the deportation by formalizing the expulsions and enacting discriminatory citizenship laws. Something akin to open warfare between the two sides began.

It was Saddam's Ambassador to China, a fellow Tikriti by the name of Issa Saleh, who described to the rest of the world what Saddam was doing. 'The Shias are more Persian than Arab', he said, referring to 65 per cent of the population of his country. The laws enacted by Saddam used lineage to discriminate against the Shias in a strange way which, if applied universally, would change the map of the world: it would be tantamount to the Celts claiming that the Anglo-Saxons were suspect Englishmen. Extraordinary guidelines were used to determine people's origins. To the regime, being a descendant of Iranians three, four or even five generations ago turned an Iraqi into an Iranian. Considering the history of the country, this covered millions of Shias. It is not that they came from Iran, for history is clear on this, most of them came from the Arabian peninsula, but of course over the years many had intermarried with Shias who had originated in Iran. Nor did Saddam's twisted use of history stop there, for the government offered 'pure Iraqis' married to anyone with Iranian blood $2500 reward for divorcing them.

Despite the harshness of the punishment of what Saddam called 'fifth columinists', and the repeated arrests of Sadr. Shia unrest did not subside. In October 1978 – perhaps justifiably, because of his incitements – Saddam deported Ayatollah Khomeini from Iraq after placing him under house arrest for a month. The Ayotallah moved to France. In 1979, having been sentenced to life imprisonment on flimsy charges, Mohammed Bakr Hakim was amnestied when Saddam became President. Soon afterwards he left the country for Syria, only to move to Iran after Khomeini's assumption of power there later that year. More members of the Hakim family were arrested and imprisoned, and a few were executed. Saddam coupled these moves with spending $50 million on redecorating the Shia shrines in Najjaf and Karbala.[53] But this gesture hardly mattered, and although Saddam's economic programmes still made a difference and guaranteed him the loyalty of many Shias, Sadr proved as determined as his opponent. Trouble was on the way.

Another problem which reappeared after 1976 was with the Communist Party. Their participation in the Progressive Patriotic Front and subscription to the National Action Charter, though it afforded the Ba'ath breathing space, did nothing to solve the ideological problems separating the two sides. Saddam's pragmatic approach ran counter to the Communists' desire to adhere to policies which precluded cooperating with conservative regimes within the Middle East. Furthermore, the temporary settlement of the Kurdish problem after the Algiers agreement with the Shah reduced the Ba'ath's need for Communist support and, as will be seen in Chapter 6, Iraq had ended its exclusive dependence on the USSR as an arms supplier.

Saddam personally was uncomfortable with the fact that the legitimacy gained by the Communists through participation in the Progressive Patriotic Front had allowed them to operate openly and attract many new members, including some in the armed forces. When the Communists criticized some of the restrictions being placed on them it was Tareq Aziz, then editor of the official *Al Thawra*, who articulated Saddam's point of view by stating, 'There is no place for a communist party in our country.'[54] Saddam followed this by ordering the arrest of a number of Communists and the execution of nineteen of them who had violated Law 200, enacted in July 1978, which stipulated that only Ba'athists could belong to the Army. To justify applying it to the Communists, Saddam ordered that the law be made retroactive to cover those who were members before its enactment,[55] even if they had subsequently changed their colours. The leadership of the Communist party fled to other countries of the Middle East, eastern Europe and the USSR. The Progressive Patriotic Front, reduced in importance already, was no more. Saddam and the Ba'ath gave up on involving others in government. The USSR, fearing a total rupture with Iraq and a consequent loss of position in the Middle East, limited its response to a few words of protest. Saddam had already announced that pleasing the Russians was not important to him.

The troubles with the Kurds, Shias and Communists, serious though they were, did not destabilize the country and interrupt Saddam's plans. In fact, for a country constantly immersed in conflict and violence, the period 1975–9 was one of stability.[56] The Army had been turned into a pliant body beholden to Saddam and placed under the command of Adnan Khairallah, Saddam's brother-in-law and Bakr's son-in-law. Not only were there commissars all the way down to platoon level, but a Directorate of Political Guidance guaranteed its loyalty to the party at higher levels too. The security forces had been expanded and sent on special training programmes with the KGB in the USSR and in East Germany, which made them better able to protect the regime. In 1974 the new Office of National Security (*maktab al amn al qawmi*), headed by Saddam, was expanded. It ran the general security apparatus, the *mukhabarat*, military intelligence and other small groups, and this added to its effectiveness. The party had been expanded and the number of members and followers was near to a record one million. Saddam found a way of putting in place party members who reported to the Ba'ath administration directly and bypassed the control of every ministry. For example, there was a Stalinist-type party member in every embassy overseas and very often, as with the USSR, they carried greater weight than the ambassador. The Popular Army under Izzat Douri was also expanded and provided with more sophisticated weapons to ensure its ability to defend the regime. In fact, it had already replaced the Army as the political force behind the party's control of power. The number of government employees rose to 410,000,[57] and along with members of the armed forces and Popular Army, they and their dependants made up a majority of the people. The state controlled everything because it controlled all the income which came from selling oil, and did not depend on taxes or the economic structure of the country. It was a classic case of what economists call a *rentier* state.

The father-leader, Bakr, became a cipher who signed pieces of paper placed on his desk by Saddam. His delegation of everything to Mr Deputy left him totally dependent on his protégé rather than the other way round. Although he would eventually challenge this *de facto* demotion, to most observers Bakr was still in a position to stop Saddam from attaining absolute power until 1975–6 – but after that it was too late. According to Dr Tahseen Mua'la, one-time Ba'athist turned opposition leader, Bakr lamented to someone that his activities did not justify the salary he was receiving. However, Bakr's mere presence meant that Saddam was not completely free. The image of the country he was trying to create needed a redefined image of the man running it. This was why, sooner or later, Bakr had to go. For Saddam, a redefinition of Iraq meant moulding it into his own personal image more than ever before.

During these years, the Ba'ath party's power as the source of government was eroded. The Revolutionary Command Council, the politburo created after the 1968 coup, became the arbiter of all things. Although Bakr was its nominal head, it was run by Saddam. The party structure, made up of Regional (Iraqi) Command and National (Arab) Command, became superfluous. The Regional Command was subordinated to the RCC and its status was similar to that of the Army, security apparatus and judiciary. The National Command was reduced to a mouthpiece for the regime, whose sole purpose was to act as counterweight to the Syrian National Command. The RCC took precedence over the cabinet and appointed and dismissed its members at will. It later appointed members of a National Assembly, a rubber-stamp body beholden to Saddam.[58] The legal system, originally made up of civil and criminal courts, dealt with insignificant matters. Everything else was referred to the military and revolutionary courts which the regime set up to deal with its enemies.

Meanwhile the security apparatus was expanded hugely, but without a published budget. In addition to the *mukhabarat*, General Security and military intelligence, widespread use was made of popular bodies to spy on the rest of the population. For example, members of the Union of Iraqi Students doubled as agents, as did members of the Iraqi Women's Federation, the various trade unions and the rest. A substantial part of the population had connections with the security system and they ranged from people who wore the dish-dash native dress to holders of Ph.D. degrees. Everybody spied on everybody, even members of the same security service. Because people who cooperated with the security system received high salaries, the only way to determine that some of them were agents was through the new cars or houses that they bought.

This elaborate system was extremely effective. People were kidnapped and vanished, others were tried and executed, some just went missing. Both inside and outside the country, people were assassinated. In July 1977 Saddam's security people finally caught up with former premier Abdel Razaq Al Nayyef and killed him in front of London's Intercontinental Hotel in broad daylight. For the thousands who were imprisoned for crimes ranging from mentioning the Deputy's name without prefixing an honorific to real opponents of the regime, the government expanded its prisons and resorted to 107 kinds of torture.[59]

The horrific range of methods included the application of electric shock to obtain confessions. Manual torture took the form of beatings, hair pulling, bastinado (beating with a stick on the soles of the feet) and the twisting of limbs until they broke. There was no end to the way psychological torture could be applied, but the commonest forms were commitment to solitary confinement and the rape of victims' relatives. Machines to saw off human limbs were put to use, as were tubes in which people were kept standing up days at a time. Another method involved applying fire to the skin and body parts of prisoners. Some prisoners were left in cold cells until their limbs froze. The number of people subjected to these inhuman methods is unknown, but given that they included Kurds, Shias, Communists and innocents who dared utter the simplest form of protest, tens of thousands must have been involved during the 1970s.

The work of the security services contributed to religious, ethnic and political divisions, but it did not stop Saddam from trying to create a uniform Iraqi personality content with Mesopotamian life and capable of facing the Iranian foe. This undertaking was to blossom after he became President in 1979. Saddam was determined to use Mesopotamian history, mythology and religion to meld a new identity for his people. He made use of all elements of earlier regional culture,[60] which among other things resulted in a plan to rebuild Babylon and to stamp his name on each brick used. The biggest single use of history to unify Iraq was the claim that he and Bakr were descendants of Ali Bin Abi Taleb, the prophet's cousin and son-in-law whose murder led to the creation of the Shia sect. Although there are no fewer than 10 million people with connections to the prophet and his family, this particular travesty was invented by Khairallah and was not believed by anybody. However, the mere resort to this lineage said a great deal about the rising importance of the Shias.

But Mr Deputy did not stop there. His propaganda efforts repeated stories about Caliph Haroun Al Rashid of Arabian Nights fame who wandered the streets incognito to check on the welfare of the poor. The people were reminded that Iraq was the country of Nebuchadnezzar, the Babylonian who sent the Jews into exile. And much was made of the fact that Hamurabi, the first man in history to codify the law and use it to protect people, was an Iraqi. Naturally, there was a suggestion that Saddam was the embodiment of all these men, but this did not become explicit until after he became President and the Iran–Iraq War had broken out. And it did not stop him from assuming, at will, the identity of a member of every sector of Iraqi society: he wore Kurdish, peasant, Shia and worker's clothes, and from 1976 the uniform of a military general. Songs and poems praised him and celebrated all these identities. Bakr watched it all with misgiving, the way Lenin watched Stalin towards the end of his life. But except for one serious attempt to stop Saddam which will be discussed later, he was helpless.

The contradictions in Saddam's approach were not as mysterious as they appeared. Like Stalin, he had an insatiable thirst for power and he was determined to drag Iraq into the twentieth century, even if half of its population had to be sacrificed in the process. Economic conditions within the country had greatly improved and gave him a feeling that he was succeeding. But instead of making him defer to the people, success made him dismissive of their wishes, and he became more inclined to use the brutal security system against them. Wealth also allowed him to make a tentative claim to Arab leadership which he was to develop later. By this time, the West was more interested in claiming Iraq as a client state to undermine the USSR, and selling him arms to do it, than in his human rights record. In most ways, his 'full bellies' maxim was being vindicated. To Saddam, 1979 was to be a year for realizing other aspects of his dream to turn Iraq into a modern state committed to him alone. This did not happen. But before examining what did happen, and why, we need to look into what Saddam was doing in another important field, his arms programme.

Marching to Halabja

As with everything else he has done in his life, Saddam Hussein explained the purpose of his arms programme in a succinct and final way: 'No country which relies on importing weapons is completely independent.'[1] Fulfilling it was a dream which he pursued with open eyes. But for small steps by Egypt under Nasser, which were constantly hampered by lack of funds, and the short-lived Arab Organization for Industry started by Sadat, no other Arab leader this century has tried to overcome this obstacle to independence by attaining self-sufficiency in the field of armaments. And Saddam reached high: he was the only one who tried to equal the developed countries in manufacturing advanced military hardware and in taking serious steps towards mastering non-conventional weapons.

Saddam's belief in this and other maxims was total. As with his beliefs that people with full bellies do not make revolutions and that one should never make threats without acting on them, he never deviated from its pursuit. Moral issues aside, Saddam's tenacity in following his dream has impressed the rest of the world. A measure of admiration is implicit in the condemnations of the United States and other countries, and even his fiercest enemies among opposition Iraqi groups speak of his efforts in this field with grudging admiration. Of course, Saddam and his inner circle would still like to be measured by their achievements in this field.

It is important to remember that, except for a brief period in the early 1960s, when Britain accommodated Kassem and supplied Iraq with some arms, since the overthrow of the monarchy in 1958 the country had depended on the USSR and the Eastern Bloc for its military hardware. But there had been occasions, such as when Saddam's 1970 agreement with the Kurds fell apart, when Moscow withheld arms from the Iraqi government as a means of applying political pressure. Saddam in particular lived in constant fear that this dependency might hamper his ability to deal freely with internal Iraqi issues, including his treatment of the Communist Party. But he wanted to avoid replacing one dependency with another. Replicating what he had done in the economic development field, Saddam decided to tap several other sources of supply.

It all began with his 1972 visit to France when he repaid that country for not opposing his nationalization of Iraqi oil by buying a small quantity of French arms. In 1974–5 Saddam had reasons to diversify and expand what he had started in 1972. In addition to trying to use the supply of arms to influence him politically, the USSR was withholding its most advanced weapons from him; further, his generals had told him that Western technology was superior to what the Communists had. Interestingly, the USSR's response was muted: they believed that political differences between Iraq and the West would protect their position as sole supplier of arms.

My own involvement coincided with my work in the civilian area when Growth International (GI) began to work with Arab Resources Management (ARM) and its chairman, Dr Ramzi Dalloul. It began in 1974, at the time of Saddam's decision to expand his purchases from France and to tap other Western armament sources in a serious way. What I did through GI and its successor company was extensive enough and important enough to reveal a great deal about Saddam's thinking and the methods he employed to achieve his aims. This provides a more accurate reading of his plans than a list of the military hardware he acquired. Although I have written about this subject in the past, most of what follows has never been told before. A collection of case studies, it provides the first complete record of how Saddam came close to military parity with Israel and self-sufficiency in manufacturing the most sophisticated weaponry.

The story begins with ARM's predecessor, Arab Projects and Development (APD), in 1973. APD was set up by Palestinian construction moguls Hassib Sabbagh and Kamel Abdel Rahman as a non-profit-making consultancy to help the Arab countries with the development projects they were undertaking as a result of the massive increase in their oil income. Both founders were committed Palestinians who contributed generously to charity and the PLO. Their purpose in sponsoring this venture was to repay the rest of the Arabs for supporting the Palestinian cause through the utilization of much-needed Palestinian talent, and to use it as leverage to guarantee continuation of this support. APD was an all-Palestinian enterprise.

Neither Sabbagh nor Abdel Rahman was directly involved in the management of their creation, but their previous business activities through the Contracting and Construction Company (CCC), the huge civil contractor they owned, had introduced them to many educated young Palestinians. The academic Walid Khalidi became APD's chairman and he was assisted by scientist Tony Zahlan, businessman Basil Aql and Ramzi Dalloul, the nephew of Kamel Abdel Rahman and future chairman of ARM. It was in general an impressive collection of talent which in turn gathered around it others of similar calibre.

APD's brief contained no ideology. The consultancy offered its expertise and help to all Arab countries regardless of political outlook. However, Iraq was more open to non-Iraqi Arabs than the rest and, although APD did undertake projects in other countries, it was there that the Palestinians made their mark. They participated in land reclamation projects, petrochemical schemes, the planning of prefabricated and other housing, and studies covering the building of harbours, airports, railways and hospitals. At one point they developed plans for overhauling Iraq's entire educational system.[2] The competence of Iraqi bureaucrats maximized their effectiveness.

One of the services that APD offered the Arab countries was the repatriation of Arab scientists and engineers to the Middle East from all parts of the word to meet local shortages. The incentives offered were straightforward: higher salaries and a chance to serve the Arab world. The response to APD's efforts was positive and a number of engineers returned to Qatar, the United Arab Emirates and other Gulf countries. Iraq, larger and more appreciative of the importance of the human factor, brought back a greater number from Germany, Brazil, France, Canada, the USA and Britain.

Soon after this undertaking started, Saddam developed a special and deserved admiration for APD which prompted him to ask them for help in repatriating scientists capable of helping him with his atomic programme – whether APD knew that he was trying to make an atomic bomb is unknown. Who in APD was responsible for responding positively to this request is also not clear and essentially unimportant; certainly Sabbagh and Abdel Rahman would not have been involved. But the answer Saddam received had a bearing on his plans for attaining military self-sufficiency. After discovering that he wanted to make atomic weapons, some-one in APD advised him to concentrate on other mass destruction weapons while continuing his atomic programme. To Saddam's advisers, chemical and biological weapons were effective and easier, faster and cheaper to make. His acceptance of this advice resulted in a merger between APD's activities and Saddam's needs.

So the consulting firm began to repatriate scientists with ex-pertise in these fields. The number of people involved is not known, and my own previous figure of over four thousand, supplied in a deliberate attempt to mislead me and adopted unquestioningly by dozens of journalists and writers, is undoubtedly exaggerated. However, further checking with former APD members who have no reason to misinform confirms that several hundred were repa-triated to Iraq.

APD liaised with two of Saddam's organizations, the Sahd Bin Heitham Establishment, better known as Al Heitham Establish-ment, and the Arab Research Institute[3]. Al Heitham, headed by Dr Sarwan Al Satidah, was already working along parallel lines. It had been cooperating with the Egyptian government to attract experts who were no longer needed after President Anwar Sadat had run down the research initiated by Nasser. Egyptian atomic scientist Yahya Al Mashed, whom the Israeli intelligence service Mossad was to kill in 1980, was part of this effort. Of course, the recruiting of Arab talent was in addition to indigenous Iraqi expertise such as scientists Ja'afar Dhia Ja'afar and Hussein Shanstari (the latter eventually opposed Saddam's plans and defected). The Iraqi scien-tists involved in the armament effort were as competent as their counterparts in the economic field.

The biggest problem facing the two Iraqi firms and APD was how to integrate the new arrivals and keep up the incentives which had brought them to Baghdad. This was to prove another success story for Saddam, one which he personally supervised. First, he made it clear that he would not tolerate any prejudice against the newcomers: they were to be treated as equals, even as honoured guests. Then he saw to it that they were placed in departments where their talents would be used to greatest effect. After that Saddam ordered that all their requirements were met satisfactorily, from housing to the type of car they wanted. Special attention was paid to making their wives comfortable, and the schooling of their children was regarded as an important factor. Saddam was protecting himself against the possibility of any of them becoming unhappy and wanting to leave. But there was another element which Saddam could not control. There is little doubt that the size of the programme must have been known to Western intelligence services and that the scientists were infiltrated. In 1976 I received an unwelcome visit from a CIA type who knew about the scientists and needed help to discover what they were doing. My refusal to be involved has influenced the official American attitude towards me ever since.

APD fell prey to feuding and accusations of individual profiteering late in 1974, before Saddam's real work started, and Sabbagh and Abdel Rahman dissolved it. Saddam was left rich in scientific talent but without people capable of handling the business aspect of his plans. He needed sophisticated international operators to procure plant and equipment for his infrastructure. Ramzi Dalloul saw the need, relied on previous connections within the Iraqi government to identify the details and created ARM to fill the vacuum. A fast learner and tireless worker, Dalloul also quickly educated himself in the area of armament procurement. ARM never had exclusivity on supplying Iraq's needs – that would have been against Saddam's policy of multi-sourcing everything – but Dalloul played an extremely important role, which elevated him to the level of adviser dealing directly with Saddam, and made him part of the inner circle overseeing this programme. Saddam gave him a horse in appreciation of his contributions; because of Saddam's fondness for horses, Dalloul understood it to be a supreme symbolic gesture.

There is no evidence of Dalloul being involved in Saddam's biological warfare programme and no evidence that his other efforts produced concrete results in the chemical and atomic fields. But his efforts were indirectly linked to the two latter areas in terms of trying to help with procuring what was needed, and he certainly participated in almost everything else to do with Iraqi conventional armament. The internal mechanisms that Saddam put into place to oversee this work consisted of the three-man Committee for Strategic Development (CSD). Run by Saddam as the political supremo, it also included Adnan Hamdani, Minister of Planning, Deputy Prime Minister and an astute trained lawyer, who was in charge of procurement, and Chief of Staff Adnan Khairallah, Saddam's brother-in-law, who was the Army representative who supervised the military input.

The team's supervisory functions reached beyond non-conventional weapons to include the purchase of aircraft, tanks and electronic equipment and the plans eventually to manufacture them. Whatever was left of the professional officership of the Iraqi Army, though all Ba'athists by the mid-1970s, were competent and favoured Western over Soviet equipment. There was a huge defence budget, and the procurement allocation increased from $500 million in 1970 to $4.5 billion in 1975.[4] But the CSD received money from other sources too, and how this special group operated without the knowledge of the RCC, cabinet and even president Bakr is an important part of the story. Keeping Bakr in the dark seems curious, but besides being slowly but methodically marginalized he was in poor health and his participation in the running of the government was diminishing by the day.

Beyond getting a share of Ministry of Defence allocations, the CSD funded itself in two distinct but related ways. First, Saddam played skimmer and ordered the Ministry of Oil to set 5 per cent of Iraqi oil income aside before it was designated national income and went in to the Treasury. This is the same 5 per cent that Saddam was accused of pocketing by former Iraqi politicians testifying in front of congressional committees in 1991 and 1992. The accusation was untrue and the fuss it generated was unjustified: the money was used to buy weaponry and nothing else. That 5 per cent amounted to huge sums which in 1981 totalled $2.5 billion, all of it deposited in a secret bank account in Switzerland called the Fund for Strategic Development. The second source of income was from commissions on arms and other deals. While Iraqi Laws 8 and 52 made the taking of commission illegal and punishable by death, these laws did not apply to outsiders – certainly not to ARM. I have personally been involved in ARM projects, including the building of the Akashat to Baghdad railroad, where the commission was to be over $100 million. However, this money was not earmarked for me or Dalloul. Each deal of this size was handled by a company set up in Switzerland exclusively for the purpose. After the commission money had been deposited in this company's account it would be transferred to the central account of the CSD, at which point the company created for that specific deal would be dissolved. When projects succeeded, ARM, with the knowledge of the Iraqis, received part of the commission, but the larger part always went to the CSD.

Dalloul's main original contact at the CSD was Adnan Hamdani, but there were also connections with Iraqi army officers though Basil Aql, the only employee of APD to move to ARM with Dalloul. As with the civilian aspects of Saddam's programme the armament strategy grew in proportion to the increase in oil income; in this case, it revealed the secret ambitions behind it. The requests I received between 1974 and 1977 covered mobile telephone systems, jet trainers, fighter-bomber aircraft, helicopters, pilotless drones, aerial defence systems, builders of military airfields, surface-to-air missiles and, above all, the purchase of nuclear plant and companies to build a chemical warfare factory. As stated before, our efforts were part of a larger programme and others were performing equally important tasks or duplicating what we were doing. But each of these requirements had political ramifications. How these requirements were pursued tells the whole story behind Saddam's, to me, not so mysterious armament programme.

The overtly innocent request for a mobile telephone system to be used by the leaders of the Ba'ath party was small in monetary terms, but had far-reaching political implications. Mobile telephones were not as common then as they are now and what Saddam wanted, undoubtedly using specifications drawn up by some of his new scientists, was a hand-held VHF system. I obtained an offer from Denmark's Storno Corporation to supply something similar, but this was rejected without explanation. The system which was accepted and bought by Saddam was a much more elaborate and sophisticated American one. Dalloul organized the whole deal. The system and its back-up equipment was provided by Karkar Electronics of San Francisco. More importantly, the sale needed US government approval and the corporation had no difficulty in obtaining it. In what might look to outsiders like a wasteful exercise, Saddam had actually obtained a similar though technically inferior system from the USSR via Yuri Andropov, then in charge of the KGB and who later became head of state.[5] Wasting money to protect against failure was something that Saddam frequently did.

The significance of buying the Karkar equipment lay in the system's intended purpose. The American mobile phones were distributed to important Ba'ath party officials throughout Iraq to use in the event of an attempt to overthrow the regime. It was part of a security system which would have allowed the Ba'athists to take steps to intercept any such move.

The year 1975 therefore represents the third phase of US–Saddam cooperation, contrary to the statements of INC Chairman Ahmad Chalabi that cooperation between the two countries resumed in the 1980s. The first phase was Cairo and CIA support for the Ba'ath to carry out the 1963 coup, the second was American assistance, tacit and otherwise, with the 1968 coup, and the third was helping the Ba'ath to stay in power through selling them equipment such as was provided by Karkar. The period of cooperation during the war with Iran in the 1980s, about which the world knows more, represented the fourth stage of this complicated love–hate relationship.

The answer to the question of whether the sale of mobile telephones worth a mere $5 million represented an important expression of US policy towards Ba'athist Iraq is a definite yes. America was trying to draw closer to the Ba'ath in an attempt to pry Saddam loose from dependence on the USSR, while the latter was competing by responding to his needs but without attaching too many strings to their offers. Saddam was successfully playing both sides against the middle. But it was what followed the Karkar deal which was much more telling and sinister and which exposed the American attitude of the time.

In 1975, the year of the Karkar project, the United States Government knowingly helped Iraq obtain the technology to build its first chemical warfare plant. This took place after the Iraqis had made an open request to buy such a plant from the USSR, a request which the Russians turned down.[6] This was unsurprising. The USSR, though trying to keep Saddam to themselves, had never approved of his non-conventional weapons plans and had no wish to help him undertake regional adventures beyond their control.

Moreover, the USSR was growing unhappy with Saddam's dupli-cative efforts, which suggested a growing closeness to the West, and had begun to suspect that his alliance with the Communist Party in the Patriotic National Front was no more than a cover. A possible third reason for the USSR's refusal to supply a chemical warfare plant was a belief that America would not provide one either.

Late in 1974, a delegation led by Dr Mohammed Al Shukri of the Iraqi Ministry of Industry, but operating under the cover of representatives of the Ministry of Agriculture, visited Pfaulder Corporation of Rochester, New York, a specialist in chemical plant manufacture. The Iraqis asked for help in refining crude drawings for a pesticide factory, which had probably been pre-pared by repatriates. Two employees of Pfaulder, Joseph M. Culotta and Morris Gruver,[7] paid a visit to Baghdad and, on their return to Rochester, provided the Iraqis with the required blue-prints and specifications.[8] Because the plant in question was supposed to make Amiton, Paraxon, Demeton and Paratheon, toxic chemicals which nobody had used for agricultural purposes in decades, it is difficult to believe that the Americans accepted this as a civilian request. As it was, after the blueprints had been provided, with US government knowledge, the State Department, without explaining its action, refused to grant Pfaulder a licence to export the needed equipment and asked the corporation not to help build the plant. Was this a rare instance of the Americans, in a hurried volte-face, adopting a moral stance in place of cynical politics? Pfaulder claims that the two sides could not agree on the building schedule because the Iraqis were in a hurry.

True or not, it was still too late. What Pfaulder had given the Iraqis was enough. A copy of the specifications found its way to Dalloul who passed them on to me, technically naive as I am, and asked me to secure the cooperation of companies to build pesticide plants near the phosphate mines at Akashat. Trained chemists know that the chemical weapons Tabun and Sarin are made from phosphate compounds, and the Belgian firm Sybatra was already mining the rich phosphate deposits in this small desert town. More elementary chemicals were needed, however, and Tabun and Sarin were for the future. Dalloul told me that the invitation to compa-nies to build the pesticide plants originated with the Ministry of Agriculture, and I paid no attention to the fact that several were needed and that they should not be built by a single contractor – after all, Saddam did things like that.

There was another novel and perhaps more important factor besides the number of plants. The construction contracts were to be negotiated, instead of tendered as was usually the case. This too was not noticed by me. Whether Dalloul shared my naiveté or not is something I have never discovered. Moreover, I was never able to determine whether he became involved in this willingly or whether he was in no position to refuse the Iraqi request.

Saddam's need for several pesticide plants at the same time prompted me to contact three companies, Imperial Chemical Industries (ICI) and Foster Wheeler of the UK and Ferrostaal of Germany. On 2 February 1977, Ferrostaal wrote me a letter (Ausland FA Lehmann/OT, ref, 2014–416) confirming their willingness to build such a plant as was specified in the Pfaulder drawings, in cooperation with the Italian company Montedison of Milan. Ferrostaal showed no reluctance to make an offer to undertake this project beyond some inquiries regarding the terms and conditions of the payment schedule. Dalloul's interests, as expressed in this letter, were to be covered through his efforts as sub-contractor, something to which he agreed. Some time later, my original ICI contact telephoned to tell me that he had examined 'the requirements' and that 'the chemicals were so hideously toxic, there was no way they were for agricultural use'. He followed this rebuke by stating that he was under a legal obligation to inform the British Foreign Office of my request. His company took a moral position and refused to contemplate participating in any such effort.

It was with considerable difficulty that I finally convinced him of my innocence, and I never heard a word from his again. However, I have no doubt that ICI transmitted the contents of my request to the Foreign Office who, probably for anti-Soviet policy reasons similar to those of the Americans, did not act on – or perhaps they already knew about the project. This makes a mockery of the dozens of reports such as appeared in the *Sunday Times* of 14 April 1991 and which – surprise, surprise – purported to show that MI5 knew about Iraq's armament effort. They certainly did, all the way back to 1975.

The reaction of Foster Wheeler differed yet again. They needed too much time to study the project and the Iraqis were in a hurry, subjecting me to a barrage of telephone calls from Dalloul. At that point, after reacting to the ICI response with 'surprise', Dalloul took that in and asked me to destroy the specification document he had given me. The atmosphere surrounding the repeated request finally convinced me of the nature of what the Iraqis wanted. (Chemical warfare was not part of people's thinking until Saddam used poison gas during the war with Iran.) I had nothing to do with the project any more, but kept hearing that the request was making the European rounds through other parties beholden to Saddam. There was no suggestion, however, that Dalloul was party to the activity. There was a report that Montedison did eventually build the plant, but a spokesperson for the company, Tiziana Zorzella, later denied it and stated that the Iraqis had lost interest.[9] In fact what happened was much simpler. The Iraqis bought the plant in sections from Italy, West Germany and East Germany, then used their scientists and assembled it themselves. The cost of the plant was around $50 million and the safety equipment alone, needed in particular for Amiton, cost around $30 million.

My connection with the chemical warfare effort, limited and unsuccessful as it was, was the accidental result of lack of technical expertise; I corrected it by withdrawing my services. But participating in an attempt to buy a nuclear reactor for Saddam was something which I willingly accepted. I cannot and will not claim that I was under the impression that this was for peaceful purposes. I knew from the start that Iraq was trying to obtain an atomic weapon, believed that it was reasonable for the Arabs to have one and made myself available to help Saddam. I suspect that the motivation behind my action was similar to that of the APD people, Dalloul, the repatriates and other Arabs who cooperated with Saddam at that time and later. We, the generation of despair which never recovered from the psychological wounds of the 1967 Arab defeat by Israel, viewed what Saddam was doing as an attempt to achieve military parity with Israel through possession of atomic weapons. Although some participants in Saddam's efforts during this period now deny it, we approved of his purpose wholeheartedly and wanted to contribute to building an Arab atomic bomb. As a matter of fact, although not a single one of us would have approved the use of an atomic or chemical weapon, being part of this effort and creating a 'balance of terror' between Israel and the Arabs gave us a special sense of elation.

Buying nuclear reactors proved to be another duplicative effort. The Iraqis had purchased a small one from the USSR in early 1975, but the Russians had put a lot of restrictions on its use and refused to supply one which could produce weapons. The Iraqi government would have turned to France anyway, but the attitude of the USSR made this a matter of urgency. Iraq's dealings with France were official, though conducted in secrecy by members of Saddam's government (often by the less than imaginative Chief of Staff General Abdel Jabbar Shanshall, a Saddam lackey) and occasionally by Saddam himself, but my brief from Dalloul differed. I was to try to obtain an offer for a nuclear reactor from Canada. My mission was a super-secret one; both Dalloul and the Iraqis told me that I would be publicly disowned should Canada make an issue of the request and go public with it.

Through friends in the United States and Canada I finally reached a potentially helpful contact who is presently a member of the Canadian government. While my contact wanted nothing to do with the project and made his misgivings known, he still wrote me a letter of introduction to A. M. Aikin, Vice President of Atomic Energy of Canada. Because of the haste which accompanied the request, I wrote to Aikin from London and invited myself to Ottawa before receiving his response. He wrote back on 4 March 1975 telling me that Atomic Energy of Canada could not consider my request because they had a heavy backlog.

Early in 1976 while on a visit to France, Saddam personally concluded a deal to purchase a uranium reactor from that country. It was to be built in the town of Ozeirak. Saddam's request had the approval of Prime Minister (now President) Jacques Chirac. The supplier was Commissart à Energie Atomique (CEA) and the plutonium reactor was called Rhapsodie.[10]

Saddam was ecstatic and, as so often, expanded the deal: at the same time he signed a Nuclear Cooperation Treaty with France which involved personnel and transfer of expertise. With that, he had attained one of his primary aims in life. Later the reactors supplied by France were renamed Tamuz 1 and Tamuz 2, supposedly to avoid any association between the names Ozeirak and Chirac. Amazingly, Saddam did not stop there. While the French were working on the reactors at Ozeirak, he initiated negotiations with Brazil to buy other reactors, obtain technical know-how and reach an exchange of atomic information agreement. As usual, he started his efforts to cooperate with this new source by offering a sweetener, the purchase of armoured cars, Brazilian models EE3 and EE9, plus some support equipment.

Where my own efforts were concerned, I reported to Dalloul on 16 January 1976 that Herr Hennig of the German company MAN was willing to cooperate with us on building atomic power stations. In 1978 Snia Technit, the little-known subsidiary of Fiat in Italy, signed an agreement with Iraq to sell nuclear laboratories and equipment.[11] Any doubt that Saddam ultimately intended to build an atomic weapon disappeared with the Italian deal, which also must have been known to Western intelligence sources. The equipment that Snia was providing would not have been needed for the peaceful use of nuclear reactors.

While the Gulf War and the ensuing United Nations Security Council resolutions focused attention on non-conventional weapons, Saddam's conventional arms programme was no less important. In fact, in the normal course of events – because they are more likely to be used – it was his purchases of conventional weapons which should have alerted the supplier nations that now feign innocence or lack of knowledge. Unlike me, they had no ostensible interest in seeing Iraq grow strong enough to 'threaten its neighbours' (I find the use of this phrase by former willing suppliers nauseating). And, as I shall demonstrate, nor are the accusations of cynicism against the French justified. Britain was as desperate for a slice of Saddam's arms programme as anyone.

Beginning in 1974, simultaneously with the major requests made to France, Dalloul and the Iraqis asked me to determine the willingness of the UK to provide the following: Rapier anti-aircraft missiles against low-flying aircraft, Jaguar fighter-bombers, Lynx helicopters manufactured by Westland, Scorpion tanks manufactured by the Alvis division of British Leyland, and companies to build military airfields with an extensive underground infrastructure to protect against enemy attacks. Except for Alvis and the division of British Aerospace (then still known as British Aircraft Corporation) responsible for Rapier missiles, the companies involved were willing to cooperate with me; in fact, they were most eager and welcoming.

In charge of selling the Jaguar at the British Aerospace Military Aircraft Division was Glen M. Hobday. A former RAF officer, he responded with undisguised glee to my inquiry regarding the acquisition by Iraq of sixty Jaguars. In the agreement between ARM and BAe, dated 29 May 1975, ARM was appointed consultants on the sale of 'versions of the aircraft, initial spares, ground support equipment and technical assistance'. In return for its assistance ARM was to receive 6 per cent of each instalment of the contract price covering its various aspects, in this case £12 million of the £200 million estimated total value of the contract. With this in hand, I arranged for Hobday to meet Dalloul; the former was so impressed with the chairman of ARM that on 23 June 1975 he wrote me a letter expressing his admiration of my associate. The agreement was deposited in a Swiss bank, to be viewed only by both sides simultaneously, and on 10 September that year Hobday sent me a letter (ref.896/GMH/LLB/4.0) confirming that this procedure had been followed.

There are several aspects to the negotiations and agreement between BAe and ARM which shed light on the atmosphere of the times which helped Saddam to succeed. First, the Jaguar was the most sophisticated aircraft of its kind made outside the USA. Realistically, because the pro-Israeli lobby would have never allowed the sale of American planes to Iraq, this was the best that Iraqi money could buy in the West, and both buyer and seller knew it. No less important were the Iraqi demands regarding the nature of the follow-up to the contract, and the great willingness of British Aerospace to accommodate them.

After the basic paperwork had been done, a delegation of Iraqi Air Force officers came to London to discuss details with British Aerospace. At the meeting which I set up, both sides agreed on the technical and delivery details, but suddenly an unexpected problem arose. The Iraqis had previously requested me to ask BAe for a British government letter addressed to them, 'guaranteeing the uninterrupted flow of spare parts under all conditions'. In other words, the British government was to keep the planes flying regardless of any war which might involve Iraq. BAe had told me that the letter was ready and would be given to the Iraqis during the meeting. But the one they gave the delegation stated that her Majesty's Government would only 'endeavour to guarantee' what the Iraqis had requested. The head of the Iraqi delegation, who had been silent until the letter was produced, looked straight at Hobday and said 'Sir, my English is not good, but either you endeavour or you guarantee.'[12]

Hobday's suggestion for circumventing the British government's obvious reluctance to give the Iraqis an open-ended guarantee was to offer to arrange the sale of the Jaguar through the French, who were entitled to do so because they were major sub-contractors on the project. But Iraqis, acting on political as well as technical and commercial considerations, refused this alternative. In particular their generals wanted the British-made navigation system, which did not go with the French version of the aircraft – and, of course, the French were already getting their share of their business. BAe, watching with dismay as the contract appeared to be slipping through their fingers, suggested a second ploy which left the Iraqi delegation and myself utterly speechless.

'Why not leak the story to the labour unions who need jobs in the aircraft industry?' they suggested. They went on to explain how this would put pressure on Prime Minister Harold Wilson – after all, the hard pressed unions might call a strike. Because this was a matter of policy, the delegation had no way of responding to this sinister suggestion. But later I obtained Baghdad's answer and to my mind Saddam was behind it. A clever example of third world smugness, it ran: 'Iraq, which resents outside interference in its internal affairs, would never knowingly interfere in the internal affairs of another country.' With this the Iraqis terminated the negotiations to buy the Jaguar and, against their better judgement, turned to the French who proved more accommodating.

As already mentioned, after the 1972 oil nationalization France had sold a small quantity of arms to Iraq – sixteen Alouette helicopters and thirty-eight Panhard armoured cars. But the new opportunity was much bigger and the French wanted the deal. The Dassault company secured the required letter of guarantee from their government in no time at all. The same Iraqi delegation which had travelled to London went to Paris and gave the French a letter of intent without finalizing the contract. Difficulties in concluding the contract to purchase the Dassault F-1 surfaced later. The Iraqis, through sources unknown to me, suspected the French of overcharging them, perhaps because the French had heard about what had happened in London. This time my brief from Dalloul was to determine the price that France was charging other countries for similarly equipped Mirage F-1s. When London's Institute of Strategic Studies was unable to help I decided to use the files of the

Peace Institute in Stockholm. For that purpose I bribed an American news correspondent who travelled to Sweden and obtained the necessary information. When Dalloul and I met in Paris to read the correspondent's report, we discovered that the Iraqis had been right. Dalloul advised them to stall.

A little later Premier Chirac visited Baghdad and had a meeting with his friend Saddam Hussein. When Chirac asked why there was a delay in finalizing the F-1 deal, Saddam Hussein pushed a large piece of paper in front of him and, with a smile, asked, 'But what about this?' It contained an analysis of French sales of the same plane to every country concerned. A combination of information from the Peace Institute and the reports of Saddam's intelligence, it proved that an attempt had been made to overcharge the Iraqis. Chirac did not question the figures Saddam provided, but volunteered – on the spot – a reduction of $1,750,000 per plane. Saddam accepted, and the gentlemen shook hands. In the Arab world, only Iraq could achieve this level of coordination between intelligence and the military to the benefit of the country, and only under the supervision of Saddam Hussein.

The second request to British Aerospace, although as important as the first, was of a different nature. The Iraqis wanted a company to lead a consortium to build military installations, in this case airfields and back-up facilities. BAe was anxious to participate in this project as the lead company using the expertise of general contractors, while providing proprietary technical know-how in the area of infrastructure including how to protect the airfields against enemy attack. On my instructions, Hobday cabled the Iraqi Ministry of Defence on 25 August 1975 expressing his company's readiness to build several airfields. This was followed by a cable (ref. 896/DMK/LEB/5.0.6.) dated 10 October from D. M. Knight to the Director of Works at the Iraqi Air Force, Colonel Nafi' Al Dirzi.

What BAe had not realized was that Saddam was duplicating once again and that, even without his inclination to protect himself in this way, the number of airfields to be built was too great to surrender to a single contractor. This led us to contact and reach agreement with the Spanish company Edes to make a similar offer. It was followed on 20 October by the usual letter (ref. 3188) to the commander of the Iraqi Air Force. BAe and Edes were not the only companies involved, and others throughout Europe were enticed into joining Saddam's airfield building programme. The efforts these European corporations went to at this time undoubtedly contributed to the difficulties encountered by the air forces of Saddam's opponents when they attacked Iraqi airfields during the Gulf War. The structures surrounding the airfields and hangars were beyond the destruction capability of the bombs initially used by the allies, though they eventually succeeded with sophisticated penetration bombs.

The cooperation with BAe had in fact followed a test request made by the Iraqis to determine the UK's interest in selling them arms. It was Saddam's usual method: first a small order, then something much bigger. As with the Atomic Energy of Canada, I was to make the initial request on my own, which would be deniable if the other side objected to it and publicized its contents. But Westland proved more willing to supply their new product, the Lynx helicopter, than I had anticipated. After contacts in London initiated by me, a meeting took place in Cairo between John Speechily, the director of the relevant division, Dalloul, Aql and myself. The result was a contract (DMD/JS/2282-1A) dated 12 December 1974, which appointed ARM as consultants on the sale of the Lynx to Iraq.

Important as all these contacts and contracts were, perhaps the most significant was the one made in 1977 by Dalloul directly to the electronics company Plessey. His expressed interest in meeting the Chairman of this company, Sir John Clark, was unusual in the way he pursued it: he simply refused to reveal the nature of the Iraqi objective behind the proposed meeting. As luck would have it, I knew Plessey's agent in the Middle East, Elias Badine, who introduced me to Michael Clark, Sir John's brother and himself a Plessey executive, who, despite the vagueness of the situation, agreed to arrange a meeting late in 1977 'to discuss certain Iraqi requests that were definitely worthwhile'. In 1976 Dalloul had moved to Paris from Beirut to avoid the civil war, and had in the meanwhile dispensed with the services of Aql.

On the appointed day, Dalloul flew to London from Paris. On his way to Plessey's headquarters in Ilford, Essex, he stopped off to see me, opened his briefcase, produced a document of about forty pages and announced that he had a surprise for the company. The contents of the document remained unknown to me until after the meeting, when Dalloul had returned to Paris. According to Michael

Clark, during the meeting Dalloul passed copies of it to all present. Sir John Clark examined the first few pages and responded in a totally English way: 'Dr Dalloul, we were under the impression that you were interested in buying some of our products, but this is much much bigger – a whole programme to help transfer Plesssey's knowledge and expertise to Iraq. We are talking about billions of dollars, are we not?'

Indeed we were. Saddam had decided to act on his transfer-of-technology ideas, probably helped by the more knowledgeable and studious Dalloul. What the document called for was the building of a whole electronics industry in Iraq. No exact figure was touted – it was to be a modular contract the size of which increased with time – but there was talk of $5 billion. Clark asked for time to study the document and assess whether what the Iraqis wanted was possible in terms of the company's willingness to transfer its expertise to foreign countries; he also wanted to consult the British government. Dalloul had expected this and agreed. Afterwards my usually polite associate visited me again and mentioned the document he had given Clark. Dalloul now had sole contact with Plessey and from this time on I was excluded.

However, the Plessey initiative never came to fruition. After many changes in specification, the contract to set up an Iraqi electronics industry was awarded to the French company Thomson-CSF in 1980 and it became the nucleus for the Sa'ad 13 complex, among the most advanced in the world. Whether or not Dalloul had a hand in this is unknown to me.

Meanwhile, the Iraqis had succeeded in obtaining direct British Government cooperation regarding a military training request. Again in 1975, they asked me to determine whether the British would be willing to train Iraqi Air Force pilots in accordance with RAF standards, as had happened before the Iraqi monarchy was overthrown in 1958. I contacted John Halbert, Chairman of the Association of British Machine Tools Manufacturers (ABMTM) which, despite its innocent name, was in this and other defence business. But someone in Baghdad had already contacted the British Embassy regarding the same request. The British gave their formal agreement and Iraqi Air Force pilots began training in Cambridge in 1976,[13] despite the fact that most of their aircraft were still Russian-made. This was typical: training programmes were another area in which Saddam was determined not to limit himself to a single source, and he always trained more people than were needed. The programme which followed the already mentioned atomic deal with France included provisions for training as many as six hundred Iraqi scientists.

The extensive dealings carried out by GI, Aburish, James and Associates, and ARM with British, French and other corporations were typical of what was happening elsewhere through others acting on behalf of Saddam. As always, it was the nature of the requests and the response of Western governments which mattered. A list of companies that were willing to help Saddam would probably include most existing defence contractors. What Saddam wanted is summarized in a statement about the arms industry he made to his biographer Amir Iskandar in 1979:

> The states that supply us with arms are friendly, but we cannot guarantee that the present will continue indefinitely. The states that supply us do not agree with us in all of our aims, for the boundaries of our aims and ambitions do not lie in Iraq but extend through the whole Arab homeland. We must therefore be prepared to manufacture arms when it is appropriate to do so, even when this conflicts with the strategy of the supplier nations.[14]

If this statement proves that Saddam had a greater appreciation of what he was doing than the rest of the world at that time, it is important to examine it as defining the strategy he followed and explaining the methods he employed. The statement makes it clear that his purpose was pan-Arab, as he proved when he nationalized oil, Saddam saw himself as a visionary Arab leader, and in a follow-up statement he distinguished between 'the leader and the technician'.[15] The technicians were no more than an instrument in the hands of the grand strategist, but if he was going to succeed, their performance had to adhere to his will and express his vision without deviation. This was the way he treated everyone with the possible exception of Dalloul, where expertise and ability proved indispensable enough to be incorporated in the leader's strategic considerations. On occasions, perhaps, what he had to say determined them.

The other experts whom Saddam used were not of the intelli

gence or ability of Dalloul, who combined scientific knowledge with business acumen. Nor – if I may say so – did they have the worldly business sophistication of an Aburish. But they did have backgrounds which fitted Saddam's design. As we have seen, these people included the repatriates of APD, scientists borrowed from Egypt and local talent. But even this treasure-house of talent was augmented in both the technical and business arenas by Iraqis, Arabs and foreigners who were deemed reliable and could be of use. Where they fitted in the scheme of things depended on their importance, and what the more valuable of them had to offer was known to Saddam himself, often without ever meeting them.

The first group which Saddam used to achieve his aim consisted of Iraqi expatriates who belonged to the *anciens régimes*, mostly the monarchy but also Kassem and the Arefs. However, members of the old regimes were seldom encouraged to go back home and Saddam used them selectively. His instincts of revenge were unforgiving, and he saw these people as renegades and outsiders who belonged to unacceptable classes or advocated open cooperation with the West or both. But, amazingly, Saddam recognized that they had expertise which he could use without re-enfranchising them politically or considering a change in their status as exiles.

For example, I know of two former Iraqi army officers who lived in London and participated in his arms procurement programme. A businessman resident in London managed to secure Saddam an offer of American Jeeps at a time when the Americans were thought to be against such a sale. (He did this through the good offices of a former American ambassador to another Arab country, who undoubtedly reported back to Washington.) Like the rest of us, the expatriate group were proudly serving Iraq, and making money. Some of the businessmen who offered their services to Saddam and his regime came from old families who scoffed at the idea of Tikrit and what it represented. It is impossible to determine the number of Iraqi expatriates who served Saddam, but it ran into the hundreds in the UK alone and there were others in the rest of Europe and the USA.

There was also a second group of people, mostly Lebanese, who contributed to Saddam's efforts. Most members of this group, including some Ba'athists, were journalists, and they became

Saddam's eyes and ears in Europe and America. Many kept him apprised of the state of relations between the West and the rest of the Arab world, while others spied for him, both on political opponents who might try to disrupt his plans and on the policies of Western corporations and governments. For example, I know of one journalist who set up an Arabic-language magazine which allowed him openly to pursue the latest developments in the arms field and to keep Saddam up to date without too much scrutiny. Other Lebanese journalists befriended Western politicians and sounded them out on what their governments were willing to sell Iraq, then reported back to Saddam. Another intimidated fellow Lebanese and Arab journalists who were opposed to Saddam, and this helped keep the lid on his human rights violations and other activities inside Iraq.

A third group of technicians used by Saddam was composed of former officers in other Arab armies. The ups and downs of Arab politics produced large numbers of cashiered army officers with undesirable political leanings (mostly Arab nationalists) who had expertise and nowhere to use it. Saddam recruited them and used their backgrounds effectively. Former Jordanian army officers advised him on Western armaments and companies because they had experience in this area while that of their Iraqi counterparts was limited to the Soviet Bloc. And even there, Egyptian officers were more qualified to assess the hardware of the Eastern Bloc than Iraqis because Egypt had started using arms from the East well before Iraq. I know of two Jordanian generals and one colonel and three Egyptian colonels who worked for Saddam, and who were rewarded both psychologically and financially. Later, during the war with Iran, Saddam managed to persuade some officers of Arab armies to resign their commissions and help the Iraqis to assess Iran's Western-manufactured equipment.

The fourth group which left its mark on Saddam's efforts was one which had been created by him. Its contribution, though indirect, was valuable. From the mid-1970s the press information officers attached to Iraqi embassies overseas were separated from their colleagues and operated independently under the cover of Iraqi cultural centres. Their ostensible brief was to introduce Arab culture to the rest of the world and many of them did an excellent job, organizing exhibitions of the work of Arab artists and others on the Arabs' contributions to civilization. But the press officers were exclusively Ba'athists and many were Tikritis. An important part of their work consisted of intelligence gathering. They too spied on individuals, companies and governments and kept Saddam up to date – hence his discovery that the French were about to overcharge him for the Mirage F-1 aircraft. Furthermore, the managers of the cultural centres established good relations with foreign correspondents covering the Middle East. A number of them depended on the cultural centres for stories and, in the process, did not think it worthwhile to report some of the more unattractive aspects of Saddam's regime.

This impressive array of talent was effective because it used both regular and unorthodox methods cleverly, and because the host countries ignored many legal but often unacceptable activities. Secrecy was the most important element surrounding these people's work. Saddam's code of secrecy, the work of an abnormally suspicious Stalinist mind, went beyond his own people and was forced on the sellers. Not a single government ever announced an arms deal with Iraq until the news got out as leaks to the press; only then were official announcements made. Of course, as the work of the Committee for Strategic Development demonstrates, the buyers operated in secret, and we still do not know what happened to its Swiss bank account. It is enough for me to refer back to my own activities and the number of occasions when the Iraqis provided me with no cover and I was left to act on my own. Dalloul's refusal to show me the document he presented to Plessey is another example. Even an old friend was not trusted for fear of leaks and having to answer for them to Saddam. Double-sourcing everything had an element of secrecy in it, and Saddam had Western intelligence services confused because they did not know what he was buying and where. In order to ensure secrecy the following elementary codes were used by Dalloul and myself during the negotiations for the Jaguar and other deals:

Kite	plane
Car	Jaguar fighter-bomber
Garage	Airfield
Car salesman	BAe director
Better Associates	British Aircraft Corporation
Arab friends	Iraq Air Force

Connoisseur	Chief of Staff
Scouts	Army
USF	Iraqi sea forces
My people	US government
Frogs	French
First essential element	Commission/fee agreement

If secrecy was important, then the availability of money for open and secret reasons was also important. People on Saddam's payroll had no problem travelling to any place in the world and spending money. Though I was never on the payroll but operated as an outsider with an agreement with ARM, I flew to Beirut, the United States, Canada and among other places Egypt. When there was a need, authorization to bribe people was given, as in the case of John Speechily of Westland. He was offered and accepted a share of the Lynx commission in return for expediting British government's approval of the sale of the then advanced helicopter. French and Italian businessmen and politicians too were offered bribes, which most of them accepted. The children of an important British businessman were sent to an exclusive boys' school in Switzerland courtesy of Saddam. (Though I was involved in some of these examples, most of them were the work of other groups.)

The wording of the agreements signed by the Iraqis with various companies contributed to this atmosphere of secrecy and efficiency. The words 'commision', 'pay-off', 'consultancy fee' and so on were very seldom mentioned. The agreements were written to guarantee secrecy on the part of the company, by making it shoulder most of the blame if the new of the deal got out. I am in possession of a copy of an agreement between me and George Wimpey Contractors dated 25 March 1975 – which could easily have been with an armaments company – in which Wimpey offered to pay me over $100 million if the already mentioned Akashat railroad contract was successful. This was in return for getting Wimpey personnel travel tickets, making hotel reservations, booking shipping space and renting equipment. Of course, there were other businesslike matters mentioned in the agreement, but the whole letter was a study in absurdity. Who would pay $100 million for such services? And would a judge accept it as 'proper compensation'? The letter was drawn up by us and Wimpey.

The size, secrecy and absurdity of the contract with Wimpey meant it had to be guarded by everyone who knew about it – disclosure would hurt all the concerned parties. However, in this case, of all the people shuttling between London and Baghdad in connection with this contract, the loophole was Sami Abuljebin, who represented a Wimpey sub-contractor which hoped to supply signalling equipment for the railroad. He and the company he represented were introduced to the project by me, despite advice not to trust Abuljebin to keep quiet. (Abuljebin and I had all attended the same school in Beirut in the 1950s.)

Dalloul was right. After some problems developed between Wimpey and the Iraqis which reflected a desire on Wimpey's part to reduce the size of the commission, the Iraqis started hearing that Abuljebin was spreading negative comments about their business methods. One day, as Abuljebin was leaving Baghdad after a brief business visit and was already aboard a plane readying to take-off, two civilian-dressed security personnel appeared inside the plane and asked him to disembark. They instructed the captain to proceed without him. A day later, and the exact date in 1976 escapes me, Abuljebin was found dead in the back seat of a car outside Baghdad's international airport. He was forty-two and had been shot at point-blank range. In announcing his death two weeks after the fact, General Security attributed it to a heart attack. It is the greatest proof of the importance that the Iraqis attached to secrecy and of their willingness to kill people to protect Saddam's operational methods and reputation. It is gratuitous to add that the security service did not eliminate people without Saddam's personal knowledge.

The secrecy surrounding the arms procurement activities, be it the absence of disclosure by supplier governments, the depositing of agreements in Swiss banks or the existence of the Committee for Strategic Development, reveal a great deal about their official nature. The deals represented state secrets to both buyer and seller. This meant that third parties, enemies of either or both sides, had an interest in knowing about them. For example, the USSR was anxious to know what Saddam was doing with the West because that had a direct bearing on its policy towards him. And Iran, which under the Shah was trying to spread its hegemony over the Gulf, was keen to undermine Saddam and prevent him from becoming a regional competitor or an obstacle to its supremacy plans. None of this escaped Saddam.

In 1976 the degree of cooperation between Saddam and the West disturbed the Iranians enough for them to try to stop it. Among contributory events was the news that General Electric of the United States had obtained approval from the Carter administration to supply engines of torpedo boats being built for Iraq in Italy.[16] Amazingly, this was happening despite America having designated Iraq a terrorist state. To the Iranians, this expression of Western–Iraqi amity ran deeper: perhaps it was part of a plan to replace Iran with Iraq as the deputy sheriff guarding the Gulf. This prompted them to initiate extensive monitoring of Iraqi activities. It was code-named Operation Adam, and among its targets was Dr Ramzi Dalloul.[17] Targeting Dalloul also meant targeting me and Aburish, James and Associates.

In the summer of 1976 my secretary inadvertently discovered that my London office was bugged. She had picked up the receiver to make a call when it played back a conversation she had had with a friend. We hired a debugging expert, who traced a wire attached to my telephone and dusted to look old down to the basement of the office building. However, because the last thing I wanted was publicity, I was unable to determine who had rented the basement room used for eavesdropping or anything else connected with the operation. Two months later, a CIA agent approached me and told me of Operation Adam. He pretended he was trying to help me and my friend Dalloul, but made plain that he could not do so unless he knew what we were up to. His offer was turned down. The man's allegations of Iranian involvement were verified to me by a former member of the Iranian Embassy staff in London who had become an exile after the Shah was overthrown and replaced by Khomeini in 1979.

It is my personal belief that Western governments knew most of what Saddam was doing. But since it represented a secret, there was nothing beyond American congressional insistence on linking Iraq with terrorism because of its backing for Yasser Arafat's former associate Abu Nidal and others. Certainly, the British knew of the activities of the Iraqi cultural centres and that Saddam was behind the assassination of former Iraqi intelligence chief Abdel Razaq Al Nayyef in front of London's Intercontinental Hotel in July 1978. (I am totally unable to determine why the people accused of this crime were released.) The Americans knew about the chemical warfare plant, approved the Karkar mobile telephone system sale and, thinking that Iraq was changing, considered selling Saddam target drones made by Teledyne Ryan Corporation of San Diego and General Electric engines for his torpedo boats. The French were as aware of Saddam's plans to develop an atomic weapon as anyone. Italy, Spain, Portugal, Brazil, Argentina and other countries received inquiries from the representatives of the Iraqi government which betrayed their purpose. Even neutral Switzerland was contacted and agreed to sell the Iraqis Pilatus jet trainers, a deal which was actually concluded after the start of the war with Iran.

If this was so, why did they all look the other way and allow Saddam to continue his efforts – which, as we shall see, were to grow more ominous after the start of the Iran–Iraq War in 1980? Indeed, the situation begs the question of whether the West's accommodation of Saddam was part of an overall policy decision, a coordinated effort or a conspiracy. In particular, what was the motivation behind helping Saddam with his plans, and was it the same for all the countries involved? And where was Mossad, the Israeli intelligence service, in the middle of Saddam's efforts? Were the Israelis aware of what was happening, or was it a case of the other countries not listening to them?

First, let me state categorically that I have failed to uncover anything resembling coordination between Saddam's suppliers, except that the Americans may have encouraged the sale of French fighter-bomber aircraft to Iraq to undermine the USSR's role as sole supplier of Saddam's air force.[18] Yet even this possibility is remote. After all, the French never listened to anyone when it came to their Middle East policy, of which selling arms to selected clients was the cornerstone. In other words, there was no conspiracy or coordination, let alone a plan. It was no different from the way the coalition which faced Saddam after his invasion of Kuwait in 1990 was formed: a rare convergence of circumstantial interest to do the same thing at the same time.

The purpose of the suppliers differed, but the buyer put them together as part of a plan and produced a result whose whole was much greater than its parts. By the looks of things, nobody had read Saddam's revealing statement to Amir Iskandar – at least nobody had taken it seriously. Though clear to him, because he was the architect and executor of the armaments programme, what Saddam was doing eluded the rest.

What the suppliers had in common was negative: an obvious lack of moral standards. There is no evidence whatsoever that Saddam's treatment of the Kurds and Shias mattered to anyone, except for some leaders of the American Congress who spoke out in the middle and late 1970s, mostly to please Israel. No one ever exposed the methods of his dreaded security apparatus. Nor did Saddam's suppliers pay much attention to his reliance on the terrorists Abu Nidal and Abul Abbas in certain overseas elimination operations. This *laissez-faire* attitude continued until he invaded Kuwait and threatened the oil supplies of the West.

Occasional Western support for the Kurds reflected the West's state of relations with Saddam and had nothing to do with their plight. The Shias never struck a chord in Western circles. Even Iraqis willing to work with the West openly were not given any attention, and this partly explains the willingness of some of them to aid Saddam's efforts. Remarkably, it was the USSR alone which, on several occasions, demonstrated reluctance to support Saddam. Although this position too was a reflection of politics rather than morality, it does reveal an ability to see the inherent danger in the character of the man. They had to protect their position with the Kurds and the Iraqi Communist Party, and did not want to be dragged into regional adventures over which they could exercise little if any control. Among the corporations, ICI was the only one justified in claiming any moral high ground. Its directors took a decision against helping to build a chemical warfare plant from the start and never deviated it from it, even after it became known that others were pursuing the business without objections from their governments.

To me the absence of a moral position by Western governments was influenced considerably by their racial attitude. Despite the unconventional nature and up-to-dateness of the plant and equipment that Saddam was seeking, the suppliers never believed that he would make sense out of what he was purchasing. Their attitude was summed up in a description of the similar Israeli attitude articulated by Saddam himself and recorded in the memoirs of Victor Ostrovsky, formerly of Mossad, *By Way of Deception*:

'Zionist circles in Europe derided the Arabs who, they said, were an uncivilized and backward people, good only for riding camels. See how today these circles say without batting an eyelid that Iraq is on the point of producing an atomic bomb.'[19] They had based their judgement on what they had previously witnessed – an Arab inability to put the most modern equipment to use during the various wars with Israel, and the fact that in Saudi Arabia and other Gulf countries, the arms supplied were more for decorative than combative purposes. Yet although there were many signs to suggest that something new was taking place, including Saddam's insistence on training programmes to accompany all purchases of equipment, few paid them attention. Even knowing about his repatriation programme made no impression on the supplier countries, because the repatriates were Arabs.

In addition to the presence of competent scientists and technicians, and despite Saddam's emasculation of his Army, Iraq was the one country in the Middle East that could master sophisticated armaments. Western intelligence sources knew about superior Iraqi generalship all the way back to 1948. The British in particular knew much about Iraqi competence because they had had a hand in their training from the 1930s. In 1967, the Iraqi Air Force was the only Arab one whose planes penetrated the Israeli defence net. Above all, the calibre of the people who trekked to the various countries seeking arms was of the highest order and should have suggested an ability to master and eventually use what they were buying. In this regard Dalloul the ideologue–dealer was a model, infinitely better equipped intellectually than the Khashoggis of this world.

These two elements combined with a purely political one which blinded the suppliers further, particularly the USA, Britain and France. The latter three welcomed Iraq's requests because they reduced Iraqi dependence on the USSR. Everything these countries did should be seen in the light of making Saddam, whom they correctly assessed to be anti-Communist, dependent on them. This attitude was strengthened by their belief that what they were providing him would never allow him to become a regional power and a danger to others. Moreover, under Kassem and afterwards, the Iraqi Communist Party had demonstrated that it was an organized, potentially major factor in the country's politics, perhaps capable of assuming and holding power.

The West opted for a stable Iraq under Saddam. To the West 'stability' is a magic word, the opposite of being vulnerable. The West did not believe in Middle East democracy because this form of government might produce situations that the West could not control. Iraq's particular make-up made it more susceptible to instability than the other countries in the region. The prospects of a fragmented Iraq were removed by Western support of a dictatorial regime. The Americans above all have never accepted the existence of an Iraqi personality that takes precedence over the ethnic and religious divisions of the country. This, more than a belief in Saddam's innocence, explains their willingness to supply the Karkar mobile telephone equipment. Except for Saddam's unpredictability, this was an expression of self-interest that did not differ from what was happening with other countries.

Of course, there was also an element of greed on the part of corporations and their governments. Selling Saddam arms was similar to what was happening with the rest of the Arabs, a process of recycling the income from the oil boom. But the rottenness of participating in this arms bazaar was sinister enough to produce an attempt to undermine Prime Minister Harold Wilson in the UK. The same rottenness prompted the Pfaulders of this world completely to ignore what they were selling or doing. It was a greed mixed with the natural competitiveness which exists between suppliers. The French wanted to claim Iraq as a client ahead of the British, the Brazilians needed help with their budding armaments industry, while faraway Chile did not want to be left out and offered cluster bombs. Even the Swiss set non-financial considerations aside and joined the fray.

The way Saddam played his hand in terms of organizing his efforts has already been detailed. But it is important to emphasize the acceptability of his political actions during this period. His refusal to come to the aid of the Palestinians in 1970 did not harm his reputation in the West. They saw in his decision not to help topple King Hussein an indication of a moderate stand, and he reinforced it by improving relations with Jordan which had been difficult since the overthrow of the Iraqi royal family, Hashemite kin of the Jordanian monarch, in 1958. His settlement of the border dispute with Saudi Arabia was another act of moderation. And except for a minor incident in 1973 which he settled quickly and amicably, he was responsible for keeping the Iraqi claim to Kuwait in check. Even his action after Sadat's Camp David agreement, the formation of the Steadfast Front against peace with Israel, was viewed with equanimity because his participation never went beyond empty Arab threats to which the West was accustomed and which he stopped after deciding not to be a full member of the Front. Only his support for terrorist groups exposed him briefly, and he eventually put an end to this as if it had never happened.

Lastly, what the Shah of Iran was doing played right into Saddam's hands. The Shah was determined to replace the West as the guardian of the Gulf. Although he was pro-West, the United States and other Western countries had no intention of ceding their hegemony over this oil-rich region to a local power. After all, it was the Shah who had initiated the massive increase in oil prices in 1973, and Iranian control over the Gulf would enable him to do it again if he chose. Supporting Saddam was another way of keeping the Shah from attaining his goal. For a while, this consideration became more important than pleasing Israel, at least under the Carter administration. Meanwhile Mossad, despite its inflated reputation, proved unable to penetrate the Iraqi security set-up by itself because Saddam had destroyed its network. Outside help did not become available until some time later.

These interim conclusions, appearing as they do in the middle of this book, are necessary to explain Saddam's later actions. Saddam had an advantage over all the countries with which he was dealing. They saw only part of the picture, while he saw the whole. He successfully played them against the USSR and each other. In competing to please Saddam and in underestimating the Arabs, they looked as if they had the same purpose when in fact they were competing with each other. The 1970s saw the first phase of Saddam's armaments programme and set the stage for the expanded programme of the 1980s and the actual use of non-conventional weapons. Towards the end of the 1970s Saddam was already well on his way to having chemical warfare capability and the suppliers knew it. But the enticements for the West to continue to help him had not changed and were to be reinvigorated by the appearance of Khomeini. The 1980s saw a consolidation and realization of the original effort. The journey down the road to the Kurdish town of Halabja, which was gas-bombed in a 1988 atrocity leaving five thousand dead, started in 1975 in Rochester, New York.

From Planning to Plotting

There is no denying the social and economic achievements of the Ba'ath's first decade in power, 1968–78, under the stewardship of Saddam Hussein. Iraq had become a welfare state[1] which was envied by the other Arabs and admired by the USSR and the West. In fact, only one thing stood between Iraq and being a model state – the human cost. The articles of the provisional constitution which purported to protect the rights of the individual – and each government which followed the monarchy had one – were never observed. But Saddam's regime differed from what had gone before. Both its accomplishments and its dictatorial ways were incomparably greater than those of the previous governments. To most Iraqis, including the Shias and the Kurds, the Ba'ath was behind the improvement in their standard of living. A minority, however, were subjected to a level of suffering that the country had never before experienced. Celebrating or condemning the Ba'athist government became an individual matter and reduced the importance of people's ethnic or religious origins.

Saddam's efficient 1970s dictatorship and its popularity with broad segments of the Iraqi people also impressed others. Outsiders too concentrated on the results and ignored the methods, a case of the ends justifying the means. The image that Iraq projected to the outside world was similar to the one celebrated by leftist Western intellectuals writing about the Soviet Union and its leaps forward in the 1930s. Like Stalin, Saddam appeared to make sense out of an unwieldy country. The improving standard of living produced stability, which in turn produced ethnic and religious harmony. Saddam was on his way to proving that full bellies would overcome and replace people's desire for a democratic system of government. Everybody agreed with him, and the tables of statistics showing economic growth figures and subsidiary achievements were better known to the rest of the world than the contents of the few reports about his human rights record.

By 1978 everything in Iraq was running smoothly under Saddam's personal control. The Army, which had been totally mechanized[2] and expanded to over four hundred thousand, was under the command of Adnan Khairallah, Saddam's cousin, childhood playmate and brother-in-law and Khairallah Tulfah's son. Although he was married to Bakr's daughter, Adnan's loyalty was to the real leader of the country, his cousin. Saddam's half-brother Barazan had become head of the *mukhabarat* branch of the security service following the Kazzar conspiracy and had claimed some of the functions of the other security departments. (The fortunes of the various branches of the security apparatus rose and fell depending in the importance of their chiefs, and Saddam trusted Barazan and depended on him.) The National Security Office, which oversaw all security functions, was run by his cousin Sa'adoun Shaker who reported directly to Saddam. Half-brother Watban had become governor of the expanded province of Tikrit, renamed Salaheddine in honour of the legendary Muslim warrior 'Saladin'. Sabawi, the last of the half-brothers, had been made deputy chief of police. The Popular Army was still under Izzat Douri, Saddam's deputy in the RCC and his unwavering obedient follower. The Popular Army was expanding even faster than the regular Army and numbered around 150,000. The number of party members, followers and supporters had increased and, though different figures have been cited, became one million strong. The Iraqi command of the Ba'ath (the Regional Command Council in charge of the country), which had been placed under the RCC, had created a structure of loyalists through the formation of seven divisions which reported directly to it: the military office, propaganda office, labour office, peasant office, student office, office of professional organizations and office for relations with the party.[3]

Saddam's Tikriti relations and a handful of unthreatening followers used the party as a front. The Ba'ath existed as a structure, but Saddam and his small group ran its various aspects on all levels. It was a merger between the family and the party, with the former using the latter as a vehicle to control the country. The party reported to the family and justified its rule, but the family acted in the name of the party. Saddam, as head of the family, needed a personality to preside over the family's pre-emption of the party. Using the colossal propaganda machinery of the government, he began to portray himself as the embodiment of every strand of Iraqi history.

Bakr was still there, but without much to do. A former Iraqi Ba'athist, who does not wish to be identified, asserts that Bakr's residence became known as 'the tomb of the well-known soldier'. Aflaq compensated for his own effeteness and inability to participate directly in the running of the country by watching the progress of his protégé with undisguised pleasure. The spiritual leader of the party limited himself to issuing what amounted to songs of praise with little philosophical or ideological content.

The opposition, made up of Kurds, religious Shias and Communists, continued to exist, and they had not changed their policies towards the regime. The Kurds kept up their demands for autonomy in their usually confused way, while the Shias wanted to participate in the running of their country and were incrementally raising their demands. The Communists were calling for 'democratic rule'. But all three groups had been weakened by the emergence of a docile, happy middle class created by Saddam. According to Iraqi historian and sociologist Faleh Abdel Jabbar, the percentage of the population that qualified to be included in this social grouping rose from 28 in 1970 to 58 in 1979.[4]

Furthermore, there was now a lack of the outside support on which all three opposition groups had depended in the past as a necessary ingredient for changing Iraqi governments or forcing change on them. Despite an occasional resort to arms, the West was not ready to back the Kurds as extensively as it had done before, and they missed the charismatic leadership of Mulla Mustapha Al Barzani who had taken refuge in the USA after the 1975 Saddam–Shah Algiers Agreement and was suffering from cancer. Iranian support for the Shias had declined considerably since the 1975 agreement, and the alliance between the anti-Shah Khomeini and the Iraqi Shias made its resurrection unlikely. The 1979 assumption of power of Khomeini was to signal a new phase in this relationship and the intensification of Shia opposition. But before that moment, relations between the Shah and Saddam had become so good that Empress Farah visited the Shia holy places in Iraq, an act which dispirited Saddam's Shia opponents. And the USSR had all but given up on the Iraqi Communist Party's chances of participating in the government of Iraq. The Communist Bloc as a whole showed more concern for saving its overall influence in the country and the Middle East from Western encroachment. This was particularly so after the Soviet invasion of Afghanistan and Saddam's open opposition to it. In 1978, the opposition to Saddam was weaker than at any other time since the Ba'ath had assumed power in 1968.

Another historical source of trouble for the rulers of Iraq, the ability of other Arab countries to influence its internal events, was in suspension. The Camp David Agreement had isolated Egypt and reduced its position as a factor in Arab politics. Saudi Arabia and Kuwait had nothing to complain about because 'brother Saddam' had been friendly and not threatened them or made claims against them, to the extent of taking no more than a day to settle several small border incidents with Kuwait. Poor countries within the Arab League, such as Somalia and Sudan, were appreciative of Saddam's financial help and wanted it to continue. Arafat and the PLO had made their peace with the Iraqi regime and were more interested in maintaining it as a backer than in anything else. They repaid Saddam by publicizing his contributions to the cause.

Saddam's inward-looking policies, which since 1973 had emphasized economics over ideology,[5] had succeeded in the Arab arena. Only Syria was still a problem, but a minor one because its supposedly leftist-leaning branch of the Ba'ath party did not have the financial means or the following inside Iraq to threaten Saddam.

It was the Iraq-first policy which guaranteed Western support for Saddam, or at least acquiescence in what he was doing. He pursued his long-term plans quietly, without any agitation that might generate Western disapproval, so the West judged him by day-to-day political happenings and decided that he was not threatening – not even bothering – anyone except his own people. Meanwhile, his crackdown on the Communists in 1977 – earned him credit in Western capitals because it was judged in political rather than human rights terms. His expulsion of Khomeini, the man who was threatening the pro-West Shah, was welcomed, even when it was accompanied by the imprisonment of thousands of Iraqi Shias.

The West perceived the Kurds as troublemakers who stood in the way of stability, the word which the West then associated with Saddam. This and the constant divisions in their ranks overshadowed Saddam's attempts to subdue them violently or to change the ethnic character of Kurdistan by resettling over half a million Kurds (the figure is disputed) in the southern part of Iraq, Nassiriya, Afaq and Diwaniya. By the late 1970s the increase in this resettlement activity, known as *mujama'at*, resembled the deportation of ethnic groups to Siberia under Stalin, and well over a thousand Kurdish villages were depopulated. To avoid being forcibly resettled, several hundred thousand Kurds escaped to Iran. The Iraqi regime, as it was to do on a larger scale later, encouraged Sunni Arabs to move to the mostly Kurdish cities of Kirkuk, Suleimaniya and others.

Even Saddam's tilt towards a market economy and his ending of collectivization could not but help him in Western circles. The one element which could have disturbed this picture, a perceived threat to Israel, was something which he studiously manipulated. During this period he never went beyond what the most pro-West of Arab countries was saying. Moreover, the hawkish Menachem Begin was now Prime Minister of Israel, and his exaggerations of the Arab threat and messianic zeal made the USA and others dismiss him – not to speak of the Carter administration's antipathy towards the Israeli leader and its desire to include Iraq in an eventual peace agreement with all the Arab countries. This background included the promotion of good relations between Saddam and civilian and military suppliers in the USA and Europe.

In one of those twists of Arab politics which leads the wise investigative writer never to take anything for granted, it was none other than Bakr who finally challenged Saddam and shattered his aura of invincibility. Bakr's move subscribed to an old Iraqi saying, '*Aydain bil qadr ma tutbukh*', which can be loosely translated as 'Too many cooks spoil the broth'. It also proved that Bakr's *de jure* position as head of state, which he had failed to utilize to control his deputy in the past, still provided him with clout. The reason that Bakr used to try to curb or remove Saddam was a legitimate one acceptable to all believers in Ba'athist ideology, and he knew that he could count on the support of most if not all members of the party. Bakr's belated move took the form of an attempt to unite Syria and Iraq as one country under a single Ba'ath Party. Even Saddam could not object to this aim; it was a perfect cover.

President Sadat of Egypt's Camp David Agreement of 17 September 1978 had provided Bakr with the real or nominal reason to attempt this move. All Arabs, including the leadership of both branches of the Ba'ath party, were agreed that the response to Sadat's peace initiative had to include a strengthening of the Arab eastern front, opposing Israel with, namely Iraq, Syria and Jordan. Jordan's special relationship with the West and vulnerability to Israeli military retaliation precluded its involvement in any unification schemes, but there was nothing to stop the other two countries responding to their peoples' wishes – and their people wanted their leaders to overcome the quarrels which had separated them and to concentrate on facing 'the common Zionist enemy'. To the average Syrian and Iraqi, creating a country big enough and strong enough to face Israel was more important then any commitment to individual leaders. They wanted to compensate for the loss of Egypt from the Arab side. Besides, the similarities between the two countries have always made this prospect more enticing than other Arab unification schemes. Misgivings based on past experience, including that of the short-lived United Arab Republic of Egypt and Syria, were set aside.

On 1 October Iraq announced that it was willing to send troops to reinforce Syria in its confrontation with Israel. This pledge was made by Bakr who, acting on his own and courageously, followed it with an open-ended offer to merge his country with its erstwhile enemy. There was no way that President Hafez Assad of Syria could refuse such an offer. On 26 October he accepted an invitation to visit Baghdad and held a summit conference with Bakr and Saddam. After condemning the policies of Sadat, the three announced a Charter for Joint National Action to coordinate their anti-Israeli efforts. On 7 November they formed a Joint Higher Political Committee to supervise their efforts. The leaders described their activities as measures aimed at turning the two countries into 'one state, one party and one people'.[6]

Behind the populist statements a struggle for power had developed which reflected the realities of the situation. To the elderly Bakr, this was a last chance to leave a mark on Arab history. He proposed an immediate union and the creation of one country under his leadership but with Assad as his deputy and successor. Although the challenge to Saddam was clear, Assad doubted Bakr's ability to deliver his part of the bargain. He knew that Saddam controlled all centres of power in Iraq, and was afraid that Iraq's natural wealth and strength would eventually play into his competitor's hands and allow Saddam to edge him out regardless of any succession arrangement reached with Bakr.

Assad refused to contemplate immediate union and declared that the dispatch of Iraqi troops to Syria was unnecessary. He came out in favour of unification but via a more deliberate step-by-step approach that would take several years.[7] Bakr tried to change Assad's mind and to circumvent the developing impasse. He visited Syria in January 1979 and reduced his demands to an immediate merger of the two branches of the Ba'ath Party as a first step. But this too was rejected by the Syrian leader. Assad, to many the most astute Arab diplomat of the century, simply refused to budge. For a while things were held in abeyance.

This state of limbo represented a threat to Saddam's position. Because the Iraqi people and the nominally important Ba'ath's Regional Command Council were in favour of union to the extent of sacrificing Mr Deputy, he had to close the door on the whole business. Acting in character, Saddam decided against leaving anything to chance. As luck would have it, this was the time of the Islamic fundamentalist victory against the Shah in Iran. Khomeini returned to his country on 12 February, and suddenly good relations between Iran and Iraq were a thing of the past. The tepid reply to Bakr's congratulatory cable to Khomeini revealed a deep level of mistrust. Bakr's wishes of regional peace were answered by a terse 'Peace is with those who follow the righteous path.'[8] This excluded the secular Ba'ath.

The Iraqi fear of emerging change in the regional balance of power stood in sharp contrast to the favourable Syrian reaction. Assad, and even the PLO's Arafat, felt that Khomeini's Iran gave the anti-Israeli forces depth. Saddam, however, saw the Islamic regime as a menace because Khomeini placed loyalty to religion ahead of loyalty to the state. He was anti-Ba'athist and committed to helping the Shias of Iraq topple their country's government. Assad's perception of Khomeini as a new ally prompted him to send the Imam a telegram to which, in contrast to his reply to the Iraqis, the latter responded enthusiastically. The developing amity with Iran lessened Assad's need to depend on Iraq. Meanwhile, Khomeini's enmity to the Iraqi Ba'ath took the form of calls for rebellion against the regime. One week after he assumed power in Tehran, he declared that he 'wanted Najjaf'[9] one of the Shia holy cities in Iraq. In response, Saddam recalled the days of the Shah's old threats to Iraq and described the cleric as nothing but 'a Shah in religious garb'.[10] But worse things were on the way.

The Iraqi–Syrian differences over the new Islamic regime in Iran turned the hitherto personal competition for position between Assad and Saddam into an ideological issue which provided Saddam with a more acceptable reason for cancelling the plans to unite the two countries. He responded in his usual methodical way to the unexpected challenge to his paramountcy within Iraq from Bakr's blatant attempt to curb his power, and to the threat posed by Khomeini's control of Iran. First, he took steps to tighten his control on all aspects of life within the country. Although the various branches of the security apparatus, Popular Army and regular armed forces had been totally Ba'athized by 1977, he conducted cleansing operations in the ranks of these organizations and eliminated anyone whose loyalty to him was suspect, or not guaranteed. This attempt to place these organizations totally in Mr Deputy's hand was carried out by Saddam's reliable Tikriti relations, and it was so pervasive it included schoolteachers. Thousands of government and party workers were dismissed and hundreds were imprisoned.

He followed this with a two-pronged attack. Unable to go back on Bakr's unification offer because of its popular appeal, he resorted to making it unacceptable. He capitalized on the Syrian leader's reluctance by presenting Assad with an ultimatum: either immediate union or the termination of all negotiations towards one. Once again, Assad read the situation correctly. He surmised that Saddam would never opt for the total merger of the two countries unless it meant that he was capable of toppling Bakr and assuming the leadership of the new political entity. When Assad did not respond to Saddam's threat, Saddam withdrew Iraqi participation from the various committees that had been set up to oversee the merger. The committees had in any case ceased to function since mid-1978; with the Iran problem they were disbanded. There is little doubt that it was Saddam who brought about the end of the discussions towards union.[11]

The time for demanding Bakr's resignation had come. According to a Ba'athist source, Saddam's first step was to surround the presidential palace with troops loyal to himself. With that and other security measures in place, he went to Jordan in early July 1979 to visit King Hussein and secure support for the physical removal of Bakr. It was Saddam's personal experience in the 1963 coup, his awareness that the CIA and others were capable of influencing events within Iraq, which made him seek guarantees against interference in the ousting of Bakr by outside powers. According to opposition INC Chairman Ahmad Chalabi, King Hussein promised Saddam support and followed that by travelling to Saudi Arabia to secure that country's blessing for Saddam's plans.[12] A former colonel in the Jordanian Army corroborates and expands Chalabi's story. He asserts that Jordanian Prime Minister Abdel Hamid Sharraf, King Hussein's cousin and an astute operator, was party to the discussions. Furthermore, during this trip Saddam also had meetings with several unnamed CIA operatives stationed in Amman.

The reason behind the attitude of Jordan, Saudi Arabia and perhaps the CIA is not mysterious: all of them were opposed to Iraqi–Syrian union. The prospect of a large, strong neighbour was a threat to Jordan's independence, or at least to its ability to follow independent policies. Saudi Arabia entertained similar fears and, as always, opposed any Arab unification schemes that might snowball to include it. And the CIA had always opposed any cooperation between Syria and Iraq lest it threaten its client states, Israel, Saudi Arabia and Jordan. Saddam's personal target was Bakr, but this did not interest the others greatly except in terms of Bakr's advocacy of an Iraqi union with Syria. In other words, Saddam offered them a package: he was willing to intercept the plans for Syrian–Iraqi union in return for a promise of non-interference in his removal of Bakr.

What started as a struggle over who would preside over a united Iraq and Syria after Bakr, ended up being something else. In helping Saddam to remove Bakr, the pro-West Arab countries and the CIA administered a blow to the ideology of the Ba'ath Party.[13] Of course, Jordan, Saudi Arabia and the rest of the Arab countries had viewed Khomeini's rise to power with unease. Though not as directly threatened as Iraq, they had already reached the conclusion that a confrontation with Khomeini was inevitable.

Saddam, unlike Bakr, agreed with them. The USA's problems with Khomeini were developing. Although the hostage crisis did not start until November 1979, Washington was already adopting anti-Khomeini policies. Along with traditional opposition to Syrian–Iraqi unity, this guaranteed American support for Saddam.

On 16 July 1979, a weary-looking Bakr appeared on Iraqi television to announce his retirement. He attributed this to personal reasons, ceded power to comrade Saddam Hussein and nominated the colourless and uninspiring Izzat Douri as Saddam's deputy. I have interviewed more than a hundred Iraqis, a knowledgeable collection of people who belong to different political groupings with different agendas, and not a single one accepts the Bakr resignation on face value. All of them insist that what took place in Baghdad in July 1979 was a coup within the Ba'ath party. To them, Saddam simply ordered Bakr to go home – under guard. Because of Saddam's history, authors and journalists accept this conclusion unquestioningly. This is indeed correct, but the activities which preceded Bakr's political demise deserve closer examination.

The fact that Saddam felt he needed outside help or acquiescence in the removal of Bakr proves that his assumption of the presidency of Iraq was opposed within the leadership of the Ba'ath Party, and that he felt insecure. Saddam attributed the 'resignation' to Bakr's loss of his wife, son and son-in-law during the previous two years and to poor health. This and the praise that he heaped on Bakr supports the allegations by Saddam's opponents that he needed to justify his action to limit the opposition to it. But Arab history and belief in individual leadership does not provide examples of presidents ceding power willingly. In fact, more solid proof that Bakr was forced to resign showed in what followed Saddam's takeover.

Before analyzing the real reasons for Bakr's removal as they manifested themselves after he disappeared to Tikrit, it is worthwhile to note what Aflaq did. As usual, he produced a pamphlet about the subject of his constant adoration and wrote on 'what God has endowed you with to make you the brave leader and inspired struggler to realize the dreams of the party'.[14] This time, Saddam's need to have his move blessed by the founder and spiritual leader of the Ba'ath had sound underlying reasons. To his comrades, Saddam's individualism and lack of ideology disqualified him. His success meant subordinating whatever ideology was left to the person of Saddam. This is analogous to what happened in Stalin's time. But in Iraq, as in the Soviet Union, the party did not cede its prerogatives without a fight.

On 28 July 1979, less than two weeks after replacing Bakr as President of Iraq, Saddam reverted to the methods he had employed during the early days of the regime and announced the discovery of a Syrian plot to overthrow him. This was followed by the trial of the conspirators in a revolutionary court and a Stalinist purge of the leadership of the Ba'ath Party. Although there had been disturbances by Shia elements in southern Iraq, Saddam began by focusing on the government and the party.

One third of the members of the RCC were shot. The party, security, Army, People's Army, trade unions, student unions, professional and other associations and departments were purged[15] of 'all suspect elements'. For several weeks, a reign of unprecedented terror enveloped Iraq. Although it had begun secretly, shortly before 'the resignation' and several weeks before 'the Syrian plot', its sheer scale precluded keeping it secret and forced Saddam into the open.

Saddam started with Muhi' Abdel Hussein Mashhadi, the Secretary General of the RCC.[16] He was relieved of his duties three days before Bakr's dismissal, but the news of his removal was temporarily withheld. In fact, Mashhadi had been arrested, tortured and convinced to turn against his colleagues. This and what followed attest to a power struggle within the party which had been in progress for months. By all accounts,[17] many in the Ba'ath command had anticipated Saddam's dethronement of Bakr through analyzing his cleansing operations of the various government departments, and had appealed to the elderly president to resist Saddam's plans. They not only refused to accept Saddam as president, but asked for time to counter his moves and stop him. Though Bakr had stood up to Saddam regarding the fate of a hundred Shia dissidents sentenced to death, and refused to sign their execution order,[18] he was too tired to contemplate another confrontation.

Bakr's inability to oppose Saddam adds to the importance of Mashhadi's removal. As Secretary General of the RCC he was capable of convening meetings to discuss the resignation and succession. With him out of the way, the party's ability to intercept

Saddam was compromised. However, to Saddam's surprise the rest of his Ba'athist opponents refused to be cowed. This forced his hand. Either he believed that their stubbornness originated in a plot against him sponsored by outsiders, or he concocted one to justify their removal and execution. Despite general agreement by writers who have analyzed the plot and agree with Iraqi political exiles that the whole thing was an invention, my first-hand experience leads me to a different conclusion. Although the first phase of my work with Iraq had by then come to an end, I was contacted by some of Saddam's security people and asked to look into the possibility that Dalloul was part of an anti-Saddam plot. It was a nonsensical request to which I never responded.

What happened on 18 July 1979 is recorded on video. Saddam personally ordered the filming of the proceedings of a meeting of the Regional Command Council and other top party officials of the Ba'ath, four hundred in all, in a conference hall which looked like a cinema that he had had built for international meetings. The film shows Saddam running the meeting by himself. He is on stage, sitting behind a large table with four microphones in front of him and a large cigar in his hand. Occupying the first row are his loyalists: Izzat Douri, his second-in-command in the Iraqi Ba'ath Party and Deputy Secretary General of the RCC; Taha Yassin Ramadan, his Vice President; Foreign Minister Tareq Aziz; and others including his cousin, brother-in-law and Chief of Staff, General Adnan Khairallah.

Saddam stood up and walked slowly, as if with a heavy heart, to a lectern with two microphones on it. He spoke to the gathered leadership in the manner of a relaxed lecturer addressing a group of supplicants. He not only announced the existence of a plot, but gestured with a wide sweep of his arm and told his followers that they would have a chance to determine the veracity of his statement. Mashhadi was summoned from behind the curtain and took Saddam's place at the lectern while the latter went back and sat behind the table, still puffing on his huge cigar.

For two hours, Mashhadi regaled the listeners with details of the conspiracy, dates, places of meetings and names of participants. It was obvious that his presentation was rehearsed. He referred to the so-called conspirators as traitors, and as he mentioned each name plain-clothed security officers were filmed escorting the person mentioned out of the hall. When one of them tried to speak to the gathering, Saddam shouted, '*Itla', itla*', or 'Get out, get out!' Heads bowed, every single one walked out with his grim-looking escorts, never to be seen again. No one said anything while the camera panned across the faces of Douri, Aziz and Khairallah.

What was happening, one of the most hideous recorded examples of the working of a dictatorship, finally became clear to the rest. Some of them stood up and started to cheer Saddam. He responded with a broad smile, twice thanked people who stood up to praise him and offer their fealty. Encouraged, others stood up to speak of Saddam leading them on a march to liberate Palestine, and the camera showed a happy Saddam content with what he was hearing.

Saddam reserved for himself the right to make the closing statement. Tearfully, he mentioned how the conspirators had tried to drive a wedge between him and Bakr and 'weaken the glorious Ba'ath Arab Socialist party'. When he repeated the names of the accused who had been close to him, Adnan Hamdani among others, he appeared to wipe tears from his eyes. The audience followed suit; Douri led the way and suddenly everyone had a handkerchief in his hand and was wiping away tears. Towards the end Saddam was in good spirits and laughed, and the whole audience laughed with him.

The most dramatic situation was that of Hamdani, Saddam's close personal friend, one-time head of his personal office, member of the RCC and partner in the Committee for Strategic Development. The camera closed in on him as he was forcibly taken out by security officers.[19] He had no opportunity to speak up for himself. The same happened to Mohammed Ayish and Ghanim Abd Al Jalil, to Saddam 'brothers who betrayed us'.

A special court was set up under Naim Haddad, a Shia member of the RCC and naturally a Saddam loyalist, who acted quickly on the leader's accusations. The secret trials lasted less than two weeks: twenty-two Ba'ath leaders were executed and well over forty others were imprisoned. Mashhadi was among those executed. Five hundred high-ranking Ba'athists who were not implicated in 'the Syrian plot' were nevertheless detained. Vagueness, inconsistencies and lack of solid proof of the charges against the accused did not matter. Although Saddam took time out during the meeting to offer Bakr fulsome praise, all of the latter's supporters and advocates of unity with Syria were now gone.[20] These moves were repeated throughout the country, and special courts were set up to deal with suspects on all levels of the elaborate party command structure. Copies of the videos of the meeting in which Saddam identified 'the traitors' and supposedly also tapes of some of the trials (I have not been able to obtain copies of the latter) were distributed to all security offices, to be shown to the public as a warning to 'other traitors and conspirators'.

If there was any doubt that Iraq was undergoing a massive purge of all anti-Saddam elements, the gratuitous execution of Abdel Khaliq Samarai put an end to it. Although he had been in prison since 1973, he was brought out now to face a firing squad with the rest. His execution by Saddam was an act of revenge by someone who knew that Samarai still commanded respect among many of the party faithful. This was followed by another commitment to revenge, one in which Saddam asked all Iraqis to join him. A special telephone number, supposedly his own, was flashed on television screens[21] to be used by informers wishing to squeal on 'enemies of the revolution'. An unknown number of innocent people fell victim to the pettiness of personal vendettas with no political content.

The way the execution of his opponents among the party leadership was carried out is an original Saddam invention. The victims were taken to the basement of the building where the plot was announced and executed by their comrades, Saddam and his supporters in the RCC and cabinet. Saddam gave every member of the *ad hoc* execution squad a handgun and asked them to participate in carrying out the hideous act. Of course, he led the way. So all of his inner circle were implicated in an act of murder, which guaranteed their loyalty to Saddam. None of them showed any hesitation, perhaps out of the kind of fear that Stalin instilled in others who carried out his crimes. In fact, Iraqi tribalism played into Saddam's hands. Because the relations of the victims would have demanded the blood of the executioners of their kin, implicating his loyalists provided Saddam with an even greater guarantee of their loyalty and subservience than would have been the case in non-Arab countries.

Perhaps what was happening in Iraq is best told through a joke which became current during that period. A twelve-year-old schoolboy stands up in class and asks his teacher whether elephants can fly. The teacher admonishes him for this stupidity and orders him to sit down. Unabashed, the boy repeats the question several times, only to receive more stern admonishments. Finally, when the class ends, he sheepishly approaches the teacher and in a hushed voice says, 'Our leader [Saddam] says elephants can fly.' The teacher looks around him and replies, 'Yes, but not for a long time.'

The executions were followed by extremely odd behaviour on Saddam's part. According to a Lebanese journalist who knows Saddam and has solid connections to the Tikriti regime which continue to this day, the new President locked himself up in his bedroom and would not come out for two days. When he finally emerged, his eyes were so bloodshot and swollen that he could hardly open them, and he had difficulty speaking. He had been crying his black heart out. I am unable to bring this story to any conclusion because, though many within Saddam's new circle knew about what he did, none of them has ever dared ask him about this episode. The reasons for it, like his reprieve of a Jew who had been kind to him when he was a poor boy selling cigarettes on the streets of Baghdad, and his generosity to an unknown Egyptian doorman, remain locked in the dark recesses of his mind.

According to the same Lebanese source – and he is definitely in a position to know – Saddam's strangeness at this time did not stop there. A few days after the executions he paid a personal visit to the widow of Adnan Hamdani, the person closest to him among the victims. He unashamedly paid his condolences, and weeping loudly, told the grieving woman that 'national considerations' took precedence over personal ones. To Saddam, her husband was a man whom he loved like a brother, but he had had no choice but to sacrifice him 'for the cause'. Continuing this incredible statement, which deserves the attention of a professional psychiatrist, Saddam assured Mrs Hamdani that 'she would never need, as long as he was alive'. Some time later he lived up to his promise and ordered the building of a substantial villa along the Tigris for the Hamdani family. My informant, a Saddam supporter, was under the impression that this story demonstrated the president's inherent humanity.

This peculiar second story was confirmed to me by six other people beside the Lebanese journalist and, like my original informant, all of them verified it on non-attribution basis because it touches on the workings of Saddam's mind. Revelations about what moved and motivated him, certainly anything which revealed human weakness, always made him dangerous and set him on the road to revenge – even when the motive of the people who revealed these weaknesses was innocent. And there is more to make this story among the most bizarre that I have ever heard. Why was Hamdani, who was utterly loyal to Saddam, executed? The answer complicates rather than solves the mystery. It is an established fact that Hamdani came from a known, well-to-do family. During their young revolutionary days he had seen to it that Saddam was never short of money. In other words, Hamdani had subsidized him. If the killing of Samarai was an act of revenge against a former senior comrade who towered about Saddam intellectually, then the murder of Hamdani was one against a benefactor.

There was a third execution which supports my belief that Saddam was intolerant of people with superior attributes or lineage to the point of eliminating them. Ghaleb Mawloud Mukhlis, the son of the man behind the Tikritis' original entry into the armed forces, was also executed during this period. Ghaleb was close to Bakr, but most people dismiss this as a reason for the execution. They believe that it was aimed at eliminating the legend of his father, to remove any risk that Saddam's success might be attributed to the older Mukhlis. Saddam had resented Samarai and secretly rejected his dependence on Hamdani, and erasing the image of the Mukhlises as Tikrit's benefactor followed. He did not want the world to know that he owed anyone anything, or that someone else was behind Tikrit's ascendance. Perhaps that was why he felt a need to repay Hamdani through attending to the needs of his widow.

The execution of Hamdani reduced the leadership of the Committee for Strategic Development to Saddam and Adnan Khairallah. That lessened its effectiveness as the supreme body in charge of non-conventional weapons development within the country and as the source of direction for hundreds of people who worked for Saddam outside Iraq. Many of the people on whom Hamdani had depended in the Ministry of Planning were also purged. Even people who emulated Saddam and saw fit to offer their condolences to Hamdani's widow were executed or imprisoned for their crime of manifesting human sympathy towards the family of a traitor. The procurement network did not escape suspicion, either, and Ramzi Dalloul was one of the victims, because Saddam never trusted him again.

Recently a number of writers have published stories about Dalloul, which include allegations that his services were terminated because he and Hamdani were realizing high commissions.[22] This is something I do not accept. Neither man put money before commitment to Iraq. If I may jump ahead of the story once again, in early 1982, during my second phase of cooperating with Saddam's government, I was questioned about Dalloul's connection with Hamdani. The Iraqis obviously believed Dalloul was politically loyal to Hamdani and that he had known about 'the conspiracy'. My reaction was to deny it; again, my knowledge of Dalloul precludes any dishonest or violent behaviour on his part.

The purge of 1979, followed by comparatively minor ones of the Baghdad-based pan-Arab Ba'ath leadership in 1980 and the consequent open abandonment of ideology, are landmarks in Saddam's leadership. Having used the party to control the Army, then merged the party with family and put relations in charge of the merger, and supported this primacy through other aspects of Tikriti, Douri and 'Ani tribalism, all power in the country was vested in Saddam's person as the head of the family and tribe. Douri, Ramadan, Aziz, Haddad and Adnan Khairallah were the new members of the RCC, but had no power except to carry out Saddam's orders. Newly appointed members of the cabinet had even less power. Aflaq, whose loyalty to Saddam made him forget the original ideology of the Ba'ath, became more decorative than ever before. The slogans of 'One Arab nation with an eternal mission' and 'Unity, freedom and socialism' became things of the past. As for Bakr, although he had been a figurehead for some time, and despite a desperate last-minute attempt to reimpose himself as leader of the country, his removal signalled the removal of the last hurdle to Saddam's assumption of absolute power.

Saddam still worked sixteen to seventeen hours a day,[23] but there was a perceptible change in the way he ran the country which showed almost immediately he became President. Unleashing government propaganda organs as if they had been held in check awaiting this occasion, the Iraqi media began calling him 'knight', 'struggler', 'leader', 'son of the people' and comparing him to Peter the Great. This was a new approach, which, for unknown reasons and until the war with Iran, dispensed with recalling the legacies of the ancient kings of Mesopotamia, famous Muslims and others.

But the change in Saddam went beyond his use of titles and comparing himself to historical figures. Instead of his former meticulous planning and precision in implementing government programmes, Saddam began issuing 'directives', 'orders' and 'national guidelines'. Because he was on television daily,[24] pompously carrying on about everything under the sun, the functional aspect of his thinking was surrendered to others, reducing the effectiveness of what he had in mind. On television, his mellow voice and slow, unemotive delivery, aimed to reassure people that their future was secure, failed to disguise the menace of his imposing physical presence. The legendary *gada*' of the Ba'ath's early days became the God Father of a ruling family, with everything that goes with this description. He was a benevolent father figure taking care of his immediate and extended Iraqi family, a poor boy with a remarkable record of achievements. But everybody whispered about how the achievements were built on the bones of the hundreds of people who dared to oppose him.

Not for the first time Saddam was reinventing himself. On the surface, his exercise of power as Bakr's Mr Deputy had been unhindered and open. But the new persona which emerged after the purge revealed that he had suffered a surprising level of frustration on most levels. The first aspect of the new Saddam concerned his personal behaviour. The suddenness with which he proceeded to indulge himself and the grandiose way in which it was expressed leaves no doubt that the presence of the fatherly Bakr and the existence of a party structure had acted as checks on his Tikriti instincts.

Soon after Saddam became President, his security people started using sticks and electric rods to administer shocks on people who wanted to approach him during his walkabouts.[25] Furthermore, he seemed to walk stiffly and in an excessively formal way, which, if intended to imbue him with an air of dignity, was self-defeating. According to others who corroborate the story about the use of sticks, this was not a security measure but a gratuitous exercise of power. So in yet another manifestation of contradictory behaviour, Saddam was maintaining the legend of the benevolent leader who wanted direct contact with the people while feeling that he was above being touched.

During the same period, it became evident that Saddam had a bottomless wardrobe. Those who watched him on television in his elegant clothes began to speak of his dandyism, something that the tough Iraqis do not admire. His former Ba'athist colleague Dr Tahseen Mua'la claims that Saddam possessed over four hundred belts.[26] In fact, Saddam had a personal tailor by the name of Haddad (also known as Sarkis Sarkis) and the rest of his clothes were tailor-made in Geneva. Soon he had a private Indian doctor, a resident soothsayer and no fewer than ten drivers. In keeping with his new image, he began to walk and talk in a more deliberate way.

The oddest Saddam story of the time is the one recalled by Dr Mahmoud Othman, the Kurdish politician who negotiated with him for nearly thirty years and whose observations of the personal and political behaviour of the Iraqi leader would fill an entire book. Following Saddam's declaration, upon becoming President, of a political amnesty for all his opponents, Othman had made an appointment to discuss the Kurdish problem. They were to meet at 7 a.m., and the meticulous Othman was at the palace on time. The previous night, Saddam had worked in his special small office in the palace until the early hours. As was his habit when he did this, he had slept in the office (which very few people had ever seen) instead of returning to the residential wing. When told of Othman's presence by an aide, Saddam told the men to apologize to the Kurdish leader and usher him in without delay, while he was still in his pyjamas.

What Othman saw – and he is probably the one person outside Saddam's personal entourage to have witnessed this – was truly puzzling. Saddam had slept on a small cot, almost military in its simplicity, in the corner of the room and had put on a robe to receive Othman, which he did warmly. But it was other things which baffled the usually unflappable Kurdish leader. Next to the bed were 'over twelve pairs of very expensive shoes. And the rest of the office was nothing but a small library full of books about one man, Stalin. One could say he went to bed with the Russian dictator.' Othman managed to hide his surprise and he and Saddam conducted one of the many meetings which marked the lives of both men, but without making any progress. To this day, Othman is unable to control a change in his voice when telling this story.[27]

There were further signs that Saddam's new persona was spinning out of control, that his image of himself as a figure of historic importance (by the looks of things modelled on Stalin) had overshadowed the real Saddam. Some time during this period he pompously told his biographer Iskandar that he was not concerned with what the people thought at the time but with 'what people will say abut us 500 years hence'.[28] He followed this with a statement to Fuad Matar which suggested that he no longer had anything to fear 'because most Iraqis are Ba'athists'.[29] In his own eyes he had become an immortal person speaking for an Iraqi people who obviously followed his Ba'athist philosophy and in the process surrendered their judgement and entrusted everything to him. According to Saddam, 'Iraq was too young for democracy.'[30]

A country too young for democracy, and obediently following its leader, needed a leader who could give it direction. Saddam decided that his television and radio monologues, often three or four hours long, were not enough. His already prodigious literary output, which eventually reached over two hundred books, articles and essays,[31] gained momentum. He 'wrote' about everything and, like his essay to justify making the birthday of Imam Ali a national holiday, the rest of his published work was aimed at creating a philosophy for what he was doing.

Surprising to most people as these manifestations of the new Saddam were, there was a small group of Iraqis who had suspected that these traits lurked within him. These people, or their children, had seen similar inherent weaknesses of character in his sons' behaviour. In 1980 Udday and Qussay were sixteen and fourteen respectively and were attending Al Kharkh Al Namouthajiya School (the Kharkh Exemplary). Until he became President, this school had been run by Saddam's wife Sajida, and her presence and the high level of education it ostensibly afforded made it a place for the privileged few. Saddam spoke of it with special pride, but, as with many other model achievements, the facade of modernity and quality hid a darker side.

Ahmad Allawi of the Iraqi National Council was a classmate of Udday, Saddam's oldest son. Tamara Daghastani's children were among the students, and one of them knew Saddam's second son Qussay. Latif Yahya was another of Udday's classmate's, who resembled the leader's son so closely in physical appearance that he was later used as his double.[32] The recollections of these three Iraqis provide irrefutable proof that Saddam's (and indeed his wife's) complexes first showed in the way they brought up their children. Although the habit of the newly rich to spoil their children to compensate for the deprivation of their own youth is well known, what Saddam allowed his children to get away with exceeded anything of which I have ever heard.

Tamara Daghastani distinguished between Saddam's two sons by stating that, according to her children, Udday was loud and vulgar while Qussay was quiet and calculating. 'Both received special treatment and never obeyed any rules or regulations. One shouted about it and the other didn't, but both of them came first in their class, though Udday never did any work. Naturally, nobody dared get near them and even the classrooms were guarded so heavily, it affected the performance of other students. Of course, leaving to go to another school was out of the question because one had to explain why they would want to leave an exclusive school attended by the president's children. It became hell on earth for others.'

Ahmad Allawi's eye witness account goes further. 'They [Udday and Qussay] always violated the dress code. They came to class in dish-dashs and Udday occasionally used a bandanna instead of a belt and had live ammunition in it. One time Udday came to class with a headdress made of bamboo sticks, and naturally the teacher said nothing and we pretended we were seeing nothing. There were so many security people, the classrooms were of a huge size to accommodate them. I was there when Udday demanded extra time to finish his test and the teacher had to obey him and gave us all fifteen minutes more. Then he finished in six minutes and told the teachers to stop the rest from continuing. The whole thing was really sick – Udday had so many cars and generated so much fuss. One time he ordered the driver to drive up about ten stairs because he did not want to walk that number of steps. Allah help anyone who had a good car the like of which Udday did not have – he'd send his guards to confiscate it. Even then their [Udday's and Qussay's] cars had special licence plates which didn't make sense – they had on them "O Salaheddine [Saladin], O Iraq", all nonsense. The rest of us were there to keep them company, that's all. When Udday broke his leg, the class moved to the lower floor to make it easy for him. Qussay was more intelligent. He did the same things, but he didn't abuse people verbally or show off like his brother.'

Latif Yahya's book confirms what Daghastani and Allawi had to say and reveals that Udday started having girlfriends quite early in life, an oddity in a Muslim society. There is a suggestion here that the girls in question had little choice in the matter. There are also stories of Udday smoking cigars at an early age, and others of him later demanding an office similar to his father's. And, of course, also to be taken into account were his arrogance, an early inclination to resort to violence and the huge sums he spent on clothes and cars.

Why Saddam, the man who for years had refused to enter Bakr's office without being announced, accepted this behaviour by his children and thought it would escape public scrutiny is unknown. To say that he was too busy and Sajida was behind her sons' misbehaviour is to excuse and absolve Saddam who, after all, was an Arab husband obeyed by his wife (in his own family, Saddam never ceased to believe in the tribal primacy of the head of the household). Moreover – and despite the fact that he might not have known about his children's behaviour because people did not dare tell either parent about it – Udday's future criminality and Saddam's acceptance of it rule this out. In reality the boys were no different from the relations of other Middle Eastern dictators, such as the over indulged offspring of the House of Saud or the Kuwaiti royal family. Their lack of proper upbringing is another testimony that even in Ba'athist Iraq, ideology was only skin-deep and family connections have always taken precedence.

When these and other stories about Udday and Qussay eventually became common knowledge, they shattered overnight an image of Saddam that many Iraqis had admired, that of a self-made family man. Together with a long list of stories about the financial manipulations of Uncle Khairallah, who used his position as Governor of the Province of Baghdad to control twenty-five companies, they dealt a lasting blow to the popularity of the new President. However much people opposed him politically, very few had ever suspected him of corruption. Even his later dismissal of Khairallah did not save him from being associated with that image of other Arab leaders.

These revelations, significant though they are in exposing Saddam the tribal dictator, should not stand in the way of detailing the other important activities which followed his assumption of the office of president of Iraq. Some of these activities contained a glimpse of the old Saddam and his commitments to populism, but others were new, forced on him by circumstances as a response to developments inside Iraq, regionally and internationally. If

Saddam the populist leader was hindered by his tribal inner mind, then Saddam the international leader was an utter disaster. But, even at the risk of pre-empting events that speak for themselves, it is well to remember that the West aided and contributed to the many problems that President Saddam Hussein bequeathed to the rest of the world.

Among his first acts as President was a decree prohibiting the use of family names.[33] This simple-sounding measure was anything but – it was an attempt at instilling equality among the Iraqi people. Except for some establishment families with solid lineage, the concept of family names was a relatively recent development in Iraq and most people were named after the town or village from which they came – the Tikritis from Tikrit, 'Anis from 'Ana, and so on down the line. Their place of birth gave them identity, and with it social status, or lack of it which could impede their advancement. For example, the poor Christians from Tel Keif in northern Iraq were janitors and servants. Saddam issued the decree to prevent people suffering because of their social origins.

Simultaneously, he expedited the end of the collective farm scheme.[34] In no time at all the only farms which remained in the hands of the government were ones which individual farmers did not want to own. To replace them, he developed schemes which gave the peasants the right to the land but saw to it that government assistance was made available. And there were other measures which were a continuation of undertakings he had started during his early years in government. All schools were ordered to install central heating, mortuaries were to be refrigerated and grocers' pricing practices were rigorously monitored. Distribution of housing was increased, although Saddam cleverly favoured Ba'ath members and put them ahead of the general public.

Perhaps it was the holding of elections for a National Assembly in 1980 which represented Saddam's most ambitious move. As already mentioned, he dangled a carrot to the people immediately upon becoming President by declaring a general amnesty. The response from the Shias and Kurds was less than enthusiastic; they simply did not trust him. But he followed this by deciding to install a National Assembly. The way he created this body does not subscribe to the Western concept of an acceptable democracy, and most representatives were appointed rather than voted in, but it was a step in the right direction which contained the seeds of possible improvement. The mere mention of every fifty thousand people being represented by someone who spoke on their behalf, and ensuring that no fewer than 40 per cent of the seats were occupied by Shias, amounted to the first serious consideration of democracy since the days of the monarchy.

These populist decrees and their consequences were taking place against a background of internal political developments which were determining foreign policy and external considerations which affected Saddam's behaviour inside his country. The two developments which occupied his mind and rendered inevitable the march towards his first regional war were the emergence in February 1979 of Islamic fundamentalism in Iran and the invasion of Afghanistan by the USSR in December that year. Both had a direct influence on the thinking of the Iraqis and their relations with the West and the USSR. And the influences of both affected the policies of other countries towards Iraq in a way which contributed to Saddam's overestimation of Iraq's capabilities, its role and his own personal importance. Both drew Iraq and the USA into a cynical embrace, the results of which remain to this day.

The appearance of an anti-Ba'ath regime in Iran encouraged Saddam's enemies, who saw it as a much-needed benefactor and backer to reignite their flagging activities against the central government of Iraq. For instance, the Kurdish leader Mulla Mustapha's sons Massoud and Idris cabled their congratulations and support to Khomeini soon after his takeover. Despite their different purposes, the contacts between Iran and the Kurds continued for years, and a while later Mulla Mustapha himself cabled Khomeini assuring him of Kurdish support against the Ba'ath. However, important as this was, the rebelliousness of the Kurds was something to which Saddam had grown accustomed and it was the Iranian revolution's influence on the Shias which threatened him more seriously.

Khomeini's exhortations to the Iraqis to overthrow the Ba'ath exceeded in both intent and intensity the usual meddling of Middle Eastern leaders in the affairs of neighbouring states. His calls to the Shias of Iraq to rid themselves of the 'non-Muslim Ba'ath' were reinforced by Iraqi Shia leader Sadr's response that 'other tyrants [beside the Shah] have yet to see their day of reckoning'.[35] Riots followed each of Khomeini's calls to religious rebellion, not only in

Iraq but in the rest of the Gulf countries which had Shia populations – Saudi Arabia, Bahrain and Kuwait. Khomeini, exaggerating
his own powers and underestimating his opponents' ability to
respond to his appeals, was pushing these countries towards an
alliance.

Once again, Saddam resorted to his carrot-and-stick tactics. At
first he stepped up the distribution of TV sets, refrigerators and
other goods in Shia areas,[36] but the magnitude of the challenge to
his authority reduced this to a hollow gesture. When Sadr openly
placed religion ahead of loyalty to the state and accepted Khomeini
as the overall leader of the Shias,[37] Saddam uncharacteristically
tried to avoid a confrontation by asking the latter to rescind his
newly declared fealty.[38] But Sadr, made of the same stuff as
Saddam, refused to do so and began issuing his own inflammatory
statements as Khomeini's deputy in Iraq.

Unfortunatley for the Shias of Iraq, Sadr's behaviour during this
period reduced their cause to a struggle between two individuals,
and his acceptance of Khomeini's leadership played right into
Saddam's hands. The chants of the rioting crowds in Najjaf and
other Iraqi cities amounted to open rebellion: '*Ash Al Khomeini wil
Sadr weddine lazim yantasser*' means 'Long live Khomeini and
Sadr, and the faith will prevail.' There was no way for Saddam to
overlook this, or the *fatwa* against membership in the Ba'ath
declared by Sadr, and survive. Slogans celebrating Khomeini were
being coined every day, among them some which touched on the
very identity of Iraq such as: '*Kulana lak fada' Khomeini*' or 'We
are for you to sacrifice, Khomeini.' This was followed by reports
that the Shias, with Iranian help, were undergoing training in the
use of small arms.[39]

For reasons which are hard to explain, Saddam's initial response, however severe or even savage, was not directed at the
source. Referring to the slogan-chanters as Khomeinites, Saddam
arrested hundreds of people and executed ninety-four, including a
ninety-one-year-old cleric. But Sadr was not touched. He had been
arrested in 1972, 1974, 1977 and for two days in 1979, but each
arrest only added to his popularity and standing among his people.
However, things were moving toward their inevitable climax.
Khomeini had followed the reports of arrests and executions in
early 1980 with an open appeal to Sadr not to leave Iraq –
probably what Saddam had hoped for by leaving him free. Sadr

had responded by assuring Khomeini that he was staying put until their common aim was achieved.[40]

On 1 April 1980, members of Sadr's Dawa Party, which had murdered a score of government officials in 1979, tried to assassinate Deputy Prime Minister and RCC member Tareq Aziz. The attempt took place when Aziz was visiting Mustinsiriya University to attend a conference of the National Union of Iraqi Students. Aziz himself was only slightly wounded, but there were an unknown number of dead and injured. Twenty-four hours later, Saddam made an announcement which ended all hope of a peaceful end to the Shia rebellion: 'Yesterday, a miserable agent caused the very dear blood of Mustinsirya students to be shed . . . Our people are ready to fight to protect their honour and sovereignty, as well as maintain peace among the Arab nations.'[41] On 5 April, when a Dawa hit squad attacked the funeral of those who had died in the attempt against Aziz and killed more people, Saddam responded by making Dawa membership a crime punishable with death. Hundreds were executed.

Saddam did not stop there. The following day his special forces entered Najjaf and arrested Sadr and his sister Amina, known to Shias as Bint Al Huda or the daughter of the righteous. Obeying shoot-to-kill orders, they overwhelmed the few who tried to oppose them and brought their prisoners back to Baghdad. There is little doubt that the cleric and his sister were tortured, but nothing short of final settlement of the problem would satisfy Saddam. On 9 April, the two were executed. There is no record of a trial. Riots broke out in southern Iraq, scores of people were shot to death and thousands arrested, many never to be seen again. Along the Iranian–Iraqi border, skirmishes between the two countries' armies became a common occurrence.

Saddam followed the executions with the rigid implementation of the nationality law which he had used against the Shias in the past. The absurd interpretation of lineage was augmented by summary deportations of 'people who had secretly entered Iraq'. Tens of thousands of poor innocents were forced to leave without their possessions. As if to prove his statement to biographer Iskandar that he was not afraid of death,[42] Saddam followed this with a visit to Najjaf to demonstrate his lack of fear and the fact that the Shia stronghold was under central government control. Having told them in 1979 that he was the grandson of Ali, founder of the Shia branch of Islam, this time he recalled his name to justify his harsh measures: 'I am the son of Ali and I kill with his sword.'[43] He went on to make declarations about the Arabism of Iraq and how it took precedence over religion.

In an attempt to gain the support of fellow Arab governments for his growing confrontation with Khomeini, Saddam dispatched personal envoys carrying explanations of what was happening in Iraq. Because Khomeini and other kinds of Islamic fundamentalism were a common threat, his envoys were received with open arms. This was particularly true in Saudi Arabia and Egypt. The former supported him because Saudi Shias in the oil-producing province of Hasa had rioted in February 1980, not for the first time, and the latter because of the growing danger of local fundamentalism. Saddam also sent his version of events to Fidel Castro in his capacity as head of the Non-Aligned Nations Conference and to UN Secretary General Kurt Waldheim. But it was what was happening behind the scenes which mattered most.

The tilt towards the Arab countries and the cynical amity with America both of which began to reveal themselves in the aftermath of Sadr's execution had in fact begun some time earlier. On 8 February 1980 Saddam announced an Eight-Point Arab National Charter, essentially a guideline for behaviour among the Arab governments. While there was nothing new in its calls for placing Arab brotherhood ahead of all else and rejecting the influence of outside powers, the charter was to become more important with the passage of time.

Saddam's rejection of the USSR had started in July 1978, while he was Vice President. In an interview with the *International Herald Tribune* he had declared that, '[The Soviet Union] will not be satisfied until the whole world is Communist.'[44] This criticism, born as it was out of his problems with the Iraqi Communist party, was followed by further condemnation after the Soviet invasion of Afghanistan. The Arab National Charter not only confirmed his rejection of the USSR's invasion of Afghanistan, it signalled an attempt by Saddam to endear himself to the moderate Arab countries. Furthermore, the charter contained an explicit commitment to settling all inter-Arab issues in an amicable way, which he himself was to violate by invading Kuwait.

While it is impossible to prove, many believe that the charter was part of Saddam's design to attack Iran and that it was aimed at pleasing the West as much as the Arab countries. The late Hani Fkaiki, the former Ba'athist turned opposition leader, told me that, with the blessing of Saddam, the CIA had opened a Baghdad office in late 1979.[45] To make the same point, others underscore Saddam's criticism of Soviet actions in Afghanistan, South Yemen and Ethiopia and his growing friendship with Jordan's King Hussein. Of course, the frequency of visits to Saudi Arabia by members of Saddam's government contributed to the theory that an Iraqi–Jordanian–Saudi–American conspiracy against Iran was in the making.

It is impossible to verify whether this 'conspiracy' was detailed or amounted to nothing more than discussions on issues of mutual interest. Kenneth Timmermann claims that what started as a mutuality of interest culminated in a July 1980 meeting between Saddam and Carter's national security adviser, Zbigniew Brzezinski in Amman.[46] Brzezinski himself denies that this meeting, first reported by the *New York Times*, ever took place. In the end, the mystery of this meeting is superseded by two proven facts. In April 1980, while Saddam was executing dozens of Shias and deporting thousands, Brzezinski declared, 'We see no fundamental incompatibility of interests between the United States and Iraq.'[47] And Saddam himself cleverly ignored certain developments of the kind which in times past had prompted him to denounce the United States and other Western countries and accuse it of complicity with Israel. In April 1979, Mossad agents blew up a ship carrying atomic reactor cores to Iraq before it left the French port of Toulon. Some time later, on 14 June 1980, an assassination with implications for the future shape of Middle East politics took place in Paris. This time Mossad killed Yahya Al Mashed, the Egyptian atomic scientist working for Saddam. The issue of Saddam's nonconventional weapons was beginning to surface.

The results of my own investigation support the conspiracy theory but do not implicate the former national security adviser. According to a member of King Hussein's cabinet, a former general in his Army and Iraqi leader Ahmad Chalabi, the meeting which took place in Amman was between Saddam and three CIA operatives,[48] Rance Haig, Tom Twitten and psychological warfare specialist Tom Alan. Saddam's presence in the Jordanian capital when the CIA men were there is an established fact. But the specifics of the actual meeting remain elusive.[49] What is undoubtedly true is that both sides met with King Hussein, and both sides and the Jordanian monarch were preoccupied with the problem of Iran. Even if a meeting between the parties did not take place, an indirect meeting of minds through King Hussein definitely did. Among the many services which the King is supposed to have provided Saddam was a meeting with Iranian opposition leaders, who assured the Iraqi leader that Khomeini's popularity was waning and that the time to attack Iran had come.

There were several other developments which confirmed that a pattern of cooperation between the United States and Iraq was emerging. Ahmad Chalabi and members of the Jordanian government at the time confirm that the USA had 'told' Hussein to stop providing assistance to the Kurds.[50] (That the Jordanian King was helping the Kurds while entertaining Saddam falls within the scope of political machinations as they occur in the Middle East.) Iraq signalled its readiness to expand commercial relations with the United States by making a request to buy five Boeing-747s, which was eventually approved by the Reagan administration in 1981. Using as evidence the news of the General Electric engines for Italian boats and the request to purchase Boeings, American business magazines began to promote business opportunities in Iraq. Above all, the improving relations between the leader of the Gulf countries, Saudi Arabia, and Iraq could not have taken place without Saudi determination that America had no objection to this happening.

Against the background of an orchestrated Iraqi media campaign condemning the 'Persian' enemy (recalling centuries-old rivalries and enmities), which had been in progress for several months, Saddam arrived in Saudi Arabia on 5 August 1980 after making a quick stopover in Jordan. He wore his military uniform, carried a gun and looked grim. His meetings with Fahd, then the country's crown prince and strong man, lasted more than ten hours. According to Saudi Arabia's Ambassador to the UK, Ghazi Al Gosaibi, Saddam told Prince Fahd of his plans to attack Iran.[51] A former Saddam aide, Sa'ad Bazzaz, supports this by making the unequivocal statement: 'We told them we're going to attack Iran.'[52]

Although both chroniclers stop there, others claim that Fahd promised Saddam billions of dollars in aid and free use of the Saudi port of Jeddah to compensate for not being able to use Basra after the start of hostilities. Even if this is only partly true, there is little doubt that Saudi Arabia encouraged Saddam and that it must bear some of the responsibility for the start of the war. Upon his return to Baghdad, the media campaign which was emphasizing Iraq's Arabness reached an unusual level of shrillness. Little doubt existed that war was on the way, and Saddam promised 'to turn Iraq into a bloodbath if the imperialists invade it'.[52] Border incidents between Iraq and Iran were taking place on a daily basis. After making several visits to Iraqi Army units along the Iranian border, on 17 September Saddam abrogated the Algiers Agreement which had ceded to Iran control of half of the Shat Al Arab waterway at the head of the Gulf. The Iraqi Army invaded Iran on 22 September 1980. The US media, though it lamented the war in the way people should, expressed its support for Saddam Hussein.

8

An Aimless War

The longest organized war of the twentieth century, which lasted eight years, pitted the two predominantly Shia countries in the world against each other and went through several mutations beyond the combatants' immediate control. The reasons Saddam Hussein started it differ from those which compelled him to continue it. By the time it ended, the war's original rationale had receded or been answered and the outcome was judged in accordance with considerations which did not exist at the beginning, or which were deliberately overlooked by the countries which had supported Saddam's original adventure and invented new reasons to continue it.

The lack of a connection between what caused the war and what ended it makes it necessary to examine Saddam's thinking for starting it. Following the course of the Iran–Iraq War (also called the First Gulf War to distinguish it from Saddam's later invasion of Kuwait) as an ever-changing multi-stage conflict allows me to examine it as the key event which revealed the true personality of the Iraqi leader. It was the major contributor to his personal and political corruption but also revealed the limits of his power. As we shall see, it was war, the great corrupter, which forced the real Saddam into the open and determined his future actions. Moreover, it lays bare the involvement of outside forces and their considerable and occasionally unchecked influence on the course of battle and the war's outcome.

Historians of the Iran–Iraq War examined its causes in academic language and broad terms of reference which need to be reduced to ordinary language that takes into account the political conditions of the Middle East and the motivations of outside powers as they existed in 1980. Many writers believe that the war reflected the general hostility between Iran and Iraq, and they cannot be faulted. This hostility has always existed, and the Algiers Agreement of 1975 was no more than an interregnum in an otherwise long history of rivalry between the two countries for supremacy in the Gulf. Other chroniclers have explained this in terms of the historic enmity between the Arabs and the Persians which goes all the way back to the Abbasid Empire (AD 749–1258). A third group of analysts changes the label yet again and gives this terrible event a racial content by viewing it as an Arab Semite vs. Iranian Aryan contest. Because the support for this explanation is how the two sides have battled each other throughout history, this interpretation is nothing more than an extension of the two previous ones. Furthermore, seeing the conflict as a Sunni–Shia struggle succumbs to the same historical interpretation with minor modifications. Essentially, a historical explanation for the war produces a single reason which appears under different names.

It is the writers who have analyzed the Iran–Iraq War in terms of the way the two countries were governed before the start of hostilities who come closer to the truth. After all, the historical justifications used for it have been in place for centuries and had been viewed with equal seriousness by former leaders of both countries without leading to conflict, except under Saddam and Khomeini. The cultural/religious enmity is indisputable, as were the conflicting territorial claims of the two countries and the wish of each to claim hegemony over the Gulf. There were the disagreements over the border between the two countries. The Shat Al Arab question and later the issue of the islands in the Gulf, the question that the 1975 Algiers Agreement overlooked but which Saddam resurrected early in 1980. The problem of state vs. religion existed under all Iraqi regimes including the monarchy, and separating the state from religion was a relatively recent development. In Islamic history, which both countries shared, the religious and state leader had been one and the same.

It was Saddam's belief in the supremacy of the state and Khomeini's view of religion as a force entitled to push aside everything in its way, especially Saddam's heretical Ba'athist regime, and how both men promoted their position, which changed the perception of the historical problems. The war was between two Middle East countries, both moving into the twentieth century but with a hard core anchored in another age which allowed individual leaders total freedom to interpret the policies of their country, including responses to outside threats. To Saddam, the threat of Khomeini's subversion was so real that there was little room for a modus vivendi between the two countries. To Khomeini, the mere existence of Saddam was a reproach to his religious beliefs which had to be removed.

Intellectually, there is little doubt that it was a cause of state vs. religion. Practically, it was Saddam vs. Khomeini. The war represented the President of Iraq, Chairman of the Revolutionary Command Council, Secretary General of the Ba'ath Party, Commander in Chief of the Iraqi armed forces, Head of Iraq's Internal Security Directorate and occasional judge and arbiter of the laws of Iraq battling an uncompromising cleric with a direct line to Allah. But because the West, Saudi Arabia, Kuwait and the rest of the Gulf states had isolated Iran and were not listening to Khomeini's argument, what the confrontation between the two leaders meant was left to Saddam Hussein. This allowed him to extend the personalization of all issues separating him from Khomeini and, probably unknowingly, he turned them into a single one: a test of will between two dictators, implacable enemies. In particular, it was the leadership of the USA and its response to being humiliated by the Iranians' holding of American hostages in November 1979, which governed the world's view of what was happening. Saddam's words and actions and the reporting from Baghdad, the first draft of history, became the accepted explanation of the war to the outside world because the USA said so. With minor exceptions, everybody was on Saddam's side and against Khomeini.

Saddam reacted in character. Emboldened by outside support, he met Khomeini's exhortation to the Iraqi Shias head on. His awareness of the hold of history and Islam on his people made him pay tribute to religion and to declare that he had 'always been on the side of belief'.[1] He ordered Koranic suras (verses) to be read more frequently on Radio Baghdad and visited mosques, praying in them with photographers in attendance. But he never accepted the idea of a religious state and his actions were aimed at pleasing the faithful among his people, the Shias in particular, without conceding anything. In fact, he proceeded to gather all historical, religious, old and new political issues into a single bundle and assumed the mantle of the world's leading advocate of secularism. This guaranteed him the continued support of major Arab and other countries. And this support produced a coalition, albeit undefined and unstructured, opposed to the Islamic fundamentalist movement of Khomeini and its threat. Ironically, this first coalition resembled the one put together after Saddam invaded Kuwait in 1990, no more than a temporary convergence of interest between disparate nation states.

The Iraqis described their massive military invasion of south-western Iran as a counter-attack.[2] This meant that it was a response to Iranian military provocations, the relatively minor border skirmishes which took place in the summer of 1980. But regardless of the language the Iraqis used to describe the commencement of hostilities, what was happening was greater than a massive and disproportionate retaliation: it was an open-ended war. Above all, more than three hundred thousand soldiers were involved – far too many for a single 'military operation'.

Yet on 11 September, eleven days before the invasion, Saddam's then Foreign Minister and present Vice President, Tareq Aziz, declared, 'We wish neither to destroy Iran nor to occupy it . . .'[3] This publicity line was contradicted by the thrust of Iraqi armour into Iran. On 23 September, one day after the Iraqi invasion started, Baghdad radio broadcasts began to refer to the Khezestan province of Iran by its Arabic name of Arabistan and the city of Khoramshahr became Mohammara. The broadcasts called on the mainly Arab population of this province, which had been under Iran for most of the twentieth century, to rise against the Persians. The calls, unlike Aziz's statement, were directed exclusively at an Arab audience.

On the same day that the broadcasts began, the European Community and United Nations Security Council appealed to both sides to cease 'armed activity'. The then Secretary General of the United Nations, Kurt Waldheim, followed with an offer of personal mediation. When the Iranians boycotted the Security Council meeting, refused Waldheim's offer and did not respond to the European plea the Iraqis gained a propaganda victory, but the long-term implications of the Iranian refusal were negative. On 24 September Iraqi minister Dr Sa'adoun Hamadi, a Shia Ba'athist of long standing, accepted the UN appeal and reaffirmed that Iraq had no territorial claims on Iran. Such conflicting utterances persisted for the rest of 1980. Iraq needed to issue different messages to different groups because what it was telling its own people differed from what it was telling the rest of the Arabs, and what it directed at the rest of the world was different again.

Saddam himself shed no light on the contradictions between statements made by the various branches of his government. For a while he remained silent. But the fighting was raging on a very large scale and there were no orders to halt it. Iraqi armour, no fewer than two thousand tanks, kept penetrating south-west Iran. On 24 September, France, with more at stake in Iraq than other Western countries, issued its own appeal to the belligerents to cease all military activity. The Non-Aligned Nations Conference added its voice to the various countries and organizations calling for an end to the fighting and Cuba, the presiding country, dispatched a goodwill mission to both sides. The Islamic Conference followed suit, and a delegation made up of Pakistani President Zia Al Huq and Secretary General Habib Shatti visited Iran and Iraq.

Meanwhile the USSR, fearing that one of the two belligerents would seek America's help, decided that the conflict was likely to produce an improvement in the USA's position in the Middle East. It did not want to lose Iraq, with whom it had a friendship and cooperation treaty, and did not want Iran to provoke unrest in its own Muslim republics. Not only did the USSR make an appeal for the fighting to stop, it declared its neutrality and a ban on the shipment of weapons to both sides. Only the United States stood above the fray and made no concrete efforts to put an end to the war. Secretary of State Edmund Muskie met his Soviet counterpart at the United Nations on 23 September, but the USA did nothing beyond issuing the usual statement expressing its wish for an end to the conflict. This was a major signal that the war might last a long time.

The second such signal occurred almost simultaneously. With some success, both combatants were directing some of their aerial attacks against each other's oil production facilities. When an Iraqi attack damaged the Iranian refinery at Abadan on 23 September the world's largest oil exporter, Saudi Arabia, increased its oil production by nine hundred thousand barrels a day.[4] As a result the panic in the oil market which usually accompanied conflicts in the Middle East did not take place. The speed with which the

Saudis responded was surprising for Saudi Arabia had always taken a long time to make up its mind about anything. The decision to increase production on this scale and the calm behaviour of the oil companies suggested that the Saudi move had been coordinated with the United States.

Saddam was caught. By all accounts he expected the war to last only a few days — to end through mediation to the collapse of Iranian resistance. This belief that a solution could be found through mediation was clear in the invitations for outside powers' involvement issued by Iraq through Tareq Aziz and Sa'adoun Hamadi. Finally breaking his silence, Saddam strengthened these appeals. In the one radio speech he gave on 28 September he alluded to Iraqi military successes and declared, 'We are not taking advantage of our military successes to formulate demands to which we have no right . . . we are asking the Iranian government to legally and virtually recognize our rights.'[5] Although 'our rights' remained vague, only one week after the start of the war it was obvious that he was already seeking a way out of the conflict.

Saddam did not know his enemy. For the believer in revenge not to take into consideration Khomeini's determination to punish him for his military arrogance and for humiliating him by ejecting him from Iraq in 1978 was nothing short of foolish. Khomeini refused to consider any efforts at mediation — to him, what was at stake was the irreducible supremacy of the word of Allah. This too was something that Saddam, the man who had responded to previous Shia religious challenges by claiming descent from Ali, should have taken into consideration. Khomeini was the same stubborn person who had called for his overthrow while in Iraq, and his assumption of power in Iran had hardened rather than softened his resolve. Perhaps, despite Iraq's acceptance of practically all mediation efforts, Saddam was hoping for a different solution, a military one.

According to former Iraqi General Wafic Samarai, the one-time chief of Iraq's Military Intelligence Directorate, Saddam had a weird fascination with the 1967 Six-Day War. He thought he could emulate Israel's defeat of the Arab armies, break Iranian resistance and force Khomeini to sue for peace in a short time.[6] Certainly his air superiority and, despite statements expressing a wish to contain the conflict, the way he committed all of his air force, armour and hundreds of thousands of troops, would support Samarai's allegation. But the reports he had received from expatriate Iranians opposed to Khomeini when he visited King Hussein before the war proved ill-founded, and the Iranian Army facing him was stronger and more united than he had thought. These factors and the geography of Iran (the country is the size of the United States east of the Mississippi) denied Saddam his easy victory. Again, he should have known better.

Except for radio speeches and occasional and unannounced forays to the front, Saddam conducted the start of the war from a bunker underneath the presidential palace. Every single military decision was in his hands, down to platoon level action and the bombing of minor tactical targets. Even his cousin and brother-in-law, Army Chief of Staff Adnan Khairallah, had to defer to him on the smallest matters. He resurfaced from the bunker three weeks later. The mediation efforts were dead or stalled and his blitzkrieg was no more than a figment of his imagination. He had miscalculated on both counts. Taking into account the evidence that America and its Saudi allies had prepared for a lengthy war through manipulating oil production, the issue of the war, how long it would last and how it would be conducted was slipping out of Saddam's hands. It was a case of war being easier to start than to stop. In reality, Saddam had no plan to end it.[7]

In combat, the American-trained Iranian Air Force put up a formidable defence. Their F-4 and F-5 aircraft were superior to anything in Saddam's arsenal, and it was a case of one-on-one aerial dogfights rather than a strategic air war. The Iraqi attacks on the oil-refining centre of Abadan and other cities did considerable damage, but close coordination with ground forces was never successful. Thus failure was the result of Saddam's personal orders: although Iraq had numerical superiority, he feared losing too many aircraft and not being able to replace them for supply or financial reasons. This was the first of the many mistakes which exposed Saddam's subordination of sound military planning to political factors and which were opposed by Iraqi generalship. Furthermore, the Iranians mounted their own air attacks on Iraqi cities with some success.

On the ground, the Iranian Army lacked a command structure because Khomeini had cashiered most of its officers who had been loyal to the Shah. But Iran made up for this deficiency by resorting to its superiority in numbers, tapping its then population of nearly

50 million, at least three times the size of Iraq's. Iran's Revolutionary Guard, Pardsan, made up of young Muslim zealots, supplied tens of thousands of recruits to fight Saddam's armour. Although their training was sub-standard, they made up for it through a willingness to die (and go to heaven) which won the admiration of Iraqi commanders uneasy about the commitment of their own troops. The Iranians did not stop Iraq's advance, but they slowed it down and made its progress costly. This limited the Iraqi penetration of Iran to ten to twenty miles, and for some time made Saddam conceal his casualty figures. Because of the length of the front, the Iraqi Army was dispersed, overstretched and unable to concentrate on achievable targets.

The Iraqi armoured units did achieve one admirable feat: four days after the beginning of the war they crossed the Karun river using a temporary bridge manufactured by Fairey Engineering of the UK. And they succeeded in crossing the river at its widest point, beyond the stretch intended for the bridge. The Iraqis had expanded its length themselves, the first of many examples of the use of Iraqi technical capabilities which were to play an important part in the war. Secretly, under the direct supervision of Saddam, the Iraqis had been successfully working to improve the performance of rockets, planes and tanks and to adapt them for the specific conditions of a war with Iran. Even turning trucks into missile launchers was possible; they converted two hundred of them to this use in the early days of the war.[8]

By early October Iran's second largest city, Abadan, was under siege. This strategic and psychological blow to his enemy confronted Saddam with a military challenge. The Iranian Army and Revolutionary Guard units would not surrender and Saddam had to decide whether to storm the city of one million inhabitants or continue to lay siege to it. Stalin's student had read a great deal about the cost of Germany's assault on Stalingrad in the Second World War, but he still decided to stay with the siege at Abadan. This meant committing a hundred thousand soldiers. On 10 October, Khoramshahr/Mohammara was also under siege and the towns of Dezful, Bustan and Susengard were under attack. In the case of Khoramshahr, Saddam's generals prevailed on him to follow their advice; the Iraqi forces drove past the city, then swung back and hit its defenders from the rear. Khoramshahr fell to Saddam's troops, a handsome victory which he made the most of.

He gave Jordan captured M-60 and Chieftain tanks as a present. The other towns held out.

But the war on the ground, despite Iraqi tactical successes, was going nowhere. Khomeini's response to military reverses was similar to his answers to the various diplomatic initiatives: he would not budge. Furthermore, the Iranian armed forces began to recover their nerve and reorganize themselves in a short time. On 30 October, in a raid aimed at exposing Iraq's vulnerability, Iranian F-4s attacked the nuclear reactor at Ozeirak. They failed to destroy it, but the raid underscored Iraq's inability to destroy Iran's Air Force and ended Saddam's dream of emulating the Six-Day War.

The failure on the battlefield was Saddam's work. There were neither strategic objectives nor sound planning, and Saddam's generals started to become demoralized well before the tide of battle turned against them. His assumption of responsibility for everything was so inclusive that field commanders were very seldom named in news dispatches, but were reduced to 'commander of sector A', 'commander of the central sector' and so on. Saddam forbade even the most imperative of tactical retreats, acted as the link between his Army and Air Force and failed to grasp the need for a military plan to replace what had begun as nothing more than an attempt to punish Khomeini. It was his war and he alone was going to run it in accordance with considerations he kept to himself and which were aimed at making him its hero.

This sudden exposure of Saddam's lack of judgement in unleashing the war and the way he was conducting it coincided with an absence of leadership and direction on the part of his Iraqi opponents. Mulla Mustapha's sons Massoud and Idris had sneaked back into Iraqi Kurdistan in 1979, but their Kurdish followers were tired and could not throw their lot in with Khomeini without having to follow him blindly and suffering the consequences. Jallal Talabani of the Patriotic Union of Kurdistan (PUK) was in pro-Iran Syria, but he did little more than issue condemnations of Saddam's actions. Moreover, mountainous Kurdistan was never a major theatre of battle and, though the Kurds were to suffer considerably later, the more serious fighting of the war was always in the plains of the south. Initially, all Saddam needed to do was to contain the Kurds.

Simultaneously most Shias, though sympathetic to their Iranian

co-religionists in some ways, proved loyal to Iraq. The Dawa Party
was unable to organize a Shia rebellion, even though Mohammed
Bakr Al Hakim was in Tehran presiding over the Supreme Council
for Islamic Revolution in Iraq (SCIRI) and was provided with
substantial Iranian backing. The other opposition groups had no
popular following and, together, all Saddam's opponents could
agree on was that they were opposed to the war.[9] To Saddam's
practical mind that did not matter; he was as contemptuous of
them as Stalin had been of the Pope having no army divisions
behind him.

The failure of the Shias to rise gave Saddam the only victory he
could hope for. The issue of state vs. religion was settled during the
first two months of the war, when a Shia uprising failed to
materialize. Judged by the reasons that Saddam used to justify
the war, he had already won it. But, realizing this, Khomeini was
now set on conquering Iraq rather than 'liberating' it and he was
adamant about the removal of Saddam. Because being conquered
was unpalatable to most Iraqis, even to the majority of the Shias,
this amounted to an Iranian failure to articulate acceptable objectives. Meanwhile, every other country which could influence the
course of the war had a vested interest in seeing it continue.

Saddam grasped what was happening. Like Stalin after the initial
shock of the German attack on the Soviet Union in the Second
World War, Saddam's manifest lack of preparation for a long war
did not stop him from re-emerging to take total control of the
situation. He was aware that he had won the battle of state vs.
religion, and that it turned into an Iran–Iraq War which promised
to last longer than he had anticipated. He acted quickly, with
dazzling deliberateness and on all fronts. His first problem was to
address the internal situation in his country, including the opposition.

Towards his opponents Saddam employed a new carrot-and-
stick policy, that of *tarhib* and *targhid*, or terror and enticement.[10]
Those who wished to rejoin him were amnestied, given their jobs
back or allowed to join the party. Others who refused the enticement or would not commit themselves faced an expanded security
service capable of imprisoning, torturing and murdering them for
'treason'. And 'treason' might be no more than airing a complaint
against Saddam or a member of the party leadership, the former
punishable by death and the latter by lengthy imprisonment. Even

mentioning Saddam's name without affixing a term of respect to it was a treasonable offence.

Simultaneously, he adhered to his maxim of keeping the Iraqis happy by filling their bellies. This much-criticized decision, with dire consequences which were to show starkly after the war ended, came naturally to Saddam. There was no way he could have gone back on the cornerstone of his internal policy. In fact, Saddam gave this maxim a broad interpretation which incorporated the new situation created by the war. Officers who showed a measure of heroism were presented with watches, naturally with Saddam's picture on the dial. Senior officers were rewarded with cars, and the families of martyred soldiers and civilians were accorded priority in housing. Instead of declining, Iraq's imports rocketed.

These two decisions in place, Saddam reverted to his old self and organized the country to meet the new situation in his usual methodical way.[11] Every Iraqi civilian was given a role and government organizations had managerial roles which harnessed the energy of individual Iraqis. For example, local party branches were put in charge of civil defence, a special department to fight crime was created[12] and the Iraqi Women's Federation organized rallies to celebrate the victories of the brave Iraqi Army. After this Saddam moved to expand the armed forces, including the People's Army. No fewer than four hundred thousand people were added to the ranks.

Using every Iraqi in the war effort while keeping the country on a peacetime economic footing and totally refusing to accept any aspect of a wartime economy created an illusion of normality. But labour shortages surfaced immediately and created a serious problem. Once again, the organizer in Saddam was equal to the task. Iraqi women were 'inducted' into the labour force. Some worked in small factories, others in government offices and yet others in farming, office cleaning and other menial jobs.

Overall, maintaining this economic policy was made possible through using the Iraqi reserves of $35 billion[13] and the grants given him by the oil-producing Arab states (the figure for this is disputed – anywhere from £15 billion to £30 billion). This Arab closeness was augmented by Saddam's decision to complement the use of Iraqi women by importing more labour from the poorer Arab countries, in particular Egypt, Yemen and Jordan. Once again Saddam devoted considerable time to accommodating non-Iraqi Arabs, in this case hundreds of thousands of people, which he used to make an implicit bid for popularity in the souks and the streets of the Arab world. With the government-controlled media relentlessly comparing him to the Arab conqueror Sa'ad Ibn Al Waqqas, he opened the doors for non-Iraqi Arabs to join his armed forces. Despite the limited number who responded to his call, it was a gesture with far-reaching implications.

With fighting raging across the plains of southern Iran, Saddam followed his internal moves by addressing himself to the rest of the Arab countries. He wanted to turn the honeymoon with their governments, which had begun in the conspiracies with Jordan, Saudi Arabia and possibly other Arab countries, into a substitute for the quick victory which had eluded him. Unlike the military campaign against Iran, this mainly propaganda effort was successful. He was always a much better propagandist than he was a military strategist.

Saddam began by redefining the Ba'ath Party in a way acceptable to the rest of the Arab governments. To him the Ba'ath was 'the soul of the nation'.[14] The war he was conducting against Iran was a second Qadisiya, the battle of AD 636 against the Persians which the Arabs won. In fact, what was taking place was a repeat of the historic Muslim Arab confrontation with the Zoroastrian Persians, known as the Magus. Saddam's ability to coin slogans was of the same standard as his organizational ability, and the struggle with Iran was aimed at 'reawakening the Arabs'.[15] The Ba'ath commitment to Arab unity was reduced to commitment to a unity through the people's realization of their Arabness.

Songs and poems in praise of Araby were written in support, both by Iraqis and by Arabs from other countries. Television dramas depicting the glorious history of the Arabs were written and produced at an amazing speed. Saddam sponsored this and much more; whatever misgivings existed regarding the war, they were overwhelmed by a countervailing image that Saddam was creating for his misadventure. It was heady stuff, and he showed every sign of enjoying himself to the extent of rapidly superimposing his person on the Arabness of the conflict, which became no more than an extension of the person of Saddam. The other Arab governments, wise to Saddam's moves unlike their people, decided that an Iraqi victory would contribute to his rising fortunes, and to them this was now becoming a source of concern.

The 'second Qadisiya' soon became Saddam's Qadisiya and he depicted himself as greater than Sa'ad Ibn Al Waqqas, the original battle's victorious general. He merged the achievements of the legendary Arab conqueror with those of the benevolent Caliph Haroun Al Rashid. These images of historical Arab figures took precedence over the Assyrian King Sargon, Hamurabi and Nebuchadnezzar, though they too were used and ceased to be distant symbols as they had been in the 1970s. Saddam became their living reincarnation. The latter non-Arab kings were still required for solidifying the resolve of the Iraqis to continue the war, the icing on the cake of a history that Saddam was making them eat. Considerably more than in past times, the object after the start of the war was to make Saddam the representative on earth of dozens of Arab and Iraqi kings and leaders.

Words and images presenting Saddam as one or other of these historical personalities appeared everywhere, naturally in addition to millions of posters depicting him as a tough general carrying a sidearm or a simple Arab in full Bedouin regalia. Moreover, Sadam's pictures, unlike those of other dictators, were unavoidable — they were present on household items, on clocks, and daily on the front page of every newspaper and in the lead story of every television news programme. It was over-kill. Whatever the concerns of the average Iraqi, Saddam appeared in the guise of a historical figure to solve them.

However superficial the propaganda, it worked. With the party expanding until one in eight Iraqis was a member, and the country committed to war, Khomeini's religious appeals sounded more hollow by the day. Members of the Iraqi National Assembly, Saddam's phoney concession to democracy, signed in blood a declaration of allegiance and support.[16] Women were shown on television donating their jewellery to the cause, children sang the praise of the hero-leader before the start of classes, and soon they were joined by teachers and factory and hospital workers. The attempt to recall the past and merge it with the present was so all-encompassing that Saddam increased the budget for the protection of archaeological sites, doubled the intake of the College of Fine Arts and broadened the curriculum of courses teaching cultural heritage.

Furthermore, Saddam very cleverly saw to it that his message reached beyond Iraq to the rest of the Arab world. Many of his exclusive interviews explaining and justifying 'the Arab–Persian conflict' were given to *Al Anba* Kuwaiti newspaper, owned by the influential Marzoug family. Jordanian papers jealously followed suit and asked for (and got) exclusives. In addition the Egyptian writer Amir Iskandar, the Lebanese Fuad Matar, Nicola Firzli and Ali Ballout, all accomplished journalists, were talked into spreading Saddam's message. But however successful Saddam's efforts in organizing the country, keeping his people economically satisfied and creating an image for himself as conquering Arab hero, the long-term consequences of the war were beginning to reveal themselves to knowledgeable observers. These consequences covered everything from the adjustment of the regional structure of the Middle East to the behaviour of members of his family, especially his wife, until his children grew up.

The Iran–Iraq War produced changes in all formal and informal alliances and cooperation agreements throughout the Middle East. These enforced changes took place as soon as the first shot was fired. The earliest manifestations were the use of other countries to front for Iran and Iraq to meet their armament needs. Because the USSR declared an embargo on the sale of arms to both belligerents, the West, except for France, followed suit by declaring a vague embargo on lethal weapons. So buying new arms and replenishing stockpiles became a problem which both sides had to overcome.

In this effort Iraq came out ahead, substantially and importantly. Egypt, ostracized because of the 1978 Camp David peace agreement with Israel, backed Iraq and agreed to help it acquire spare parts for Russian military hardware. Egypt was switching to American-made equipment, and President Anwar Sadat was willing to cannibalize his old Communist-made tanks and planes (T-72s and Mig-21s and Mig-23s) and sell them to Iraq. Beyond expecting Iraqi help in ending its isolation from the other Arab countries, the Egyptian leadership was confronted by a growing Islamic fundamentalist movement at home which received both direct and indirect assistance from Khomeini.

Jordan too acted as a supplier of military equipment to Iraq. First, more Jordanian officers were seconded to the Iraqi Army to help it determine its needs in the West. Secondly, King Hussein had connections with Amman-based international arms dealers who were willing to assist Iraq to meet its requirements from the West – and, except for the USSR, the East too. The task of the arms merchants was made easier because King Hussein provided them with end user certificates, documents which claimed that Jordan was the buyer and final destination. Though many supplier countries knew this was a sham, they still accepted the certificates as a legal way of circumventing the embargo. Italy used Jordan to sell Iraq recoilless guns and South Africa, anxious to gain support against its international isolation, followed suit and sold Iraq 130mm ammunition. Jordan became Iraq's major arms channel.

Saudi Arabia was not far behind. Initially it provided Saddam with intelligence information, and later with military hardware. From the onset of the war the Saudis, with American approval, provided Saddam with summaries of Iranian military capability, based on information obtained from the United States.[17] Importantly, they kept Saddam up to date on the arms flow to Iran. From 1981 the AWACS surveillance planes, leased to Saudi Arabia by the USA but operated by Americans, provided information on Iranian troops and naval movements. Moreover, the Saudis shipped howitzers, 130mm artillery shells and other arms to Iraq, even at a very late stage of the war. As expected, Kuwait followed Saudi Arabia and provided all it could, as did the small states of the lower Gulf. Some did no more than allow Saddam to use their harbour facilities and provide him with the cover of their end user certificates, two elements which grew in importance as the war ground on.

Iran could not equal Saddam's list of countries willing to front for him in the arms procurement field. The two Middle East countries which sided with Iran, Syria and Libya, were less acceptable in the West than Saddam's backers. Both had been accused of supporting terrorism, and their support for Iran made them even more unacceptable. Furthermore, in practical terms neither country had experience with Western military hardware or spare parts, which Iran needed. Both had depended on the Eastern Bloc for their armaments, and it took a great deal of time for the Iranians to acquaint themselves with Communist-made equipment. Neither country had sophisticated arms dealers such as those headquartered in Amman and Saudi Arabia. Syria intermittently closed the Iraqi oil pipeline to the Mediterranean, and did so in a final way in May 1982, but the long-term economic effect of that action had been anticipated. Saudi Arabia and Kuwait were producing oil in the Neutral Zone between their two countries (an entity set up as part of the post First World War Sykes–Picot Agreement) and giving it to Iraq to sell, so that closing the pipeline caused little dislocation.

The one country in a position to come to the aid of Iran was Israel. Because Khomeini was religiously bound to liberate Jerusalem in the name of Islam, and had made declarations to that effect on several occasions, the Iranians were in a bind. However, emulating Saddam, they placed military need ahead of ideology when shortages became acute. The intensity of the fighting and the consequent rapid use of ammunition forced Iran to accept Israel's secret offers of help. The Israelis had set aside Khomeini's pronouncements and sold Iran F-4 aircraft and spare parts in 1980, shortly after the start of the war. This was done with the knowledge of the United States.[18]

The supply contracts between America and Israel stipulated that the manufacturing country must approve the transfer of the arms in question. But even if Israel had acted on its own, as some writers allege, the Israeli supply operation was too large to be carried out without US knowledge. In 1981, despite the fact that the United States ostensibly wanted the flow of arms to Iran to stop (beginning in 1982, the move to block arms to Iran was called Operation Staunch), Israel sold Iran $100 million worth of military hardware.[19] The evidence is clear: the United States was indirectly supplying both sides with arms.

In fact, the USA was opposed to a quick Iraqi victory,[20] or to enough of an Iraqi military success to force Khomeini to the negotiating table. Moreover, America used the preoccupation of Iraq with the war, and Saddam's inability to respond to its actions except in a subdued way, to intercept his atomic programme. On 7 June 1981 Israeli F-4 aircraft flew over Saudi Arabia, managing to avoid detection by the AWACS surveillance aircraft leased to the Saudis by America, and destroyed the Iraqi atomic reactor at Ozeirak. There is evidence that CIA director William Casey supplied the Israelis with photographs of the atomic facility.[21]

Saddam was furious – according to a former aide, 'hopping mad' – but he could not do anything. He did not even issue a condemnation of America. The Saudis feigned anger, particularly because the Israeli planes had violated their air space, and King

Khalid offered Iraq funds to rebuild the reactor. Meanwhile communications with the USA continued, at the United Nations, between Sa'adoun Hamadi and Assistant Secretary of State Morris Draper. Among other things, the two discussed the restoration of diplomatic relations, severed since the 1967 War, and Iraq wanted to be taken off the list of states named as sponsoring terror. Saddam's room for manoeuvre was growing smaller and smaller.

In fact, the apparent American cynicism was true of all the outside powers involved in supplying arms to maintain the belligerents' capability to fight. Egyptian political considerations aside, the rest of the Arab countries used the war to avoid or delay the threats posed by both combatant countries, the explicit Iranian one of by-passing governments and appealing directly to their people and the implicit Iraqi claim to Arab leadership. While Syria and Libya believed they needed Khomeini to confront Israel and considered Saddam an obstacle, the other countries which ostensibly lined up behind Saddam had other things on their minds. Though fear of Iran came first, Saddam's reassurances and manifestations of amity were never totally accepted by them. They wanted him contained, through using Iraq to fight Iran. In fact, their fear of Saddam manifested itself in a clear and vital way.

In January 1981, in the middle of the stalemate in the fighting, Saudi Arabia, Bahrain, Kuwait, Oman, the United Arab Emirates and Qatar announced the formation of the Gulf Cooperation Council (GCC). This new political and economic alliance was nothing more than a rich countries' club with a special relationship with the West that separated it from the rest of the Middle East. The GCC's two main aims were to protect member countries against outside threats and internal uprisings. Iran and Iraq were excluded from the alliance and identified as sources of danger to the new political grouping, which was headed by Saudi Arabia.

Excluding Iran, a non-Arab country, was not the same as excluding Iraq. Saddam had wanted to join this regional alliance and Iraq had attended a preliminary meeting in Oman in early 1979.[22] Ironically, the idea had been discussed between Saddam and Kuwaiti Crown Prince Sa'ad Bin Abdallah in April 1980, when the latter paid an official and highly publicized visit to Baghdad. Furthermore, Kuwait had advocated including Iraq in the GCC[23] because it was the country most threatened by Saddam's growing strength.

But now Saddam had to accede to what was happening.[24] The GCC's member countries had not dared create the alliance without Iraq until Saddam had started his war with Iran, so that he was no longer a military threat and was dependent on them for financial support. Meanwhile, they offered him dollars and empty words to compensate for Iraq's growing isolation. The press in these countries, expressing the positions of their governments, were full of praise for 'the courageous Arab hero'. The Saudi Minister of the Interior, Prince Nayyef, declared, 'You're protecting the Arab nation.' Crown Prince Fahd made a clearer statement and cabled Saddam, 'We're with you every step of the way.'[25] And in July 1981 Saudi Arabia approved the building of an Iraqi pipeline to carry oil through its territory. Everyone was making sure that Iranian and Iraqi blood would continue to be shed.

By the beginning of 1981 it was becoming evident that any further military advance in Iran was beyond Saddam's capabilities, even if he had a military objective. His armed forces were at their peak in terms of numbers and the quality of their military equipment, but geography, Iranian resistance and lack of plans stopped them. Meanwhile, Iran was improving its military command structure and continuing to field more people. More importantly, the economic situation in Iraq was deteriorating very fast. Iraqi oil income declined from £26 billion in 1980 to £10.6 billion in 1981, a year which saw imports soar to £21.6 billion.[26] The military and economic situations produced a further need for Arab and outside support and were determining Saddam's policies as never before.

Despite his extensive programme to reward 'heroes' and the families of dead soldiers, the mounting Iraqi losses were beginning to demoralize Saddam's forces.[27] Furthermore, though Iranian counter-attacks in early 1981 were limited they were also successful, pushing the Iraqis back a few miles and stablizing the line between them. From March the Iraqis were on the defensive. Saddam responded by sending missiles against Iranian cities. In 1981 there were sixteen such attacks, and the number increased in 1982. Some writers[28] claim that two of the 1981 strikes involved the use of chemicals, in violation of the 1899 Hague and 1925 Geneva Conventions, but this has never been satisfactorily verified for that year, though Saddam certainly used them later. What is easy to verify is Saddam's resort to executing officers who complained, disobeyed orders or exhibited cowardice. Fifty-five officers were executed in 1981, including senior officers Muwafeq Jabbouri, Adnan Musawi and Naqib Muludes.[29] There were no trials: Saddam acted on the notion of 'treasonable behaviour'. These actions only added to the Army's demoralization.

Conditions were also deteriorating inside the country. There were already 208,000 people in the employ of the security apparatus and the presidential office – more than 15 per cent of all government employees.[30] Saddam expanded both offices and kept the numbers secret. His brother Barazan headed the dreaded *mukhabarat* branch of security and expanded its functions. A sign of insecurity over what was happening, Barazan used what amounted to a mobile office – he changed his headquarters regularly, perhaps once a month.[31] This, however, did not prevent the Dawa undertaking an assassination attempt against Minister of Information Latif Nassif Jassem on 12 April 1982. Saddam hit back by imprisoning hundreds of Shias, and many were never seen again. Nor did he limit himself to the perpetrators; soon afterwards, 140 members of the Patriotic Union of Kurdistan (PUK) in Abu Ghraib prison were executed.[32] Overall, 1981 and 1982 saw the execution of over three thousand civilians.[33]

In March 1982 Saddam was to carry out what has become one of the most widely reported and notorious acts of his life. He personally killed his Minister of Health, Riyadh Ibrahim, in the middle of a cabinet meeting. Saddam called Ibrahim out of the meeting, ostensibly to discuss a private matter, took him to the waiting room, shot him dead and returned to preside over the cabinet as if nothing had happened. While all this is true, the reported reason for the murder, that Ibrahim asked Saddam temporarily to step aside in favour of Bakr to facilitate negotiating peace with Iran, is not – a man who could speak in this way to Saddam would never have been appointed to the cabinet in the first place.

By chance, and not from any official source, I am privy to the real reason for Ibrahim's execution. While Saddam was preoccupied with playing general, the one-time adherence to anti-corruption Laws 8 and 52 had become a thing of the past and profiteering was rampant. Ibrahim had a business associate in the

W2 postal district of London who was supplying the Iraqi Army with medical equipment and sharing his commission with the minister. This greedy man, who had the initials A-M. F., supplied the Ministry of Health with many items including out-of-date penicillin, which resulted in the deaths of dozens of soldiers. When the news reached Saddam, he had no problem in personally acting on it. The source of this story is the death merchant himself, and while nothing could conceivably excuse Saddam's assumption of the roles of judge, jury and executioner, it does shed light on this notorious incident.

The disappearance of all legal constraints, which allowed Saddam to execute generals and others, the imprisoning and killing of hundreds and the spread of wartime corruption was matched by a removal of all inhibitions on personal behaviour by members of Saddam's family. The most obvious signs of the family's growing degeneracy came from Saddam's wife and his father-in-law. Very early in 1981 Sajida secretly visited London with an entourage of twenty. The reports on this trip are sketchy, but Mrs Hussein appears to have spent millions shopping. She is reputed to have paid several visits to Hermès in Bond Street.

But it was Sajida's trip to America which gave the world a picture of how far things had declined from the golden days of the mid-1970s. In March 1981 she arrived in New York in a private Boeing-747 owned by the Iraqi government in the company of her cousin and future son-in-law Hussein Kamel and an entourage of thirty.[34] This time she fell in love with Bloomingdale's department store and spent more millions of dollars there. While she was in New York, Saddam telephoned her every day to check on how she was doing.[35] In an act which reveals the divisions in his mind between commitment to his programmes and the personal corruption consuming his immediate relations, Saddam had authorized Hussein Kamel to use the trip to establish contacts with American businesses. The latter did establish contacts with a company by the name of American Steel, which, though not in the armaments business, was prevailed on to front for Iraq in buying ammunition from Brazil and other countries.[36]

In Baghdad, during his last days as Governor of the capital's province, Sajida's father, the infamous Khairallah Tulfah, was setting up more and more companies to capitalize on the war economy. Khairallah, who always fancied himself as a writer, was also given free rein to express himself in the national press. Among the gems produced by him during that period was a statement about the three things Allah should not have created, 'Persians, Jews and Flies'.[37] It was a period of corruption from which the family would never recover, Saddam's son, the infamous Udday, grew up in the shadow of Sajida and his grandfather.

The early pattern of the war continued until the middle of 1982. In May, the Iranians reoccupied Khoramshahr in a human wave assault which the Iraqis could not repel, and during which ten to fifteen thousand Iraqi soldiers were taken prisoner.[38] Saddam could think of nothing to do except blame his senior army officers and several more were executed,[39] including General Saleh Qadi and Brigadier Jawad Assad. As this defeat occurred when US help to Iraq was increasing, it needs to be explained in terms of the secret and open cooperation between the United States and Iraq.

In April 1981, Secretary of State Alexander Haig openly praised Saddam for his understanding of the USSR's threat to the Middle East.[40] That year the United States stepped up its supply of food to Iraq, and the number of Iraqi students in the United States on government grants trebled. Simultaneously, Iraqi pilots carrying Jordanian passports began training in the USA.[41] On 24 April, as if in coordination with Haig and in justification of the emerging cooperation between the two countries, the *Wall Street Journal* declared in favour of Saddam because Iraq believed in 'Western values and technology'. Soon afterwards, the United States approved the sale of the new B-747s which had been requested in 1980. Tom Twitten, the CIA chief stationed in Amman, became a frequent visitor to Baghdad and had access to Iraqi officialdom. In March 1982, there were reports that William (Bill) Casey, head of the CIA, visited Baghdad[42] and there was a marked increase in the American intelligence data reaching Iraq.[43]

These reflections of an increasing American tilt towards Iraq dramatized the Iranian victory in Khoramshahr and smaller military achievements and generated fear of an Iraqi collapse beyond US control. When Iraq's second largest city, Basra, came under fire a week after the retaking of Khoramshahr, it was Saddam and only Saddam who kept his head. He acted on several fronts and with his usual speed. In June 1982, Saddam gave Turkey the green light to invade northern Iraq and put down a budding rebellion by the

Kurds, who had finally organized themselves enough to try to take advantage of Saddam's predicament. And he initiated moves on the regional and American fronts to divert attention from his critical military situation and earn yet greater US support.

On 3 June a Palestinian gunman shot and wounded the Israeli Ambassador to the UK, Shlomo Argov. On the 5th Saddam, anticipating a major Israeli retaliatory attack on the Palestinians in Lebanon, announced a total Iraqi withdrawal from Iran and appealed to Khomeini to order a stop to the fighting and to join him in facing the common Israeli enemy. Most writers have claimed that the Argov assassination attempt was organized by Saddam as a diversionary move[44] in anticipation of the Israeli response. This remains the general perception of the incident and of the hard-to-resist appeal to Khomeini which followed it.

However extensive research has not uncovered anything to support this thesis, and certainly a terrorist act which put the Americans in a difficult predicament after Israel invaded Lebanon on 6 June would have been noted and acted upon by the Reagan administration. The evidence is against an elaborate plot by Saddam, but he did act on this God-sent, unexpected event which gave him the needed cover to listen to his generals and withdrew from Iran. Among other things, Saddam the supreme organizer was too methodical to depend on the terrorist Abu Nidal to shoot Argov and he could not have predicted the Israeli reaction with certainty. Although the meaning of major strategic decisions occasionally eluded him and exposed his lack of education, he seldom left the outcome of such operations to chance.

At about this time, I was called on by the Iraqis to help them foster US relations by using official contacts and by presenting Iraq's story to the American people. There was a problem with congressional leaders, who were never as enamoured with Saddam as the Reagan administration and who had called for him to be punished because of his human rights record. Little of what was happening within Iraq was known to me – like the rest of the world, I knew nothing about the execution of army officers and hundreds of civilians, and stories about the use of chemical weapons were suspect. What I did know reduced my choice to acting in one of two ways: refusing the Iraqi offer because of my deep anger over the execution of Hajj Sirri, Hamdani and the rest of the Ba'ath Party command in 1979, or accepting it because I feared a Khomeini victory as much as most of the world did. I took the latter path but, unlike my 1970s work with Dalloul, only with trepidation and voicing my reluctance. This is not to excuse what I did, for it was as callous, short-sighted and unjustifiable as the behaviour of the countries supporting Saddam.

In late June 1982, responding to a request from Saddam's Ministry of Information, I arranged for a team from *Time* magazine to visit Baghdad to interview Saddam. He had not given an extensive interview to Western journalists for some time, *Time* was anxious to delve behind the day-to-day news, and Saddam wanted to transmit a specific picture of Iraq, the status of US–Iraqi relations and what was needed to end the war. Fortunately for Saddam, *Time* dispatched senior editor Murray Gart and correspondent Dean Brelis, an impressive combination who knew the Middle East and the workings of the American government in Washington. Although what Saddam wanted, a *Time* cover story, did not materialize, it was the longest interview that he has ever given anyone, a total of seven hours, and the most revealing in terms of his perceptions of Iraq, the Middle East, US relations and where he personally fitted in the scheme of things. Excerpts from the interview, given on 6 July 1982, are reproduced below: telling the world about Iraq and his achievements during the 1970s was foremost in Saddam's mind.

Iraq has a special character because of the past fourteen years . . . we want people to understand what happened in Iraq . . . the image you have outside doesn't exist . . . ask a taxi driver and people like that . . . it [talking to ordinary people] tells you more about conditions in Iraq . . .

The private sector is very important, alongside the public sector . . . the private sector is flourishing, but we provide financial help with no interest for people to develop their business . . . [we] also do the same for agriculture, otherwise we will have big ownership [of land] . . . collective farms was a Soviet mistake . . . pure socialism doesn't take into consideration the problem of acceptance . . .

I went to a collective . . . the people asked that it be stopped . . . I agreed, cancelled collectives . . . told them if the party man insists [refuses to obey] handcuff him and send him away . . . the incident was televised . . . people became aware of the general conditions I corrected . . .

In the past, we depended on ministers, on leadership without technical efficiency, but now that traditions and ideas [as to what to do] are clear, we need technicians . . .

A party member is no different from any other citizen . . . Have you gone to popular parts of Baghdad? . . . Enter their [the people's] houses and see whether they love the regime or not . . . nobody can force them to put Saddam's picture up . . . Iraq is entering a new age of democracy . . . Dawa followed Khomeini . . . depended on his ideas. . . . The strength of a party is not in numbers . . . is Dawa capable of closing shops and organizing demonstrations? No, their effective action is tactical, not strategic . . . Dawa does not represent a danger . . . if a party is only two hundred but it acts [it is effective] then it is successful . . .

We have built hospitals in Kerbala and Najjaf . . . churches in the north . . . the people have changed the name of Al Thawra [Revolution] City to Saddam City . . . We are building schools and theatres . . . Haifa Street is the biggest [housing] construction project in the world . . . we will have to move the British Embassy [in the process of building] . . . sixty to eighty thousand people will live there . . . [the works of] artists will be everywhere . . .

When Gart and Brelis started making their excuses to leave because it was Ramadan, the President was fasting and they had been there for three hours, Saddam insisted that they stay and asked them if there was more they wished to see. After personally driving the journalists to a building constructed to accommodate a meeting of the Non-Aligned Nations Conference, with a dozen cars full of security people trying to catch up with this impromptu gesture, Saddam continued with the interview. He pointed out the murals on the walls of the huge building:

I don't like to stay put . . . yes [I move a lot] . . . This [pointing to a mural] is the story of Aladdin and forty thieves . . . fishing without getting the fish . . . how many people know it happened in Iraq . . . I grew up on this story, like American children. [But] do they realize the story came from Iraq? Like the hanging gardens of Babylon . . . Iraq is old and new. . . This is the cinema hall, I don't like it [because] it is without our heritage . . .

According to Gart, and unrecorded on the audiotape in my possession, Saddam followed up the tour of the impressive conference hall with visits to a Shia mosque, a shop, the house of a woman who hailed him when she recognized him and the spot in Rashid Street where he had tried to shoot Kassem in 1959. In the Shia mosque he opened his hands and offered a prayer and the people there, surprised to see the President, applauded and cheered him. By the time he crossed the street and entered the grocery store, the security people and the translator had caught up with him. The shop owner was frightened but managed to offer an effusive greeting. Saddam reached over to one of the shelves, picked out a can of foods and suddenly addressed the owner with some agitation. Although the translator was at first reluctant to tell Murray Gart what had happened, he eventually relented: 'You see, the tin had one month of shelf-life left. The president told the shop owner to sell it before the expiry date, otherwise he would have to throw it away. If he doesn't then the president would take his head off.' Gart and Brelis remembered this without taking notes.

Later Saddam bought watermelon and, when a woman saw him at the stand and spoke words of singular esteem, he followed her into her house in the presence of the correspondents. She offered them tea, asked Allah to prolong Saddam's life and, by the sound of her, made known her admiration and love for the hero-President. However contrived it may seem now, the exchange between Saddam and the woman was too choppy to have been set up in advance.

At the site of the assassination attempt against Kassem, Saddam was in his element. Walking jauntily and gesturing, he went into details of who the assassins were (without a word of what happened to them later), repeated what he had told his biographers and gave a graphic account of how he had escaped and the aftermath. To both corespondents, it was obvious that Saddam viewed his participation in the assassination attempt as a formative event.

Earlier, in the main body of the long interview, Saddam had devoted considerable time to discussing the war with Iran and his relations with the United States, the USSR and the Arab countries. It was obvious from his comments that he lumped the United States

and Israel together, believing Israel's actions to be totally dependent on what America approved.

> Every month that passes confirms the correctness of our decision
> [to start the war with Iran] . . . Had there been any way to avoid
> it we would have been wrong, but there wasn't . . . We had to
> maintain the independence and dignity of Iraq, it would have
> been shameful not to fight . . . They started a war against us on a
> large scale . . . We took away their arrogance . . .
>   Khomeini is superficial . . . he has no logic . . . We're stronger
> than they are . . . US allies and US intelligence played a special
> role to help Iran with military contracts, not government to
> government, but indirectly . . . you made a deal on the hostages
> which involved [giving time] credit and [fulfilling] previous
> military contracts. [the Regan administration had by this date
> secured the release of American hostages held in Iran in February
> 1981, but the Iran–Contra affair had not yet started]
>   Peace is possible to achieve . . . when Iran realizes [that it is
> possible to achieve it] . . . We want peace with Iran, this or any
> [other] regime . . . We will not interfere in their internal affairs
> . . . Khomeini thinks he destroyed Baghdad [loud laughter] . . .
>   Yes, our policy of guns and butter . . . we have to do it . . . they
> are trying to stop it . . . if they achieve this [a change in our
> policy] then they [will] have succeeded . . . Iraqis will not tire of
> the war with Iran, even if it were [to last] ninety years. . . [At
> stake] is the stability of our country and our way . . . I was the
> first to ask for peace, on 28 September 1980 . . .

When the interview turned to the other Arab countries, Saddam
reflected pride in Iraq and a wish to avoid alienating the rest of the
Arabs. 'Syria [the one Arab country most opposed to Saddam] has
its aims . . . they are hostile . . . the battle is on Iraq's shoulders,
militarily and financially . . .'
Referring to financial support from the Arab oil-producing
countries, mainly Kuwait and Saudi Arabia, he said:

> What we have taken are loans . . . we will pay them . . . I can't
> tell you the figure . . . Bankruptcy [due to the war and the guns-
> and-butter policy] is not on . . . there are priorities, we'll stop
> development projects, if we need to . . .

> All Arabs are the same . . . foreigners too [are the same] when they aggress against the Arabs.

Saddam was trying to say that the Arabs have a common identity as witnessed by the common attitude that foreigners hold towards them.

Afterwards Saddam was asked about a Saudi initiative, the Fahd Plan, to end the Arab–Israeli conflict. Presented in final form in 1982, it was one of the first such Arab plans to accept UN resolutions as a basis for ending the conflict. 'The Saudi initiative is private . . . we favour it with minor adjustments . . . We favour what the Palestinians accept.'

The final and most extensive part of the interview concerned relations with the USSR, USA and Israel, and some comments about Iraq's nuclear programme. The USSR, concerned about developments on the battlefield, had just announced its resumption of arms shipments to Iraq.

> Iraq is close to the Soviet Union . . . the Soviet Union said frankly that they are interested in preserving Iraq . . . the Soviet Union itself is not involved, but Soviet arms reach Iran . . .
>
> I have nothing personal against the US . . . There are no relations [diplomatic] with the US . . . we want relations with the US, good [relations] . . . The position of the US regarding Arabs and Iraq is [no longer] hostile . . . until now it was hostile . . .
>
> We have a special stand in implementing politics [restoring diplomatic relations] . . . all steps [must be taken] in a clean and clear atmosphere . . . we are not weak, we're not begging, when the time comes we'll restore relations . . . it is on the agenda, it is unnatural not to have relations with one of the superpowers . . .
>
> My advice to Reagan regarding his Middle East policy is don't accept Israel's stick or use of the big stick . . . don't exaggerate Israel's strategic importance . . . the Arabs will continue to develop . . . our [military] quality is greater than in 1967, the competence of [our] fighters is different . . . the US should not use Israel as a club against us . . . it would lose in the long term . . .
>
> You tell me how Iran gets satellite pictures? . . . No, I have no information regarding the Soviets providing them [to Iran] . . .

Saddam's mother, Subha Tulfah Al Musallat. Her first husband, Saddam's father, disappeared before the birth of her son, and not long after she married Hassan Ibrahim.

ie young Saddam in the
e 1950s, the early days
his Ba'ath Socialist Party
embership.

Major General Abdel Karim Kassem, Iraqi leader (1958–63) and target of Saddam's failed assassination attempt in 1959

Saddam (ringed) with fellow Iraqis in exile in Cairo, 1960.

Robert Anderson, US Secretary of the Treasury under Eisenhower. He supposedly acted as intermediary between the United States and the Ba'ath Party in the 1968 overthrow of General Abdel Rahman Aref's government.

...addam with General Ahmad Hassan Al Bakr, his political mentor and predecessor ...s president, with an unknown officer in the background.

At the front in February 1983, as the Iran–Iraq conflict enters its third year.

Ayatollah Ruhollah Khomeini, leader of Iran from 1979 until his death in 1989. His rule covered the inconclusive eight-year war with Saddam.

ith Qussay Saddam Hussein, Saddam's younger son and most likely successor as
esident.

ddam's family. He later had his sons-in-law, Hussein Kamel and Saddam Kamel,
anding on the left, executed.

Saddam with King Hussein of Jordan and President Hosni Mubarak of Egypt, at a meeting of heads of state of the Arab Co-operation Council in Baghdad.

At the front in Kuwait, October 1990, inspecting Iraqi armed forces. Several hours later the United Nations issued a deadline for Iraq to withdraw from Kuwait.

...ssing the Koran. Saddam sways towards Islam to pre-empt opposition political parties.

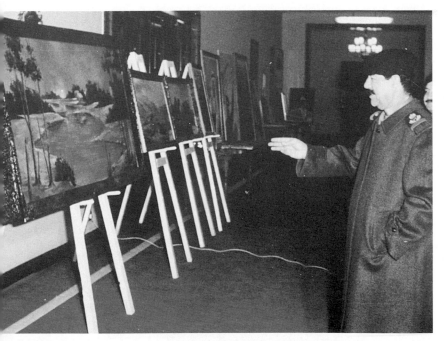

...a painting contest on the theme of the Shat Al Arab waterway, in south-eastern Iraq.

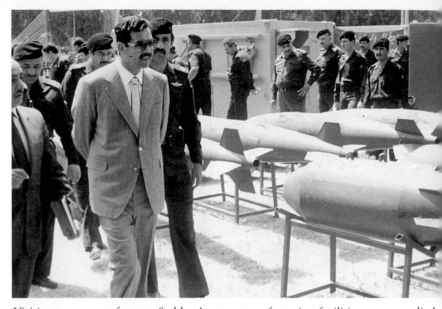

Visiting a weapons factory. Saddam's arms manufacturing facilities were supplied largely by the West.

On a visit to the northern town of Salahuddin. Saddam's hats – not a traditional Arab trait – are all lined with Kavlar bullet-proofing.

Suddenly Saddam stopped halfway and refused to complete what he had started – an accusation that the USA was providing Iran with satellite pictures.

> I don't know . . . it is probably third parties . . .
>
> Encirclement of Beirut [the Israeli invasion of 1982 in response to the Argov assassination attempt] will produce more long-term effects . . . contrary to this dirty operation . . . [When it comes to that] . . . we've always been with Arabs against foreigners . . . you must increase cooperation and respect the rights of the Arabs to choose their own course, independence and dignity . . . if we have a relationship of mutual respect, then commercial exchanges increase . . . there are commodities and technology which the US alone possesses . . .
>
> We have signed the nuclear non-proliferation treaty . . . we shall try to buy more than one [reactor] . . . we shall try to continue our programme . . . this is our right . . . we accept international supervision . . . but relations with the suppliers continue . . .

Then, towards the end of the formal interview in his office, he delivered the shortest and most telling line of them all: 'If the two superpowers wanted to stop the war, they could have.' Saddam knew that he had started something which was beyond his control, that he was nothing more than a pawn in a game of international power politics.

The interview, in abbreviated form, appeared in *Time* magazine on 19 July 1982. Soon afterwards I was dispatched to Washington to explore further Iraqi moves aimed at enhancing the image that the *Time* story had created, above all that Iraq was not a socialist country. Among my most important briefs was to look into the opening of a service office by an American bank in Baghdad, a confirmation of Saddam's capitalist inclinations. During my investigations I met with former Secretary of the Treasury and Federal Reserve Chairman William (Bill) Miller. There was considerable interest by American banks and I nominated the Mellon Bank; however, the Iraqis did not adopt this recommendation. Furthermore, there was no shortage of people in Washington willing to advise me on how to improve the overall Iraqi image, to offer me their understanding of the current military situation, to stress the importance of restoring diplomatic relations, and much more. The Americans knew I was working with Iraq and wanted to help. On the other side, I was led to believe that my reports received Saddam's personal attention.

Soon after my Washington junket, the Iraqi Establishment of Television and Cinema (IETC) transmitted a request to me which reflected the division between high policy and the pettiness of personal aggrandizement which was always part of Saddam's thinking. IETC had made a feature film starring the British actor Oliver Reed and a six-hour documentary of Saddam's fictionalized biography *The Long Days*, but the head of IETC wanted a film director of major standing to do the final editing and to make the documentary of 'international standards that would prompt other countries to air a film of the life of the hero-president'. This absurd request originated with Saddam; there was no one to tell him that other countries' television companies had no interest in airing a six-hour romanticized version of his life. Saddam had a relatively clear idea of how to deal with the USA, but his self-image was so inflated as to be laughable.

I travelled to Baghdad in the company of Terence Young, an established director who had made the first two James Bond films and whose reputation was known to the Iraqis. Irish, elegant and with the gift of the gab, Young was a hit in Baghdad and we had meetings with a number of important people including Dr Samarai, the director of IETC, and Dr Latif Nassif Jassem, the Minister of Information. I kept looking for signs that Iraqi officialdom viewed the request with misgivings, but there were none. Right in the middle of the war, they were devoting considerable time and energy to promoting the image that Saddam had created for himself.

The day before Young returned to London, Dr Samarai asked him to talk to the IETC employees about his plans for *The Long Days*. The small cinema there was so full that I had to stand in the back. Young gave an impressive speech: 'Why not, the Iraqis have a great story to tell, how their glorious history merges with the personality of their President. Everybody in the whole wide world wants to know more about the President and his incredible achievements and how he is standing up to the devil in Tehran.'

Taking a deep breath and speaking with emphasis, Young concluded with one of the most ridiculous comments I have ever heard: 'My friends, this is a great day for Irish–Arab relations.' He got a standing ovation.

Saddam had reduced life to farce. The film was completed and shown, but only in Iraq, and Young was paid handsomely. Saddam was played by a Tikriti cousin, look-alike and future son-in-law, Saddam Kamel, whose fate will be detailed later.

A month after the film episode, in December 1982, a weary Saddam summoned an Arab journalist who had acted as a go-between with the USA, performing similar duties to mine. The journalist had written a report recommending the establishment of an Iraqi office in Washington DC to liaise with the centres of power there, particularly Saddam's opponents in Congress, which the Iraqis eventually did with considerable success after the re-establishment of diplomatic relations in 1984. The report had gone to the Iraqi Foreign Ministry and from there to Saddam, who was intrigued enough to want to know more. The journalist had been told of the reason for the summons from Saddam.

This is a summary of the journalist's recollections.

He sat on a couch, asked me to sit opposite him and told me to speak clearly. He clasped his hands around his middle in the manner we have seen in many pictures – it obviously comes naturally to him. I had met him once before, but very briefly, and was a little nervous. There was no idle talk, no Arab expressions of welcome, no offers of tea or coffee, but he was there and there was no mistaking the power he emitted – not charm but power. He plunged into the issue right away, he told me that he had my report, appreciated its contents and wanted to know more. What he wanted was an explanation of the American governmental system of checks and balances.

I told him it was complex and it would take a long time to explain. He looked at me with steely narrow eyes and said he had time and hoped I did as well. It took me about fifty-five minutes to go through a rough sketch of the system. He never missed a beat, but there was something strange. He never stopped me at the point where he wanted to clarify something; he always waited half a minute or so and then asked the question. He was trying to determine whether I was telling the truth – the conspirator in the man is not far below the surface. When I finished, he made as if he were sighing then looked at me and asked me to tell him which branch of the American government he should work with. When I told him that there was no option but to work with the executive branch, he shot back, 'But they lie to us all the time.' With that he ended the meeting. I had to walk backward to get out of his office – it was like an audience with a king. But there is little doubt about it, the Americans had managed to confuse him.

Saddam's expression of concern about US policy towards him was justified. Contrary to common belief, the American support was never open-ended and was always accompanied with moves to balance the picture. Despite the resumption of arms shipments to Iraq from the USSR, Saddam always believed that the key to peace with Iran lay in America's hands and that, for the most part, it depended on an American willingness to stop its client states in the Middle East from pumping enough oil to compensate for the decrease in Iraqi and Iranian production. To him, only an oil shortage and consequent need for Iraq's oil would prompt the West to force peace on both sides.

But the USA, with Saudi Arabia in tow, never made any moves in that direction. In December 1982, while Saddam was at a loss about how to gain full American support, the State Department approved the sale of sixty Hughes helicopters to Iraq. Ostensibly they were for use in agriculture, but everybody knew that converting them to military use was within Iraq's capability. During this period, Mobil Oil Company was exploring for oil below Baghdad, with the blessing of the hero of nationalization. Mobil came out with a report that Baghdad East was floating on a sea of oil, something that the Iraqis had always claimed and the rest of the world consistently dismissed. But the implicit offer to the Americans to lift Iraqi oil led nowhere. Because an oil glut had been engineered by Saudi Arabia from 1978,[45] the Americans were not ready to go further than assessing Iraqi reserves, with the exception of leaning on Turkey to allow Iraq to build a pipeline through its territory to compensate for the closure of the one across pro-Iranian Syria.

Once again, in late 1982, the United States appears to have been determined to maintain a balance between Iraq and Iran without tilting too far in favour of Iraq. Though the level of activity of its Baghdad CIA station suggested closeness between the two sides, its help to Iraq was selective and changed depending on how the fighting was going. Saddam's frustration drove him to devote his energies to running the war, and his continued insistence on making all decisions suggests he thought his military talents would make a difference.

Meanwhile, the running of the country was placed more and more in the hands of his relations, mostly his half-brothers and Generals Khairallah Tulfah, Ali Hassan, Al Majid, and gradually Hussein Kamel (Sajida's New York companion) and his actor brother Saddam. The most serious attempt to assassinate Saddam took place some time during this period, though the exact date is unknown. Highly organized, it took place while he was visiting the town of Dujail in the Balad district of Iraq. In the ambush, which lasted over two hours, several of Saddam's companions and eight of the attackers were killed. A few days later the whole of Dujail was razed and its inhabitants relocated to a new town built for them by the government.[46] The assassination attempt was carried out by Dawa assassins, who called it Operation Bint Al Huda after the sister of Imam Mohammed Bakr Al Sadr; both had been executed by Saddam in 1980. The perpetrators were never apprehended, but hundreds of people were arrested and, once again, some of them were never seen again.

This was the end of Saddam the populist, for after Dujail he never made another impromptu visit anywhere. This must have come as a blow to him – by all accounts he truly enjoyed doing so and engaging people in spontaneous conversation. The stalemate in the war, the interest of the regional powers in seeing it continue and the refusal of the superpowers to end it isolated him as a player in the international arena. Developments inside Iraq and the emerging threats to his safety isolated him from his people. There was little he could do about either.

Saddam was left with one outlet for his undoubted mental and physical energies. He ordered a stepping up of his non-conventional weapons programme. Among other efforts, a contract signed in 1981 with Thyssen Rheinstahl Technik to build a laboratory for toxic substances in Salman Pak was being fulfilled[47] and the lethal chemicals Tabun and Sarin were being manufactured in Samara.[48] Obviously Saddam saw the speedy development of chemical and biological weapons as a possible solution to his predicament. He was preparing to unleash a new phase of devastation and destruction on a horrific scale.

9

Illusions of Alliance

The beginning of 1983 provided considerable proof that war without plain or clear objective is the costliest and cruellest of them all. The recapture of Khoramshahr by the Iranians had been a turning point, after which the Iranians were on the offensive. Iranian attacks were mounted, Iraqi defences were strengthened, but movement was slow and the number of dead and wounded, the abstract statistics of human shame, were substituted for military achievement. Because the Iranians resorted to using costly human wave tactics to compensate for an inability to match Iraqi firepower, the Iraqis suffered fewer casualties and could claim they were winning.

Returning from the front after a one-week visit, *Time*'s Dean Brelis told me that the Iranians suffered 'over ten thousand casualties in twenty-four hours'. Nobody seemed to care; certainly the horrific increase in casualties produced no concrete efforts to end the conflict, just more empty appeals with nothing to back them. The only real manifestations of outside interest consisted of both secret and open attempts at guaranteeing a stalemate. My shameful personal experience attests to that.

In January 1983, a well known and well connected English businessman invited me to lunch at the Arts Club in London's Dover Street. I found him in the company of a distinguished-looking elderly but alert gentleman, impeccably dressed and full of old-fashioned graces. The guest was introduced as Marshal of the Royal Air Force Sir ————, former chief of the RAF. In introducing us, our host exaggerated my importance in Iraq and asked his other guest to tell me the purpose of the meeting. What followed was rehearsed – the former RAF chief spoke succinctly and wasted no time.

'Sir, this is a personal offer, strictly so. Mr ———— tells me that you have a direct line to the authorities in Baghdad. I am an old soldier and like all old soldiers I follow wars when they occur, and they unfortunately do. Of course, I have a special interest in air wars and how people use their air forces. I have been watching the Iraqis from a distance and I am sorry to say I don't believe they have used their air superiority effectively. There is an obvious lack of coordination with ground forces – they should be able to do much better. ———— here tells me that your friends might be amenable to receiving outside help. I am willing to help them. I should like to tell you my history . . .'

I listened for five minutes. The man on my left was one of the most qualified military airmen in the world and he was willing to go to Baghdad to help the Iraqis. This was a more important offer of help than was represented by the many arms deals in which I had been involved. But, however attractive his offer might seem to a layman, I was also aware of the inherent Iraqi opposition to hiring outsiders, because they suspected them of being spies. Notwithstanding that objection, I decided that the Iraqis should know about the offer. I agreed to play messenger and transmitted what I had heard with as many caveats as I could muster; I feared Iraq would accuse me of promoting a spy.

The Iraqis responded within a week – a very short time by their standards. The hero-President was grateful for the information, but Iraq was determined to conduct its own war by itself and did not need outside experts. Nevertheless, I was to maintain contact with the ex-RAF officer. My business friend was clearly disappointed and there was no further contact.

I have never satisfactorily verified whether this was a British or a personal offer. Would the Marshal of the Royal Air Force have made it without the knowledge of Her Majesty's government? I doubt it. At the time, the press was full of stories about Iraqi failures and many of them were attributed to poor use of their Air Force. In fact, there were reports which claimed that no amount of military hardware could turn the tide in favour of Iraq unless Saddam used his Air Force more effectively.

Two or three weeks later, I travelled to Washington with a direct request from Saddam. His conspiratorial mind had developed a plan to unnerve the Iranians. Through a trusted military adviser, Saddam wanted me to make an official request to the US government to buy two hundred M-16 rifles for his Presidential Guard. He was not interested in acquiring M-16s made under licence by other countries, but wanted only American-made ones. Of course, even Saddam's allies were not to know about this. The significance of this request eventually dawned on me. The rifles were of no military consequence, but Saddam wanted his personal guard to be photographed parading with them. He wanted the Iranians to find this out and to surmise that he and the Americans were close enough for the USA to equip his personal guard.

The man at the State Department's Iraqi desk read me a statement about America's 'neutrality in the conflict', and the request was turned down. I could do nothing but return to London and transmit the news to Baghdad. When I inquired from my Iraqi contact how Saddam had responded, he gave me the standard Iraqi reply: 'The hero-President was informed of your efforts and thanks you for them. The President does not react to these small matters.' This may be so, but the President certainly reacted with unusual speed to an American offer which was transmitted to me in late February 1984, after Iranian forces had moved into Iraq in October 1983 and a short while after an Iranian attack had succeeded in capturing the Majnoon oilfields, a militarily valuable and psychologically significant development.

The caller from Washington was unknown to me, but he identified himself as a major arms dealer and hurriedly added that he 'didn't lift a finger without the US Government's knowledge and approval'. Would I be interested in purchasing $250 million worth of Harpoon missiles? 'My brother,' – and it was a disarming use of the word – 'the Exocet missile the French gave your big friend and which Iraq is using now is an ancient weapon compared with this.' Yes, I thought, the US Government knows all about this, otherwise he would not contact me. I had been selected because Saddam was suspicious of the other avenues, including King Hussein (which explains why the M-16 request had come to me). 'Of course, Mr Aburish, I will send you written confirmation of this.'

The following day the man faxed me confirmation in the form of a letter from the Harpoon manufacturer. McDonnell-Douglas Corporation. The language was careful, no more than a statement that they were led to believe that 'the United States Government would view with favour a request for the supply of Harpoon missiles to Iraq.' Knowing that the Iraqi Embassy in Athens was in charge of arms procurement, because it was geographically located to buy from both East and West and because the Greeks were rather lax in controlling the embassy's activities, I telephoned Saddam's man there, a fellow Tikriti, and told him of the American offer. I was asked to come to Athens with the letter, which the then ambassador took from me after determining that I had overlooked making a copy. After a two-day wait, during which a messenger flew to Baghdad to tell Saddam of the offer, I was told to fly Concorde from London so as to get to Washington as soon as possible to buy the Harpoons.

I went to the State Department accompanied by the caller, who, though he verified the story to Patrick Cockburn of the *Independent* newspaper in 1994, shall remain anonymous.[1] Once again – but this time it came as a surprise – the Iraqi desk made a statement about America's neutrality. The person with whom we had our meeting feigned lack of knowledge of the offer. As we left I expressed my fury with the arms dealer, who kept talking to himself and asking, 'What happened? What the hell happened?' In the end we agreed to discuss the matter over dinner in a few days' time.

Very soon after my abortive trip to the State Department I received a telephone call from an old Beirut friend, a CIA operative. He advised me to have dinner with him instead, promising to tell me 'all you need to know'. When we met, my old friend told me the story behind the offer and the change of mind. When the offer had been made, twelve days earlier, American satellite pictures had shown that the Iraqi lines were about to break under the pressure of an Iranian attack. However, by the time I got to Washington the situation had changed and new satellite pictures showed them holding the line. The offer was genuine – the Americans would have supplied the Harpoons had the danger persisted. Saddam, he said, should know that the USA would do everything to stop the Iranians from winning the war.

The message was not transmitted to Saddam. I returned to London and resigned. The stories that Iraq was using chemical weapons were gaining currency and supported by more and more neutral reports. But, cynically, governments both within and outside the Middle East had shown little interest in investigating these claims or in acting on the findings of independent groups.[2] I could no longer justify having anything to do with Saddam: the combination of killing and cynicism had gnawed on me until I could not function. I resigned at a time when Saddam's government and the Establishment of Television and Cinema owed me hundreds of thousands of pounds sterling, the price of films I had purchased on their behalf. Like many blind supporters of dictators I had woken up too late, but better late than never. To the Iraqi government, I was a traitor who was abandoning 'the cause'. To me the cause had ended a long time ago, in the 1970s. I was not a traitor; I was on the edge of bankruptcy and mental breakdown.

The lack of specific objectives and the strategy to achieve them, from which both Saddam and Khomeini suffered, were true of all parties with an interest in the outcome of the Iran–Iraq War. The Arab countries, the United States, the USSR, France, Britain and even China had an interest in Iraq's survival but, with the possible exception of an oil-hungry France, they had no interest in supporting Saddam to defeat Iran. Because the United Nations reflects the will of the countries which comprise it, particularly the permanent members of the Security Council, it too was rendered impotent by the obvious lack of will to end the conflict by member countries. The stalemate stretched on.

Beginning in 1983, simultaneous with the stalemate in battle which favoured Iran, the decline in the price of oil engineered by Saudi Arabia (Saudi oil income had plummeted from $113 billion in 1981 to $40 billion by the beginning of 1984)[3] resulted in a precipitous squeeze on the income of the oil-producing countries. The Arab oil producers reduced their financial support to Saddam. In 1983–5 their help consisted of $9 billion in revenue from the oil they were able to sell on his behalf from the Neutral Zone between Kuwait and Saudi Arabia. In March 1983 Crown Prince Abdallah of Saudi Arabia sounded as if he was providing Saddam with moral support to compensate for economic aid: 'Iran cannot enter Baghdad. It would mean war with all the Arabs.' But this did not give Saddam enough to underwrite his guns-and-butter policy. The Iraqi reserves which he had had at the beginning of the war were all but used up. Tareq Aziz had set the tone earlier by complaining that 'our brothers have stopped helping us'.[5] The Iraqi press followed suit, and there was mild criticism of the people who made continuations of the war possible through pumping too much oil.

The United States, contrary to common belief and the analysis of experts, had always been wary of Saddam's unpredictability. It stepped in to fill the gap, but only after that became an imperative. The US government began to expand its credit facilities to Saddam to buy more food through the Commodities Credit Corporation. The food aid programme which had been set up in 1981[6] was stepped up to compensate for the decline in Arab subsidies. America's decision to become the primary source for filling Iraqi bellies increased Saddam's dependence on US support. The British followed the American lead, and in 1984 the Export Credit Guarantee Department began extending credit facilities to Iraq.

Saddam reciprocated. Anti-Israeli rhetoric in the Iraqi media was toned down. Secret contacts with the Israelis aimed at achieving peace took place,[7] but were unfruitful. In the middle of 1983, Saddam expelled the terrorist Abu Nidal and ordered other terrorist groups headquartered in Baghdad, such as the Palestine Liberation Front, to cease their activities. Of course he also continued his privatization programme, to the Americans the ultimate indicator of a dictator's intentions and soundness. Saddam's clear gestures of appeasement were aimed at pleasing the Reagan administration and blunting the criticism of the Iraqi regime by congressional leaders. In substance, it resembled Saddam's pragmatic moves towards the Arab countries at the start of the war.

According to one-time director of the Establishment of Television and Cinema and Saddam confidant Sa'ad Bazzaz, this was concurrent with 'secret attempts by American firms and their agents to re-establish diplomatic relations between the US and Iraq' which were in progress.[8] In December 1983 Donald Rumsfeld, the American administration's special envoy to the Middle East, visited Saddam and gave him a handwritten letter from President Reagan. In November 1984, after other friendly gestures on both sides, diplomatic relations between the two countries were restored and Foreign Minister Tareq Aziz visited Washington, delivered a message from Saddam to President Reagan and met with Vice President George Bush, Henry Kissinger and Secretary of State George Shultz. Aziz capped his visit by confirming Iraq's new position of moderation vis-à-vis Israel, and announced that Iraq would accept 'a just, honourable and lasting settlement'.[9] Liberating Jerusalem was a thing of the past; not for the first time Palestinian rights were being auctioned.

Both sides were acting in accordance with the unwritten rules of an alliance of convenience. On Saddam's side need dictated his attitude, and even his commitment to Palestine was part of the price he was willing to pay to maintain it. Iraqi Ambassador to Washington Nizar Hamdoun went out of his way to gain the support of pro-Israeli organisations and convince them that Iran and not Iraq was a threat to Israel. In 1987, he was to produce a phoney map showing that the aim of Iranian military attacks was reaching Jerusalem[10] and that Iraq therefore deserved help. But all these surface signs of an alliance were subordinated to basic policy which never changed. In 1984 a State Department memorandum to Vice President George Bush favoured continued support for Iraq but unequivocally stated, 'Victory by either side would have far-reaching consequences' on the balance of power in the area.[11] It was the fighting and the fear of the consequences of an Iraqi defeat which were determining the degree of American help to Iraq. This was the fourth stage of US–Saddam cooperation, after 1963, 1968 and the mid-1970s.

Here it is important to point out that corporate America, often for supporting Iraq, was acting on overt US policy without much knowledge of the covert cynical policy. The US government did encourage the formation of organizations to nurse the relationship along, ostensibly to capture Iraq as a market. The leading organization in this field was the US–Iraqi Business Forum. Headed by former diplomat Marshall Wiley, it counted among its members Amoco, Exxon, Hunt Oil, Brown and Root, Chemical Bank, General Motors, AT&T and defence contractors Bell Textron, United Technologies and Lockheed. Among the participants in the Forum's efforts was former head of the Senate Foreign Relations Committee Charles Percy. This and other bodies knew nothing of the secret, undeclared policy of the United States as followed by Bush, Casey and others.

Because all gains in the fighting between 1983 and 1985 were tactical in nature, detailing them is an unnecessary diversion. They are significant only in terms of their effects on the policies of the countries whose behaviour had a direct bearing on the overall conflict. Saddam continued to follow a strategy of 'no retreat'.[12] This was not exclusively the result of a lack of military education, for he always saw the war with Iran as one for the hearts and minds of the people and believed that the Iraqis saw retreats as defeats regardless of their military merit. Forty thousand Iraqi soldiers of all religious persuasions and ethnic backgrounds had defected.[13] A retreat by an army which was not organizationally sound might increase the number of defectors and lead to total demoralization of his armed forces.

To hold the line, Saddam depended on three different but related things. First, he relied on his superiority in arms, including chemical weapons. Secondly, he devoted more effort to utilizing the superior intelligence information he was getting from Arab countries and the United States. Thirdly, he tried to counter Khomeini's advantage in having followers within Iraq (though the great majority of the Shias proved loyal to the nation, there was a hard core of religious people who accepted the Iranian message) by waging psychological warfare to attract secular elements within Iran. Of course, his programme to acquire more weapons, including non-conventional ones, was still receiving a great deal of his attention.

In the armament field, Saddam had an advantage which went beyond the numbers in planes, tanks and artillery. Twenty-nine countries were supplying him with arms and nine others were fronting for him whenever such cover was needed.[14] Very early in 1983, though it was not announced until September that year, the French began fulfilling a secret agreement to lease to Saddam five Super Entendard extended-range aircraft equipped with Exocet missiles. Saddam put them to use immediately and his Air Force attacked the oil facilities in the lower Gulf, including the very important terminal of Kharq Island, which forced a reduction in Iranian oil production. As when using chemical weapons tactically and missiles against cities, Saddam believed that this would force Iran to the negotiating table; the French agreed with him.

But once again Saddam had misjudged his enemy. All that this escalation of the war produced was an Iranian threat to close the straits of Hormuz to oil shipping to punish 'Saddam's Western supporters'. It was at this point that Saddam considered using chemical weapons against Iranian cities.[15] The use of Exocets, though it administered a severe blow to the Iranian economy through reducing oil exports, did not stop Khomeini's forces from mounting one of the heaviest attacks of the war in October 1983. For several days Saddam received news of the Iranian attack and waited. He was in constant touch with the battlefield, practically with his hand on the trigger. His eventual decision not to use chemical weapons against cities was taken after the Iraqi Army managed to stop the Iranians. The casualties of what he had been contemplating, could have run into hundreds of thousands.[16]

In 1983–4 Saddam – once again listening to his own voices instead of following the advice of his generals – resorted to psychological warfare.[17] He decided to counter the Ayatollah's hold on a small number of Shias by appealing to anti-Khomeini elements within Iran. His target for countering Khomeini's advantage was the Iranian Air Force, comprised as it was of modern people who rejected Khomeini's Islamic ways. His generals saw logistical problems in organizing the defections of Iranian pilots which Saddam was hoping for, but this did not stop him. He persisted in beaming special broadcasts to them, and the final result was the defection of eight Iranian aircraft with their crews.[18] It was a small victory, the importance of which Saddam inflated.

Along with this, Saddam began spending lavishly on Mujahadeen Khalq, an anti-Khomeini leftist Islamic group with a confused ideology which merged the teachings of Marx and Mohammed. The leader of the group, Massoud Rajavi, signed a cooperation pact with Iraq; he also moved several thousand of his followers, mostly from France, and based them there. Again, Saddam made more of this than was militarily justifiable, to the chagrin of his generals. And even at this point of reaching for subsidiary victories through airing questionable propaganda and sponsoring Iranian dissidents, Saddam ignored the obvious lack of response to his appeals to the ethnic Arabs of Iran and continued to waste money on this futile exercise.

The other side of Saddam's quirky military behaviour concerned the creation, in the middle of the fighting, of a special army beholden directly to him. Early in 1984 he used Egyptian help to create Special Forces 888 and 999.[19] Then he turned this effort into one to expand the now infamous Republican Guard, until early 1983 a mere two brigades. The Special Forces disappeared within the Guard, but the Guard itself was expanded and given special treatment. It was equipped with the best tanks, T-72s, T-

62s and T-55s. French manufactured self-propelled 155mm guns and more advanced ground-to-air missiles, as well as receiving special training and better salaries. The members of the Guard were imposing physical specimens, tall, lean and strong, and totally dependent on Saddam for their existence. Their social background was the same as Saddam's, from the Sunni lower class.

Slowly but methodically Saddam set up this special army and justified its creation by assigning to it difficult military situations. The command of the Republican Guard – and as usual Saddam bypassed the Army command structure and made this decision on his own – was given to General Abdel Sattar Tikriti, as the name suggests a *baladiati*, someone from Saddam's home town, and a loyalist. Members of the Guard were expected to join the Ba'ath Party. But, importantly, even the Republican Guard was never allowed passage through Baghdad, their officers were not allowed to carry sidearms and, except when ordered into battle, they had no ammunition. The fate of the rest of the Army, over one million in strength by 1984, was no better. The constant executions, removals and rotations of officers made it weak and near impotent. It was so reduced in importance that only the Minister of Defence, Saddam's cousin Adnan Khairallah, and the unimaginative Chief of Staff Abdel Jabbar Shanshall were invited to meetings to discuss the war. Khairallah had been elevated to his position after being promoted to field marshal ahead of many more qualified soldiers.

Saddam's creation of the Republican Guard, his guard against army attempts upon him or his regime, was not an isolated event. For some time he had been concentrating on expanding the already pervasive internal security apparatus, putting more and more power in the hands of his relations and reducing the functions and importance of all other centres of power in the country. The planned contraction of his powerbase, which he started as a response to the assassination attempt in Dujail, signalled the final transfer of power from the party to the family. Even the pliant Michel Aflaq responded to this transfer of power by stating, 'I no longer recognize my party.'[20] In reality, there was no longer a party to recognize.

In 1984, a short time before he expanded the Republican Guard, Saddam created a new department in the General Security Directorate, *amn khas* or Private Security. Three security offices, General Security, *mukhabarat* and Military Intelligence (*istikhbarat*), had already been in place since the mid-1970s, but the number of people who worked for them and their budgets were not published. With the emergence of a fourth organization entrusted solely with guarding the person of Saddam, and the estimated growth of the membership of the various security departments to between sixty and eighty thousand,[21] there was suspicion that the Security Directorate claimed a higher percentage of the national budget than any other similar service in the world.[22] Certainly they showed no signs of economizing, and instead of a single telephone number for people to call to squeal on their neighbours there were now several.

Saddam's Private Security fared as well as his special army, the Republican Guard. The recruits came from reliable backgrounds, the Sunni lower class loyal to Saddam. Their training, on Saddam's instructions, was focused on guarding against subversion. If their name was not enough to reveal their function, then Saddam's insistence that they study every single coup and revolution which had taken place in the twentieth century[23] eliminated any doubt. For Saddam, what happened elsewhere was not going to happen to him. To ensure success he made Sa'adoun Shaker, a trusted relation, head of this privileged service. Later Saddam Kamel, his cousin and son-in-law, assumed this position, only to be replaced by Qussay, the second and more intelligent of Saddam's two sons.

This emphasis on security was a reflection of conditions within the country. It followed disturbances in Baghdad and the arrests of members of the Dawa, Kurdish and Communist parties. Many of them were executed, once again including members of the Hakim family. The atmosphere had become so brittle that an Iraqi Army helicopter flying over the presidential palace was attacked with anti-aircraft fire.[24]

In 1983, obviously in an attempt to discourage conspiracies against the regime and demonstrate their futility, Saddam's half-brother Barazan published a book about the various attempts which had been made on the life of the Iraqi leader. *Attempts to Assassinate Saddam Hussein* listed nine, in a haphazard manner and without providing acceptable proof. Among them were schemes by the security apparatus, former politicians, the Army, Syria and Islamic groups, and ones sponsored by Iran and the CIA. While the authenticity of some of them is doubtful, instead of serving its intended purpose Barazan's list merely highlighted the level of opposition to the regime.

Additional procedures were now put in place to guard against future attempts. The days of Saddam emulating Haroun Al Rashid and wandering around Baghdad to check on his flock were over. He took to wearing hats lined with Kevlar bullet-proof material, and his food taster began to accompany him on trips. Even a minor medical problem found him depending on Indian rather than Iraqi specialists. Visits to villages and towns never subscribed to a fixed time. Cars similar to his, with blackened windows and contingents of guards, would arrive in a make-believe effort to draw out assassins. According to Dr Heidar Abbas of the Dawa Party, Saddam began using doubles extensively.[25] Abbas claims that a Saddam double was killed in 1984 in the town of Taji, but there is no further verification other than vague statements by other Iraqi exiles including Udday's former double, Latif Yahya. General Samarai recalls seeing one of the doubles wearing native clothing and substituting for Saddam in a minor function.[26] Three armed battalions travelled with Saddam whenever he went,[27] and an area of five square miles around the place he was visiting was swept with mine detectors. Of course the party faithful, when they were informed, were entrusted with reporting any suspicious people or unusual movements.

The security system which guarded against assassinations and coups was extended to include the armed forces, still the major source of worry for Saddam despite their emasculation. Orders to Army units were three-tiered. They originated with Saddam himself, followed by clearance by the military office of the party and then approval by the Army command. When relocating, Army units had no ammunition. And even then each contingent included a representative of the Army security who reported to a director in the President's office, a member of the Military Intelligence (*istakhbarat*) and a commissar. Not a single Army unit was stationed within 100 miles of Baghdad; the security of the capital was in the hands of the Republican Guard and Private Security, *amn khas*. Naturally, no officer of these services stayed in command long enough to develop a relationship of trust with his troops.[28] All this made the Army unable to rise against Saddam, but it also vitiated its effectiveness in fighting Iran.

Nor did Saddam trust modern methods of communications to

transmit his military orders about the conduct of the war. His fear that they might be intercepted by the Iranians or other enemies made him resort to using couriers. From 1984, orders to divisional commanders were delivered by hand.[29] What prompted Saddam to create his special security force and the Republican Guard increased his reliance on his extended Tikriti family. But this did not solve the problems created by the war and unhappiness with the way he was conducting it. Reliance on the family merely became another reason for opposing him. And that opposition ran deeper than simple nepotism, for the private and public behaviour of the Al Majids, Ibrahims and Tulfahs had got completely out of control. Saddam ignored their misdeeds in order to keep their loyalty. Saddam the one-time energetic enactor of anti-corruption Laws 8 and 52 was condoning family corruption to protect what had become a Tikriti state.

In 1984 a family incident exposed Saddam's and his family's inherent tribal instincts, the superficiality of their modernity. Despite Saddam's promotion of equality for Iraqi women, the female members of his household were subservient and, beyond indulging themselves and spending money, did what they were told. Among other things they were given away in marriage at an early age. Saddam agreed to the marriage of his daughter Raghid to his cousin and confidant (and eventual victim) Hussein Kamel. An army officer of limited talents, Kamel had endeared himself to Sajida Hussein and her daughters and had become their unofficial sidekick. Pleased with his cousin's commitment, Saddam had promoted him several times until he became a full colonel. But for Hussein Kamel to marry Raghid created a problem. Saddam's half-brother Barazan wanted Raghid as a bride for his son.

What ensued was a family feud which threatened the foundations of the Iraqi state. With Barazan fuming and threatening to eliminate Kamel, the family which was running Iraq and successfully supervising its non-conventional weapons programme, including the development of an atomic bomb, reverted to the behaviour of a primitive clan. Barazan's threats against Kamel led the latter to complain to Saddam who, angry that anyone would dare question his decision, responded by firing Barazan from his position as head of the *mukhabarat* and exiling him as Ambassador to UNESCO in Geneva. The *mukhabarat* was the largest of the four security branches; it controlled overseas intelligence, ran all the regime's informers, and administered counter-intelligence and the activities of foreign embassies in Iraq and Iraqi embassies overseas. The security of Iraq, a country in the middle of a colossal war and one which Saddam wanted to force into the twentieth century, was subordinated to tribal instincts anchored in an ancient past.

Later in 1984, Saddam's mentally underequipped older son Udday graduated from the College of Engineering of the University of Baghdad with an average grade of 98.5. Tutors who would not give him the highest grade possible, such as Mazen Zaki, were tortured and lost their jobs. Udday's behaviour became the talk of Baghdad, but Saddam still proudly appointed him director of the Olympic Committee. In fact, his duties were more extensive: Udday acted as Saddam's Minister for Youth and was later promoted to that position. Towards the end of the year Udday married his cousin Saja, the daughter of his uncle Barazan, in what seemed an attempt to end the family feud. But the marriage lasted only three months, after which Saja went to join her father in Geneva. According to knowledgeable private sources, she arrived in Switzerland 'half black and blue'. Udday, in an omen of worse things to come, had beaten her savagely. One could say that the family had not progressed since the days of Hassan the Liar.

A year later, Rana, Saddam's second daughter, married Saddam Kamel, Hussein Kamel's brother and another cousin. This event too added to Saddam's estrangement from his half-brothers; they wanted Rana as a bride for one of their sons. But Saddam Kamel, the hero of *The Long Days* television series, was similar to his brother in endearing himself to Saddam's immediate family by playing servant. Sajida's influence and Udday's quarrel with Barazan over the treatment of Saja decided the issue. It was Saddam's second son Qussay who broke the mould and married Sahar, the daughter of one of the few heroes of the war with Iran, General Maher Al Rashid. Still, Rashid was a fellow Tikriti and highly dependable. This marriage too was political in essence, and was dissolved after it produced two children.

Marriages aside, both boys (though definitely not the girls) cut a swathe through Baghdad's social scene. Stories of Udday's heavy drinking and summoning pretty girls for a night of pleasure became common fare. He used the roof discotheque of the Melia Mansour Hotel as his hunting ground. Qussay manifested more specific inclinations and imported blondes from Scandinavia.[30] When Udday took to using a helicopter to make public visits, Qussay competed by using a tank. Ostensibly both boys were doing their part in promoting support for the war.

Even Saddam, the one-time family man who celebrated home life with thousands of pictures on the front pages of newspapers, did not remain immune to temptation. In 1984 he established a liaison with Samira Shabandar, the blonde wife of Iraq Airways General Manager Nour Eddine Al Safi. How they met is unknown, but it was an affair rather than a dalliance. Samira eventually divorced her husband in early 1986, became Saddam's second wife and bore him a son named Ali, after the revered founder of the Shia sect, Ali Bin Abu Taleb, from whom Saddam claimed descent. But the affair with Samira, known to all because it was carried out in the open and caused Saddam's first wife Sajida to dye her hair blonde to compete, led to many more such relationships. It appears as if Saddam's children had indirectly introduced him to the joys of sex, not indiscriminate but wide-ranging. Moreover, he eased his subscription to his religious pretensions and began drinking Old Parr whisky in the company of his cousin Adnan Khairallah, whose excessive drinking was well known. It was another case of Saddam following the family's ways.

In 1985 what amounted to a whole town to house the family was commandeered along the banks of the Euphrates. The owners of the valuable houses and land were paid sums of money determined by Saddam's family rather than in line with market conditions. When the gossip about this reached Saddam, the one-time opponent of corruption reacted angrily, in the manner of a desert sheikh. 'They were without jackets and shoes before me,' Saddam is supposed to have answered.[32] He followed this by decreeing that insults to members of his family were punishable with heavy prison terms. His insensitivity had become so ingrained that he gave away most of the two hundred suits he ordered every few months from Switzerland.[32] To him this was charity, but there were more signs that Saddam had completely lost touch with his people.

A boy who had taken a liking to his daughter Hala and showed it was arrested, buried up to his neck and stoned to death.[33] Hala, his youngest and favourite child, was what Svetlana was to Stalin, and on many occasions the Communist dictator had punished his daughter's suitors. Brother-in-law Adnan Khairallah, the Minister of Defence, collected a huge fleet of expensive cars.[34] He imported a dozen Mercedes at a time and had a chauffeur for each. His nephew Udday noted this and began emulating him, though concentrating on sports cars. It was during this period that Saddam, dizzy with power, preoccupied with war and totally oblivious to the rot surrounding him, declared, 'We have grabbed the lines of the sun and we will not go.'[35]

Along with the contraction in his powerbase, the dependence on the family and fear of outsiders, signs were multiplying that the war was not going well. Yet Saddam still maintained undivided control on the levers of power which allowed him to limit the effectiveness of the opposition, to continue his non-conventional weapons programme and to secure enough foreign help to stay in power. The state within a state that he had created depended on the family and the loyalty of the Republican Guard and the Security Directorate, both of which acted as instruments of oppression against civilians and military alike. The opposition was divided and weak and unable to mount an open challenge to the regime. And continuing his non-conventional weapons programme and obtaining support to stay in power depended on outside powers whose determination to deny Iran victory was more important to them than any desire to control the monster they were creating.

The family's behaviour has been detailed in part, and the size, function and almost unlimited budgets of the Republican Guard and security services have been analyzed. But it was Saddam's personal involvement and attention to detail which made all the difference. He devoted considerable time to both services. Saddam personally oversaw the training of the Republican Guard and the indoctrination programme which accompanied it. Films of the special forces of the USSR, other European countries and even Egypt were selected by him. More experts from Eastern Europe were imported to train his security people. Again, he selected the films to be studied and, responding to local conditions, provided the local services with money to bribe informers. Among the people who spoke out, General Hamid Mohammed Tikriti, a divisional commander and deputy chief of military intelligence, was eliminated and it was labelled suicide. Brigadier Tareq Abdallah, *chef de cabinet* and later Minister of Industry, died in an 'accident'. Many others who objected to this diversion of energy and money suffered similar fates.

Disappointingly, the Shia opposition offered very little resistance. Above all, they failed to establish any connection whatsoever with army officers who might try to remove Saddam. What they did was peripheral and required time to produce results. Khomeini, aware as he was that Saddam's closeness to America meant a reduction in Iraqi commitment to the Palestinian cause, had begun to name his various military campaigns after the holy city of Karbala, suggesting that the liberation of Palestine was his final aim: his constant cry was that he would liberate Karbala first, then move on to Jerusalem. But this challenge to Saddam over the issue of Palestine[36] did not produce any results because people were preoccupied with things closer to home. The Dawa, though it tried to make use of Saddam's relegation of Palestine to the back burner, did not go beyond the occasional hit-and-run incident. Greater oppression kept them down, and Shia leaders operating outside Iraq were eliminated by Saddam's extensive intelligence network. Between 1986 and 1988 Iyad Ambassi, Sami Abdallah Maher and Mahid Hakim were killed in Pakistan and the Sudan. Outside powers ignored these murders because their cries against state terrorism did not cover such matters.

It was in Kurdistan that a more substantial opposition to Saddam began to manifest itself. The geography of the region afforded the Kurdish leadership a measure of autonomy which placed them beyond the reach of Saddam's armed and security forces. Both the Barzanis and Talabani were now in northern Iraq and, because of Saddam's preoccupation with Iran and inability to wage war against them, the Kurds were more immune than ever.

In May 1983 there was Turkish incursion into northern Iraq to subdue the Kurds and stop them attaining total autonomy, and this was undertaken with Saddam's blessing. An unwritten agreement between the two sides granted Turkey the right of hot pursuit into Iraqi territory without objection from the Iraqi government. When the effects of this move proved to be only temporary, Saddam tried to divide the Kurds. He established contacts with Talabani of the PUK and offered him a deal which invested him with sole leadership of the Kurds. Talabani saw in this a way of superseding the Barzanis of the KDP and accepted, despite the fact that Saddam had killed two of his nieces.[37] In December 1983 the two sides signed a truce and Talabani, along with the Iraqi Communist Party, was invited to join a government of National Unity.

Talabani should have known better, but his wish to assume overall Kurdish leadership came ahead of other considerations. The death of his nieces, along with the murder of Barzani's sons Luqman and Obeidallah, made no difference to him. Talabani persisted even after Saddam told him not 'to insist on Kirkuk being Kurdish'.[38] Nor was there any shortage of other signs that Saddam was using the Kurdish leader to implement his own Kurdish policy. Saddam followed this by strengthening his own position with the Kurdish tribes through providing financial support to the important Zubeir and Jaff clans which were feuding with the Barzanis,[39] labelled by Saddam the Descendants of Treason, and expanding the Jash (mules) Kurdish militia which he had created and which now numbered nearly fifty thousand.

In 1985 the deal between Saddam and Talabani unravelled when Saddam failed to implement any of its articles, and there was no follow-up on the idea of a government of National Unity. Following that, a number of villages in the Suleimaniya district of Kurdistan were razed. By November 1985, the number of villages razed had increased to almost two hundred.[40] The *cordon sanitaire* that Saddam was building to stop Iranian incursions, particularly in the area of Hajj Umran, was broadened. Local resistance came to an end with the imprisonment and murder of hundreds of Kurds, and thousands more villagers were moved to concentration camps in the plains of southern Iraq. Saddam had gained time. The Kurds, as divided as ever, did not start moves towards a unified position to include all their feuding factions until 1987.

Simultaneously with devoting time to reorganizing his internal structure under the cover of war and through the various means he used to deal with the opposition, Saddam was continuing to build up his conventional weapons and to develop his non-conventional armaments programme. It is worth repeating that, except for the French policy which deserves praise for its openness if nothing else, the guidelines governing the supply of arms to both Iraq and Iran were ridiculously loose and subject to interpretation. Even the words 'lethal weapons' were never strictly defined by the British government which used them selectively; in this they were emulated by other governments. While Iraq was the chief beneficiary of this vagueness, it was not until 1986 that Britain stopped training some Iranian military personnel and later, in September 1987, it closed the offices of the Iranian National Oil Company in London, the front organization for Iranian armament procurement.

With France espousing a policy of open opposition to Khomeini, the UK was providing substantial military help to Iraq while pretending neutrality. Reports of Iranian responses to still limited Iraqi chemical attacks found the UK agreeing to sell Iraq protection suits[41] against chemical, biological and atomic warfare. To Prime Minister Margaret Thatcher, this fell within what became known as the Howe (Sir Geoffrey, Foreign Secretary) Guidelines on selling to Iraq. Indeed, so did the sale to Iraq of a Plessey-manufactured elaborate electronic command system worth £370 million to render its Army more effective.[42] Improving the Iraqis' ability to kill Iranians did not matter as long as the weapons were not lethal.

There were also the cases of the British companies Matrix-Churchill and Astra. Initially both were used for general arms procurement purposes. In 1987, Saddam bought the machine tool maker Matrix-Churchill and Technical Development Corporation and turned them into his primary front organization for buying material for his non-conventional weapons programme. It did so successfully through London and its American subsidiary. Astra, Britain's second largest seller of military equipment after the official Foreign Military Sales, became totally dependent on Iraqi business. It used all types of methods to give the Iraqis what they wanted, acting as a respectable worldwide purchasing agent.

The British government knew about the activities of both companies and allowed them to continue their work after infiltrating them with secret agents. The Iraqi dependence on Matrix-Churchill and Astra in the UK was similar to its use of the American Steel Export Company, Al Haddad Trading in America and a Chilean with impeccable CIA connections by the name of Carlos Cardeon. Western corporations were fronting for Saddam, augmenting the work of arms dealers and friendly countries. With France and the USSR openly supplying Saddam with military hardware, this meant that the four major arms suppliers in the world were supporting him.

Britain's use of intelligence operatives to infiltrate Saddam's front organizations proves that he was never a trusted ally but a convenient tool who was fending off a more dangerous evil. Unsurprisingly, the Americans too kept an eye on what he was doing by following individual arms deals and through their intelligence presence in Baghdad. The American policy was the most cynical of them all. The US aid programme to Iraq, ostensibly to buy food, freed other funds which Iraq used to buy arms. By the mid-1980s the credit extended to Iraq by the Atlanta Branch of the Banca Nazionale di Lavoro (BNL) was over $600 million and increasing at an incredible speed. The machinations of manager Christopher Drogoul, still subject to controversy, were considerable, but it should be remembered that it was through these credit facilities that the USA exercised influence on Saddam. Having started by offering Iraq loans under the Commodities Credit Corporation (CCC) guidelines, basically a government guarantee of private bank loans, Drogoul proceeded to advance Iraq unsecured ones which eventually amounted to $4 billion. There was nowhere else Saddam could obtain this kind of money except through printing more of it and risking the total collapse of the Iraqi economy. Without the BNL loans, the war with Iran would have ended.

Saddam knew how to use this money. He had expanded his nonconventional weapons programme, replaced the first atomic reactor that France had sold him with another one from that country, and continued to pamper his scientists and engineers and push them forward. He joined the executive branch of the US government in trying to avoid congressional censure as advocated by Senators Claybourne Pell and Jesse Helms. He avoided violating the embargo rules in a blatant way and followed his scientists' advice by hiding behind the curtain of dual use – equipment requested was ostensibly for civilian purposes but could be used in his military programme. When acquired as civilian equipment it was not embargoed. This was a more sophisticated form of buying a pesticide plant in order to build chemical weapons, as he had done in the 1970s.

The success of this method, undoubtedly unknown to the US government, is best demonstrated by the fact that 241 dual use American licences were granted from 1985 onwards. Just six applications were turned down,[43] and only because their civilian use was marginal. Among the equipment imported under dual use licences were machine tools, computers, fungus for biological plants, fuel air technology for bombs and oscilloscopes for radar.

The following is a list of companies which received US export licences to import dual use equipment: Nassr State Establishment,

Badr General Establishment, Al Kindi Research Complex, Salaheddine Establishment, Al Qaqa Establishment, Hutteein Establishment, Al Qadisiya State Establishment, Al Yarmouk State Establishment, Auqba Bin Nafi Establishment, Samar Establishment, Al Qheim Establishment, Salman Pak, Al Muthana Establishment and Sa'ad 13, 16, 25 and 38 manufacturing complexes.[44] The equipment supplied to Saddam for his pet projects contributed to modifying Scud missiles, building explosives and rocket fuels, the nuclear programme, equipment to manufacture chemical and biological weapons, the building of ballistic missiles, making tank parts and contributing to the building of the 'Supergun'. The Americans knew these companies were exclusively military in nature; none of them was manufacturing civilian goods. Even the sale of strains of anthrax, cholera, typhoid and botulism was covered by this system.

Simultaneously four thousand Iraqi military personnel, many in disciplines related to the non-conventional arms programme, were being trained in the UK and Switzerland through the good offices of Astra.[45] The exact number of people employed in the Iraqi arms manufacturing establishments was unknown, but a former participant estimates that it was sixty thousand, over seven thousand of whom were involved in the atomic programme. Impressive and effective as these organizations were, Saddam still reached out to other countries to expedite the mastery of non-conventional and sophisticated weaponry. He secured Brazilian help in extending the range of the Russian-made Scud B missile and began cooperating with Egypt and Argentina to build the long-range Condor missile.

In fact, in 1986 there was an important change in Saddam's list of priorities among non-conventional weapons. He never stopped his extensive development of chemical, biological and atomic weapons, but he did reduce his use of chemical weapons in order not to alienate the US Congress. He balanced this by improving his rocketry and the effectiveness of his Air Force. Chemical weapons were used selectively to counter the human wave Iranian attacks; for the first time he had successfully put lethal chemicals in artillery shells.[46] With Iran finally responding by using chemical weapons on a small scale, criticism of Saddam's conduct of the war by human rights organizations and Congress came to a halt. (In an interview with me in 1998, Assistant Secretary of State Richard Murphy, a gentleman diplomat who had been appointed special envoy to liaise with the Iraq Government, stated that Saddam's reported use of chemical weapons 'came as a shock' and added that the Iranians were using these weapons as well. Unlike other writers, I am inclined to accept Murphy's words. Field diplomats were often kept in the dark by the CIA and others who pounced on the Iranian use to justify Saddam's behaviour. Throughout the war, US policy was always divided into an overt one and a covert one.)

Meanwhile, still in need of a technological edge, Saddam devoted more time to rocketry. His fascination with long-range rockets with unusually heavy payloads led him, through his extensive procurement network, to establish contact with the Canadian maverick Dr Gerald Bull. The Iraqis were introduced to him by Sarkis Soghanlian, an Armenian–American arms dealer with shady connections to the CIA, and evidence that the USA did not object to the Bull–Iraq cooperation.[47] What ensued was a duplicative effort of huge dimensions which found Iraq sponsoring the building of several 'superguns' through Bull's two organizations, the High Altitude Research Project and Advanced Technology Institute. The Canadian was an eccentric scientist who wanted to use artillery to place satellites in outer space; Saddam wanted the same artillery pieces to deliver tons of explosives to Iranian cities, including those that had been out of reach of his rockets.

Short of funds after alienating several governments now unwilling to sponsor him because of his eccentric behaviour, Bull found Saddam a more willing benefactor. Britain, Spain, Austria, Greece, the Netherlands and Switzerland had earlier contributed to Bull's efforts, which included the making of a number of huge guns including one with a massive 600mm barrel capable of firing on Tehran from Iraq. Saddam's son-in-law Hussein Kamel, promoted to supremo of the armaments industry, was in charge of overseeing Bull's efforts, but the real movers on the Iraqi side were scientists Shabib Azzawi and Dr Samir Sa'adi. But as usual, when the project began to show signs of yielding results Saddam personally took over its management and made it a priority.

Saddam's superiority in arms changed the nature of the war without changing its course. The attacks which followed his acquisition of long-range Super Entendard aircraft, begun in 1984, blossomed when French suppliers leased more of them. By 1986, Iraqi attacks on Iranian tankers and oil terminals were sufficiently heavy and effective that this phase became known as the 'tanker war'. Incredibly, according to the veteran correspondent John Cooley, the US fleet in the Gulf aided the Iraqi effort by jamming Iranian radar that was protecting ships and terminals and cancelling its effectiveness.[48] By late 1986, the Iraqi attacks had become so successful that Iran had to respond in kind. Because Iraq was now exporting oil in safety through Turkey, the Iranians attacked the tankers of Saddam's supporters, mainly Kuwait.

The Iranian response and the prospect of a broader war sent shivers through the oil market. Lacking congressional support, the Reagan administration, though tempted to do so, stood aloof from joining the fighting openly. But when the USSR responded to the Kuwaiti pleas for help by agreeing to 're-flag' Kuwaiti tankers and give them protection against Iranian attacks, the Americans offered a similar deal: from then on, most Kuwaiti tankers flew the US flag and had US naval escorts. Saddam had the edge, for the Iranians had no one to protect their tankers. Iraqi planes roamed the Gulf unopposed – so much so that in May 1987 an Iraqi aircraft attacked the American frigate *Stark* and killed thirty-seven American servicemen. Unbelievably, the Reagan administration described the incident as nothing more than an Iraqi error and blamed it on Iranian aggression.[49]

The tanker war, although it was going Iraq's way, could not conceal the two over-riding realities of the war on land, and American cynicism. On 9 February 1986, at huge human cost, the Iranians managed to cross the Shat Al Arab waterway, sever the road between Iraq's two major cities of Baghdad and Basra and occupy the strategic island of Fao. It was a daring and totally unexpected attack which caught Saddam napping, and it was the kind of defeat that he feared most. It could have led to the collapse of his demoralized Army. Having taken place after the tanker war had been expanded, it left Saddam in a quandary as he had nothing left up his sleeve.

Saddam's orders to his generals consisted of one short sentence; 'Fao must be reoccupied.' But the Iraqi Army, despite one of the heaviest bombardments in history – according to some, forty thousand rounds in one day – could not dislodge the Iranians. According to General Wafic Samarai,[50] then head of military intelligence, Saddam lost weight and became so agitated that he telephoned Samarai six times in one day. The failure to recapture

Fao was followed by the usual execution of generals and the dismissal of General Maher Abdel Al Rashid, father-in-law of his son Qussay, a war hero and fellow Tikriti. But blaming the generals was not enough, and Saddam followed it by accusing America of providing him with false information about Iranian military intentions. Iraqi Vice President Taha Yassin Ramadan publicly stated that the satellite information supplied to Iraq by America had been doctored.[51]

The defeat on the ground was coupled with a huge psychological blow which left Saddam reeling and convinced him of US perfidy. On 3 November 1986, Beirut's *Al Shira*' weekly published a report about secret American–Iranian negotiations aimed at freeing Western hostages being held by pro-Iranian Shias in Beirut. According to the report the United States, in the persons of National Security Adviser Robert MacFarland and Colonel Oliver North, had visited Iran several times to negotiate such a deal. This was the beginning of what came to be known as the Iran–Contra affair, the selling of arms to Iran under the auspices of the United States and the use of the money illegally to fund the operations of the Contras in Central America. By all accounts negotiations between the USA and Iran had been in progress since the beginning of 1985, a time so critical for the Iraqis that both King Hussein of Jordan and President Mubarak of Egypt saw fit to visit Baghdad to offer Saddam moral support.

Iran–Contra was not a one-off deal. It began with the Reagan administration approval of the sale to Iran in November 1985 of much-needed Tow anti-tank missiles held by Israel.[52] In October 1986, with Saddam escalating the tanker war to compensate for the loss of Fao, and former CIA director William Colby and a member of the National Security Council openly stating that 'It is important that Iraq withstand the Iranian attacks,'[53] Oliver North, with or without authorization, was once again in Tehran telling the Iranians that 'Saddam must go.'[54] Practically at the very same moment that North was advocating the removal of Saddam, the US Navy was increasing its participation in the tanker war and, according to some sources, had destroyed one-third of the Iranian Navy.[55]

Saddam the calculating conspirator behaved in a remarkably restrained fashion,[56] both regarding Iran–Contra and in response to a massive Israeli attack on the PLO headquarters in Tunis which killed over thirty people. Not only did he refuse to allow Iran–Contra and the attack on the PLO to derail his dealings with America, he overlooked Saudi involvement in the Iran–Contra affair in the person of arms dealer Adnan Khashoggi, the man used by North and the Israelis to facilitate the transfer of arms to Iran (King Fahd sent him a message telling him that Khashoggi did not have Saudi government sanction). However, from that moment on, Saddam knew that his aims and those of the USA and its allies were irreconcilable. The believer in revenge never truly got over the Iran–Contra affair and it was the legacy of this American betrayal, and to a lesser degree the Saudi one, which was to affect his future behaviour.

As 1986 turned into 1987 it looked as if no degree of indirect US support would save Saddam. America had gone from providing him credit (1982–4) to supplying him with arms (1984–6), but after that it set all reluctance aside and became a temporary military ally. Its involvement, initially slow and secret, came into the open after July 1987 when Iranian pilgrims to Mecca rioted and four hundred of them were killed by Saudi security people. This gave America a much-needed excuse openly to change the nature of the help it was giving Saddam. Claiming that Khomeini was threatening their Saudi ally, the USA joined the battle. But while this emboldened Saddam and eliminated any check on his use of chemical weapons and his arsenal of rockets in ways which violated international conventions, the USA still wanted to win the war and control Saddam at the same time.

The United States signalled its change of policy by prevailing on the Israelis to stop the flow of arms to Iran. Operation Staunch, aimed at stopping arms sales to Khomeini since 1983, was finally put into effect and forced on the Israelis. US aircraft began to fly over Iran, locating targets[57] and adding this information to what the AWACS and satellite pictures provided. The US Navy increased its harassment of the Iranian Navy and made it difficult to supply their garrison in Fao. On the diplomatic level, in July 1987 the United States backed a strong resolution in the United Nations Security Council (resolution 598) calling for an immediate end to the war and the settlement of outstanding issues afterwards. Moreover, working through its Arab allies, with Saudi Ambassador to the USA Prince Bandar acting as messenger, America prevailed on them to place the Iran–Iraq War at the top of the agenda of an Arab heads of state meeting in Amman in November 1987. (A fuming Arafat came close to boycotting the meeting.) But – and it is as well to remember this – the United States halted one of Saddam's projects, the Condor long-range missile, by stopping Germany and Italy from supplying irreplaceable parts.[58] This increased Saddam's dependence on Bull.

In 1988 the new US policy to end the war took the concrete form of assisting the Iraq attack to recapture Fao. The Iraqis succeeded on 16 April, but only after considerable direct American military help against Iranian positions and the Iranian Navy.[59] On 3 July, the USS *Vincennes* shot down an Iranian airliner carrying over three hundred civilians while on a scheduled flight to the United Arab Emirates. There had been no aerial activity in the region, but, unlike in the Iraqi attack on the *Stark*, America criticized Iran for allowing the plane to fly in a war zone.

But Iranian pressure persisted in the northern part of Iraq which was beyond America's reach, and Saddam now directed his attention to the deteriorating situation with the Kurds there. The initial inertia and failure of the agreement with Talabani had been replaced by a united Kurdish front which, with Iranian help, threatened the north. To counter this, in March 1987 Saddam appointed his first cousin, General Ali Hassan Al Majid, commander of his forces in the northern sector. Unlike other generals, Majid had Saddam's full trust and was given absolute power to put down any and all signs of resistance to the regime.

In April, Majid used chemical weapons in Sheikh Wazzan and Suleimaniya. Thousands of Kurds were killed, but the combined Kurdish–Iranian offensive continued, with the Iranians using chemical weapons on a much smaller scale than the Iraqis and making some progress. Later in April, Kurdish forces took over the important town of Karadagh and Iranian troops occupied a chunk of Iraqi territory. Responding to this in the middle of 1987, acting on order 4008 dated 20 June, Al Majid, already the bearer of the dubious honour of being called Ali Chemical, began a more extensive depopulation programme of Kurdish villages than had ever been seen before. Three thousand villages were razed and five hundred thousand people were moved to concentration camps in southern Iraq.[60] By early 1988 the number of towns and villages depopulated was to reach four thousand and the number of Kurds moved south had risen to 1.5 million.[61] This operation against innocent civilians was called *anfal*, after the 8th sura of the holy Koran, one which celebrated Muslim victory in the battle of Badr. As a travesty, there is nothing in Arab or Muslim history to equal it.

Saddam's use of chemicals against the Kurds and his deportation programme were augmented in February 1988 by starting what was known as the War of the Cities. With the help of his own scientists, Gerald Bull and foreign governments he had built up a substantial arsenal of extended-range Scud B missiles. He had used rockets against Iranian cities earlier, but gave up on it in 1985 and 1986. Now, rejecting the advice of generals who feared Iranian retaliation, he resumed this tactic – but this time his rockets had a longer range and were more lethal.

He was proved right. Tehran and other cities hitherto out of range were hit with a steady barrage of rocketry, in which thousands of people died, and the Iranians were reduced to a state of panic. They hit back, but they could not match the Iraqi firepower, Saddam managed to deliver 150 rocket attacks in a period of two months. However, the Iranian government which had shown an ability to cope with chemical weapons was determined to withstand all that Saddam threw at them. Khomeini would not countenance ending the war and giving Saddam a military and psychological victory.

In March 1988, the Kurds and Iranians achieved yet another victory. A combined force captured the town of Sari Rash, moved on to capture Halabja and threatened the strategic dam at Darbandikan. Saddam responded swiftly and ordered his cousin to show no mercy. Ali Chemical reacted without hesitation: the town of Halabja was repeatedly attacked with chemical weapons which caused many thousands of casualties. Incredibly, the United States put the blame for the attack on the unfriendly Iranians and issued a report to that effect from the US War College.[62] In a bizarre move the USA, playing both sides against the middle, still tried to maintain a line to the Kurds and in June 1988 held secret meetings with their leader Jallal Talabani.[63] As usual, the UK was not far behind. Soon after Halabja, Her Majesty's government approved £340 million in extra credits to Iraq.[64]

Because Halabja has become a prime example of Saddam's criminality, it is well to reproduce some of the words of film producer Gwynn Roberts, the man who unearthed conclusive evidence that the attack was the work of Saddam.[65] 'There is no doubt that the onslaught was a retaliatory attack by the Iraqis who had been forced out of the city by the PUK [Talabani fighters]. Iranian Army units swept in hours later . . . I brought back an Iraqi gas mask which seemed to prove the opposite [of the American claim]. It showed that it was effective against Tabun and Sarin and hydrogen cyanide . . . It was analyzed by me at Porton Down, Britain's chemical defence establishment.' Roberts proved that the gas masks which the Americans had used to accuse the Iranians were manufactured to protect the Iraqis against chemicals such as were made in Iraq. American cynicism knew no bounds.

The Kurds and Iranians were demoralized, and the northern front against Saddam collapsed. The Iranians, stung by the dishonest and later feeble American reaction, feared the use of chemicals against their cities. It became obvious to them that the cries of human rights organizations and individual Western leaders mattered little in the face of American determination to help Saddam. In May 1988, equipped with US intelligence information and making use of their superior firepower and chemical weapons, the Iraqis drove the Iranians out of the southern city of Salamcheh and Majnoon Island and once again started moving into Iran.

Belatedly, the mullahs in Iran managed to transmit the significance of the new military realities to Khomeini. It was not Saddam who was winning the war but the Great Satan, as Khomeini called the United States. On 18 July 1988, nearly eight years after the start of the war, Khomeini accepted UN Security Council resolution 598. On 22 July the guns fell silent. Khomeini spoke of drinking a poison chalice and retreated into silence. Saddam declared victory. The boy from Tikrit was so delirious that victory rendered him incomprehensible. He was the knight on a white horse. He gained weight, smiled a lot, walked with a swagger, gave speeches in praise of his fighting men, announced plans to build monuments, received Arab guests offering their congratulations and on one or two occasions spontaneously joined crowds in performing the *chobbi* native dance. That over 360,000 Iranians and Iraqis had died and over 700,000 had been injured,[66] and that the war had cost an estimated $600 billion, were temporarily forgotten.

Behind the noise level orchestrated by Saddam to celebrate his victory, Iraq was now a different country. Like many nations which suffer the consequences of long wars, the Iraqi people were asking questions which even a dictator could not neglect. Chief among them was whether Saddam's victory was real, and what might follow it.

10

The Friend–Foe Game

During the Iran–Iraq War, it was Henry Kissinger who articulated the attitude of outside powers towards the conflict and lamented the fact that both sides could not lose.[1] He was wrong. Both belligerents did, and the almost universal wish of plague on both their houses did come true. Because it was beaten on the battlefield and its principal aim of spreading Islamic revolution was halted, Iran's defeat was recognizable. That of Iraq was disguised, but it was structural and equally profound. Saddam's propaganda deliberately exaggerated what he had achieved, concealed the considerable damage suffered by the Iraqi nation state and claimed victory. In strictly personal terms, it was.

But in reality, the war had set back the clock and cancelled both the tangible and intangible accomplishments of Saddam's pre-1980 Ba'athist regime. Somewhat similar to victorious Britain after the Second World War, but without the advantage of a democratic system, he presided over a disrupted society and a bankrupt country. Iraq's treasury was depleted and it was deeply in debt. The price of oil was low, and whatever income the oil exports generated was not enough to service Iraq's existing debt and meet the country's burgeoning needs. Saddam's powerbase had narrowed and his family had pre-empted the Ba'ath Party's functions instead of acting as its front and manager. When the party's ideology was invoked it was totally perverted and reduced to a vehicle for Tikriti tribal primacy. Corruption was widespread, and Saddam would not and could not control it because that meant acting against his corrupt family, his primary source of support. The Arab countries' obligations and willingness to help Iraq ceased with the disappearance of the Khomeini threat. Iraq was no longer their front line, and the drastic decrease in their oil income precluded acts of brotherly Arab generosity.

Furthermore, the absence of Khomeini's menace changed the nature of outside support for Saddam. The support of the USA and other Western countries stopped being a matter of urgency, while the USSR lacked the financial muscle and was preoccupied with its own internal problems. With Iraq's survival guaranteed, the Western powers began responding to internal pressures by Congress and other groups who wanted to focus on the nature of the Iraqi regime, the neglected issues of human rights and democracy, and Saddam's use of non-conventional weapons.

Meanwhile, Saddam was left with a standing army of over a million men and nothing to offer them. Parades and celebrations provided nothing more than a transitory substitute for soldiers' expectations of the fruits of victory, and Saddam had no civilian jobs for them. Furthermore, their expectations were matched by the civilian population's anticipation of a better life. For a short period, Saddam resorted to lies and cover-ups such as announcing that he was building a Baghdad subway and railroad network at a cost of $40 billion. But when he did not have enough money even to start the projects, the lies were exposed. Although he had not planned for a long war, Saddam had nevertheless staked everything on its outcome. The outcome, too, created problems for which he had not been prepared.

Except for resorting to remedial action with limited results, such as using soldiers in some rebuilding projects, acting to reverse the effects of the war exposed Saddam to greater danger then leaving them untouched. Political considerations stood between him and curbing the corruption of his family and the abuses of the security apparatus under them, the focus of complaints by the people. The country's considerable debt and low credit rating meant he could not borrow more money except on prohibitive terms. Mortgaging the country's future oil income or going back on nationalization amounted to accepting the ways of Western oil companies, destroying his most notable achievement and committing political suicide. Changing the attitude of the Arab countries or influencing the policies of outside powers required a payment in kind, adopting new policies that would have reduced Iraq to an also-ran and cancelled Saddam's previous efforts to build a new modern state and to become a leader of the third way between East and West.

Two courses of action offered Saddam an indirect way out of his predicament. Although both needed time to implement and depended on non-interference by outsiders to succeed, they could have forced the Arabs to respond to his financial needs and made the West more inclined to help him. Counting on non-interference was a gamble, but Saddam had no choice. The first option was to continue his non-conventional weapons programme and turn Iraq into a regional power strong enough and menacing enough to assume a position of leadership among the Arab countries, the Gulf states in particular. Saddam felt this would prompt the Gulf states to provide him with much-needed financial support in return for leaving them alone, and would stop the rest from coming to their aid. The second option was to assume a position of Arab leadership by adopting the Palestinian problem and appearing to confront Israel. This too contained the potential of forcing all the Arabs to back him for fear of appearing soft on the Arabs' common enemy. Moreover, the West too might grant him a financial lifeline in the form of generous credit terms to stop him disturbing the fragile regional balance of power and starting another Arab–Israeli war.

The development of non-conventional weapons never suffered from lack of funds. Before, during and after the war with Iran Saddam always gave this work precedence over other programmes and diverted precious money to it at the expense of civilian needs and other military programmes. The decision to assume responsibility for the Palestinian problem was timely, aided by developments between the PLO and the United States and universal Arab fears over the increasing number of Russian immigrants to Israel who were competing with Palestinians for limited areas of land. The immigration problem had existed before the end of the Iran–Iraq War, but the other Arab countries had done nothing beyond issue protests which proved ineffective and unpopular with their people. Saddam used Arab inactivity to try to place the PLO under his aegis before the end of the war, and after it he hurried to capitalize on the failure of the PLO and others to stop further Jewish immigration through dialogue with the USA. Beyond using this deadlock to advantage, he gave the PLO more money than he could afford and worked to gain acceptability for it with third world and African countries friendly to Iraq.

The Iraqi–PLO amity which flourished as a result of these moves had its origins in what happened on 1 October 1985, when Israeli aircraft attacked the PLO headquarters in Tunisia, killed a number of Palestinians and rendered the country unsafe for the rest. It was a pro-Saddam faction of the PLO, the Arab Liberation Front led by the infamous Abul Abbas, which retaliated by hijacking the Italian cruise ship *Achillo Lauro*, killed a crippled passenger and generated widespread international and Arab condemnation of Palestinian methods, which were equated with terrorism. Vulnerability and isolation increased PLO leader Yasser Arafat's need for support and a safe haven beyond Israeli's military reach. Quietly, Saddam offered the PLO facilities in Baghdad and the latter accepted the offer and moved many of the PLO personnel and offices to Iraq.

The importance of Arafat's famous comment made at the time that he 'can't sleep peacefully except in Baghdad'[2] escaped most people. The assassination of Arafat's second-in-command, Abu Jihad, by an Israeli hit squad which sneaked into Tunisia on 16 April 1988 resulted in more PLO functions, including the military ones, being transferred to Baghdad. Saddam, setting financial pressures aside, showed no hesitation in paying the PLO's expenses. But Arafat did not accept Saddam's adoption gestures wholeheartedly and still pursued a diplomatic solution. The numerous attempts at dialogue between the USA and the PLO during this period, 1985–8, faltered over the problems of the PLO's recognition of Israel, its insistence that Jewish immigration be stopped and Israel's unwillingness to negotiate with the organization as the sole representative of the Palestinian people. Saddam, though opposed to these efforts, made no attempts to stop Arafat. Instead, he continued to ignore his country's financial state and redoubled his efforts to woo the Palestinians; he gave Arafat another $50 million to support the uprising known as the intifada.[3] This was a larger donation than the richer Arab countries had given, and Saddam topped this by telling Arafat that he had fifty-four Army divisions ready to fight Israel.[4]

Arafat's attempts to avoid Saddam's close embrace were unsuccessful. The PLO's feelers towards America were producing few results and in the period 1988–90 the Palestinians and Iraq drew closer together at the expense of Arafat's traditional relationship with Egypt, the advocate of dialogue.[5] Arafat, responding to various initiatives (the Baker, Mubarak and Shamir plans among others), made what he considered a declaration of recognition of Israel in Stockholm in December 1988, amplified this in Geneva a few days later and sent the White House various peace messages through Palestinian and other intermediaries. For a while – to Saddam's chagrin – the PLO and USA had a dialogue. But it had little chance of success and was practically dead before the pro-Saddam Palestine Liberation Front of Abul Abbas raided a Tel Aviv beach on 30 May 1990, an event which prompted Secretary of State Baker to suspend the negotiations with the PLO in retaliation for Arafat's failure to condemn the raiders. Whether Saddam instigated the raid or not is unknown, but each failure of Arafat's every diplomatic move was a victory for Saddam. By the time of the 1990 Gulf crisis, Arafat and the PLO had accepted Saddam as the chief advocate of their cause.

Saddam's policy towards the PLO did not take place in isolation. After the end of the Iran–Iraq War, all the Arab leaders visited Baghdad to congratulate Saddam on his victory except arch-enemy Hafez Al Assad of Syria and the Emir of Kuwait. Saddam's commitment to his long-term aims precluded confronting these visiting Arab leaders with financial demands or expressing Iraqi anger over their failure to continue to help him. Instead, he used the opportunity of their visits to re-establish his country's relations with them on a new and friendlier footing. It was during the Saudi King Fahd's visit to Baghdad that the Iraqi leader insisted on a non-aggression and non-interference pact between their two countries. It was eventually signed in March 1989, during a second visit to Iraq by Fahd. A month before concluding the agreement with Saudi Arabia, Saddam used the visit of Kuwaiti Crown Prince Sa'ad to Baghdad to propose a similar deal with Kuwait. The Kuwaitis considered it but never responded.[6] Determined to improve relations with Kuwait, Saddam none the less agreed to provide Kuwait with 350 million gallons of drinking water a day and another 50 million gallons for agriculture.[7]

Saddam, undeterred, succeeded in talking President Hosni Mubarak of Egypt, King Hussein of Jordan and President Saleh Ali of the Yemen into starting negotiations towards the formation of a new alliance comprising Iraq and these three countries, to be known as the Arab Cooperation Council (ACC). This belated response to the Gulf Cooperation Council (GCC) came into being in Baghdad in February 1989, after the leaders of the member countries had exchanged several visits. Lacking a clear purpose, the new bloc was just another attempt by Saddam to enhance his standing in the Arab world.

In the absence of problems between the two countries, the non-aggression pact with Saudi Arabia was symbolic. But Saddam's two other moves, hegemony over the PLO and the formation of the ACC, were significant. Saddam had wanted the latter to be a military as well as an economic alliance since he was keen to enhance his role as the Arab leader preparing to confront Israel, but Mubarak had refused to accept this.[8] The West, though it briefly welcomed the ACC as a force of moderation[9] and hoped to exercise some influence on it, had made known its opposition to a new anti-Israeli military bloc.

Despite the failure of what must have been his primary purpose of forming a new military alliance, Saddam nevertheless continued to court Egypt. In May 1989 he prevailed on an Arab League Heads of State Conference meeting in Casablanca to readmit Egypt as a full member (its membership had been suspended since the Camp David Agreement). And moving ahead of the ACC, he initiated steps towards increasing trade with Cairo and giving favourable treatment to importing Egyptian goods. His trips to visit Mubarak in Cairo became frequent and were highly publicized.

These inter-Arab moves could not but generate a considerable amount of speculation regarding Saddam's aim. Realistically, nobody had anything to offer towards solving his more pressing internal problems, and the PLO presence was costing him money. But, unlike his past moves to endear himself to the Arab people, this was a most deliberate bid to build on his own perception of Iraq as the new protector of the Arabs and to lead the Arab governments. However, the illusion that the limited military victory over Iran created in Saddam was not shared by others. During this period Kuwait watched him uneasily and kept its distance. Taking no notice of this, Saddam interpreted the silence of most Arab countries as an implicit acceptance of what he was doing, and decided that only Syria and its Ba'ath Party stood in the way of his claim to Arab leadership.

To the dismay of other Arab states which had welcomed his moderate moves and taken them at face value, Saddam began sponsoring Christian elements in Lebanon against Syria's presence in that country. Using PLO offices and know-how, he opened offices in Cyprus and elsewhere which supplied the Christians with arms, attacked the 'Syrian occupation' of Lebanon during Arab League meetings, and spent precious money sponsoring Islamic movements opposed to Assad. This was a clear sign that Saddam was determined to pursue his Arab leadership claim at all costs, but it was widely ignored.

The concentration on Arab issues, particularly that of Palestine, appealed to many Iraqis. Like Saddam, most of them believed that Iraqi human and financial sacrifices had saved the Arabs from Khomeini's Islamic fundamentalism, entitled them to a position of leadership and placed the rest of the Arabs under an obligation to repay Iraq for saving Araby. But, unlike Saddam, they could not overlook their immediate needs and were unwilling and unable to follow long-term policies to force the rest of the Arabs to recompense Iraq. Nothing could for long hide or replace what was happening economically and politically inside Iraq and which, in addition to Arab neglect, was made worse by the deterioration in relations with the United States. Saddam had secretly accepted the Arab attitude and its consequences, but it was America's failure to provide him with more help, exacerbated by the increasing control and abuse of power by members of his family, which intercepted his planning and determined his future actions.

Violating his famous maxim, Saddam was willing to tolerate some internal pressures and to try to achieve his regional leadership aim while the Iraqis' bellies were only half full. But the sudden unreliability of US policy towards Iraq – the calls by a vociferous Congress and press to punish him by imposing sanctions on his regime and deny him loans, credits and dual use equipment – made for an explosive situation with potential consequences beyond his control. Fear of empty bellies and not being able to continue his non-conventional weapons programme cut across Saddam's improvised strategy to lead the Arabs. This was what forced him to respond to the mounting pressures on his government well before realizing either of his aims.

The non-interference in his plans that Saddam had counted on, which would have allowed him to manipulate the policies of the oil-rich Gulf, was an unrealistic dream. Moreover, despite the Bush administration's efforts to help while containing him, the congressional campaign to deny him credit, and the various interceptions of his acquisitions of non-conventional weapons equipment, succeeded in stopping him. With his plans thus shattered, the reality of what the Iran–Iraq War had produced and a convergence of dozens of coordinated or accidental events ended Saddam's twin approach. What Kissinger had hoped for, an Iraqi defeat, became an undisguised reality. After that there was no grand design. Most of Saddam's decisions represented uneducated reactions to what others did, and became unintelligible.

To understand Saddam's sudden incoherence in dealing with conditions within Iraq and his growing isolation, one must begin with the pure results of the Iran–Iraq War. Although different figures have been used by various writers and journalists, all of them attest to the huge human losses suffered by Iraq during its eight-year conflict with Iran. Dr Abbas Nasrawi, among the more reliable sources, places them at 105,000 dead and 300,000 wounded[10] plus tens of thousands of prisoners. Iraq's population was somewhere near 16 million, so these losses were the equivalent of 1.4 million people in the UK and between 7 and 8 million in the United States. They represented over 3 per cent of Iraq's population.

The financial losses too were staggering. Iraqi reserves had disappeared: $35 billion was owed to the West, $11 billion to the USSR and, in addition to outright cash grants and gifts of oil produced in the Neutral Zone, more than $40 billion to Kuwait and Saudi Arabia.[11] Because of the peculiarities of the Kuwaiti–Saudi loans – neither expected to be paid interest – the figure for servicing the overall Iraqi debt, though substantial, is elusive. Though this extremely serious financial situation could be deferred – at least Saddam thought so – his refusal to contemplate an austerity programme, his determination to continue to try to fill bellies, and the imperative of keeping up generosity to the families of dead and wounded soldiers made everything worse.

When the war ended in August 1988, the price of a barrel of oil had been hovering around the $17 figure. An elementary calculation using an Iraqi level of production of 2.3–5 million barrels per day, and taking production costs into account, would suggest that Iraq's annual oil revenue would have been less than $14 billion, considerably less than the $26 billion per annum that the country had realized at the start of the war in 1980.[12] Servicing the non-Arab debt and underwriting the million-strong Army required more than the oil exports were generating. Recalling Churchill's post-war fate in Britain and awareness of internal conditions precluded reduction in spending left Saddam in need of immediate economic relief. Long-term planning aside, he needed an increase in the price of oil or to borrow more money.

Well before he embarked on his improvised programme to lead or coerce the Arabs, on 9 August 1988, one day after the announcement of the ceasefire between Iran and Iraq, Kuwait increased its oil production.[13] The price of oil declined and put Iraq under greater economic pressure. When the United Arab Emirates followed Kuwait, the problem became worse. On the same day as the Kuwaiti action, the United States Senate rejected the appeals of the Bush administration and tried to impose sanctions on Iraq, though unsuccessfully. The Senate's proposed measures included controlling the flow of all equipment with dual use potential, a direct threat to Saddam's non-conventional weapons programme. Saddam felt as if he was being choked, but he continued his inter-Arab efforts, initiated some internal political liberalization and persisted in following his disastrous economic policies.

Because the Kurds and Shias had been subdued and there was little chance of internal rebellion, Saddam was relatively safe. None the less, a few days after the cessation of hostilities with Iran he dispatched several Army divisions to Kurdistan.[14] Because he had already ended the *anfal* campaign,[15] at least officially, this was more of a precautionary move to guard against future trouble and to get the Army out of the way. The rest of the Army was already in the Shia south, where things were quiet and there was no need for special action. With both Kurdistan and the south quiet Saddam announced a liberalization programme which included more privatization of industry and a general amnesty for all political opponents except Jallal Talabani of the PUK (to punish him for reneging on their agreement and helping Iran). He invited all the political parties to re-enter the political arena and participate in elections.[16]

Nobody took Saddam's perestroika seriously, but the elections were held on 1 April 1989 and produced the expected overwhelming Ba'athist victory. Through new economic policies, a number of companies were privatized and hundreds of licences were issued for people to start up construction and other companies. But that too had little effect. The money generated by privatization was comparatively small, and whatever building took place was insignificant because funds were earmarked for the more immediate needs of importing food and consumer goods. These unsuccessful programmes had the twin purpose of easing internal pressures and appeasing outsiders, the US Senate in particular. But discovering that his concessions to the pressures enveloping him produced nothing more than interim remedial measures, Saddam soon gave up the whole effort.

It was economic conditions with political implications which were determining Saddam's course of action, rather than the other way round. A demobilization programme which released two hundred thousand soldiers was halted when discharged men desperate for jobs started street brawls with Egyptian workers in which dozens died. Coming early in 1989, when Saddam was promoting the ACC, this embarrassed him and threatened his image in the Arab world and his new friendship with Mubarak.[17] Rightly seeing the soldiers' riots as a time bomb which threatened his position, the firm believer in security increased the number of his personal guard to fifteen thousand.[18] As if this overloading of the military establishment was not taxing enough on an empty treasury, Saddam increased the number of people working in the area of military industrialization to a hundred thousand. In 1989 military expenses, including those of the industrialization programme, represented 88 per cent of the value of oil exports.[19]

Neglecting his own contribution to the economic problem and realizing that his long-term policies needed time to mature, Saddam now concentrated on diverting attention to more immediate issues, the overproduction of oil by fellow Arabs and American policy. He began by attacking the US military presence in the Gulf and accused Kuwait and other oil producers, to him America's agents, of conspiring against him. It was at this point that Saddam told Yasser Arafat that the USA was out to overthrow him.[20] Members of his government, in particular Minister of Information Latif Nassif Jassem, began repeating his words.

There is no way to judge Saddam's many statements on the subject of America (and the West), Israel and Kuwait without examining in some detail the welter of events which began to converge after the end of the Iran–Iraq War, and spun so completely out of control as to affect Saddam's judgement and produce the Gulf War. Nor is there any consistent pattern to these state-ments and whether they were justified by what supposedly prompted them. The background to Saddam's behaviour was the gratuitous Kuwaiti and UAE overproduction of oil and the limitations eventually placed on Iraq by the US Senate, which were followed by similar actions from Britain's Export Credit Corpora-tion and a French refusal to reschedule debts.[21]

But the actions of America, Britain and France came late in the day, in 1990, after the governments of these countries had tried to accommodate Saddam despite the nature of his own government. What Saddam and nobody else could understand was the series of incidents, which, often but not always, smacked of coordination, and which were undoubtedly directed against him. Like Ahmad Chalabi of the Iraqi National Council,[22] I believe that the Gulf War resulted from miscalculations by both sides. The reader will have to decide who miscalculated more, under what circumstances, and the innocent or suspicious nature of the miscalculations which elevated them to disaster.

However, miscalculations, like new policies, do not occur in a vacuum. As we have seen, the colossal political and economic consequences of the war with Iran, Saddam's phoney determina-tion to equate his and America's military achievement with total victory, the inability and unwillingness of rich Arabs to help him, and the West's refusal to accept him as a supreme Arab leader, all merged to isolate him. His questionable long-term strategy never had a chance. What was happening inside Iraq, and at the begin-ning of 1989 it included high unemployment and food shortages, left the Iraqi people confused. But, however confused, they were agreed that the replacement of the Ba'ath Party by the Tikriti clan had brought them nothing but disaster. This emerging universal hatred for their leader and his family was a major factor in the deteriorating situation which governed Saddam's thinking. It is part of the background to the series of miscalculations.

In October 1988, a drunk and ranting Udday Hussein broke into an official function attended by the wife of Egyptian President Hosni Mubarak and shot and killed one Hanna Geogo, his father's food taster and sometime pimp.[23] To the Iraqi people, it was worse than going without food; their legendary pride would not accept any of it, especially the humiliation they felt owing to the presence of an Arab guest. Once again, the reasons behind the crime were tribal and primitive. Udday had blamed Geogo for introducing his father to Samira Shabandar, the blonde who had become Saddam's second wife in 1986, and on seeing Geogo at the party he decided to avenge the affront administered to his mother. Although there had been many other stories of Udday's misbehaviour during the war, this was an unforgivable act of murder by a psychopath.

What followed this affront to Iraqi dignity and human decency subscribed to the old Arab saying that the excuse is worse than the crime. Initially Saddam reacted to the outcry against his son by imprisoning him, then banished him to Switzerland, both for a total of four months, and the press carried stories of these punishments. Later, on the intercession of Udday's mother Sajida, he was allowed to return home and granted a presidential pardon. According to Saddam's media, the family of the victim had invoked a tribal custom and appealed to the hero-President to spare them the life of Udday. Supposedly Udday was like a son to them, and family feuds and misunderstandings often lead to killings which are forgiven. That Udday, Sajida and the rest of the Tikriti tribe would follow this convoluted, totally out-of-date logic was in character, but for Saddam to accept it reconfirmed the suspicion that his modernity was only skin-deep. Moreover, this episode represented a landmark. Saddam never again tried to control or limit the behaviour of members of his family.

On 5 May 1989 General Adnan Khairallah, Minister of Defence, Sajida's brother, Udday's maternal uncle, Saddam's boyhood idol and the one family member who was popular within the armed forces died in a helicopter crash while returning to Baghdad from visiting Army units in Kurdistan. The official explanation spoke of an unexpected sandstorm and a mechanical failure, but every single person interviewed by me alleged that Khairallah was murdered by Saddam because he too had sided with Sajida and objected to the Shabandar marriage. However, these stories cannot be verified and there was indeed a sandstorm on the day of the crash.

But this matters less than the Iraqi people's acceptance of the murder accusation. Not a single Iraqi believes otherwise. The Shabandar factor is less important to them than their belief that Khairallah's popularity with the Army had made him a threat to Saddam. This follow-up to Udday's blatant thuggery made the Iraqi people reel with embarrassment and shame. Even Khomeini's death on 3 June 1989 was overshadowed by that of Khairallah, and there were no Iraqi celebrations.

Some time after being pardoned, in another fit of anger Udday Hussein beat up his cousin Mohammed (son of Barazan) so badly that he damaged his liver and left him unconscious.[24] The once committed populist looked the other way and pretended that his son had done nothing. Encouraged by his father's total permissiveness, Udday began gathering around him a collection of thugs, including Palestinian elements, who smuggled drugs originating in Iran and arms discarded by the Iranian Army to the rest of the Middle East. In a more obvious move, he began buying foreign currency on the official rate and exchanging it on the black market; and these transactions, which took place on a regular basis, realized millions of dollars in profit. He ordered all football players to join the Alawi Football Club, of which he was chairman, and beat up players when they lost.

Udday's final insult to Iraq was directed at its Army. Udday Saddam Hussein, aged twenty-seven, demanded that all army officers, however senior, address him as *sayyidi* (sir). Afraid for their lives, they obeyed him. The only son of a dictator in modern history whose behaviour resembled Udday's was Vasya, Stalin's favourite son, like Udday, a drunk and a rapist, who insisted on being called Prince Vasya. Prince Udday used millions of dollars earned through illegal trade or exchanging currency to build himself a palace right behind Baghdad University. His palace office was the same size as that of his father.

In June 1989, Michel Aflaq died of natural causes. Saddam tried to make the most out of the death of the spiritual father of the Ba'ath, but, despite media exhortations to mourn him, the Iraqi people showed very little interest. When the obvious indifference to the death of his mentor reached Saddam, the people were told that the Christian Aflaq had converted to Islam soon before his death; but after-the-fact conversion too failed to generate a sympathetic reaction. Like many other adoptions of Islamic rhetoric which Saddam incorporated in his propaganda during and after the war with Iran, the Islamization of Aflaq was perceived as a diversion. To the people, Ba'athist ideology as represented by a Christian or a Muslim Aflaq had ceased to matter.

In fact the Iraqis' dismissiveness of Aflaq's death reflected a much wider picture. While the RCC, the National and Regional

Commands of the Ba'ath and the cabinet continued to hold meetings to address the problems facing the country, they had ceased to exist as anything except collections of people who were photographed under the chairmanship of Saddam. His person had so replaced all political structures in the country that members of these organizations were reduced to a castrated cabal of yes-men. When holding individual meetings with Saddam they would not sip their tea until he had done so, and there are unverified rumours that one of them, Hanza Zubeidi, paid dearly for forgetting this. Though he smoked cigars sent to him from Cuba by Castro, Saddam's visitors refrained from doing anything similar. Their subordination to family members was demonstrated by their walking after Udday at official functions. Hussein Kamel was introduced to visiting dignitaries ahead of Izzat Douri, nominally Saddam's second-in-command in the party hierarchy. Whatever non-family members managed was carried out in accordance with Saddam's orders and was aimed at promoting his personal image.

What interested the Iraqi people more than the death of Aflaq and the living dead who surrounded Saddam was their leader's personal behaviour. Except for his participation in the endemic political violence from which Iraq suffered, his personal behaviour had once been considered exemplary; but now it began to resemble that of other members of his family. Much as he had discovered the joys of extramarital sex through emulating his sons, he now joined them in ordinary depravity. Although he openly admitted that corruption had become a national and familial malaise,[25] this did not stop him from personal involvement. Clearly, in his own eyes he had become a sheikh or an emir and accorded himself a position above that of normal mortals. In 1988, he ordered the building of a huge new presidential palace that would take eight years to complete.[26] In August that year, celebrating the official end of the *anfal* campaign against the Kurds, Saddam built an Iraqi equivalent of the French Arc de Triomphe.

The ultimate monument to bad taste, it resembled two human arms modelled on Saddam's own which sprang out of the ground holding swords and joined to form an arch. Each arm was 54 feet in length and weighed 40 tons, while the swords were each 66 feet long, twenty-four times the length of a regular sword. The total height of the monstrosity was 130 feet.[27] It was designed by Saddam himself who, carried away by his newly discovered architectural talents, emulated the frustrated architect in Stalin and began to design other monuments and palaces.

According to Iraqi historian Faleh Abdel Jabbar, this use of Saddam's artistic talents had another purpose behind it: the multiplicity of palaces was part of his new security set-up because nobody knew where he slept any more.[28] Of course, reaching his office within any of them was a complicated exercise which resembled negotiating a maze. Opposition personality Ahmad Allawi, while accepting security as a factor in Saddam's designs, points out that Saddam was importing blue marble from Argentina at a cost of $3000–4000 a square metre in the middle of his country's financial crisis.[29] Though he was outwardly calm and still sensible in the conduct of his regional and international policies, Saddam's perception of himself as a new Arab conqueror did affect the way he behaved. After the end of the war, the Iraqi media announced that people saw Saddam's face on the moon.[30]

The utter lack of control over their personal behaviour from which Udday and Saddam suffered did not stop with them. In 1988, son-in-law Hussein Kamel became a member of the cabinet. He presided over the merger of the Ministry of Industry and Military Industrialization Department, which became known as the Ministry of Industry and Military Industrialization (MIMI). His appointment amounted to a twin exposure of family corruption. Unlike his predecessors in these departments, he expected a commission on every armaments deal[31] including those for Saddam's non-conventional weapons. Furthermore, his appointment to head of this organization was a more serious act of corruption which amounted to undermining the most important programme of Saddam's regime. Hussein Kamel was meagrely educated and scientifically illiterate. His previous work experience had been a brief stint as head of the *mukhabarat*. Once again, the comparison with Stalin forces itself; the Russian dictator had appointed Beria, head of the dreaded NKVD, forerunner of the KGB, to oversee his acquisition of atomic weapons.

It was the United Nations which struck the first blow against Saddam immediately after the ceasefire with Iran. On 29 August 1988, the UN issued a report which detailed Iraqi use of chemical weapons against the Iranians and Kurds and called for punitive measures against Iraq. Several think-tanks issued similar reports. A month later, an explosion in the Iraqi city of Hilla destroyed a suspected chemical and biological warfare plant and resulted in the deaths of hundreds of people. Saddam, totally convinced that 'foreign hands' were behind the UN and other reports and the explosion in Hilla, reacted in an unusually subdued manner. He ignored the chemical warfare reports, insisted that the explosion in Hilla was inconsequential and withheld the casualty figures.[32]

Simultaneous with the Hilla explosion, US Customs officials were organizing a sting operation with CSI Technologies, a defence contractor which had been approached by Saddam's agents to buy nuclear triggers.[33] Operation Argus, the code name for this set-up, was aimed at intercepting and exposing Saddam's purchases of non-conventional weapons. Although it reached its conclusion sixteen months later, after Saddam's relations with the US government had deteriorated, it began at a time when the American administration was still defending Saddam against congressional and other criticism. Shortly afterwards, in November 1988, the US Department of Energy announced that Iraq was pursuing the development of nuclear weapons. After years of toleration, the sudden awakening to Saddam's activities within the USA, and how it started, remains a mystery to this day.

In December 1988, Assistant Secretary of State John Kelly visited Baghdad and had an audience with the Iraqi leader. Saddam used the occasion to register a complaint about the propaganda campaign being waged against Iraq in Congress and by the American press. The attempt to impose sanctions on his country was something he took seriously enough to remind Kelly that Iraq had signed the nuclear non-proliferation treaty. (Obviously the Lebanese who had briefed him on the American system of checks and balances had done a good job.) Saddam also spoke of the adverse effects of overproduction of oil but without mentioning Kuwait by name. And, of course, he made an implicit appeal for financial help.

All this occurred after George Bush had been elected President but before he assumed office. Like Reagan, Bush opposed congressional censure of Iraq and manifested little interest in Saddam's use of chemical weapons, his human rights record and internal politics. Whether or not Kelly was aware that immediately before their meeting Saddam had executed officers Aydan Mustapha, Tareq Ahmad Abdallah and Fadhil Jabbouri for conspiring to overthrow him is unknown. This and two other attempts to otherthrow Saddam were not mentioned, nor was there any American reaction to the dismissal from Army service of two of the leading heroes of the war with Iran, generals Maher Al Rashid and Thabet Sultan. But Kelly was reassuring regarding the administration's intentions towards Iraq to the extent of describing Saddam as 'a force of moderation'.[34] This was the first example of the difference between open US policy and what was happening in the background, Operation Argus.

In January 1989, a report by ABC journalist Charles Glass caused a substantial stir when it alleged that Iraq was developing biological weapons near the town of Salman Pak, south-east of Baghdad and close to Hilla where the explosion had taken place. There were several aspects to this important report which merited examination. Glass had been tipped off by a disaffected senior Iraqi diplomat, but the State Department had denied the existence of such a plant. ABC's contacts with the US–Iraqi Business Forum produced more denials. Eventually, because of the importance of the story and proof supplied by the informer, ABC paid for satellite time, focused on Salman Pak and took detailed pictures of what looked like a modern military structure in an otherwise dusty town of mud huts. Armament authority Anthony Cordesman told ABC that the pictures showed a biological warfare plant, and his claim was supported by scientists hired by ABC and confirmed by some military people who helped ABC on an individual basis. This was the second example of the Bush administration not knowing or disguising what were established facts. Moreover, its overall position regarding chemical warfare differed from ones accepted by the UN, members of independent think-tanks (among them the reputable Washington Institute) and military experts.

That Saddam was determined to ignore the economic circumstances of his country and outside criticism of his regime's military programme and pursue the image of the leading military power in the Arab world became clear on 28 April 1989, his birthday. That was when, two months after the formation of the ACC, he organized what amounted to a military trade fair under the supervision of his son-in-law Hussein Kamel, it was called the First Baghdad Exhibition for Military Production. The United States arms manufacturers were not officially represented, but the US–Iraqi Business Forum was there and its members played guide to major US corporations such as General Motors.[35] One hundred and sixty-eight British corporations were there to show their wares, as were the French, Soviets and everyone else from China to Chile.

The exhibition was a stunning success. What Sa'ad Bazzaz called 'the biggest transfer of technology in the twentieth century'[36] had yielded results. The Iraqis exhibited two rockets, the Hussein and the Abbas, respectively with ranges of 650 and 950 kilometres. They had given the Soviet-made Mig-23 extra range and equipped it with French rockets which made it considerably more lethal than the original model. They had also developed their own advanced warning system and fitted it on several models of aircraft. It was the first disclosure to foreign experts of what Iraq had achieved, and Saddam's message that Iraq was the undisputed regional military power was accepted. But this was accompanied by a measure of shock at the degree of Iraqi success. Reports to the State Department by diplomats and CIA agents using the cover of businessmen cautioned against Saddam's growing military strength.[37]

But the contradictions continued. All warnings aside, in 1989 the United States supplied Iraq with helicopter engines, vacuum pumps for a nuclear plant, sophisticated communications equipment, computers, bacteria strains and hundreds of tons of unrefined Sarin.[38] Furthermore, the pro-Iraq activities of the US–Iraq Business Forum, led as it was by former diplomats with solid connections with the State Department, were augmented by the work of Kissinger Associates, the consulting firm headed by former Secretary of State Henry Kissinger. Representing companies such as Volvo, Fiat and Hunt Oil, this firm was staffed by other insiders who took their signal from the government. Two of the insiders, Brent Scowcroft and Lawrence Eagleburger, were to join the Bush administration in the spring of 1989, the former as National Security Adviser.

There is no overstating the Bush administration's efforts to underwrite the survival of Saddam by continuing to resist the calls to impose sanctions on him, affording him Banca Nazionale del Lavoro CCC credit, encouraging American corporations to trade with him, selling him dual usage equipment and disregarding his threats to his neighbours. On 17 July 1989, tiring of trying to convince Kuwait to reduce its production of oil, Saddam used the anniversary of the Ba'ath's assumption of power to issue a stern warning. Alleging the existence of a conspiracy against Iraq, he declared, 'We have warned them. It is a conspiracy to make us live in famine.'[39] The 'them' was not identified and this coincided with internal reports of another attempt to topple him; another twenty officers were executed. Obviously he was responding to more than one conspiracy, but nobody paid any attention to 'them' and having enemies, or creating them, suited his need to look beleaguered.

In fact, whatever game outsiders were hatching against Saddam continued. In August 1989, Federal agents raided BNL's Atlanta branch and seized cases of documents on the bank's loan programme to Iraq. Though the contents were to be exposed later, enough was already known to reveal a pattern of illegal practices, lending beyond accepted limits and without adequate clearance by the bank's or the country's responsible authorities, which would have prompted most governments to refrain from persisting in the policy which created the situation. But there was more than persistence: what followed amounted to a government-inspired cover-up. Meanwhile, on 13 September, an incident took place in Iraq which reflected the brittle atmosphere of Saddam's relations with the West. Though it was to reverberate later, the arrest of *Observer* journalist Farzad Bazoft while investigating the nature of the Hilla explosion attested to the tension which had developed between Iraq and the West.

Despite the mounting case for the contrary, the Bush administration still refused to change its policy and moved a dangerous step further in its efforts to help Saddam. On 2 October, George Bush signed a secret order (National Security Directive 26) which offered Iraq political and economic incentives to moderate its behaviour and guarantee the flow of oil from the Gulf. The directive also contemplated something else: it was the only official document to broach the subject of US–Iraqi military cooperation.[40] Yet, days after NSD 26, in all likelihood on 22 October, two Kuwaiti officials undertook a secret trip to the United States during which they held a high-level meeting with officials of the CIA. One of the Kuwaiti emissaries, Brigadier Sa'ad Al Ahmad Al Fahd Al Sabah of the royal family, later wrote a report to the Interior Minister, his cousin Salem Al Salem Al Sabah, about meetings with CIA Director William Webster. The report, exposed after the Gulf War, makes a clear statement about CIA–Kuwaiti cooperation and states: 'We agreed with the Americans that there should be visits and exchanges of information between the administrations on the security of state . . . We're agreed with the American side on the necessity to exploit the deteriorating economic situation in Iraq.' The CIA conspiracy against Iraq as revealed by this memorandum calls for closer cooperation between Kuwait and Iran to undermine Saddam, perhaps to replace him.

The obvious question can no longer be delayed. Was there a conflict within the US administration regarding Iraq? The differences of opinion between Congress and the executive branch were there for all to see, but little is known about who was behind Operation Argus, the military people who cooperated with ABC when the State Department would not, and why the CIA was conspiring against Saddam at the same time that Bush was doing everything possible to use him as guarantor of the American position in the Gulf. In November 1989 dual purpose equipment was still reaching Iraq. In December, what began as a raid on BNL became 'Saddamgate', an open-ended questioning by Congress of the behaviour of corporations and government officials towards Iraq. On 5 December, the Iraqis sent a 90-foot three-stage rocket weighing 82 tons and capable of carrying a satellite into outer space. On 8 December a somewhat baffled State Department spokesperson who had previously questioned it confirmed the Iraqi achievement. The year 1990 was to be an eventful one.

On 11 February 1990 John Kelly was back in Baghdad, but this time fulsome praise had given way to implicit criticism. Unlike the situation at past meetings, Kelly's audience with Saddam found him registering misgivings about Iraq's human rights record and, for the first time on the part of an American official, mentioning the use of chemical weapons. Whatever Saddam's on-the-spot response, he could not overlook what followed Kelly's visit. A mere four days later the Voice of America, using information contained in a State Department report, broadcast a scathing criticism of the Iraqi government human rights record and compared it to the crimes of other dictatorships.

Even without the benefit of knowing about the secret Kuwaiti visit to Washington, Saddam decided that he was the target of a conspiracy. US Ambassador to Iraq, April Glaspie's, open apology to the Iraqi Foreign Office was brushed aside by him; among other things, he could not understand why the people responsible for the broadcast had not been punished.[42] Moreover, though it had not been publicized, Saddam connected what was happening with a serious attempt on his life while in his car in Baghdad in early January.[43] Throwing all caution to the wind, on 19 February Saddam responded in kind by giving an exclusive interview to Jordanian television; in it he attacked the American presence in the Gulf, advocating instead Arab control of the Gulf and its resources under the leadership of Iraq.[44]

On 21 February the State Department's report resurfaced through a different channel. Disregarding Glaspie's diplomatic apology, the House Foreign Relations Sub-committee aired the full report on human rights in Iraq, condemned Saddam's regime and proposed sanctions against his country. When the Bush administration declared its opposition to the proposals of the congressional committee, Saddam's conspiratorial mind told him that Bush's objections to the congressional action were part of a cover-up. Accepting the content of the reports of his able ambassador to Washington, Nizar Hamdoun, Saddam was convinced that it was 'an imperialist–Zionist conspiracy'.[45]

That Saddam was more focused on Israel than on Kuwait as being part of the scheming against him is attested to by an earlier statement about American–Israeli complicity that he had made to King Fahd of Saudi Arabia. The Saudi monarch had been reassuring, particularly regarding the intentions of George Bush.[46] But Saddam was not one to take the word of others. On 23 February, a mere two days after the House Committee's action, he arrived in Amman in an unmarked plane and, for obvious security reasons enhanced by the January attempt on his life, without announcing the exact time of his arrival.

Wearing a military uniform and looking grim, Saddam had ostensibly come to Amman to celebrate the first anniversary of the ACC with King Hussein and President Mubarak. But instead of making the usual pronunciations of friendship, he immediately turned the event into an anti-US, anti-Israeli propaganda-fest. In a heated speech he again attacked the US presence in the Gulf, demanded money from the rich Arab states and capped it all by declaring his purpose: reversing the 'rape' of Palestine. 'From here in Amman I see the lights of Jerusalem,' he declared, and followed it with a promise to punish the usurpers.[47] The speech did not differentiate between America and Israel, nor did Saddam make any effort to disguise his intentions to lead the Arabs into a new anti-Israeli crusade.

Hosni Mubarak of Egypt, dependent as he was on US economic support and opposed to going back on the Camp David Agreement with Israel, took strong and open exception to Saddam's exhortations and demands. Sounding as if he were lecturing a child, he told Saddam that 'this kind of talk is not permitted'. Then he described Saddam's demands that $30 billion worth of debts to other Arab countries be cancelled as 'unjustified'. He followed his reprimand by announcing that he was going home. King Hussein's intercession stopped Mubarak from leaving the meeting, but the issue between the heads of the two leading Arab countries was irreconcilable. They were never to trust each other again, and the differences in their policies on regional problems were to have serious consequences for their countries and the rest of the Middle East.

What followed the fiasco in Amman can be judged in terms of the total absence of any attempts to repair the damage to US–Iraqi relations and to intercept the march to disaster. The string of inexplicable incidents which followed also made undertaking such efforts impossible. After so many years of direct, indirect, open and secret cooperation, US–Iraqi relations still suffered from lack of mutual trust which manifested itself in an inability to engage in a constructive dialogue. Strange as it may sound, there was not a single person within the American administration capable of assuming the role of intermediary to resolve problems, which increased the tension between the two countries.

Because Saddam suspected him of being part of the wider conspiracy against him, John Kelly was no longer an acceptable channel. April Glaspie was hampered by her position; according to former Assistant Secretary of State Richard Murphy, Saddam thought that dealing with people below cabinet rank was beneath him.[48] Members of the US–Iraqi Business Forum were so taken aback by developments that they could not think of anything to do. In Washington, Nizar Hamdoun was finding it more and more difficult to operate effectively within the developing atmosphere of belligerence. Mubarak had decided that Saddam was too unreliable and unpredictable, and refused to play mediator. Rather than enhancing his position, King Hussein's relations with both sides neutralized him. Each side wanted him to promote their point of view, and he did not want to alienate either. For a while, until the Americans prevailed on Saudi Ambassador to the USA Prince Bandar to visit Saddam in an attempt to defuse the situation, nothing was happening on the diplomatic front.

However, what was fuelling the fires of discord was substantial, damaging and occurring with disturbing and suspicious frequency. On 10 March 1990 the journalist Farzad Bazoft was sentenced to death for spying, and his companion, a nurse by the name of Daphne Parrish, to fifteen years' imprisonment. That the trial was a sham is undoubtedly true. But the noise generated by the Western media and the blind insistence that this relatively uneducated journalist with a questionable background was innocent were not justified by the facts, not only that, they were inflammatory. In fact, the protests and accusations against the Iraqi regime backfired and Bazoft was hanged on 15 March.

Despite my wish to adhere to the tradition of never criticizing fellow journalists, the importance of the Bazoft case leaves me no option but to examine it. The outcry of the press in the UK, USA and elsewhere and the shrill insistence that Bazoft was not guilty did irreparable damage to Iraq's image in the world. Had the accusations against Iraq been limited to Saddam's system of justice the press would have been on solid ground, but presuming Bazoft's innocence is something else. Not one of the six journalists interviewed by me regarding the Bazoft case – and they include former colleagues on the *Observer* – believed that he was innocent. He had been sent to Iraq to cover an important story when more qualified journalists were available for the assignment. He was Iranian by origin, a bad writer with a criminal record and suspicious contacts, and when in Iraq he had resorted to questionable methods to reach the site of the explosion. Moreover, the two leading authorities on the subject, journalist Simon Henderson and intelligence historian Rupert Allason, have suggested that Bazoft had intelligence connections.[49] Even the Saudi-owned daily *Al Hayat*, like Henderson and Allason not given to supporting Saddam Hussein, accused Bazoft of spying on 8 May 1991.

On 22 March 1990, a week after Bazoft's execution, Gerald Bull, the Canadian armaments scientist and Saddam's adviser on rocketry, was assassinated in Brussels. While irrefutable evidence is lacking, most people accept that the Israeli intelligence service, Mossad, was behind this killing. To Saddam, the two murders (without a fair trial for Bazoft his execution becomes murder) were related. Bazoft had been caught trying to get earth samples to prove that the Hilla explosion had involved a non-conventional weapons plant, and his capture and execution were used against Saddam; Bull was killed because he was helping Saddam develop his rockets and his murder generated little protest; and the perpetrators were never apprehended. Of course, the suspicion that Mossad was involved added to Saddam's belief that there was a conspiracy,[50] to him one involving the USA and Israel.

On 28 March five people were arrested at Heathrow Airport while trying to smuggle krytons, capacitors, that could be used in triggering an atomic device. The UK customs officials had acted after being tipped off by their American counterparts, and this was the culmination of Operation Argus (renamed Quarry at this point). Two days later Saddam Hussein, proudly holding a kryton, told the world that Iraq had all the krytons it needed. He blamed the Heathrow interception on Zionist and imperialist elements, and vowed that Iraq would continue its efforts in the arms field.

On 2 April Saddam held a televised press conference in which he listed a number of complaints against the West. He used the reaction to the Bazoft execution, the murder of Bull, the threats to apply sanctions and the interception of the krytons to support a case of conspiracy against Iraq. To Saddam, the enemy behind it all was Israel. Convinced that Israel was considering attacking Iraq and destroying its non-conventional weapons,[51] he responded by issuing the most blatant military threat of his career. Admitting that Iraq possessed binary chemical weapons, a particularly lethal form, he declared, 'We'll devour half of Israel by fire, *if it tries to attack Iraq.*' Yet Saddam still left the door open for the crisis to be defused. On 5 April he invited the Saudi Ambassador to the USA, Prince Bandar, to visit him in Iraq. At their meeting, he asked the Prince to intercede with Washington to stop an Israeli attack on Iraq.[52]

The United States described the speech as inflammatory, and the rest of the world began paying attention to the developing crisis. But the dual game of appeasing Saddam while exerting economic pressure on him and stopping the flow of non-conventional weapons to Iraq continued. On 11 April the British government announced that a shipment of steel tube to make a supergun had been intercepted. This was followed almost immediately by similar actions involving different components of the supergun in Spain, Greece, the Netherlands, Turkey, Switzerland and Italy. To this day, there is no plausible explanation as to who coordinated these moves or why the relevant departments in these various countries all woke up at the same time.

But whatever was happening was obviously not part of the policy of the executive branch of the US government. On 12 April, ten days after Saddam's famous but conditional threat, a congressional delegation led by Senator Robert Dole had a meeting with him in the northern Iraqi city of Mosul. (Saddam was in fact there on his honeymoon after marrying his third wife, Nidal Al Hamdani, the manager of the solar energy department at the Iraqi Ministry of Industry and Military Industrialization.) The Americans had been encouraged to make the trip by none other than President Bush[53] and their purpose was to promote better business and political relations between Iraq and the USA. Saddam repeated his complaints about the Voice of America broadcast, overall press coverage, the fuss over Bazoft, threats of sanctions and exaggeration of the Iraqi threat. The senators, determined to please him, told him that President Bush's policy differed from what the press was saying; Senator Alan Simpson confirmed this by telling Saddam that his problem was strictly with the press.

In another reassuring move on 24 April, John Kelly appeared in front of the House Foreign Relations Sub-committee and made an appeal against applying sanctions against Iraq. But Saddam, definitely suffering from a dizzying case of confusion beyond his intellectual capabilities, had reason to be suspicious. General Norman Schwarzkopf, chief of the US Army's Central Command, was making regular visits to Kuwait during which he was critical of Iraq and identified it as the enemy.[54] In addition, the Iraqis had received news that the Central Command's Army exercises were based on scenarios which identified Iraq as their target, in place of the USSR. Other reports reaching the Iraqis suggested that CIA chief William Webster had made several visits to Kuwait during which he had meetings with the Emir, and that after each meeting the Kuwaitis increased their oil production.[55]

It was these moves, coupled with successful US legislation to suspend loans to Iraq on 21 May, which shifted Saddam's focus from Israel to Kuwait. The split in American policy between a pro-

Saddam executive branch and an anti-Saddam Congress, press and perhaps intelligence service, hard to understand especially for a dictator, was accepted by Saddam until the total suspension of American loans. He could not survive without them while Kuwait and the United Arab Emirates continued their overproduction of oil. Despairing of changing the American attitude without having to pay for it through unaffordable political compromises, he turned his attention to Kuwait.

Until the reports of Schwarzkopf's and Webster's visits and the suspension of American loans, Kuwait had continued its over-production of oil and Iraq had continued its protests. The last open Iraqi protest against overproduction was registered on 3 May. When that failed, Iraq called for an Arab League Heads of State meeting and offered to host it. Though it opposed the holding of the meeting, Kuwait agreed to attend. Meanwhile Saddam, once again relying on his intelligence to formulate policy, discovered another aspect to the 'Kuwaiti conspiracy'. His agents in the Emirate sent back a report which merited his personal attention. It claimed that Kuwait was offering to sell the Iraqi debt notes incurred during the war with Iran to the British Lloyds Bank at a considerable discount.[56] What this meant was simple: Iraq could no longer borrow money on the international market because its credit rating was unacceptable. Despite an open agenda calling for discussions on Jewish immigration, the attacks on Iraq by the Western media and the denial of sophisticated technology to the Arabs, it was this secret report and Saddam's unexpected demands which determined the outcome of the Arab League meeting in Baghdad on 28–30 May.

The first ominous sign that this was no ordinary summit came when Saddam suggested that the sessions should be held in secret. He prevailed, despite the objections of others. He opened the first session with a long, improvised speech in which he lashed out at Kuwait and the United Arab Emirates for producing more oil than was allocated to them by OPEC. Citing Kuwait as an example, he wondered out loud why it had to produce 2.1 million barrels a day instead of its share of 1.5 million. He followed this by openly accusing Kuwait of declaring economic warfare against his coun-try, stating that wars are not necessarily fought with tanks and planes.[57] Then, cleverly, he offered Kuwait a way out – the cancelling of debt; the leasing of two islands at the mouth of the Gulf, Warba and Bubiyan, to give Iraq a sensible sea outlet; and a payment of billions of dollars. His summation was a combination of threat and appeal: 'I ask my Arab brothers not to declare war on Iraq.'[58] Whatever shock Saddam wanted to administer to the Arab leaders worked, with one exception. While the others scurried around, objected to the extent of Saddam's demands, said that they found the issuing of threats unacceptable and offered comments of reconciliation, the Emir of Kuwait remained utterly unmoved.[59] Many analysts of the events of May 1990 describe the Kuwaiti behaviour as 'strange'.[60]

I am indebted to a member of the PLO's delegation to this conference, who spoke on non-attribution basis, for a most revealing record of a small meeting within the larger Arab meeting which was held to settle the issue between Iraq and Kuwait. With minor modification, what occurred was confirmed to me by Pierre Salinger, a leading historian of the Gulf War, in February 1992. Those present at the small meeting were Saddam, the Emir of Kuwait, Yasser Arafat, King Hussein of Jordan and King Fahd of Saudi Arabia. President Mubarak of Egypt, angry over Saddam's opening outburst, had refused an invitation.

With Saddam and the Emir of Kuwait silent, the other Arab leaders called for a 'brotherly' solution. Specifically, they wanted Kuwait to keep to its oil quota and to refrain from asking for repayment of the $8 billion that Iraq owed it. Certain issues were not raised: Iraqi demands that the debt be cancelled; the lease of the two Gulf islands to Iraq; and that Iraq be given a substantial infusion of funds to compensate it for its efforts during the war with Iran and for Kuwaiti pumping oil from the disputed Rumeillah oilfield. Saddam, waiting for the Kuwaiti reaction, said nothing. But the Emir of Kuwait, still unconcerned and speaking haughtily, refused to commit himself to any reduction in oil production, rejected the principle of compensating Iraq for oil extracted from Rumeillah, spoke of the sanctity of Kuwaiti territory and insisted that the Iraqi debt be paid immediately.

It was Arafat who realized the gravity of what was happening. Shaking with anger, he wagged a finger at the Kuwaiti and told him that the consequences of his attitude endangered peace in the whole Middle East. This too failed to generate any reaction; the Emir showed no interest in compromise. He did make a passing comment about Iraq accepting a final border between the two countries and made plain that internal considerations stood between him and accepting a delay in the repayment of the debt. With that the meeting broke up; Fahd and Hussein lamented the divisions in Arab ranks, while Arafat seethed with anger. The following day, the Emir of Kuwait approached Saddam during one of the larger meetings and asked to discuss the border issue between the two countries. The Iraqi leader put his arm around him and said that he had a surprise for him,[61] that all would be well.

Saddam, humiliated by Kuwaiti arrogance, was dead-set on exacting revenge. This became clear in a passing comment he made soon after the meeting to the Saudi Minister of Petroleum: 'I'll never allow my people to starve.'[62] Without articulating it, the believer in full bellies had once again reverted to his tribal instincts of *darb al a'naq wala qata' al arzaq* (chopping necks is preferable to denial of livelihood), an old Arab saying. Though the crisis with Kuwait was escalating, there was evidence that Saddam had still not made up his mind regarding his way out – whether it was still preferable to provoke a crisis with Israel. A month after the Arab summit, during an Islamic conference in Baghdad, he expanded his warning to Israel against attacking Iraq by stating that he would 'strike Israel if it attacked any Arab country'.[63] The emblem of the Islamic conference was Jerusalem's Dome of the Rock.

The Arab Summit in Baghdad marked the beginning of an unstoppable march towards war. In a last-ditch effort, Saddam sent his trusted adviser Dr Sa'adoun Hamadi to the various oil-producing countries to ask them to curtail their production. The Kuwaitis not only refused to listen, they signalled a hostile policy by inviting Iranian Foreign Minister Vilayati to visit their country and closed Kuwaiti airspace to Iraqi civilian aircraft. President Mubarak, King Hussein, Yasser Arafat and other Arab leaders continued their efforts to reach a negotiated settlement between the two sides, but the Kuwaitis would not compromise on anything.

The Kuwaiti attitude deserves close examination. According to Middle East historian Dilip Hiro, everyone was telling Kuwait to hold the line – and in this case 'everyone' meant the USA and UK.[64] In fact, British Prime Minister Margaret Thatcher's support for Kuwait was open and her encouragement that Kuwait should reject Iraqi demands was contained in a cable to the Emir. Norman

Schwarzkopf openly warned the Kuwaitis against Iraq.[65] Even Kuwaitis share the puzzlement and suspicions of outsiders as to what prompted their government to adopt such a dangerously uncompromising position. After the Gulf War, several of the more educated and knowledgeable among them expressed their misgivings to writer and Middle East expert Milton Viorst. The Kuwaiti economist Dr Jassem Al Sa'adoun accused his government of following 'the wrong oil policy'. Businessmen Ali Al Bedah saw the whole thing as a plan 'to get rid of Saddam'. And professor of politics Dr Massima Al Mubarak stated that none of Saddam's demands amounted to 'violating our [Kuwaiti] national interest'.[66] That something, in all likelihood US guarantees, led the Kuwaiti government to behave in a 'strange' way is accepted by everyone.

The puzzlement that prominent Kuwaitis express regarding their government's attitude prior to the invasion by Iraq is made more curious by the attitude of the Gulf Arabs. A telephone conversation between King Fahd and Sheikh Zayyed of the United Arab Emirates that was intercepted by the Iraqis revealed a dismissive attitude to the crisis, which the two men attributed to Iraqi bad temper and inclination to create problems.[67] This telephone call and a manifest lack of interest in finding a solution betray a conviction that Saddam would not invade. Meanwhile, the efforts of other Arabs were getting nowhere, while the West was supporting Kuwaiti stubbornness and doing little else. Saddam's frustration was becoming more acute by the minute.

On 10 July, during a conference of Gulf oil producers in the port city of Jeddah, the two countries appeared to have reached a solution. The Kuwaitis, in the presence of Iran and Saudi Arabia, agreed to reduce their oil production to the OPEC-permitted level. But this did not last long; only hours afterwards, the Kuwaiti Oil Minister announced that his country would subscribe to the agreement for a mere three months.[68] On the international market the value of the Iraqi dinar plummeted by 50 per cent. Sa'adoun Hamadi, the able Iraqi economist who had negotiated the agreement, joined those people who believed Kuwait was behaving strangely. The makers of Kuwaiti policy were too arrogant to realize they were dealing with a Tikriti who was accustomed to taking risks.

On 15 July, Iraqi Foreign Minister Tareq Aziz lodged a complaint against Kuwait with the Arab League. In it he repeated

Saddam's claim that every one dollar reduction in the price of a barrel of oil cost the Iraqis a billion dollars at a time of dire economic conditions. The Arab League proved as impotent as ever; nothing happened. But in an important development with eventual far-reaching implications, Hosni Mubarak of Egypt visited Saddam and, according to the Egyptian President, secured a promise that force would not be used against Kuwait while there was room for a negotiated solution.[69]

Whatever promise Saddam Hussein gave to Mubarak – and it was disputed by Saddam and subsequent events – the Iraqi leader knew that a real solution lay in the hands of the United States. Desperate for a way out, and losing face over the confrontation with Kuwait was unimaginable to him, Saddam decided to determine the American attitude to the crisis for himself. On 25 July, thinking that she had been summoned to a meeting with Tareq Aziz, the Arabic-speaking US Ambassador to Iraq, April Glaspie, was taken to see Saddam Hussein.

This was to become one of the most controversial diplomatic encounters of all time. But, while it is impossible to analyze Saddam's purpose accurately, the record of the meeting is available. Saddam's many complaints – and he certainly was complaining – were summed up in two simple statements to the Ambassador: that Kuwait was overproducing oil, and that the United States supported this policy which was tantamount to economic warfare against Iraq. He followed this with a review of US–Iraqi relations and, importantly, complained bitterly about the Iran–Contra Affair.[70] Saddam could not understand why America's Congress and media were against him, why America had stopped viewing him as a friend; but, threatening to retaliate against Kuwait's economic policies, he was not servile. The most important point in the meeting, the one for which Glaspie has been criticized mercilessly, was her admission that the USA had 'no opinion on Arab conflicts'.[71] In fact, this was in line with American policy and less significant than her overall assessment that Saddam was extending a hand of friendship and her decision to follow the meeting by going on holiday.

The statement regarding the absence of a commitment by the USA to defend Kuwait represented US policy and was not Glaspie's own invention. One day before the Glaspie–Saddam meeting, State Department spokesperson Margaret Tutwiler had admitted that there were no treaty obligations for the USA to protect the Gulf countries. This had been the line followed by Assistant Secretary of State John Kelly throughout, and one he repeated two days before the invasion of Kuwait. Glaspie's statement did not give Saddam a green light to invade Kuwait – it confirmed that the light was already green. Even with Glaspie's report in his possession, George Bush sent Saddam a friendly message on 27 July 1990: it reconfirmed America's good intentions towards Iraq and its leader.

The flurry of Arab diplomatic activity taking place during this period of open Iraqi threats against Kuwait was making little progress. Saddam's conspiratorial instincts, dramatized by the seemingly unsolvable economic problems of his country, took precedence in his mind to the assurances of Glaspie, Kelly and Bush. He was bewildered by the Kuwaitis' attitude and convinced that the country was being used as base against him. According to a former aide now resident in London, Saddam remembered how Kuwait had been used against Kassem in 1963 and how the CIA had supported the Kurds against the Ba'ath, and made much of American duplicity against Iraq during its war with Iran.

The only hope of averting war rested on a proposed Saudi–Kuwaiti–Iraq meeting scheduled for 31 July in Jeddah. The high-level Iraqi delegation to the meeting was headed by Deputy Secretary General of the RCC Izzat Douri, and the Kuwaiti team by Crown Prince Sa'ad. King Fahd was supposed to chair the negotiations, but showed little interest and ceded the function to his brother, Crown Prince Abdallah. Instead of being a venue of reconciliation, Jeddah became a battleground of recrimination. Each side upped its demands and Abdallah proved unable to bridge the gap between them. The Iraqis eventually resorted to threats which Sheikh Sa'ad of Kuwait answered with a blunt warning of his own: 'Don't threaten us, Kuwait has important friends',[72] something that the Kuwaitis had told King Hussein when he had tried to defuse the crisis. The meeting broke down on 1 August, a day when a shipment of sophisticated US-made transmission equipment reached Baghdad.[73] Twenty-four hours later, Iraqi armour and paratroops invaded Kuwait and in a most efficient operation occupied it in four hours. Though it had already gone on for months, the crisis caught the world unprepared and the

Kuwaiti resistance, though nobody expected them to hold the line for long, was so feeble that it precluded dispatching immediate help to forestall the invasion.[74] The Kuwaiti royal family quickly escaped from their country in accordance with a plan which had been worked out with the Americans months before.[75]

11

An Abundance of Pride,
A Shortage of Intellect

Saddam Hussein's plan to confront the world with a *fait accompli* ended with the escape of the Emir of Kuwait. The survival of the Emir simplified the dilemma for Saddam's opponents and reduced their problem to one of restoring the legitimate government of a member state of the Arab League and the United Nations. Saddam's occupation of Kuwait amounted to the acquisition of territory by force, a clear violation of international law which would have to be reversed. With the Emir free, it could be undone without conceding anything to Saddam or changing the regional political structure.

As with the war against Iran, when Saddam invaded Kuwait he overestimated his position and failed to take into consideration all possibilities and their consequences. Once again, Saddam's evaluation of the intelligence reports reaching him and his personal assessment of what his action might produce were wrong. The vital issues of the regional balance of power and importance of oil temporarily aside, his miscalculation became obvious when he was turned down by the individuals he had counted on to form a new Kuwaiti government capable of giving his action the veneer of legitimacy. He had not consulted any of them.

His leading candidate to run Kuwait had been Fahd Al Ahmad Al Sabah, the younger brother of Jabber Al Ahmad Al Sabah, the Emir. But Fahd Al Ahmad was the one Kuwaiti royal who did not flee the Iraqi onslaught and he died defending Dasman Palace, the family seat. Although he was unlikely to have accepted Saddam's offer, the death of Fahd Al Ahmad denied Saddam a chance to personalize his problem with Kuwait by blaming it on the older Sabah. He had convinced himself that dethroning the Emir would be welcomed by many people, including his royal relations. Saddam now offered the position to a member of the Kuwaiti National Assembly and occasional critic of the Kuwaiti government, Aziz Al Rashid, but he rejected all cooperation with Saddam. Saddam's third candidate was Faisal Al Sanii, a Kuwaiti Ba'athist. But he too refused to equate his belief in the Ba'ath's call for Arab unity with acceptance of military occupation.[1]

This completed Saddam's first Kuwaiti defeat. His initial expectations were similar to believing that the Iran–Iraq War would be short-lived and having no other plan. Again, what followed was improvized rather than thought out. Saddam found a willing collaborator in a little-known officer, Colonel Ala' Hussein Ali, and eight of his colleagues who belonged to the large group of disenfranchised Kuwaitis called Bidoons who, because of their forebears' nomadic border-crossing existence had never been offered Kuwaiti citizenship. He made Ali Emir and claimed that Iraq had invaded Kuwait at the request of Ali and his clique. According to this, they had overthrown the Kuwaiti government and set up a provisional one in its place. Nor did Saddam limit himself to this absurd story, he proceeded to give the world mixed signals about his real intentions. He received the hapless Colonel Ali in Baghdad, showered him with praise and embraced him in front of photographers, but told the rest of the world a different story.

Reacting to UN Security Council (UNSC) resolution 660 which condemned the invasion, demanded an immediate Iraqi withdrawal from Kuwait and threatened sanctions, Saddam assured King Hussein of Jordan of his willingness to pull out of Kuwait if the Arab League did not censure his move. The Jordanian King had hurried to see Saddam hours after the invasion, following consultations with other Arab leaders and after securing a promise of inaction for forty-eight hours from President Bush. The King returned to Amman a day later, thinking that he and Saddam had reached an agreement. But the rather vague offer to withdraw elicited no response from other quarters. Secretary of State James Baker and Foreign Minister Edvard Shevardnadze of the USSR, by chance in Irkutsk, Siberia, to discuss other issues, released a joint statement calling for unconditional Iraqi withdrawal, the restoration of Kuwaiti sovereignty, the freezing of Iraq's and Kuwait's overseas assets and the withholding of arms deliveries to Saddam. They repeated this in Moscow the following day. On top of UNSC resolution 660, this allowed America to request Saudi Arabia and Turkey to stop the flow of Iraqi oil carried by pipelines running through their countries. Moreover, US naval units were now heading towards the Gulf.

An emergency meeting of Arab Foreign Ministers in Cairo duplicated the demands of others, but opposed any foreign intervention in an Arab dispute. Acting on King Hussein's report of his meeting with Saddam, they refrained from attacking Iraq and announced that a mini summit meeting of Saddam, King Fahd, King Hussein and President Mubarak was to be held in Saudi Arabia on 5 August. Its purpose was to settle the problem by rolling back the Iraqi invasion, but Saddam made his agreement to attend it conditional on the Arabs refraining from condemnations or attacks against him in the meanwhile. The following day Mubarak, despite a promise he had made to King Hussein,[2] publicly denounced Saddam and the Iraqi invasion and called for unconditional Iraqi withdrawal. This occurred after King Fahd of Saudi Arabia had told Mubarak that he was for an Arab solution and against the stationing of foreign troops in his country. It amounted to an unnecessary raising of the stakes. Mubarak was taunting Saddam, forcing him into a corner and endangering the proposed meeting. Saddam's over-reaction, which ought to have been expected, prompted Fahd to consider calling for outside help. To King Hussein, the Egyptian President's tirade was wholly responsible for Saddam's failure to keep the promise he had secured in Baghdad.[3] An inter-Arab war of accusations and recriminations followed and exposed the divisions among the Arab states. The resulting deprecation of King Hussein's mediation role provided outsiders with a chance to become involved and to control the direction of the crisis. The United States moved into the breach.

A day after confirming to Yasser Arafat his acceptance of King Hussein's proposals for a mini summit of Arab leaders,[4] on 4 August, President Mubarak followed his denunciation of Saddam by quietly dispatching a small contingent of Egyptian troops to Saudi Arabia.[5] This serious decision had been preceded by telephone conversations with both President Bush and King Fahd. When King Hussein and Arafat objected to being undermined by the new Egyptian attitude, Mubarak accused Saddam of having lied to him during the pre-invasion crisis, of having told him that he would not resort to military action. But despite that, every Arab leader except Mubarak was still committed to an Arab solution and the Arab governments still acted in accordance with the explicit caution adopted by the Arab Foreign Ministers during the meeting in Cairo on 3 August.

Mubarak's various actions had become a test of will between the Iraqi and Egyptian leaders. The idea of the mini-summit died a natural death when Fahd followed Mubarak and demanded an unconditional commitment to withdrawal from Saddam prior to meeting him. On 5 August, in another attempt to extricate himself from the crisis he had created, Saddam, with the perfunctory backing of the RCC, told King Hussein he was pulling some of his forces out of Kuwait. Ten thousand Iraqi troops, including units of the Republican Guard, did indeed withdraw from Kuwait.[6] A day later Saddam held a meeting with the US chargé d'affaires in Baghdad, Joseph Wilson, reassured him regarding the foreigners in Iraq and Kuwait whom he was holding as hostages, stated that he had no intention whatsoever of attacking Saudi Arabia, and hinted at the possibility of withdrawal. When Mubarak and Bush ignored the gestures and maintained their demands, Saddam announced the formation of eleven more Army divisions to augment his armed forces. Mubarak had succeeded. King Fahd, until then still in favour of using Arab forces instead of foreign troops to protect his country, began tilting towards the Mubarak–Bush axis.

In examining this short period crammed with confused and contradictory hourly developments, I am struck by the fact that Mubarak's personal accusations that the Iraqi leader was a liar took precedence over any concessions towards a peaceful solution and saving the world from a catastrophe. Mubarak's attitude and Saddam's reactions betrayed a rare animosity between two arrogant men that resembled the behaviour of Mafia godfathers. Mubarak was a vain man who spent hours dyeing his hair and attending to his looks, and he considered that his position as leader of Egypt, the most populous and arguably most important Arab country, afforded him special status. On the other side, Saddam was the knight on a white charger, a tough uncompromising settled

Bedouin who saw himself as a victor over the Persians and thus the natural heir to proud Arab history. He resented the Egyptian leader's subservience to the West and his ingratitude regarding Iraq's help to Egyptian workers and Saddam's sponsorship of the readmission of Egypt to the Arab League after its expulsion following the Camp David Agreement. Above all, the post-invasion messages between the two men reveal a haughtiness on the part of Mubarak who wanted Saddam to leave the Egyptian leader to determine the nature of a satisfactory settlement.[7] Saddam's response was to terminate all contact between them. What had started in Amman during the second anniversary celebrations of the ACC, the conflict between the two men over basic policies, was to escalate into mutual accusations of treason. Behind the personal factors lay the historical competition for Arab leadership between Egypt and Iraq. There was no way that Mubarak would miss a chance to deny Saddam and Iraq Arab leadership, and denying the Tikriti (and Mubarak used that term) Kuwait's oil riches opened the way for Egyptian reassumption of Arab leadership and intercepted Iraq's bid to claim it. What Saddam had hoped for by creating the ACC, acceptance of his primacy in the Arab world through pulling Egypt away from the USA and getting it to cancel the Camp David Agreement, was in tatters. Not for the first time, Saddam's inflated image of himself and his achievements made him misjudge how others, Khomeini and Mubarak in particular, assessed them.

On 6 August, British Prime Minister Margaret Thatcher, on holiday in America, had a meeting with President Bush in Aspen, Colorado at which she emphatically urged him to take a strong, uncompromising stand against Saddam. Bush's earlier reaction after the invasion had been that he was not ruling anything out or in while making precautionary moves, but Thatcher was of the opinion that Saddam should be stopped, and by the use of force if necessary. Thatcher's was a totally British attitude, one that has become a national trademark since the failure to appease Hitler in the 1930s. On 7 August, US Secretary of Defence Richard Cheney met with King Fahd and, equipped with President Bush's Thatcher-inspired instructions, requested the stationing of US troops in Saudi Arabia against the possibility of an Iraqi invasion.

Much has been written about Cheney's success in his efforts, and how he used phoney satellite pictures which showed an imminent (but non-existent) Iraqi-threat to Saudi Arabia, and how Crown Prince Abdallah had not joined King Fahd in accepting his presentation. But this is irrelevant, because the Egyptian move which preceded the Cheney–Fahd meeting had already provided the monarch with the mandate needed to invite foreign troops into his country. The initial rejection of foreign troops was a reflection of the feared reaction of the Saudi people, and the presence of Arab–Muslim troops was used as a justification. What Mubarak provided[8] with studied deliberateness was an Islamic–Arab cover. Even an offer by King Hussein to station Jordanian troops as a buffer between Kuwait and Iraq after a pull-out was dismissed out of hand by Mubarak, who had somehow become the spokesman for the anti-Saddam Arabs. Despite that, the acceptance of US troops by Fahd was conditional. President Bush himself declared that the presence of US forces in Saudi Arabia was wholly defensive, and this was what King Fahd understood and claimed.[9]

On 8 August, the alley boy in Saddam surfaced. He responded to the uncompromising moves aimed at forcing his immediate withdrawal from Kuwait without even a safe conduct for his troops by annexing the country as the nineteenth province of Iraq. He still declared, however, that he harboured no designs against Saudi Arabia. Instead of the local emir, Ala' Hussein Ali, Saddam's cousin General Ali Hassan Al Majid (Ali Chemical) was appointed governor of the 'new province'. This produced another UN resolution of condemnation and reinforced the previous international demands. But more important for Saddam was the loss of the USSR as a friend and potential neutral intermediary. The USA and USSR found themselves in total agreement regarding what was happening, and produced repeated rigid demands for his immediate withdrawal.

Unlike when he started the war with Iran, Saddam was now totally bereft of major friends and his only hope lay in an Arab solution. But it was a fading hope indeed and his customary arrogance was unpalatable to the rest of the Arabs, particularly in the circumstances. Even Ba'athist Syria which, though opposed to Saddam, had uneasy relations with America, was conducting anti-Saddam negotiations with Washington. These culminated in Syria joining the coalition against Iraq in return for a free hand in Lebanon together with financial help from Saudi Arabia and the exiled royal family of Kuwait.

The Arab League heads of state met in Cairo on 10 August in lieu of the originally proposed mini summit. But Saddam's last hope for escaping an Arab League censure turned into a fiasco. On Mubarak's orders the Iraqi delegates, headed by Vice President Taha Yassin Ramadan and Vice Premier Tareq Aziz, were accommodated in Al Andalus, a small, decrepit hotel with a defunct telephone switchboard[10] which prevented the Iraqis from lobbying other Arab delegations. During the meeting proper, a suggestion by King Hussein aimed at finding an Arab solution was turned down summarily by Mubarak,[11] which led to a shouting match between the two leaders. The PLO was stopped from presenting a proposal aimed at forming an Arab mediation committee.[12] Another bout of shouting, this time between the Iraqis and Kuwaitis, made the Emir of Kuwait faint. Finally, King Hussein lost his temper. He reminded Mubarak that they had agreed on an exclusively Arab solution and followed this with accusations that the Egyptian was obeying outside order.

The only resolution which was brought to vote was one presented – most unexpectedly – by the Egyptians. It was passed by twelve of the twenty-one members, and not unanimously as stipulated in the rules of the Arab League. Nothing more than a validation of what Egypt had already done, it supported the sending of Arab troops to defend Saudi Arabia as a cover for the American troops – and US Air Force planes were already arriving in the kingdom. But the resolution was a phoney one – no one had been told about it or had had time to study it thoroughly, and it was obvious to most of the Arab leaders that the text had been translated from English into Arabic in a hurry.[13] In fact, the Egyptian writer Mohammed Heikal takes this matter a step further and suggests that Mubarak had pressured Bush into acting against Saddam speedily to pre-empt the Arab streets exploding in support of the Iraqi leader.[14] The Egyptian leader certainly showed no signs of considering a compromise, and three weeks after the Arab League meeting he lashed out at King Hussein and his Arab solution proposal in front of a visiting US congressional delegation. Meanwhile, the UN was issuing another resolution, this time against the annexation.

On 12 August, the side of Saddam which betrayed calculation and caution took over from the impulsive street fighter. He announced a willingness to withdraw from Kuwait in accordance with UN resolutions, in return for Israeli acceptance of similar ones demanding their withdrawal from the territories they had occupied in 1967. The attempt at linkage was turned down by all parties concerned, including the Arab countries. A few days later, Saddam granted Iran all it had demanded to end the state of war with Iraq, including navigation rights in the Shat Al Arab waterway. Unlike his other daring but improvised moves, the linkage between pulling out of Kuwait and the Israeli occupation of Arab territory was a masterstroke. Adopting it on the heel of demonstrations through the Arab world against the behaviour of the anti-Saddam Arab governments – and the average Arab was opposed to Western interference in the crisis – he drove a wedge between the Arab people and their leaders. Even Palestinian leaders who had objected to Saddam's occupation of Kuwait – and they included Arafat's second in command Abu Iyyad and PLO Executive Committee member Jaweed Ghossein – were taken aback by the action.

In Morocco, Jordan, Egypt, Tunisia, Algeria, the Sudan, Yemen, the occupied territories and countries as far east as Malaysia, people demonstrated against the planned military campaign against Iraq. Many of them disapproved of Saddam's adventurism, but they accepted his claim that the West was following a double standard. However, that provided Saddam with little comfort. His oil exports had ceased and food, most of it imported, was running out. A US military plane carrying troops or war materials was landing in Saudi Arabia every ten minutes. Despite reports that the Iraqis were deploying in defensive positions inside Kuwait[15] (they certainly refrained from appearing to do anything that suggested attacking Saudi Arabia) the announced number of foreign troops needed to protect the oil kingdom kept increasing. It went up to four hundred thousand, and the number of countries willing to participate in the coalition against Saddam kept rising too. Moreover, countries which sided with Saddam suffered the consequences of America's belligerent mood. Secretary of State Baker told Yemen that its UN stand against punishing Saddam was the most expensive vote it would ever cast.[16]

The end of August and early September saw several disjointed attempts to stop the slide towards war. Saddam, knowing that the Americans were monitoring his troop movements, tried to impress them by withdrawing more men from Kuwait. On 31 August, finally waking up to the crisis swirling around him, UN Secretary General Perez de Cuellar held a meeting with Iraqi Vice Premier

Tareq Aziz in Amman. Incredibly, except for admitting that even a partial use of force against Iraq needed a specific UN resolution, he had nothing to offer. Instead of manifesting initiative through capitalizing on the United Nations' moral authority, he merely repeated what was contained in the old Security Council resolutions. After two days of discussions he casually told journalists that there had been no progress. Meanwhile, the International Red Cross admitted that the sanctions as applied against Iraq, which prevented food and medicine from reaching the country, were in violation of international law.

Through contradictions and uncoordinated action, September saw the death of serious attempts to resolve the crisis diplomatically. On 1 September Prime Minister Thatcher announced that Saddam would be charged with war crimes against humanity, while Saudi Minister of Defence Prince Sultan declared that foreign forces stationed in Saudi Arabia would not be used offensively against Iraq. But despite Sultan's statement Saudi Arabia and Kuwait vetoed the Arab League seven-point plan to settle the conflict. (In this case two members were allowed to veto a resolution, while nine could not during the heads of state meeting.) On 3 September Chadli Klibi, the Secretary General of the Arab League, despairing of uniting the Arab house, resigned. Clovis Maksoud, the League's representative in the United States followed suit, on 9 September. The same day a Bush–Gorbachov meeting in Helsinki produced a joint anti-Iraq position and gave America a green light to act in accordance with UN resolutions and punish Saddam, if necessary.

The only regional development which offered Saddam a measure of comfort was the killing of nineteen Palestinians and injuring of over one hundred on the Haram Al Sharif Temple Mount compound in Jerusalem on 8 October. The impact of this event went beyond the number of victims – it dramatized Saddam's point regarding the Israeli occupation. Briefly, the Jerusalem incident threatened the shaky Arab coalition against Saddam, and followers of the Mubarak line feared that the outrage might escalate into a major conflagration which would force them to line up against Israel to the benefit of Saddam. But this did not happen, and Saddam's isolation continued.

The period which followed the initial whirlpool of activity centred around three points: whether Saddam was willing to withdraw from Kuwait; the foundations for the massive military coalition which was being assembled to eject him from that country; and the propaganda campaign set in motion by America which made it impossible either for intermediaries to succeed or for people throughout the world to understand what was happening.

According to *Newsweek* magazine of 3 September, President Bush ordered the CIA to develop plans to overthrow Saddam Hussein a day after the latter invaded Kuwait. In other words, the initial American hesitation did not include covert operations. On 20 August, Michael Emery of the *Village Voice* reported that Saddam had made an offer to withdraw from Kuwait which had been turned down by the US administration. On the 22nd, well after the US had been granted the right to station troops in Saudi Arabia 'for defensive purposes', the *New York Times* reported that the US was blocking all diplomatic efforts towards a peaceful settlement of the crisis. The 10 September issue of *Time* magazine admitted openly that Saddam Hussein was indulging 'in a flurry of activity to negotiate a settlement'.

Certainly, Saddam had made his willingness to withdraw known to visitors to Baghdad including former British Prime Minister Edward Heath, the Yugoslav politician Budimin Loncar, the Reverend Jesse Jackson, former Texas Governor John Connolly, former West German Chancellor Willy Brandt and a host of other dignitaries. In fact, although holding foreigners hostage was an utterly counterproductive act of thuggery, Saddam was half-hearted about it while making up his mind. He allowed most of his political visitors to return home with a number of the hostages as a token of his intentions (he eventually announced the release of the rest of the hostages on 18 November and allowed them to leave during Christmas, after alienating the rest of the world). Whatever Saddam Hussein's intentions – and what he wanted was not shared with others and subject to doubt – he never refused to discuss withdrawal. According to private PLO sources, he authorized several Arafat associates with American connections to carry messages with peaceful intent to the White House. They were rebuffed.

The other development which revealed that a war against Saddam was being prepared involved the number of countries bribed to include themselves in what came to be known as 'the allies'. This effort began when Kuwait set aside $22 billion to defray the costs of a military campaign and after Saudi Arabia had assured America of its willingness to provide more funds. Of course, money came from other sources too and the United States prevailed on rich countries such as Germany and Japan to contribute to what amounted to a 'saving the world from Saddam fund'. Unsurprisingly, the first payment was from the USA to Egypt, and it amounted to $7.1 billion. Soon afterwards, Secretary of State Baker promised Turkey a payment of $2.5 billion dollars, and the country also received $8 billion worth of military equipment from the Americans. On 9 September President Bush promised to provide the USSR with an undisclosed financial package, which was followed by Kuwaiti and Saudi payments amounting to $6 billion. Later the informal grouping of industrialized nations known as the Paris Club wrote off the $10 billion financial debt of Egypt, and the GCC gave Egypt and Syria another $5 billion.[17]

The bribes offered to various countries to join the alliance against Saddam took different forms. Syria was allowed to use force to remove the President of Lebanon, General Michel Awn, and to turn the country into a dependency.[18] This was part of a wider pattern of non-cash encouragement. US complaints about China's human rights record were toned down in order to guarantee the country's support for UN resolutions. Malaysia received a break on its exports of textiles to the USA.[19] Altogether, the creation of the alliance was underwritten by the largest bribe in recorded history – probably in all history. Only Jordan, the Palestinians and Yemen stood by Saddam against the rest of the world. And Yemen was punished in a most savage way which violated international law. Eight hundred thousand Yemeni workers in Saudi Arabia, including some who had been born there, were ejected from that country in one of the harshest ethnic cleansing campaigns of modern times. Naturally, most of the Western media ignored this event.

Press reporting of what was happening was contaminated by disinformation from the Pentagon and other departments of the US government soon after President Bush began dismissing all efforts aimed at finding a peaceful solution. Saddam's holding of hostages, undoubtedly the prime example of his stupid policies and misjudgement of Western feelings, was rightly described as barbaric. But reports of their mistreatment were unfounded, and the *Sunday Times* report of 19 August 1990 that Saddam intended to starve the babies of hostages is either outrageous or laughable. The efforts against Saddam were described as 'halting the advance of evil'. Halabja, flagrantly ignored by America in the past, became a rallying cry, and using chemical weapons 'against his own people' became another anti-Saddam slogan. Bush repeatedly equated Saddam with Hitler and invoked the image of the German dictator to justify his actions. Others used similar terms to characterize him including Stalin, Kaiser, criminal, barbarian, butcher, psychologically deformed, beast, lunatic and incarnation of evil. It became difficult to separate news from propaganda.

Two other elements deserve mention as representative of the hysteria aimed at demonizing Saddam. Although the Iraqis were most definitely guilty of considerable looting, some cases of rape and the killing of Kuwait resisters, the figures used for these hideous and utterly unjustifiable crimes were constantly exaggerated. Among other things, Kuwaiti resistance involved an embarrassingly small number of people. And some stories were fabrications, in particular the killing of dozens of Kuwaiti children in incubators.[20] Unreason reached its height when the US and UK governments arrested Arabs living in their countries, without due process of law, on suspicion of sympathizing with Saddam. In the UK twenty-seven suffered this fate; one of them, the respected writer Abbas Shiblaq, was a Palestinian who had attacked Saddam when America supported him. The Western disregard for Arab life was summed up in a statement by General Norman Schwarzkopf carried by the *Independent* of 9 September 1990: 'I hope they're hungry, thirsty.' The success of these efforts allowed President Bush to use a television speech on 16 September to describe what was happening as a struggle between the world and Saddam Hussein.

As with Mubarak's demands, everything was aimed at creating the image of a monster with whom one could not negotiate. Even waiting for the sanctions to take their toll – and the Iraqis were forced to ration food as early as 2 September – was dismissed. Every international body, former President Carter, Secretary of Defence John Schlesinger and even CIA chief William Webster spoke of sanctions working. A reliable inside witness, the Iraqi writer Nuha Radi, devoted a good part of her book *Baghdad Diaries* to that issue. But the American campaign appeared to be a psychological rather than a practical expression of policy: the number of troops dispatched to Saudi Arabia was increased yet again and supported by contingents from other countries before any reports on the effectiveness of sanctions were published. Slow to react after the invasion, Bush, once committed, would not entertain anything short of destroying Saddam militarily. Or perhaps the Americans expected him to fall in the face of the pressure they were applying.

As we have seen, Bush had been a Saddam supporter, both under Reagan and after he became President. It was his diplomats and State Department which had defended Saddam's human rights violations and use of chemical weapons. It was the Bush administration which had backed loans to Saddam, accepted him as a lesser evil than Khomeini, resisted congressional attempts to censure him and wanted to initiate military cooperation with him. But now George Bush was following the opposite line, the one developed and put into action after the war with Iran by other departments of the US government, the advocates of weakening Saddam, or destroying him. The new Bush policy was an extension of the policies of those who had urged Kuwait to pump more oil and who had intercepted shipments of non-conventional weapons to Iraq. But it was Saddam's lack of understanding of world politics which forced George Bush to do a 180-degree turn. A patrician American who could not accept that a third world figure whom he had supported and tried to befriend would defy the USA and the West, George Bush felt personally betrayed and he too put pride ahead of all else. In fact, on 7 August he told French Defence Minister Jean-Pierre Chevènement that he was determined to go to war.[21] For Bush, personalizing the issue and allowing pride to guide him was possible because of the negative image the Arabs and Muslims have in America. In fact, confronting Saddam was vastly popular,[22] and opinion polls showed it.

The final failure of Arab efforts and Gorbachov's solid support for the USA while undertaking minor diplomatic moves to resolve the crisis left Saddam with a single option, to convince French President François Mitterrand to fill the gap.[23] The unreported record of secret Iraqi–French discussions regarding a French initiative is based on off-the-record interviews with two former French ministers, one who was called out of retirement to initiate a dialogue with Iraq and a deputy minister in the then French cabinet. Below are some of the recollections of the former French politician delegated by Mitterrand to negotiate with the Iraqis because of his friendly relationship with them when he was in office:

I met with Tareq Aziz in Tunisia, I think without anybody knowing about the meeting. My first question to him was the obvious one: 'What made you do it, Tareq?' I had to repeat it several times before he told me the truth. It had been a Saddam decision which most members of the RCC had opposed. Saddam firmly believed that Glaspie gave him a green light to occupy Kuwait. [Saddam was later to make the same claim to the Turkish newspaper *Itilaat*.][24] According to Tareq, nobody could talk him out of it, counsel him or oppose him.

The other half of it, according to Aziz, was Saddam's belief that the Americans were using Kuwait to plot against him. This sounds as if it contradicts the first reason, but in fact it produces the same results. He had to invade Kuwait either way, because it was acceptable to America or to intercept America's plans. Aziz said that after the Iran–Contra affair things were never the same again, that Saddam thought of the Americans as plotters. Aziz also believed that Kuwait had declared economic warfare on Iraq and cited past history when issues between the two countries had been settled easily. To Aziz, this time a solution was not possible because someone was behind the Kuwaitis. Yes, a conspiracy, he thought.

Acting on the instructions of President Mitterrand, I told Aziz that Iraq must withdraw from Kuwait, and without expecting anything in return. I made it clear to him that France would try to mediate, but that when the chips were down France had to side with the allies and could not take a position against them. This is what Mitterrand believed; the allies came first. On the other hand, France was willing to help Iraq extract and sell more oil.

Aziz appeared to understand this, he even accepted it. But he was insistent that an honourable way must be found, to protect the Iraqi Army during and after withdrawal and for Saddam to save face. He made much of both and I understood him, particularly on Saddam not appearing as if he were defeated, the issue of pride.

This is something the Americans never understood, the Arab need to maintain dignity. The Arabs attach a great deal to pride, it comes ahead of the practical things Americans understand. You see, I know Saddam. Saddam is a simple man, quite uneducated really, but he has his ways. Whenever I visited him before the crisis, he always gave me a present before every meeting, and sometimes we had four or five meetings. This is not a worldly man, this is a real Arab.

You say that the Americans, the CIA, had made a psychological profile of Saddam. I don't know anything about it, but whatever it was it was wrong. If it had been right then they would not have wanted him humiliated. Wanting to humiliate him is the same as not wanting a peaceful solution to the problem.

I told Aziz that Mitterrand would try, but that Saddam must help him. I repeated what I said about France's commitment to the alliance and to Mitterrand this was more important than to other French presidents. I did not think Aziz would get Saddam to move. The space for him to change direction without losing his pride was not there.

My conversation with the other French politician was revealing in a different way:

You're absolutely right, Mitterrand was committed to the alliance. But look, the Americans did not want Saddam saved . . . off the hook. The Americans – the British don't matter really – wanted him stopped, gone. He was of no more use to them and he was becoming strong.

Our colonialism was geographic, the American one has to do with oil and that was what Saddam threatened. They had to control the oil, they have to control the oil. Perhaps not physically, but there was no chance of allowing Saddam to . . . dictate to them on oil. He was becoming a problem for them . . . not for us, by the way, because he needed us for making the oil work. He needed technical help and we were good – not as big as America, but good.

The Arab situation, oh, what a disaster. You see, we were unable to say attacking Saddam was against the Arabs because Arab leaders were against him. Egypt wanted to be leader again and that was bad for Saddam. . . . Perhaps he should not have allowed them back in the Arab League . . . what a mistake – for him, of course.

Mitterrand tried, he tried more than you think, but no use. It was impossible. He gave up. No one supported him. If the Arabs had said for Mitterrand to continue and they were behind him, it would have been different. Nothing happened.

Following a Security Council resolution authorizing the use of all necessary means against Iraq (SCR 678, 29 November 1990) and giving Iraq a 15 January deadline to withdraw from Kuwait, Saddam offered to meet Bush face-to-face to discuss all outstanding issues between their two countries. This suggestion was laughed off. Later there was an effort at mediation by President Chadli Benjedid of Algeria. Saddam accepted his good offices, but King Fahd, bowing to US pressure,[25] refused to receive the Algerian leader. President Mitterrand had addressed the United Nations on 24 September and presented a four-stage plan. Except for giving Iraq a sensible amount of time to withdraw without being attacked, it contained nothing new. The Iraqis accepted it as a starting point for dialogue, but the rest of the Western world did not respond. Rebuffed but committed to side with his allies, Mitterrand made an appeal in November to give sanctions time to work, then in January 1991 dispatched special envoy Michel Vauzelle to Baghdad. When no one showed interest in what he was proposing, he elegantly gave up without making any announcements.

A trip to Baghdad by Yasser Arafat during this period produced an incident which supported the assessment that Saddam had originally acted alone and that he did not understand the Western position. Saddam, in one of their many meetings, turned to Arafat and asked the PLO leader whether Western threats to attack him were real. Arafat, facing opposition to his pro-Saddam policies within the PLO, would not give a clear answer and referred Saddam to special adviser Bassam Abu Sharif. The latter said that the West would indeed attack, and to support his position cited cover stories on Saddam in *Time* and *Newsweek* magazines. At this point Saddam turned to his own advisers and asked them why no one had told him that he had been the subject of these stories. This proves that the unsoundness of Saddam's original analysis of the Western position was made worse by being isolated and by the fear of his associates of sharing facts with him. Amazingly, Arafat was not deterred by any of this, and soon afterwards he contributed to the atmosphere of unreality by giving a speech in which he three times repeated the phrase: 'Welcome to war.'

But time was running out for Saddam, and extricating himself from what he had started was becoming more difficult, if not impossible. By 2 January 1991, Iraq had made new announcements in the name of the RCC and modified its position several times, totally accepting the principle of withdrawal in return for promises of safe conduct for its troops. The Iraqis stopped demanding immediate action on the Palestinian problem but only asked that it should be addressed soon. This offer too was turned down. After considerable debate as to venue and scheduling, Secretary of State Baker and Tareq Aziz met in Geneva in a highly publicized attempt to negotiate a solution. The attempt failed; according to some writers, Baker had drafted the statement rejecting Iraq's position the day before the meeting of 9 January.[26] On 11 January, after a lengthy period of total and inexplicable inactivity, UN Secretary General Perez de Cuellar travelled to Baghdad for a meeting with Saddam Hussein at a time when Congress was authorizing Bush to use force. The meeting, which took place on 13 January, was distinctly cool. Perez de Cuellar undiplomatically admitted failure, and flew to Paris to dissuade President Mitterrand from undertaking new efforts towards peace. He even neglected the obvious – a call for the UN to meet after the expiry of the 15 January deadline. This is what should have happened, and indeed had become imperative once the US Congress had, following much debate, authorized George Bush to use force on 12 January.

With the countdown to 15 January approaching, the only party acting towards a peaceful resolution of the crisis was the USSR; it was pursuing efforts which it had started in a small way in October. Internally and regionally Saddam was short of options. Finally accepting that war was on the way, he reverted to using symbols. He ordered that 'Allahu Akhbar' (God is greatest) be painted on the Iraqi flag, added the words 'Be the Arab saviour, Oh Iraq' to the national anthem, described the impending battle as one between believers and non-believers, and made plain that he would respond to any attack by firing rockets against Israel. Of course, family idiocy was part of this propaganda campaign and Udday exchanged telegrams with his father about going to the front to fight.

With sanctions biting[27] and crippling Iraq, these gestures of defiance were accepted by Arabs elsewhere but not by Saddam's own suffering people. The only possible way to avert war was for him to swallow his pride, pretend the USSR was still a friend and encourage its mediation. Otherwise, Saddam had the options of playing martyr or using non-conventional weapons and risking atomic retaliation. But he did not see it that way, and members of his inner circle were too afraid to speak to him. To Saddam, the Arab people would somehow come to his help and stop the West from attacking him, or he would go down in history as a hero-martyr and achieve what had eluded him in real life. The second possibility took into consideration America's Vietnam experience. Saddam thoroughly believed the USA was not ready to enter into another costly war which would produce similar casualties, and this was something he repeated to Arafat and other friendly visitors.

Led by the United States, the allies refused to extend the deadline of UN Security Council resolution 678, and massive aerial attacks against Iraq began on the morning of 16 January 1991. Operation Desert Storm entered the language. The multinational air forces targeted military formations in Kuwait and throughout Iraq, the Ministry of Defence, the presidential palace, petrochemical plants, airports, oil refineries, bridges, power stations, food processing plants, textile factories, railways, sewage plants, markets and monuments. The non-military targets had been included at the last minute, when the allies' list of strategic targets was increased from 57 to 700;[28] the declared purpose of ejecting Iraq from Kuwait was subordinated to punishing a third world upstart.

Saddam, thinking that he personally had been targeted, took to moving from one palace to another, and all of them had bunkers. His Air Force failed to put up a credible fight and his air defence system proved unequal to the electronic sophistication of the attacking aircraft. On 22 January he managed to fire some modified Scud rockets against Tel Aviv, Haifa and Riyadh. Though they caused little damage, they gave his supporters a psychological lift. In Jerusalem I was told by a Palestinian that he 'had lived long enough to see Arab rockets hit Israel'. Even Egyptian and Syrian soldiers stationed in Saudi Arabia were reported to have cheered at the news.[29] But what the USA had expected – that Saddam would use chemical weapons[30] – did not happen.

Arguably, the bombing was heavier than the tonnage dropped during the Second World War and it horrified the world. Demonstrations broke out in Germany, Scandinavia, France, the UK, the USA, all the Arab countries and at least a dozen more Western countries. In Morocco four hundred thousand marched in protest, the largest event of its kind since the country had become independent, and in Egypt there were bloody clashes at Cairo University. Nobody was willing to overlook the 'indiscriminate' nature of the bombing.[31] Napalm and depleted uranium were being used and the list of civilian targets included electrical generating plants, irrigation pumping stations, 28 schools and several hospitals.[32] In the town of Amiriya 47 civilians died and 163 were injured. In Hilla, the local clinic received a direct hit[33] and there were many casualties. In total, until the ground war started on 22 February 1991, the allies flew 110,000 sorties and dropped 85,000 tons of explosives.[34] In the middle of it all, General Schwarzkopf responded to criticism over the intensity and nature of the attacks by saying, 'We're ethical people.' This came in the wake of President Bush's declaration that the USA had 'no dispute with the Iraqi people'.[35]

On 26 January, on Saddam's personal orders, an Iraqi armoured unit stationed in Kuwait attacked and occupied the nearby Saudi town of Kafji, only to be ejected two days later after sustaining over 50 per cent casualties. It was a suicidal mission and the tired, hungry Iraqi soldiers who surrendered told stories of the suffering of their comrades in Kuwait and other places. Some units had gone without food for days at a time and were ready to surrender. On the civilian side things were no better: the destruction of roads, bridges and hospitals led to shortages of all kinds, and thousands died for lack of medical care. Many political analysts argued that Iraq was on its way to collapse but that was dismissed by the allies' leaders and did not influence their military planning.

Sensing the futility of the situation, Saddam ordered most of his Air Force to escape to neighbouring Iran. Simultaneously, he ordered Vice Premier Tareq Aziz to redouble his efforts with the USSR, but the unavailability of an air route forced Aziz into a schedule of slow-paced shuttle diplomacy. He travelled to Iran by car, after which he flew to Moscow and then, because of lack of safe communications, had to return to Baghdad in person to report to Saddam. He had no decision-making powers. The slowness of the process aided the purpose of those opposed to easing the bombing who called for turning Iraq 'into a parking lot'.

Time and again, Soviet Foreign Minister Bessmertnykh and Chairman Gorbachov protested that the allies were exceeding their UN mandate, but there was no let-up. Indeed, the most concentrated air war in history found its planners totally unwilling to accept any criticism. For example, the report on the destruction of a baby-milk plant was unusually interrupted: CNN correspondent Peter Arnett was simply cut off. Angry retorts, refutations and accusations that the plant was manufacturing chemical weapons followed and there were verbal attacks on Arnett, a seasoned journalist and Pulitzer Prize winner. Another attack on a shelter which caused nearly four hundred deaths was also refuted, with the allies claiming that it had been a command centre.[36] The level of destruction was so extensive that several Arab countries, Egypt among them, called for a halt to the bombing on humanitarian grounds – or at least limiting it to military targets. But, it was no use, even after Tareq Aziz's effort had been reinforced by several visits to Baghdad by USSR special envoy Yevgeny Primakov, a former Tass correspondent in Baghdad who knew Saddam and his ways. Though time was running against the Iraqis, Saddam reverted to being Tikriti and began to trumpet the coming Mother of Battles, perhaps his unique contribution to everyday language. This aside, on 15 February the RCC accepted UN Security Council resolution 660, the original resolution calling for unconditional withdrawal from Kuwait, in its totality. President Bush described it as a 'cruel hoax' and called for the overthrow of Saddam Hussein.[37] Afraid that Saddam might announce a unilateral pull-out which could result in popular pressure to stop the bombing, the Bush administration demanded the withdrawal of hundreds of thousands of Iraqi troops in a matter of two days – a physical impossibility.

On 17 and 18 February Tareq Aziz was once again in Moscow, and this time Saddam had instructed him to accept any plan that would stop the allied forces waging a land war.[38] On the 19th, after lengthy meetings with Aziz, Gorbachov announced a revised plan which took into consideration all previous American objections to previous Soviet suggestions. It called for an unconditional Iraqi commitment to withdraw based on UNSC resolution 660, a ceasefire to begin immediately, the completion of the withdrawal in twenty-one days, the cancellation of punitive UN Security Council resolutions, the release of all prisoners of war and the use of UN observers to oversee the implementation of the whole plan.[39]

Saddam accepted the plan on 21 February, upon Aziz's return, and asked for one week to pull out of Kuwait City. But Bush demanded that all Iraqi forces should withdraw by noon on 23 February, another impossibility, or face a ground war. Gripped by anger and despair, and determined to preserve the appearance of doing something, Saddam set the Kuwaiti oilfields on fire and began an oil spill of unprecedented size. It was a totally criminal act, akin to a primitive reaction, and it backfired. On the 24th the ground war began, even after Gorbachov made a personal telephone call to Bush asking for a short delay to reconcile the Soviet and American positions under the auspices of the UN. When that failed, Saddam announced that Iraqi forces were withdrawing from Kuwait, but Bush ordered the fighting to continue until the Iraqi Army had laid down its arms. On 26 February, Iraqi civilians and military personnel were attacked while retreating from Kuwait City. On the 27th, hours after the liberation of the city, George Bush announced that hostilities would cease at midnight; several American companies made immediate announcements that they had contracts to rebuild Kuwait.[40] Instead of drawing lessons from what Saddam had undoubtedly initiated, his apologists attributed the poor performance of the Iraqi Army, a near repeat of its defeat by the British in 1941, to a threat by the allies to use nuclear weapons against it.[41]

Neither propaganda nor the attempts to stifle voices of dissent had prepared the world for what accompanied the Iraqi attempt to withdraw from Kuwait on 26 February. In the words of former Carter administration National Secretary Adviser Zbigniew Brzenzinski, the war had been 'over-personalized, over-emotionalized and over-militarized'.[42] In London, speaking on BBC Television the night the air attacks began, the veteran journalist Patrick Seale was near desperation: 'What everybody has forgotten is that Iraq is a third world country.' The words used by the knowledgeable diplomat and the experienced foreign correspondent – and both had first-hand knowledge of Iraq – to describe the attitude of the Bush administration, strong as they were, do not measure up to how the American military translated their government's hatred for Saddam Hussein and used it against innocent people. Central to this was the confusion of Saddam's person with the Iraqi people, something which has never changed to this day.

Iraqi civilians and military personnel, with Palestinians who feared Kuwaiti reprisals for Arafat's idiotic support of Saddam, began leaving Kuwait on 25 February, hours before the official order to evacuate. Their only way back to Iraq was Highway 80, the route linking Kuwait with the city of Basra. With the Iraqi Army collapsing all around them, what began as an evacuation turned into an unorganized stampede including over two thousand mostly civilian vehicles.[43] The escapes had no air cover and no defence, and General Norman Schwarzkopf had already declared that his forces would not attack an army in retreat.[44]

The US Air Force, roaming the skies freely and using everything from F-16s to B-52s and 1000lb. bombs, attacked the head and tail of the convoy and trapped everyone and everything in between, in a place which allowed no room for escape, the Mittlah Ridge. The attack lasted forty hours, until 28 February and Bush's announcement of a ceasefire, and left very few survivors. Most people were incinerated in their cars, trucks, tanks or whatever mode of transport they were using. The world watched aghast and the USSR issued a statement describing the Americans as 'twentieth-century barbarians'.[45] But much more important than criticism from outside sources was the total lack of interest shown by the Americans in restraining their pilots. In fact, most American airmen described what was happening as a 'turkey shoot' and viewed it with glee.[46] Even American news sources recorded the barbarity of it all and *Triumph without Victory*, the record of the Gulf War compiled by the editors of the right-wing *US News and World Report*, carries this statement by Major John Feeley: 'We've hit the jackpot.'[47] Another US Air Force major, Robert Nugent, stated that 'even in Vietnam I didn't see anything like this'.[48] To the White House, the escapees were 'torturers, looters and rapists'.[49]

It was Secretary of State Baker who followed the failure, planned or not, of his negotiations with Tareq Aziz in Geneva by threatening to return Iraq to the pre-industrial age. The mass killing at Mittlah Ridge was confirmation of what the US government had in mind. The hideousness of what was happening was recorded by Stephen Sackur and Jeremy Bowen of the BBC, Tony Clifton of

Newsweek, Greg LaMotte of CNN, Michael Evans of *The Times*, Colin Smith of the *Observer*, Edward Pearce and Martin Woolacott of the *Guardian* and dozens of other journalists. According to the noted Egyptian writer Mohammed Heikal, some British pilots were so disgusted by what was happening that they refused to continue bombing the Mittlah Ridge entrapment.[50]

But American officialdom, despite a degree of popular disgust over the television reports being shown, offered no justification, let alone excuse. In view of the fact that the USA had suffered a total of 97 deaths and 213 wounded, any attempt to absolve themselves through calling what happened a reprisal would have sounded idiotic. In fact, a different but still idiotic excuse was not long coming. The *Sunday Telegraph* of 3 March quoted President Bush as saying that the ghost of Vietnam had been exorcised. In other words, after declaring that his military objectives had been met, George Bush restored pride to America. No one spoke of what happened being in violation of all international conventions, the 1874 Brussels, 1907 Hague and 1949 Geneva ones in particular, which protected civilians caught in the middle of fighting. There was no military logic to it. Greg LaMotte and Stephen Sackur had to suffer the disbelief of the anchormen of their networks, who viewed their reports with misgivings. Jeremy Bowen was accused by a British politician of being an apologist for Saddam. Only the *Guardian*'s Martin Woolacott's pre-massacre assessment of 15 February can explain Mittlah Ridge: 'The destruction of Iraq will continue as long as Saddam is in power.' Demonstrating insensitivity but consistency, President Hosni Mubarak of Egypt said the death of civilians was sad, 'but that happens in time of war'.[51] According to some sources, he was talking about the thousands of people who died on the road to Basra.[52] A much more humane reaction consisted of the resignations of French Defence Minister Jean-Pierre Chevènement and Italian Foreign Minister Gianni de Michelis, and the demonstrations which broke out throughout the world. Journalists, a select group of politicians and the average person showed greater concern for human life than the players – Saddam Hussein, the instigator himself, Bush and Mubarak.

On 3 March 1991, in a tent at the desert village of Safwan, American General Norman Schwarzkopf and Saudi General Khalid Bin Sultan accepted the surrender of their Iraqi counterparts,

Generals Sultan Hashim Ahmad and Salah Abid Mohammed. The allied forces were well into Iraq, but lacking the necessary mandate, aware that other countries would not support them and with no coherent plan to replace Saddam, they had stopped short of Baghdad and ceased all military activity. The surrender document that the Iraqis signed accepted all UN resolutions, and it was agreed that the allied forces would pull out of Iraq as soon as possible. In a last-minute gesture which escaped the American and Saudi victors, and which, like everything else, originated with Saddam, the Iraqis had requested and been granted the right to fly helicopters. In accordance with UN resolutions all fixed-wing aircraft were grounded. Saddam Hussein, Udday, Ali Chemical and the rest of the unlovable Tikritis were in Baghdad, presiding over an army without an air force except for helicopters. President Bush began trumpeting his idea of a New World Order.

Bush's military defeat of Iraq was total and American pride was restored, but the US administration had given no thought to what to do next. In this, as in so many other things, Bush's thinking resembled that of his former ally, Saddam Hussein. On 11 October 1990 President Bush had declared, 'We all want Saddam removed, I hope the Iraqi people do something towards that.'[53] His open calls for the Iraqi people to overthrow Saddam were repeated throughout the crisis and the actual war.[54] The US President was not alone, and General Schwarzkopf, hardly someone who understood Middle East politics, appealed to the Iraqi people 'to rise up in revolt'.[55] The US Air Force backed this by dropping leaflets printed with similar sentiments.[56]

On 5 March 1991, a mere two days after the signing of the surrender agreement, the Shias of southern Iraq rose in open rebellion against Saddam.[57] It had started at the time of signing, supposedly when a tank commander angrily shot off a huge poster of Saddam in Sa'ad Square in the city of Basra, and gathered momentum. Demonstrations turned into armed insurrection in Basra and Nassiriya, and thousands shouted anti-Saddam slogans. When the uprising spread to the Shia holy cities of Najjaf and Karbala it became a civil war. The rebels resorted to slogans such as: *Saddam shil idak, sha'ab al Iraq ma yredak*', or 'Saddam, lift your hand, the people of Iraq do not want you', and '*La illah illa Allah, Saddam 'Adou Allah*', 'There is no God but God and Saddam is His enemy'. The cities of Basra, Nassiriya, Najjaf, Karbala, Amara, Kut and Hilla fell to the rebels in four days. The Kurds, initially reluctant in their northern redoubt, joined the rebellion after a few days. By 14 March they had succeeded in occupying the oil centre of Kirkuk and Suleimaniya. The lines were not clearly drawn, but over 60 per cent of Iraq was now in rebel hands.

Success or failure depended on the behaviour of the three Iraqi parties to the uprising, which became known as the 1991 *intifada*. Internally they were the rebels, the Iraqi opposition, and Saddam himself. In early March, the rebels in Najjaf issued an appeal for the allies to help them, but there was no response.[58] President Bush simply refused to interfere. White House spokesman Marlin Fitzwater shamelessly announced that the Americans had no guilt 'over not helping'.[59] According to a former Iraqi Army major[60] who defected and joined the rebels the Americans were not neutral – their behaviour amounted to malevolent interference without the use of arms. He quoted four examples of such activity. In Nassiriya, US aircraft flew over Iraqi helicopters and gave them protection. American troops stopped the rebels from reaching an arms depot to obtain ammunition. The American and French troops still in southern Iraq dug trenches to slow down the rebels and stop them pursuing Saddam's troops. Finally, American troops provided Saddam's Republican Guard with safe passage through their lines to attack rebel positions.

Former Iraqi General Wafic Samarai and opposition leaders Dr Tahseen Mua'la and Dr Heidar Abbas confirm much of this. Others speak of unverified reports that the Americans provided Saddam's Republican Guard with data on rebels' hiding-places. Even General Norman Schwarzkopf admits, without delving into details, that the allies provided Saddam with help to crush the rebellion. But he had made his position clear on 3 March when he declared that the people of Iraq were not innocent because 'they supported the invasion of Kuwait and accepted Saddam Hussein'.[61] In the middle of the uprising, President Bush had nothing more to say than, 'I did not mislead anybody'.[62] Later, after Saddam got the upper hand and prevailed on the Shias and Kurds, forcing 2 million of the latter to flee to Turkey while television cameras recorded the event, Marlin Fitzwater articulated Bush's policy in terms of 'We don't want to involve ourselves in the affairs of Iraq.'[63] What lay behind this baffled everybody. To most people it was a case of the Americans not meaning what they said when they called for the overthrow of Saddam, or changing their mind under pressure from friendly Arab governments who feared the consequences of Saddam's disappearance.

In reality, it was the nature of the uprising which determined the behaviour of the Bush administration. Although it was the plight of the Kurds which was publicized, and which led British Prime Minister John Major (he had replaced Thatcher) to pressure Bush into providing them with a safe haven and attempting to stop Saddam's attacks, the *intifada* was, in origin and in terms of its ability to topple Saddam, a Shia uprising. In a case of better the devil you know, Bush was against helping a Shia rebellion[64] because he believed the Shias were surrogates of the Iranians and he did not want them replacing Saddam, particularly the Tehran-based Supreme Council for Islamic Revolution in Iraq (SCIRI). During battles in the south, some US Army officers told rebel Shias, 'You're with Iran, we can't help you'.[65] Moreover, according to Iraqi opposition leader Ahmad Chalabi, what the Bush policy had called for was 'the replacement of Saddam [the person] and not the regime'.[66] In other words, the USA was happy with an Iraqi dictatorship, perhaps under a Saddam relation or follower, without the person of Saddam. This acceptance of Saddamism without Saddam, essentially a refusal to contemplate a Shia-controlled Iraq, was later confirmed in an interview given to ABC journalist Peter Jennings by former National Security Adviser Brent Scowcroft: 'We would have preferred a coup'.[67] Well after the fact, on 30 October 1994, the *New York Times* published a report which purported to show that the Bush administration had intercepted a Saudi attempt to help the anti-Saddam rebels. If this was true, then it was American rather than Arab blind prejudice which ruled the day. (The Shias now constitute nearly 65 per cent of the population.)

The allies' refusal to come to the aid of the rebels made the *intifada* an exclusively Iraqi affair between Saddam and his compatriot adversaries. He never panicked, wavered or, contrary to rumours, considered leaving the country. Just hours after news of what was happening in Basra and Nassiriya reached him, he appointed his cousin, the infamous Ali Chemical, Minister of the Interior, gave him command of the southern forces and ordered him 'to crush the centres of treason and perfidy'. In Baghdad itself,

Saddam's cousin and son-in-law Hussein Kamel and Vice President Taha Yassin Ramadan were given responsibility for the security of the capital, and issued shoot-to-kill orders to the special forces and the Popular Army. Disturbances in the capital were nipped in the bud, but a dozen or so people were killed.

In the north, Saddam issued orders to contain the Kurds. He decided to delay action against them until things in the south were under control. Saddam did not sleep, used radio and television to attack his opponents, spoke with calmness and certainty, issued orders for army units to regroup and reorganize, distributed responsibilities to the inner core of family and party faithful and used his helicopters against the thinly armed rebels with remarkable effectiveness. He made a special appeal to the thousands of people who had defected and joined the rebels, offering them amnesty and asking them to rejoin their units. He also dispensed with the security people around him and became visible, occasionally driving his own car, which lifted the morale of his supporters. In addition to Ali Chemical, RCC Vice Chairman Izzat Douri and Vice President Taha Yassin Ramadan, his half-brothers Watban and Sabawi were at his side and so were the rest of the RCC. On 23 March, he capped his efforts to crush the rebellion while appearing reconciliatory by appointing Shia Sa'adoun Hamadi Prime Minister.

The rebels, though they probably represented the most popular uprising in the history of modern Iraq, suffered from several disadvantages which became apparent very early. First, Iran, their most likely source of support, shied from coming to their aid because it was aware of US opposition to its hegemony over Iraq and knew what the American reaction would be. This was followed by an Egyptian warning to America from Mubarak to stay aloof from the civil war. On the ground the rebels were inadequately armed; the allies prevented them raiding arms and ammunition depots and on occasions disarmed them. They were no match for Saddam's well-trained troops. Sometimes they bravely faced his tanks with sticks and stones.

Secondly, the rebels played right into Saddam's hands. They executed security people and Ba'ath Party members without trial. The Kurdish rebels, the Peshmerga, murdered three hundred soldiers,[68] and in Karbala in the south the Shias threw some innocent soldiers in the river and executed seventy officers.[69]

Unfortunately, the rebels 'tortured, decapitated and dismembered'[70] hundreds of people. This united the army and the Sunni Muslims against them and stopped some willing members of both groups from joining them. Even former politicians capable of giving the movement substance shied from joining it because it gave the appearance of being exclusively Shia and Kurd and threatened the unity of Iraq.

The third reason for the failure of the *intifada* was its structural weakness. Years of repression had left the people inside Iraq without leadership and a central command. Even the most organized area of the internal opposition, the Iraqi Communist Party, could not rise to the occasion. The Shia religious leadership in Najjaf and Karbala did not give the movement their wholehearted support because they feared the dismemberment of the country, objected to some rebel excesses and thought that Saddam would prevail. In addition, the opposition residing outside the country, though it claimed leadership of what was happening,[71] failed in its role. The Joint Action Committee of Iraq (JACI), a coalition of thirty-two opposition groups founded in Damascus in December 1990, met in Beirut on 11 March 1991, at the height of the uprising, but failed to produce anything beyond condemnations and appeals to outside powers. They set up Radio Iraq and the Voice of Free Kurdistan and settled for trying to match Saddam's propaganda machine. Essentially, they were too diverse and divided to be effective.

So not for the first time in his life, Saddam was saved by Western inaction and divisions among his opponents. Unlike when dealing with outside matters beyond the scope of his intellect, he was a master strategist and tactician in dealing with events inside Iraq. Ali Chemical used the three intact divisions of the Republican Guard in full view of allied forces and reconquered the south. He personally reoccupied Basra, while Hussein Kamel's and Taha Ramadan's tanks blasted their way into Karbala and Najjaf and damaged their holy places. Izzat Douri reclaimed Nassiriya.[72] Saddam reserved for himself the honour of formalizing the end of the Shia rebellion, by visiting Najjaf and firing his handgun in the air in celebration.[73]

Thousands of people perished; in Najjaf alone there were more than fourteen hundred dead.[74] Nurses who had treated *intifada* wounded were molested. Fifteen hospitals were destroyed. A whole family was thrown out of a helicopter alive. Shia clergy, though they had called for moderation throughout, were singled out for punishment. By the end of the *intifada*, during the last week of March 1991, their number had declined to a few hundred from ten thousand in the early 1970s.[75] Some people suspected of sympathizing with the *intifada* had their foreheads scarred while others had an ear lopped off. Army officers who had joined the *intifada* or wavered were executed without trial (they included Colonels Kazem Rashid, Abdel Amir 'Ebais, Bassem Al Abboud and Tewfiq Al Yassin). Estimates of the number of people killed in southern Iraq range between fifty thousand and three hundred thousand. Meanwhile, allied troops were pulling out of Iraq.

With the south subdued, and its people's fate now in the hands of his revenge-bent security people, Saddam turned his attention to the north. The Kurds also, despite the defection to their side of most of Jash, the Saddam-sponsored Kurdish militia, were no match for the Republican Guard. Kurdistan was reconquered in less than two weeks and the cities of Kirkuk and Suleimaniya reoccupied on 28 March. The Iraqi Army, encouraged by President Bush's continued non-interference policy, went on an orgy of killing. In some villages the number of people killed precluded proper burial and they were bulldozed into mass graves.[76]

On 1 April Kurdish leader Massoud Barzani issued an appeal to the West for help. There was no response – Washington was still against involvement in the affairs of Iraq. British Prime Minister John Major, responding to television reports showing hundreds of thousands of starving Kurds escaping into Turkey, flew to Washington and made a personal appeal to President Bush to stop Saddam. On 3 April the UN Security Council passed resolution 687 which, along with setting up inspection teams to stop Iraq from continuing to develop weapons of mass destruction, demanded that hundreds of billions of dollars in compensation be paid to the countries which had suffered at Saddam's hands and ordered a cessation of violent acts against the indigenous population of Iraq. It was followed on 10 April by Operation Provide Comfort, which protected the Kurds, gave them a safe haven and imposed a no-fly zone north of the 36th parallel. This action was undertaken by the USA, Britain and France, without the backing of a UN resolution. American and allied troops entered northern Iraq forty-eight hours later. The number of Kurdish losses before this intervention, also unknown, is estimated at one hundred thousand dead and wounded and 2 million displaced. Most of the refugees, however, eventually returned.

Significant as Provide Comfort was and still is, Saddam emerged as the undisputed leader of most of Iraq. On 25 April, in a most important development which undermined Saddam's Iraqi opponents and demonstrated lack of faith in what the West was doing, Kurdish leader Jallal Talabani of the PUK visited Baghdad and signed an autonomy agreement with Saddam. He had pre-empted his leadership rival Barzani, who was willing to do the same. Abdel Kassem Al Khoei, a ninety-two-year-old imam, was brought to Baghdad to meet Saddam and appear as if he was offering his fealty. Talabani's agreement was short-lived, however, and people knew that the venerable Al Khoei was acting under duress, but that mattered very little. The behaviour of the West at the end of the Gulf War sanctioned the survival of Saddam. In early May, Special Adviser for National Security Affairs Richard Haas dissuaded Majid Al Khoei, a Shia leader, from starting a new anti-Saddam rebellion[77] on the pretext that a coup was on the way. On 20 May, Saddam replaced Libya's Muamar Qaddafi as US public enemy number one. George Bush stated that sanctions would remain until Saddam was removed.[78] A day later, other members of the Bush administration began to repeat his words. But very few people believed them.

12

Principality of Stones

Although UN Security Council resolution 678 authorized the 'use of all necessary means' to eject Iraq from Kuwait, none of the resolutions contained anything about toppling Saddam Hussein or changing the Iraqi government. However, by the middle of 1991 President Bush's call for the overthrow of Saddam had become the declared intention of the United States and Britain. Both countries were giving the UN resolutions spacious interpretations, serving notice that they did not feel restricted by them. In this, they were once again in agreement with Saddam Hussein. Although military defeat left him with no option but to accept the UNSC resolutions, he had no intention of obeying all their articles – certainly not the ones demanding the destruction of non-conventional weapons and a stop to the repression of his people.

Saddam's behaviour and attitude towards the resolutions was in character, but the stance adopted by the USA and Britain represented a functional breakdown in the workings of the world's two leading democracies. Instead of prompting them to adopt coherent policies, the failure to support the Iraqi *intifada* made the US and British governments behave more illogically. Despite the absence of change in the reasons which had stopped them from supporting the *intifada*, the leaders of both countries elevated the overthrow of Saddam Hussein to a national aim. They promised this to their people without developing any sensible plans for achieving this aim or coping with the consequences of an unexpected internal coup in Iraq. Nothing was done to reconcile the public position of the USA and Britain with the realities of the situation which were known to their countries' leaders.

In America in particular, though not exclusively, the official propaganda had been a success. Saddam Hussein had ceased to be a person and had become an institutionalized monstrosity, and the public was demanding his head. President Bush and Prime Minister Major were caught in a vicious cycle. The more they insisted that Saddam should go, the more their public wanted them to do it, and public demands were forcing them to escalate their promises. Bush's and Major's private and substantial fears that Saddam's overthrow might lead to the disintegration of Iraq or its fall to Islamic fundamentalist groups were complicated matters which they could not explain to their respective nations without sounding as if they were backtracking.

Saddam's main problem was also embedded in the nature of the governmental system over which he presided. He was a dictator who had been defeated in battle, but who had succeeded in putting down an uprising by his own people. Saddam knew that he had to answer for both the defeat and the victory, that his country had become isolated, weaker and poor and that his constituency had become considerably smaller. Unable to keep people's bellies full, he blamed their misfortune on the siege imposed on Iraq by UN resolutions and enforced by outside powers against an Arab Muslim country, not a secular Ba'athist one. Changing the identity of the country to a nationalist/religious one was Saddam's way of appealing to a wider segment of his people and it was accompanied by more frequent recitals of the Koran on Radio Baghdad, but he knew that this was not enough. Greater repression, the tried guarantor of his survival, followed.

Iraq was under two sieges: one comprised of the United Nations sanctions applied to their harshest degree by the USA and Britain, and the second an internal one imposed by Saddam against the majority of the Iraqi people. Meanwhile, all the other forces were marginalized. The USSR had ceased to exist, and what had replaced it was weaker and less influential. France was independent, supported a literal, legal implementation of the sanctions and protection of the Kurds, but from the very beginning had never viewed the sanctions as instruments of punishment in American or British terms. Without the backing of the rest of Europe, which it sought and failed to gain immediately after the cessation of hostilities,[1] France was reduced to a lone voice of dissent with limited effectiveness. China had its opinions, which also varied from those of America and Britain, but it was not ready to confront the United States over Iraq. The Arab countries had no power whatsoever except when they were needed to provide logistical support for the forces stationed on their land to maintain the external siege. Even the countries with no Western troops, such as Egypt and Jordan, suffered from growing dependence on the USA for protection against internal dissent by Islamic militants, which made them more compliant than usual. The rest of the world behaved like disinterested parties. The field was clear for a confrontation between activist America and Britain on the one side and Saddam Hussein on the other. This situation has not changed.

Despite the *intifada* and its bloody aftermath, eliminating Saddam's weapons of mass destruction (the broad term used in UN resolutions) and ballistic missiles came ahead of everything else. A United Nations Special Commission (UNSCOM) was created for this purpose on 18 April 1991. Along with the International Atomic Energy Agency (IAEA), UNSCOM was mandated by the United Nations to locate and destroy all the arms which fell under both definitions. It was staffed by chemists, biologists, weapons experts and diplomats from over twenty countries. But no commission was created to stop Saddam's repression of the people of Iraq. One could say that the potential danger to Iraq's neighbours was perceived as a more important issue than the on-going repression and consequent crimes against the Iraqi people.

On the same day that UNSCOM was created, Saddam's government, barely recovered from the *intifada*, willingly submitted an extensive list of the mass destruction weapons it supposedly possessed. The list was voluntarily amended on 27 April and again on 17 May. In early June UNSCOM and IAEA inspectors, headed by Executive Chairman Rolf Ekeus, a distinguished Swedish diplomat, began arriving in Iraq to perform their duties. But between 21 and 28 June Iraqi soldiers obstructed the work of an IAEA team headed by American inspector David Kay, and the confrontation turned nasty when the soldiers fired over the inspectors' heads.[2] This pattern of cooperation and obstruction reflected Saddam's acceptance of the resolutions without meaning to obey them, and set the stage for the next eight years.

There were reasons for Saddam's behaviour. His inability to understand democratic systems of government made him dismissive of the grave situation facing him, and he had benefitted from American and British inaction, if not help, in putting down the *intifada*. Understanding the hardening of their positions which resulted from the demands of their free press and people was beyond him. Moreover, he believed that the Kurdish leaders Jallal Talabani's and Massoud Barzani's wish to make peace with him reflected their knowledge of American and British plans.[3] He also interpreted the departure of the last US troops from southern Iraq in May 1991 as another significant signal of a Western desire to reach an amicable settlement with him. Although this was followed by the imposition of the no-fly zone covering Iraqi Kurdistan, he viewed as more important the fact that Tareq Aziz was already discussing the lifting of sanctions with the UN Secretary General.

In August, acting on the Secretary General's recommendations, the UN responded to the human suffering inside Iraq. It granted Saddam's government renewable permission to sell $2 billion worth of oil to buy food and medicine under UN supervision. The UN stipulated how much of this money should go to the Kurds as reparations and how much towards the cost of maintaining UNSCOM, and even ordered Saddam to pump his oil through the Turkish pipelines to generate income for that country as well. The components of what Iraq had to pay out from exporting oil fluctuated, but without the UNSCOM cost they represented about 30 per cent of total receipts.

Saddam turned the oil-for-food-and-medicine offer down. The country which imported 65 per cent of its food needs and as much as 80 per cent of its medicine was denied both. Saddam refused to accept the deal because it infringed on Iraqi sovereignty and consequent right to control its oil and the income generated from its sale. Of course it did, and all the parties concerned knew that. Saddam was not exposing an unknown fact but reacting to what he interpreted as the UN's carrot-and-stick tactics – the most that Britain and America were willing to allow. A master of this game and other balancing acts, he chose to haggle in the hope of hearing the offer improved.[1] It was not, mainly because the USA and Britain refused to budge.

The two countries missed an opportunity here. Giving the Iraqis more could have been used as a demonstration of concern for the welfare of the people despite Saddam and not because of him. Alleviating human suffering without easing the pressure on

Saddam or aiding his cause should have been tried. More food and medicine could have been provided under stricter UN control and without Saddam, desperate for a deal as he was, having a say in the matter. The UN, instead of Saddam, would have got all the credit for feeding the Iraqi people. This would have eliminated the argument of whose siege was producing the misery that the Iraqi people were and are still suffering. In their confrontation with Saddam, America and Britain have betrayed a stubborn inflexibility which perpetuated their inability to separate the dictator from his people.

The international response to Saddam's attempts to intimidate the UNSCOM inspectors came fast, and further UNSC resolutions, 707 and others, ordered Saddam to afford them 'unconditional and unrestricted' access to all areas, facilities and everything within them. Unlike the exclusively American and British calls to overthrow Saddam, this was a UN resolution supported by all the major powers and, as became obvious with time, Saddam always gave in when faced with the united front of the major powers. Shortly afterwards, the unconditional and unrestricted ability of the inspectors to carry out their mandate produced impressive results. In September UNSCOM was able to begin pursuing Iraq's biological warfare programme after endlessly hounding the dowdy woman in charge of it, Dr Rihab Taha (she was nicknamed Dr Germ while the man in charge of chemical weapons, Dr Ghazi Faisal, was called Dr Gas). In October, Iraq itself admitted having a programme to build an atomic bomb and supplied some details of its uranium enrichment programme. This was followed in November by what Iraq described as a 'full and final disclosure' of its weapons of mass destruction.

That Saddam was lying about his substantial stock of weapons of mass destruction is too well established to warrant discussing, but there was nothing new in this. In dealing with the outside world, especially the USA, Saddam was bargaining in the manner of a souq Arab – the disclosure-and-denials tactic were extensions of his carrot-and-stick ones. Like a souq Arab, he actually thought that the other side would tire and give in. Unfortunately, this was not a hypothetical situation but a time-consuming exercise with direct bearing on the fate of a people already short of food, medicine and even clean water. The Iraqi people were at the mercy of a test of wills between a dictator determined to use the suffering of his people to advantage, and two outside powers who were punishing his people for allowing him to exist. The old Iraqi phrase of '*amara al hijara*, or 'a [poor] principality of stones', was an apt description of what the once-wealthy country had become.

The background to the Iraqi-UNSCOM problem was the US efforts to depose Saddam, which began immediately the Gulf War ended (disgustingly, at the same time that the USA was turning its back on the *intifada*), but the Americans wanted 'a suitable replacement', in other words someone they would control. Unbelievably, America's first move consisted of direct contacts with Saddam's half-brother, the infamous Barazan Ibrahim Tikriti, onetime head of the dreaded *mukhabarat* whom he had exiled to Geneva and made Ambassador to Switzerland and the UN institutions in that country.[5] The CIA were now considering promoting him as a replacement for Saddam. The American who contacted Barazan was an Arabic-speaking agent, operating under the cover of a business consultant, who was related to a highly placed US official – high enough for copies of his reports to reach the White House.

Concurrently, the CIA succeeded in convincing the Kurds to join forces with the other Iraqi opposition parties to form a united front against Saddam, which eventually replaced the Joint Action Committee of Iraq and became the Iraqi National Council (INC). These efforts culminated in a CIA-sponsored meeting of the opposition in Vienna in June 1992. It was a pretentious convention at which over forty groups participated and, with American approval, issued declarations which predicted the imminent downfall of Saddam. The world greeted this prediction with glee, but some of the delegates knew better. When a quorum was needed to take a decision in one of the meetings, an opposition personality brought in his twelve-year-old daughter and she voted for the resolution in question.[6] The overall programme adopted by the opposition was vague and beyond their ability to implement. Vienna was no more than a pretence, a subsidiary effort to justify what America and Britain were saying – that things were happening.

As if this march of folly was not enough, the CIA tried to establish contact with another of Saddam's security criminals, Dr Fadhil Barak. The former Director of the *mukhabarat* from 1983 to 1989 had been fired for mysterious reasons and retired to

Tikrit and a small farm. This brilliant man, who had a PhD from the University of Moscow and had been trained by the KGB and Stasi in East Berlin, was the chief architect of a joint command for Saddam's security apparatus and a firm believer in using torture. Because, accidentally or by design, Saddam had eliminated most CIA agents operating under ethnic cover, the Americans tried to reach Barak through a UN personality in 1991. Some months later, in September 1991, he was arrested by members of the department of which he had been the longest-serving head, subjected to a dose of his own medicine and then executed.[7]

Despite the mainly propaganda support for the INC and Iraqi opposition groups in general, the USA clearly had no intention of allowing democratic forces or organized political movements to otherthrow Saddam. The Barazan and Barak contacts were more important to the Americans than Vienna, and represented proof that the USA was looking for someone similar to Saddam. Further evidence of this came in early 1992 when a group of Iraqi politicians using Tehran as their headquarters and cooperating with military and civilian elements within Iraq tried to organize an internal uprising to overthrow Saddam. Only the conclusion of this operation is known: the death of one Safar Mukhlis, the son of Mawloud Mukhlis, the politician who decades earlier had put Tikrit on the map by sponsoring the entry into the Army of many of its young men. Safar was arrested and executed by Saddam in April 1992. A few months later Sa'ad Saleh Jaber, the head of the Free Iraq Council, son of a former Prime Minister and an esteemed member of the Iraqi establishment, announced that the plot against Saddam had been betrayed by the CIA.[8] Though information about this plot is scarce, to the Americans its planners would have had two black marks against them – belief in democracy and links to Tehran.

The British were not directly involved in trying to overthrow Saddam, but the authority given them by their long experience in Iraq provided them with an opportunity to influence the atmosphere and nature of the confrontation with Saddam. Unfortunately the British government, under both John Major and Tony Blair, was more keen to play to its home audience than to take responsibility as the provider of expertise and sound judgement. There were many British Orientalists, diplomats and academics who knew the political structure of Iraq and who were capable of differentiating between Saddam and Iraq, but tapping this wealth of knowledge was subordinated to their government's wish to please the British public and to its blind acceptance of the 'special relationship' with America. Moreover, many British politicians totally dismissed the effects of what was happening in Iraq in terms of human suffering and its potential political consequences, and some believed in the power of Britain to redesign the country it had created in 1921.[9] The British refusal to listen to its experts was as significant in the prevailing situation as the CIA's bungling, and indeed contributed to the background which made the CIA's clumsy efforts possible.

British 'expertise' began to assert itself when the Marsh Arabs rose against Saddam in June 1991 in an on-off rebellion which continues to this day. Colourful and brave, the Marsh Arabs occupy a huge area the size of Wales, formed by the confluence of the Tigris and Euphrates where they flow into the Gulf. As with the Kurds, the terrain affords them protection; in their case, the lush tall grass, lakes and streams make it difficult to detect their movements and to use tanks and helicopters against them. Furthermore, this area is adjacent to Iran, and because the border between the two countries is not strictly delineated the Marsh Arabs can cross back and forth and count on the help of their co-religionists. The historical involvement of the British in Iraq led them to assume the role of interpreters of this continuing rebellion, and to create an image for it which extended the demonization of Saddam.

The uprising by the Marsh Arabs – and on this everybody is now agreed – was not purely political. They rebelled when Saddam diverted water feeding the marshes with the creation of a third, 300-mile-long river which acted as a drainage channel to carry away the salt and thus to make the waters of the Tigris and Euphrates usable for irrigation. He named the drainage channel the Saddam River, exaggerated the amount of land his government would recover by the consequent draining of the marshes, and responded to the uprising by dispatching his Republican Guard to put it down without mercy. Saddam did not make plans to relocate the Marsh Arabs but mercilessly pushed them out and killed those who resisted. Thousands died and tens of thousands more fled. Draining the marshes meant the end of an ancient way of life and to the Marsh Arabs this, rather than ideology, was reason for them to rebel. Except for the inexcusable savagery of Saddam's response, the conflict between the central government and the local way of life was similar to other such clashes throughout the world.

The plan to drain the marshes was presented by the British as another example of Saddam's political criminality. Politicians, human rights activists, some Orientalists and an assorted collection of anti-Saddam forces continue to claim this as reason enough to hate Saddam, depose him and try him. But romanticizing the Marsh Arabs, who represented only 1 per cent of the total Iraqi population of some 20 million, is similar to the British penchant for romanticizing and exaggerating the importance of the Bedouins. The British objection was to the idea of draining the marshes rather than to the way it was being carried out, and they regarded the welfare of the Marsh Arabs as more important than the biggest land reclamation project in the history of Iraq. The Iraqis told their side of the story but, understandably, the world did not accept it. In this case, what made the British outcry against Saddam especially cynical is the fact that it was they who were behind the plans to drain the marshes.

It was British companies who drew up plans to drain the marshes for the Iraqi monarchy in the 1940s.[10] The Cambridge-based company Mott MacDonald worked on the overall draining of the marshes in the 1970s. These efforts produced no protest. The Kut–Naminyah stretch of the project, the Dalmaj, reclaimed some 200 square miles of land. The Sweiyrah and West Gharaf part of it have been on the books for ages, and the whole scheme would have been finished in the 1980s except for the Iran–Iraq War. The studies conducted on the Iraqi marshes by British companies told the same story: the water table is close to the surface, salinity is high and Iraq would do well to build a third river/canal and divert the salty water to the huge Khor Abdallah depression. That would enable the water of the Tigris and Euphrates, now desalinated, to be used to irrigate and thus reclaim land.[11] Saddam resurrected the diversion project in 1991 because he had tens of thousands of soldiers with nothing to do, and he used them as labourers and killers. But he was following British plans. The British government ignored this fact and used the situation for further demonization of Saddam which made it difficult to advocate easing the sanctions.

The British had another chance to administer an indirect blow to the image of Iraq in July 1991. They flatly stated that they would not support the lifting of sanctions against Iraq unless British businessman Ian Richter, imprisoned in Iraq since 1986 on bribery charges, was released.[12] The Richter case was not political and, while a miscarriage of justice under Saddam was commonplace, the British government turned the affair into an anti-Saddam human rights issue at a time when UN representative to Iraq Prince Saddureddine Khan and the French Foreign Ministry were pleading for an easing of the sanctions to avoid a human catastrophe. Richter was released in November 1991, but the British government did not vote for easing the sanctions.

The third opportunity for the British to assert themselves came during the negotiations regarding the Iraq–Kuwait border which immediately followed the war. It was a United Nations task, but British expertise was needed because Britain had been responsible for demarcating this border in the 1930s. Acting on British advice, the Indonesian head of the UN commission responsible for settling the border dispute recommended squeezing Iraq northward and giving Kuwait more than it had asked for before the war. The recommendation was accepted. 'This recipe for disaster', as the Iraqi writer Sa'ad Bazzaz called it,[13] will come to haunt us in the future. What it meant was that most of the huge Rumeillah oilfield, one of the issues which ignited the Gulf War, was ceded to Kuwait. Regardless of political persuasion, no future Iraqi leader will ever accept this situation, nor will the Iraqi people, though Saddam nominally did. Except for deriving some psychological satisfaction out of still being capable of influencing the design of countries in the Middle East, Britain's keenness to award so much land to Kuwait makes no sense.

The inclusive and punishing external siege of Iraq consisted of legitimate UN efforts to make Saddam obey Security Council resolutions and American and British determination to give their resolutions a broader interpretation. The United States and Britain followed their own interpretations even when the rest of the United Nations took exception to them. The USA was openly trying to create an Iraqi government beholden to it, while Britain was in charge of reinvigorating the image which justified maintaining the punishing sanctions. The division between the UN and the Anglo-Saxon countries presented Saddam with an opportunity to drive a wedge between the two by fully complying with the UN resolutions and using this compliance to encourage France, the Russian

Federation and China to sponsor an easing of the sanctions and other punitive measures. But Saddam, emulating the refusal of the USA and Britain to appeal to the Iraqi people over his head, would not do so and continued to deny UNSCOM and IAEA full cooperation. Saddam used the issue of national sovereignty as an excuse and, though this argument had and still has basis in fact, what he was relying on most was his continued possession of weapons of mass destruction and the implicit threat of using them in the event of a final showdown.

Meanwhile, the internal siege continued and the noose choking the Iraqi people was getting tighter by the day. After Saddam's defeat of the forces behind the *intifada*, the three sources that could restrain him and his family were too weak to capitalize on the reduction of the country to a principality of stones. The RCC command was made up of weaklings and sycophants, and the Ba'ath structure beneath it reported to Saddam and members of his family. Even cabinet changes made no difference whatsoever. Except for the Shia Dawa Party and its ally the Tehran-based SCIRI, unacceptable to the USA and Britain because of their religious bent and pro-Iranian sympathies, the opposition had no street following and were left dependent on Kurdish leadership. Because Kurdistan had been autonomous on a number of occasions in modern times, severing it from the control of the central government, as was done by Operation Provide Comfort, was not a traumatic process. Furthermore, the ephemeral support provided to opposition groups by the Kurdish leadership reduced their alliance to showmanship. Even the October 1992 meeting of forty opposition groups under the auspices of the INC in Suleimaniya in northern Iraq, and the setting up of radio and television stations in the region (the names change but there are only two of them), had a greater effect on Western perception of the Iraqi situation than on conditions within the country. Thirdly, Iraqi civilian society as a whole has never been cohesive enough to mount an organized movement of civil disobedience against the central government, and the repression imposed by Saddam's security apparatus added to the social divisions.

Meanwhile, Saddam turned to the corruptible tribes to augment his Tikriti powerbase. By bribing them with the promise of total control over their flock he gained the support of the Harb, Aqaydat, Khazraj, Azza, Jabbour, Shaman, Tuma and Sa'adun tribal federations. Saddam had no money to give them but he allowed the sheikhs to revert to their old ways, to treat their followers like slaves and register all the tribal land in their individual names. Whatever land reform programmes had been enacted in the past are no more.

Once again, the only realistic prospect of ridding Iraq and the rest of the world of Saddam, rested exclusively on possible moves by the Army or the will of an individual assassin. This was what the USA wanted, a pliant colonel or a killer, but organizing either eluded it. Individual officers and small groups acting on their own plotted Saddam's overthrow time and again, but the task proved beyond them. Some of these plots were Saddam inventions, excuses to rid himself of potential sources of trouble, but two serious attempts were made during 1991 and Saddam's motorcade was ambushed in 1992.[13] To the knowledgeable Dr Heidar Abbas the reason for the plots' failures is clear: the maximum number of people who could meet and plan anything without rousing suspicion was three.[14] But there was another reason too: officers do not change the government of their country when it is under siege by outside powers and when the institution to which they belong, the Iraqi Army, is being attacked by these outside forces.

Aware of the real danger to his position, Saddam tightened his grip on the Army and security apparatus immediately after the Gulf War. The system of commissars and party informers within the Army was effective, but among Saddam's first acts in 1992 was the creation of the Golden Division or Special Republican Guard.[15] This new privileged army within the bigger privileged Republican Guard was expanded, paid higher salaries and accorded priority over normal mortals even in getting food and prescription drugs.[16] Saddam's new creation bridged the gap between the regular Army and the security apparatus; the main task of the Special Republican Guard was to work with the Special Security to protect Saddam, and together they became the Organization of Special Security (OSS).

In addition to his new, expanded OSS he imposed greater family control on the various elements of the Army and security apparatus. His half-brother Watban was made Minister of the Interior, while his second half-brother Sabawi was made head of his private office and given special security duties which eventually elevated him to head of the *mukhabarat*. Son Udday's duties were expanded dramatically: this semi-literate was made head of the journalists' syndicate and editor of the newspaper *Babel* in addition to his job with the Olympic Committee chores, and briefly he was made head of National Security. Cousin Ali Hassan Al Majid (Ali Chemical) was made Minister of Defence, while Saddam's son-in-law Hussein Kamel already held the post of Minister of Industry and Military Industrialization and his brother, Saddam's second son-in-law Saddam Kamel, headed a mysterious section in the security department. The prize position eventually went to Saddam's more thinking son Qussay, who was put in charge of the OSS and presided over the merger of Special Security and the Special Republican Guard. Of course, half-brother Barazan, the diplomat/conspirator, was in Geneva overseeing what money remained in Swiss banks from the now defunct Committee for Strategic Development. These funds were used to take care of the family and perpetuate its hold on power.

Except for Saddam's son Qussay and his half-brother Barazan the family group made for a most unimpressive collection of people, but their exalted positions had nothing to do with talent. In fact the other members resembled a mafia family. They stole and looted when the Iraqis occupied Kuwait.[17] Their homes contained valuable Kuwaiti Persian rugs, gold fittings and fixtures and even furniture, not to speak of the dozens of Kuwaiti cars including Ferraris in Udday's garages. Furthermore, the state of dual siege provided Udday and Hussein Kamel with an opportunity to profit from the ensuing conditions. Udday struck an alliance with the Palestinian terrorist Abul Abbas, who had past connections with the Russian mafia, and the two created an elaborate smuggling organization. Udday and Abul Abbas supplied the Russians with drugs from the Middle East and as far away as Colombia.[18] Udday also got involved in selling on the open market and in Jordan some of the food and medicine given Iraq by humanitarian organizations. Hussein Kamel too was involved in smuggling and the MIMI, still the recipient of precious funds and trying to continue the unconventional weapons programme, yielded him a considerable income in kickbacks.[19]

Saddam himself was surrounded by one of the tightest security protection systems in modern history. The system of doubles blossomed and Saddam had no fewer than eight of them which, amusingly and more frequently, allowed him to be in several places at the same time. But it was when receiving visitors that the extent and madness of it all was exposed. The procedure of driving Saddam's visitors around in a car with blackened windows remained, and it was done for several hours so that the visitors lost all sense of direction. After they had arrived at a palace unknown to them they were strip-searched. This was followed by medical examination to detect what they might have swallowed – perhaps an explosive. Then their fingerprints and photographs were taken. Even then, they were transferred to another place for the meeting itself.

The office in which visitors met Saddam was always equipped with secret cameras and recorders. The cameras were focused on Saddam's handsome side, and the people in charge of them faced the prospect of execution if they inadvertently showed the President in a bad way. Nobody was allowed to speak except in response to what Saddam said, and then only briefly unless encouraged to continue by the leader. Visitors only sat down after Saddam sat down, sipped their hospitality drink after he did and never budged from the position they occupied when they entered Saddam's office – the one he selected for them. They did not cross their legs or move their hands and maintained a rigid, uncomfortable position. They addressed Saddam as 'Hero-President' or 'Master' but never simply as 'Mr President' or, as in the past, with the traditional Arab 'Abu Udday' (father of Udday). The meetings ended at Saddam's pleasure and the departure procedure, naturally walking backwards, duplicated the one which had to be endured before arriving. No visitor ever knew where he or she had been, and a five-minute meeting with Saddam took a whole day to implement.[20]

The combination of a pervasive all-seeing security system and strict precautions allowed the family to continue in its hideous ways and prompted Saddam to brag, 'I know a person who betrays before he does.'[21] Hundreds of people perished during this period, most without knowing that they had betrayed Saddam – because they had not. Thousands suffered detention and humiliation for belonging to political parties, for the suspicion that they belonged to parties or for being related, even distantly, to people who had an association with parties. Ordinary people fared much better than suspect army officers, clerics and members of the bureaucracy, because Saddam expected undivided loyalty from these groups and deemed them dangerous.

Baghdad province commander Omar Mohammed was executed for reasons no one can fathom and so was General Barek Abdallah, one of the heroes of the war with Iran. Religious leaders Abdel Aziz Al Badri, Aref Al Basri, Mohammed Al Sahi, Ali Al Azzouni, Hassan Shirazi and many others were executed. Dr Raja Al Tikriti – as the name suggests, a fellow townsman of Saddam's – who became Minister of Health offended Udday so much that he was given to a bunch of starving dogs which ate him. In fact, despite Tikriti supremacy, more of that town's residents than outsiders suffered at the hands of Saddam, simply because many of them occupied sensitive positions which put them in harm's way. When Finance Minister Hikmat Hadithi refused to transfer to Udday's personal account money desperately needed to feed people, Saddam told him never to forget that 'Udday was his master', denied him the use of his official car and made him walk home.[22] When it came to acting with utter craziness, the family was determined to stretch the limits of human credibility. Saddam's son Ali, the son of Samira Shabandar and still only a child, took to parading with units of the Special Republican Guard, and soldiers saluted him. And there was a nineteen-volume publication called *The Life and Struggle of Saddam Hussein*[23] which the more ambitious members of the Iraqi bureaucracy had to read. Meanwhile, government departments were running short of paper for official use.

That the internal siege complemented the external siege is un-doubtedly true. There were no signs whatsoever, despite dozens of reports by non-governmental aid organizations, the UN and others, that much thought was given to easing the sanctions in a way which separated Saddam from the Iraqi people. The USA and Britain vetoed all such moves. One could even say that the external siege made the internal siege possible. Without it, people would have thought of Saddam's crimes against them instead of thinking about where they might find something to eat. A less inclusive external siege would have permitted more overt action to be taken against Saddam without harming the Iraqi people. Furthermore, the channelling of the available money to Saddam, certainly a vital aspect of what was happening, allowed his family, the special forces and security people to benefit from it. This and the absence of any effort to help the Iraqi people themselves made him strong and the rest of the population weak. This suited Saddam, but a principality of stones should have been unacceptable to others. By accepting this situation, the American and British leaders validated the allegation that what was happening amounted to shooting down a plane full of innocent passengers in order to get at the hijacker.

The Iraqi opposition was not and is not a contributor to the dual siege of Iraq, except through allowing themselves to be instruments in the hands of the CIA as in Vienna and Salaheddine. However, as the visible if not viable alternative to Saddam, and, to many, an important component of the Iraqi situation which should be taken into consideration, they deserve close examination. While they are not directly involved, it is their ineptness and inability to organize which contributes to the twin state of siege that has determined everything since 1992. I am in possession of a document[24] which lists eighty-two separate Iraqi opposition groups, from serious political parties with long histories, to the Communists and disaffected Ba'athists, to former ministers of the Iraqi government who believe that they will eventually be called on to save their country. And there are former officers with no following who believe that their military rank is enough to guarantee them a position in the future of Iraq.

There is a lack of cohesion and unity among the opposition: all the groups exaggerate the little things they do achieve, and in most cases their programmes reflect no more than the self-interest of their leaders. Furthermore, the divisions between them run deep. Some object to cooperation with the CIA and accuse those willing to work with it, or with other branches of the American government, of treason. Others accuse SCIRI of treason for cooperating with Iran. Many are beholden to other Arab countries and follow their directions at a time when those countries do not have a sensible political programme to change things in Iraq. This is particularly true of people who receive Saudi and Kuwaiti funding. Most have become professional opposition personalities – they earn their living through receiving financial assistance to speak out against Saddam.

This is not to suggest an absence of honour and intelligence among the opposition. Dr Ahmad Chalabi's call for an eventual Iraqi confederacy of Kurds, Sunnis and Shias is totally sensible, and such a confederacy would not come about without democracy.

But, while cooperating with the USA, he himself admits that the United States 'is against a confederacy and is promoting stability and not democracy';[25] in other words the USA is promoting the emergence of another dictator. Salah Omar Al Ali, Adnah Pachachi and Sa'ad Saleh Jaber, though they occupy different political positions, speak eloquently of the future of Iraq and democracy, but that automatically denies them foreign and Arab help. One cannot but be impressed by Dr Latif Rashid and Dr Fuad Ma'asoum of the PUK, who make an impressive case for the Kurdish position in future Iraqi politics.[26] But this still does not stop their leader, Jallal Talabani, from subordinating Kurdish interests to his personal leadership and playing Saddam against the USA and vice versa.

The only area of success for the opposition has been in creating an expatriate Iraqi community of 2 million people composed of the *crème de la crème* of Iraqi society, among others the doctors, engineers and oil experts needed to save Iraq in the future. According to Dr Amneh Murad there are two thousand Iraqi physicians in the UK alone, while Dr Tareq Shafiq speaks of Iraqi oil expertise – once the best in the Middle East – having left the country for good.[27] In other words, those who can do so have already left Iraq. As a result, except for the Army there is nothing within Iraq that could lead to change. The opposition did not create the state of siege, but its weakness and total dependence on outsiders solidifies it.

Since mid-1991 the Iraqi situation has been judgeable in accordance with two yardsticks: the misery inflicted on the Iraqi people, and the behaviour of the people who control and contribute to the sieges creating these appalling conditions. The sieges started biting very early because Iraq was already bankrupt from the war with Iran when it started the Gulf War. The effects of this worsening situation will be detailed later, but serious signs of deterioration were already showing by the middle of 1991. According to Patrick Cockburn of the *Independent*, death among infants increased from 36.5 per thousand in 1989 to 120 per thousand in 1991.[28] Eye witness Nuha Al Radi tells of many middle-class people already on the streets begging for food.[29] Only a change in the behaviour of all countries, individuals and organizations capable of influencing 'the Iraqi situation' can stop this descent into despair.

By the end of 1991, with many Arabs and Westerners expressing admiration for Saddam's powers of survival, none of the other parties involved had developed a plan to resolve the impasse which had developed. Not only was it a situation which desperately needed a solution, but no two parties were in agreement on what needed to be done. UNSCOM was facing greater and greater Iraqi resistance over the totality of its mandate, and Saddam was trying to redefine what 'unrestricted' and 'unfettered' meant. His attitude to UNSCOM changed weekly, and most of the time secretly. Dependent on the reports of UNSCOM as it was, the United Nations could do nothing except restate the contents of its resolutions. The Iraqi opposition, exposed through being over-optimistic if not careless in its predictions, became more and more dependent on the United States for financial and other support. The Arabs, Egypt and Saudi Arabia in particular, though facing a growing sympathy for the plight of the Iraqi people, still had nothing to offer in terms of a solution – certainly nothing that others would accept. Saddam, rightly convinced that he was being personally targeted by the sanctions, had no incentive to cooperate with anybody, and his acts of obstruction and demands that the sanctions be lifted became louder and more blatant. To the USA and Britain, Saddam's mere existence amounted to a failure; this prompted them to tighten the squeeze on Iraq and Saddam without new plans. France, Russia and China, angry because no one was listening to them, distanced themselves from the USA and Britain and complained bitterly. France's cooperation in implementing the no-fly zones became selective. In essence, it was still a confrontation between Saddam and the USA and Britain. But lack of success by either side made them raise the stakes, which meant escalating gratuitously and behaving more irrationally.

In August 1992, ostensibly reacting to the plight of the Marsh Arabs, the USA, Britain and France imposed a southern no-fly zone and thus closed most of Iraq to Saddam's helicopters. Unable to respond to the perpetrators, Saddam acted against the inspectors. He denied them access to the Ministry of Agriculture, the traditional front for acquiring chemical and biological weapons, and to the air base at Habaniya, and followed that by sending troops into the area around Um Al Kasr, the no-man's land separating his country from Kuwait. The UN passed more resolutions, the USA and Britain responded by attacking Iraqi facilities, and this purposeless tit-for-tat replaced a more measured reaction to the provocations.

This gamesmanship was elevated to a new level in the spring of 1993 in an incident which, because it reflected unreason on both sides, merits examination. Bill Clinton had defeated George Bush in the November 1992 presidential election, which was notable because the failure to remove Saddam and exposure of the corrupt cooperation between the two countries prior to the Gulf War had contributed to Bush's defeat. Saddam responded by appearing on the balcony of his palace and firing his gun in celebration. According to an Iraqi ambassador overseas, Saddam's tribal mind had exaggerated the importance of this event and he thought there would be an easier, less personalized US policy towards him. But Secretary of State Warren Christopher made clear that there would be no change in policy; even had Clinton wanted it, the demonization of Saddam was too entrenched and attempts at easing the pressure on him would have been extremely unpopular.

In April 1993 George Bush made a ceremonial visit to Kuwait. The government of that country announced that Iraqi intelligence had plotted to assassinate him during his trip and that several Iraqi agents had been apprehended. On 26 June Clinton retaliated. Twenty-three Tomahawk guided missiles loaded with thousands of pounds of explosives, and costing a million dollars each, were fired on the *mukhabarat* headquarters in downtown Baghdad. Several missiles went off course and killed many civilians including Layla Al Attar, one of Iraq's leading artists. In the USA the death of the civilians was ignored, and the press and public considered the attack a success. 'He's learning on the job,' crowed the *Wall Street Journal*, and applauded Clinton's first act of war.[30]

What followed was considerably more important than the original allegation. Kuwait, which had proved itself unreliable during the Gulf War and afterwards regarding the notorious baby incubators allegations and the trials of so-called collaborators, was believed by the Americans without question. The mechanics of smuggling the bomb to Kuwait, cumbersome even had the border been open, were doctored to prove Iraqi culpability. The confessions extracted from some of the suspects were taken under duress and no independent people were allowed to see them. More importantly, the attitudes of Sandy Berger and Martin Indyck, Clinton's advisers on this case, were formed before the FBI report on the case was completed.[31] They wanted an attack on Iraq. Later, after the Americans attacked Baghdad, the Kuwaitis sentenced four of the accused to death and carried out the sentence.

This was a case where the evidence and the accuser were highly questionable, where the deaths of Iraqi civilians were dismissed as unimportant, where the execution of the accused did not merit press coverage and where Clinton's baptism of fire was celebrated by the Americans because Saddam Hussein was on the receiving end. Furthermore, attacking Iraq from the air did not stop with this retaliation. Military operations carried out in response to specific crises have a tendency to repeat themselves and, in July and August, the USA carried out more air attacks – because Iraqi missiles had supposedly been moved into the southern no-fly zone. Attacking Iraqi installations became a habit, even when it produced civilian casualties.

In the Middle East, people lamented the attacks on Baghdad. The executions elicited a lot of sympathy and very few believed the Kuwaitis or had faith in their legal system. In souqs and streets truths and exaggerations about the suffering of the Iraqi people were constantly recited. But the Arab governments still said nothing. Arab governments and the West had a different viewpoint on Iraq from that of the average Arab, and the divide was growing wider by the day. What Saddam Hussein achieved during the Gulf crisis and subsequent war – gaining the support of the Arab masses – was growing in strength by the day. Saddam was slowly becoming the only Arab leader with a constituency beyond his own borders. Palestinians, Jordanians, Egyptians and even North Africans named their sons Saddam.

Beyond the deepening misery of the Iraqi people, the period until March 1995 was a repeat of what had happened before. Saddam would deny access, make false claims, interfere with inspections and threaten Kuwait and the Kurds by word of mouth or by moving troops. Ekeus would persist, coolly present the Iraqis with solid evidence and get them to change their minds. He and UNSCOM were successful in getting Iraq to accept a difficult requirement of permanent inspection installations including sophisticated monitors, in allowing UN inspection flights to continue, in completing the removal of all irradiated nuclear fuel from Iraq and in maintaining a cordial relationship with Iraqi officialdom. Even the occasional US attack on Iraqi installations did not disrupt the work of UNSCOM and IAEA. Ekeus had a total appreciation of his mission and knew that it had a clear objective in sight: the total elimination of weapons of mass destruction that would lead to a lifting of sanctions. He did not respond to US and UK calls for making the otherthrow of Saddam part of the UN requirements to lift the sanctions; he simply ignored them. In a way he followed the legalistic interpretation of UN resolutions adopted by the French. And here it is well to remember that the French supported the original no-fly zones but refused to use them as an excuse to attack Iraq.

In fact, the attitude of Ekeus and the rest of the world took into consideration the deteriorating human conditions within the country, something which the US, UK and Iraqi opposition were determined to ignore. With the deadlock over the oil-for-food offer continuing and no sign of compromise, a catastrophe of huge proportions was enveloping Iraq. Most means of modern life were gone. There was no drinking water. Electricity became a precious commodity and power was on for only three to four hours a day. The transportation system broke down and people could not get around. Medical care in the country was collapsing: in one place two doctors were caring for eighty thousand people[32] and most basic medicines, antibiotics in particular, were not available. The shortage of paper was so severe that staff of government departments wrote their memoranda on the other sides of old documents from their files which resulted in the destruction of most of the government records. The per capita caloric intake was half of what it had been before the war, and the streets were full of garbage and beggars. Even well-to-do families were selling their precious belongings in order to eat.[33] An Iraqi artist friend sold his collection of modern prints for less than one-tenth of its value in London or New York. Crime became so widespread that in 1993 alone thirty-six thousand cars were stolen.[34] Life expectancy among Iraqi men declined by twenty years and among women by eleven.[35] In 1991, the Harvard School of Public Health issued the first report of human suffering. Later, UNICEF estimated that in 1993 between eighty thousand and one hundred thousand children died because of the sanctions.[36] Five thousand five hundred institutions of education were badly damaged and in need of equipment to function.[37] The statistics contain enough evidence to justify the invocation of the articles of the Geneva and Hague conventions against starving civilian populations, not to speak of the UN Genocide Convention. More specifically, in defining the embargo, UNSC resolution 661 – the original one from which the rest flowed – exempted what needed to be imported for 'humanitarian circumstances'.

Everybody except the USA and UK was in favour of easing the sanctions. Meanwhile, the gentlemanly Ekeus was heading in the right direction. In September 1992 IAEA inspector Maurizio Zifferero announced that Iraq was in compliance with the requirements of the UN regarding atomic weapons.[38] The American members of IAEA and several British ones attacked him publicly. In 1994 Ekeus, along with most UN diplomats believed the embargo would be history within a year.[39] This was followed by a more open-ended statement from Ekeus in which he announced that 'with the exception of biological [weapons] it was all clear'.[40] Of greater importance was Ekeus's faith in the monitoring equipment that he and the teams had installed to keep Iraq from pursuing their previous programmes – equipment similar to that which had been used in the various international disarmament agreements.

What followed in 1995 exposed both the powers opposed to relaxing the sanctions and Saddam Hussein as liars. Both sides had secret agendas. Saddam was concealing weapons of mass destruction to protect himself. The Americans, with British knowledge, were planning to intercept the lifting of the sanctions even if it meant that more Iraqi civilians would suffer. In fact, the more the Americans and British spoke, the more it became apparent that their purpose was to destroy Iraq's ability to make non-conventional weapons – a huge step ahead of destroying the weapons in Saddam's possession. Because buying equipment to make chemical and biological weapons is relatively easy and costs little, destroying Iraq's ability to make non-conventional weapons meant destroying the people capable of making them. Admitting this would have amounted to a call for murder; it was avoided, and remains a closed subject. Amazingly, most of Saddam's scientists stayed in Iraq, though the *Observer*, *New York Times* and *Sunday Times* ran stories about a small number of defectors (Sharastani, Abbas, Al Huddani) and re-ran warmed over stories purporting to show Saudi support for Saddam's programme in the 1970s and 1980s.

(Saudi King Khalid had openly offered Iraq money to buy a new reactor after the Israeli attack on Ozeirak in 1981.)

In early March 1995 the INC under Ahmad Chalabi, Talabani's PUK and Barzani's KDP – after full consultation with the Americans and, according to some, securing their agreement and a promise of support[41] – decided to begin a military campaign against Saddam in northern Iraq. Having contacted SCIRI leader Sayyed Mohammed Bakr Al Hakim in Tehran, they expected the first signs of success to prompt the Dawa and other Islamic splinter groups to join them in a southern campaign. The INC and PUK forces commenced hostilities at the agreed hour, but Barzani balked and refused to commit his forces. This discouraged Hakim, who refrained from joining the uprising.

Despite Barzani's defection, the combined PUK–INC forces augmented by Assyrians and Turkoman dissidents made considerable progress. Town after town fell to them and they pushed back three of Saddam's divisions, mauled the 38th and took seven hundred prisoners in the process. The new forces had the benefit of the knowledge and leadership of a new defector, General Wafic Samarai, former chief of Saddam's military intelligence department. However, Barzani, fearful that a Talabani success would undermine his own leadership, decided to switch sides completely and ordered his forces to attack his Kurdish rival. Barzani fought Talabani in the towns of Banjawin and Nalbrize, killed two hundred of his men and occupied the towns. More significantly, the promised American help never came. The campaign collapsed, the old lines were restored and the Kurds continued to fight each other. Kurdish perfidy and American inaction settled the issue at a time when the Iraqi Army demonstrated a lack of will to defend Saddam. Hundreds of Saddam's soldiers were happy to defect. What the USA had in mind in sanctioning this operation without any intention of supporting it is yet another inexplicable act of cynicism.[42]

The lack of reason on the American side in 1994–5 was matched by equally illogical behaviour on the part of Saddam and his primitive family. In October 1994 he had set up a militia of young people called the Sadamyoun, the Saddamists. These teenagers were indoctrinated in special schools to worship Saddam as a messianic, unseen saviour in tight seclusion. They regularly received special stipends and instilled fear into the hearts of ordinary citizens. For Saddam it marked a reversion to the use of thugs in the days of his youth when he headed Jihaz Hunein. Udday was made commander of this force, the numbers of which were multiplying with considerable speed. Although lightly armed and militarily insignificant, the Sadamyoun complemented the various special forces which fell directly under family control. They extended Udday's influence and, except for refraining from poaching on the territory of his more able brother, he tried to use them to control the rest of the family.

Udday's primacy was opposed by his uncle and Minister of the Interior Watban, brother-in-law Hussein Kamel of MIMI, and Kamel's brother (also Udday's brother-in-law) Saddam Kamel, the hero of *The Long Days*. In May 1995, after several open attacks on Watban in the newspaper *Babel* which forced his resignation, Udday, in another drunken fit, shot his uncle and seriously wounded him in the leg, at the same time killing three of his companions. Watban, fearing for his life, claimed it was an accident; later his leg had to be amputated. Hussein and Saddam Kamel, also in fear of their lives because of Udday's repeated threats against them, chose another route: they decided to defect.

Hussein Kamel's position as head of MIMI afforded him contact with outsiders, through whom he organized his own and his family's escape. First, he established contact with the CIA through a Western journalist.[43] Then, feigning illness, he travelled to Jordan for two days, supposedly for medical treatment, and completed the arrangements. On 5 August Hussein and Saddam Kamel defected to Jordan with their wives (Saddam's daughters Raghid and Rana) and children. In terms of press coverage it resembled the defection to America in the 1960s of Stalin's daughter Svetlana. But in this case everybody expected the family divisions to lead to Saddam's overthrow.

Hussein Kamel had a meeting with King Hussein, a party to arranging the defection, and spent his first two weeks in Amman closeted with CIA agents who were in the city to debrief him. Kamel, Saddam's cousin, son-in-law and trusted aide and the man responsible for Iraq's non-conventional weapons programme since the end of the war with Iran, told the Americans everything they wanted to know. Hitherto undiscovered plants for making chemicals were exposed, companies fronting for the biological warfare programme were identified, documents confirming that Iraq had been working on the lethal VX nerve gas were provided, and individuals and departments in charge of these programmes named. He had little new information about the nuclear area; the IAEA had been relatively successful. The CIA handed Kamel over to Ekeus after they were through with him and the Swedish diplomat got more out of him because he knew the right questions to ask.

On 17 August, Saddam accepted the inevitable. Angered to the point of not being able to eat, losing weight and ignoring his associates with an icy silence, Saddam brooded. Finally, he dismissed Udday from most of his positions, spoke of the family being hurt 'mentally and deeply'[44] and declared a *tabaru'* (disowning) of his relations. He followed with another final declaration about his weapons of mass destruction which included data on biological weapons (anthrax and botulism) and VX nerve gas, and gave details of Iraq's crash programme to acquire nuclear weapons. A standing Iraqi threat to throw UNSCOM and IAEA inspectors out because Iraq had met all the requirements of UN resolutions and wanted the sanctions lifted was rescinded. Ekeus had no choice but to start all over again, but he did so without fanfare. He went to work to destroy what had been exposed by Hussein Kamel. The new Iraqi declaration was accompanied by thousands of pages of data, according to Baghdad what Hussein Kamel had been hiding without authorization.

Not for the first time, for the real antagonists the confrontation was back to square one. America and Britain cried foul and wanted to get rid of Saddam, but still stopped short of supporting popular forces. In Amman the CIA squeezed Hussein Kamel and his brother for all they were worth, then dropped them; even Jordanian government officials stopped seeing them. Kamel tried to contact Iraqi opposition groups throughout the world, particularly in London, to offer his cooperation, but nobody wanted anything to do with him. He made noises about supposed promises made to him by the CIA, but nobody listened. He, his brother, Raghid and Rana lived in isolation in what amounted to a miniature leper colony.

Hussein Kamel, once touted as a successor to Saddam and often described as the second most powerful man in Iraq, suffered a nervous breakdown in January 1996. He was treated in Amman by Dr A.S.,[45] but neither the CIA nor the Jordanians showed any interest in helping him. In February 1996 Kamel and his brother, donning the uniforms of Iraqi army officers and accompanied by their families, returned to Iraq. A third brother refused to accompany them. Television cameras were there to record the event and there was talk of Saddam having forgiven or amnestied them, but this was not true. When the group reached Baghdad, Raghid, Rana and the children were separated from the Kamels, who were allowed to proceed to Tikrit.

The two men stayed at their father's house and relations stood guard all around it. Four days later, a raiding party led by Ali Hassan Al Majid (Ali Chemical) attacked the house. The father, two defectors, two daughters and their children were killed, along with one of the attackers. According to the official announcement, the murder was carried out by members of the Albu Nasser who wanted to redeem the tribe's honour. Saddam accepted 'the family's' decision and spoke of 'the deep shame inflicted upon us'.[46] Months later, in May 1996, Saddam the sloganeer started speaking of them as having been 'martyrs of wrath'.[47] His own daughters, spared martyrdom, have not been seen since. In assigning martyrdom to people and speaking of his wrath, Saddam was behaving in a God-like way. A few days later, with failure staring him in the eye, His Divinity accepted resolution 986, the one governing oil for food. This confirmed his acceptance of the outside siege but allowed him to manipulate the programme in a way which afforded him full control of the internal siege which complemented it.

For a brief while, Saddam was on good behaviour and there were no incidents with UNSCOM because the inspectors were busy pursuing Hussein Kamel's disclosures and the official admissions which followed them. In fact, in June 1996 Ekeus was developing a programme aimed at finishing the inspections and ending the sanctions with the help of Iraqi Deputy Premier Tareq Aziz.[48] However, there were significant developments regarding the Kurdish area and again within the family. The bitterness which followed Barzani's betrayal of the PUK–INC campaign to defeat Saddam turned into intermittent fighting between the two major Kurdish factions. In August 1996, the PUK got the upper hand and pushed Barzani's forces into a corner. The latter appealed to Saddam for help and the first week of September found him going to war again. His Republican Guard and Special Republican Guard units managed to mount a substantial surprise attack which routed the PUK forces, pushed north-east towards Iran and occupied the regional capital of Irbil. For Saddam it was more than a return to Kurdistan; his troops captured hundreds of INC followers who were operating under direct CIA control and thousands of documents which revealed the combined plans of both sides. Most Iraqi CIA operatives were executed, but hundreds were saved and taken to the United States and exile.

America responded in character and Secretary of Defence William Perry announced that it would not interfere in the fighting. Later, it blamed Saddam without mentioning that he had been asked to help by a Kurdish group, the KDP, a traditional ally of the West. Nor did the fact matter that since 1995 Turkey had been making massive incursions of between twenty thousand and forty thousand soldiers into northern Iraq in pursuit of the PKK, the Kurdish movement in Turkey which was asking for no more than the Iraqi Kurds had long since attained. To the USA and Britain, the PKK were terrorists. Having made up its mind, the United States unleashed another cruise missile against Iraq and, with the expected British support, extended the southern no-fly zone to the 32nd parallel on the outskirts of Baghdad. Furthermore, the Americans requested a suspension of the oil-for-food programme. The world was aghast. This time the French officially served notice that they would not patrol the extended no-fly zone, the Russians vetoed another punitive UN resolution prepared by the USA, the Arab League unanimously condemned the attacks, and even Iran expressed grave concern over unrestrained attacks against Iraq by America and Britain. In fact, only Kuwait and Israel backed the attack and the extension of the zone and, though the Kurds unsurprisingly made up and Saddam had to evacuate Irbil, the damage had been done. Militarily, in obtaining secret documents, undermining the PUK and INC and through the support of others, Saddam was able to claim victory.

The Iraqi Kurdish leadership, as foolish as ever despite possessing a totally just cause, handed Saddam a victory, but the brave men of the Dawa Party served dramatic notice that Saddam and his family would never be acceptable. On 12 December 1996, while driving in the middle of a convoy of Mercedes cars through Sa'adoun Street in central Baghdad, Udday Hussein was attacked by commandos of the Dawa and seriously wounded. Two of his companions including his driver were killed, and he was left paralyzed from the waist down. All the members of the hit squad escaped and Saddam, stunned and visibly disturbed, blamed the attack on the Iranians. Though this was untrue, what matters most was that the event drew attention to the vulnerability of the family. After that date none of them would ever drive through Baghdad's streets in an identifiable car or convoy again. They now move around in secret and irregularly. Promise after promise that Udday was on the mend proved to be false. If his personal behaviour did not finish him, his paralysis from the assassin's bullet did.

The early part of 1997 was relatively uneventful, but a fifth Iraqi 'full and final disclosure' was made in September. This time it included extensive information about the biological programme and VX nerve gas. Although the constant changes in the disclosures and addition of new data are testimony to Saddam's dishonesty, this latest disclosure did answer vital questions raised by Rolf Ekeus and represented a desperate attempt by Saddam at cooperation in order to have the sanctions lifted. Sadly Ekeus, who had done his utmost to keep the lid on things by separating his inspection efforts from America's attitude, had retired in July 1997 to become Sweden's Ambassador to Washington and been replaced by the Australian diplomat Richard Butler. Instead of continuing along the same lines, Butler immediately served notice that he was not bound by what Ekeus had accepted. The clock was set back.

Butler's contribution to the maintenance of sanctions resembles Mubarak's contribution towards the start of the Gulf War. His actions followed a punitive rather than a legalistic line, which played right into the hands of those who were advocating the overthrow of Saddam. Abrasive and certainly undiplomatic, he repeated that the sanctions 'would end when they ended'.[49] In October 1997 he came out of a meeting with Tareq Aziz to speak crudely of the Iraqi and would not use his title or position. He enjoyed the limelight (my unverified count saddles him with more press conferences in sixteen months than Ekeus's in six years) and gave the impression of being combative, of viewing the Iraqis with disdain and of playing up to the Americans and British. His objections to certain Iraqi actions were reported by Washington before the United Nations announced them. He was clearly the wrong man for the job; to a people who believed in dignity and pride, he was a walking, talking old-fashioned colonial officer determined to humiliate them. The Egyptian writer Mohammed Heikal, writing in *Rose Al Yussef* magazine of 16 February 1988, accused Butler of being given the job of 'finishing off Iraq'. Instead of being a problem-solver, Butler himself became a problem. He insisted that Iraq was not in compliance, kept adding to the list of the places to be inspected because he had received information about them from sources he would not disclose, and went as far as reinspecting places which Ekeus had cleared in the past.

In March 1997 US Secretary of State Madeleine Albright, speaking at Washington's Georgetown University, had declared, 'There would be no predictable end to the economic embargo.'[50] This followed the cruellest statement of all about the suffering of the Iraqi people, when Albright, appearing on CBS's *60 Minutes* programme on 12 May 1996, told the world that 'the pain [of the Iraqi people] was worth it'. British Foreign Secretary Malcolm Rifkind was clear without being crude; he said that, 'We won't lift the sanctions while he's [Saddam] in power.' Later, Prime Minister Tony Blair was to repeat similar statements every time the issue of Iraq came up. How Saddam was supposed to cooperate with the UN against this background of belligerence is unknown.

Butler's intransigence and seeming wish to please America and Britain created two new issues on which the future of the relationship between UNSCOM and Iraq rested. The first one had to do with spying, an old Iraqi accusation which went back to 1992 when inspector David Kay submitted Iraqi documents to the United States before giving them to the UN.[51] Of course, the American U-2 planes performed spying functions for the Americans. The issue of spying was resurrected more seriously in 1997 when Iraq claimed that some inspectors were intelligence agents in the pay of foreign powers, including Israel. In Iraq's eyes that should have disqualified the inspectors, and it justified Saddam's refusal to opt for full cooperation. Naturally, Butler thought it was beneath his dignity to consider this and he defended the inspectors, claimed they were innocent and accused the Iraqis of fabricating falsehoods.

The second problem was exclusively Butler's creation. He insisted on extending his inspection mandate to include the presidential palaces. The Iraqis refused to accommodate him and in turn insisted that it was a fabricated issue involving their honour. Both cases were exaggerated, and the American and British press rose to defend the purity of the inspectors and to fill their pages with stories about Saddam's palaces. The existence of the palaces rather than their possible use to conceal non-conventional weapons became the issue. In fact, Saddam living in palaces at a time when many of his people were starving was an undoubtedly criminal act, but to the Iraqi leader the palaces had become a symbol of defiance, living testimonies to the fact that he was alive, well and living in luxury despite American-British actions. In a strange way, most Iraqis supported this perverse notion and wanted these monuments of defiance.

What made this cat-and-mouse game deplorable – and neither side showed any signs of caring – was the genocide being inflicted on the people of Iraq.[52] In December 1997 the United Nations Secretary General, the wise and activist Kofi Annan, who had succeeded the ineffectual Perez de Cuellar and the incompetent Butros Butros Ghali, responded to the reports of suffering inside Iraq. He proposed to double the amount of oil that Iraq was allowed to export in return for food and medicine to produce revenue of $4 billion every six months, and suggested a delay in the payment of some reparations to allow the Iraqis to use the money to meet their pressing needs. It was a noble gesture, but one of limited effectiveness because the Iraqi oil facilities had been so short of spare parts that they could not pump so much oil. It was the buying of spare parts that had become a problem. As with every other request for food and medicine, the Iraqi needs had to be cleared by the United Nations through every single member of the Security Council. The USA and Britain took to turning down many requests and to delaying others. Even the ones that passed – no more than 20 per cent of what was needed – took more than twenty weeks to be handled. In March 1997, only nine out of thirty-seven applications for food and medicine were approved.[53] Although the situation has since improved, Iraq is still unable to pump all the oil permitted by the United Nations because of a shortage of equipment.

On the ground, conditions between 1991 and 1997 had deteriorated so badly that the Iraqis were now poorer than the people of Bangladesh. The per capita income of $4083 in 1980 had declined to $485 in 1993 and has fallen further since.[54] Inflation rose to 1000 per cent a year.[55] By 1993, because of the prevailing conditions, diabetes had increased by 135 per cent in people over fifty years old. Present estimates put the increase at 500 per cent. Cholera had disappeared from the country in the 1980s, but there were 2100 cases in 1996; the incidence of typhoid increased ten times. In its 1 March 1997 edition, the *British Journal of Independence Studies* placed the number of Iraqis who had died as a result of the sanctions at 1.5 million, half of whom were under five years old. Even as far back as March 1991, the World Health Organization (WHO) reported to the UN Secretary General that 'Iraq has been relegated to the pre-industrial age'. Another WHO report, of 1 March 1996, spoke of 'the majority of the population living on a semi-starvation diet for years'. In 1995 the Food and Agricultural Organization of the UN reported that individual Iraqis were receiving only 34 per cent of the caloric intake required to survive.

While Saddam, his family, his special forces and members of the Iraqi security apparatus escape the results of the sanctions, these statistics are the direct results of the outside siege imposed by America and Britain through a perverse interpretation of the UN resolutions. This is not to suggest that Saddam Hussein has ever told the truth or shown interest in anything except his survival, but to expect him not to favour the people who maintain him in power is tantamount to believing that dictators are choirboys. As the world entered 1998, Madeleine Albright was making announcements about looking forward to working with a new Iraq government that would succeed Saddam. It was a stupid statement, but not as stupid as the actions of members of Congress who wanted to overthrow Saddam through spending money on the Iraqi opposition without controlling how the opposition used that money. Refusing to listen to the executive branch of government, members of Congress eventually started debating the Iraq Liberation Act which would give the opposition in exile millions to propagandize against Saddam and to try to topple him. The only visible result of this was the creation of Radio Free Iraq, located in Prague, modelled after Radio Free Europe and with relay stations in Kuwait. It was an act of foolishness. Some of the people who promote the Iraq

Liberation Act speak of 'Eye-rack' and have no idea what the country is all about. Before 1998 the idea of removing Saddam Hussein from power needed a solid plan behind it. What happened during this crucial year made removing him close to an unattainable dream.

No Exit?

The period from the end of 1997 until the beginning of 1999 was marked by further deterioration in the conditions within Iraq, and a hardening of positions by both Iraq and UNSCOM which translated into acrimonious accusations and counter-accusations. The two sides were arguing over the corpse of the Iraqi people. There were further increases in the number of people suffering from malnutrition and disease and a decline in the ability of Iraq's health services to cope with the growing catastrophe. Even ambulances had no wheels to carry sick people to health centres. Meanwhile, UNSCOM chairman Richard Butler was determined to expand the areas of search and demanded fuller disclosures on VX nerve gas and biological weapons, while Saddam's government resisted both requests, repeated their accusations that many UNSCOM inspectors were spies and demanded the removal of the Americans among them because they were more suspect than the rest.

Once again, it was the atmosphere of the situation, the total absence of goodwill, rather than its realities which governed what was happening. Butler made much of having access to eight presidential sites and used the American Major Scott Ritter to conduct unannounced raids on suspect laboratories, storage facilities and hitherto cleared buildings. Unfortunately for the United Nations, Butler demonstrated a measure of ineptitude and ignorance. Among other things the size of the eight presidential sites in question kept increasing, from 70 square kilometres to 240. And Ritter, an aggressive former US Marine, had fought in the Gulf War and was known for his hard-line views regarding the

Iraqis. An Iraqi argument that the Americans and British, advocates of maintaining the sanctions as they were and still are, were over-represented in UNSCOM and should be replaced by inspectors from neutral countries was something that Butler refused to consider. Moreover, his answers to the spying accusations were less than satisfactory. I remember hearing him answer a question about alleged UNSCOM cooperation with Israel on CNN by stating that UNSCOM worked with several UN member countries. He not only refused to exclude Israel from UNSCOM helpers (Iraq still maintained a state of war with Israel), he later gratuitously and crudely involved them by stating that Saddam could hit Tel Aviv with his biological weapons.[1] Unfortunately, the US and British media had once again contributed to the rising level of tension by making similar unverifiable inflammatory accusations that Iraq had used biological weapons on Iranian prisoners of war during the war with that country.[2] Moreover, the media's coverage of Saddam's palaces was considerably greater than its coverage of the human catastrophe that the sanctions were producing.

The Iraqis eventually withheld cooperation from the Ritter group within UNSCOM and demanded their withdrawal. Butler still insisted on their inclusion in the inspection efforts. However, by late January 1998 it was becoming clear to Butler and Madeleine Albright that Ritter's methods were creating constant crises with Saddam Hussein[3] which might get out of control. Nevertheless, in early February Butler and UNSCOM decided that Iraq had not revealed the full extent of its various non-conventional weapons programme and recommended UN action to force the country into compliance. With the American and British press and public fully behind Butler and urging their governments to administer a hard, perhaps fatal, blow to Saddam the stage was set for yet another confrontation. In fact, most people had lost track of what was causing the constant state of tension between the two sides.

The issues of the palaces, sovereignty, hidden weapons and other daily matters were the tip of a huge iceberg. Even had they been settled, there were elements within the UNSC resolutions which could have given countries disinclined to lift the sanctions and ease the pressure on the Iraqi people ample excuse to maintain them. Among others, resolution 678 spoke of punitive measures staying in place to 'restore peace and security in the region' and of a need to establish 'Iraq's peaceful intentions'. These inexact requirements could have been used to keep the sanctions in place for ever. This explains the actions of the Iraqis. They were going beyond the small incidents to draw demarcation lines, to get the United Nations to identify what it would take to have the sanctions lifted. Claiming that they had met the requirements regarding weapons of mass destruction, they wanted this issue – unwisely dramatized by the USA and Britain at the expense of other important aspects of UNSC resolutions, the establishment of peace and security and determination of peaceful intentions – to become the determining factor for lifting the sanctions.

The crises created by Iraq's demands to know what it would take to lift the sanctions and Butler's expansion of what was needed to determine Iraqi compliance with UNSCOM's particular mandate regarding weapons of mass destruction manifested themselves in ways which focused on the palaces and other small issues. Eventually, the palaces inspection problem was defused by the respected and independent-thinking Kofi Annan. With only the USA and Britain in favour of continuing to punish Iraq and the rest of the Security Council in favour of sanction easing, the UN Secretary General felt free to dispatch his own survey team to Baghdad to determine the nature of the problem and the size of the palaces. Against US wishes, Annan followed the dispatch of the survey team with a personal visit to Baghdad.[4] Certainly US congressional leaders, in particular Senate majority leader Trent Lott and chairman of the Armed Services Committee Jesse Helms, behaving as if the inspection mandate originated with the USA and not with the UN, opposed the visit and saw it as interference in America's affairs.

The quiet, dignified Annan was in Iraq from 20 to 23 February, met with Tareq Aziz and Saddam Hussein, and came out with an agreement which intercepted American and British threats to attack Iraq. The Secretary General's visit was a signal victory for Saddam because it renewed his claim to legitimacy. Annan cleverly announced the agreement while in Baghdad, without consulting the Americans, and left them with no option but to accept it. In fact the Security Council accepted it on 8 March, and on the 27th the stipulated inspection of presidential palaces under the supervision of Annan's representative began.

Soon afterwards, the chief antagonists were at it again. Annan was criticized by US lawmakers for dealing with Saddam, and on

19 April this made it possible for Butler to announce that 'no progress has been made'. The Iraqis had expected the opposite, that providing the UNSCOM team with access to the palaces, in reality no more than 40 square kilometres in size, would lead to a total lifting of the sanctions. This was not written in the agreement with Annan, but the friendly atmosphere of the talks had implied that a serious review of the sanctions aimed at lifting them in total would follow Iraq's compliance on the palaces.

With Butler publicity undermining Annan's quiet diplomacy and the Iraqis resorting to intransigent public pronouncements, the Secretary General came to the conclusion that both sides were unwilling to compromise and decided not to intervene again. In June, Butler and Aziz met to try to find a way out of the impasse, but the brittle relationship between the two men was not conducive to reaching an agreement and they did not. Instead, both held press conferences presenting their points of view and criticizing the other side. Aziz, an articulate diplomat, made an excellent case for Iraq. He succeeded in presenting the maintenance of the sanctions as the exclusive work of the USA and Britain. Another Aziz–Butler attempt to ease the tension was made in August (the issue of the sanctions was subject to bi-monthly reviews) and this time it produced a stormy meeting the like of which Ekeus would not have contemplated.[5]

In the background, the USA and Britain were defending the maintenance of sanctions and, despite protests by other UNSC members, making declarations that they did not need a new UN resolution or mandate to punish Iraq for its intransigence. To them, past resolutions were enough. Saddam responded in kind and, on 17 September, the rubberstamp Iraqi National Assembly voted for withholding all cooperation from UNSCOM. The Iraqi act of defiance was matched by the other side. On 29 September Scott Ritter, who had resigned in anger because of the constraints placed on him, admitted that UN inspectors had indulged in spying all along.[6] He later expanded his admission and spoke of visiting Israel several times while with UNSCOM and sharing information with its intelligence services. Eventually he accused Butler and Secretary of State Albright of being behind some of the efforts to curtail his inspectors efforts. Not to be outdone, the hawkish US Congress – and most members leaned towards Ritter's point of view and behaved as if the UN and Annan did not exist – voted the

Iraqi Liberation Act into law on 1 October. Among other things, this piece of legislation allocated $97 million to Iraqi opposition groups. The same day Denis Halliday, the United Nations humanitarian aid coordinator to Iraq, resigned in protest over the obstacles placed in his way and the conditions of misery created by the sanctions against Iraq.

Congress's allocation of money to politically deserving but ineffectual opposition groups, the multiplying admissions of spying and Halliday's resignation were picked up promptly by the world press. Saddam Hussein was handed a handsome victory. Many members of UNSCOM were revealed as spies and the USA, which had the greatest number of them, was clearly following policies outside of UN resolutions. By the end of October the USA and UK, isolated from other members of the UNSC and unable to secure Arab support for continuing to mount attacks against Iraq and maintenance of the sanctions, were reverting to the obsolete methods which had yielded no results since the end of the Gulf War. Even before that, in July that year, insensitive to world reaction to her statement, Secretary of State Madeleine Albright had announced that the United States had no intention of ceasing its attempts to change the Iraqi leadership.[7]

During October, at a time when the US administration was being accused of indulging in 'fantasies'[8] hundreds of members of the Iraqi opposition responded to US government invitations and trekked to Washington 'for consultations'. The government was undertaking another attempt to unite the feuding anti-Saddam Iraqis. Several of those who attended the Washington meetings returned to London complaining about American preference for certain individuals, favouring them with money which they simply pocketed.[9] The Kurdish leaders Jallal Talabani and Massoud Barzani refused to meet with Dr Ahmad Chalabi in the INC and called him names in public. The whole attempt to unite the Iraqis was a huge failure. Moreover, according to a well-placed source in Washington, the United States was producing psychological profiles of opposition personalities which showed that some of them were totally lacking in intelligence; according to my source, they were 'idiots'.

The embarrassing Iraqi opposition behaviour was followed by reports that the USA was once again relying on the CIA to engineer a coup in Baghdad.[10] Meanwhile, American newspapers were waking up to their country's failure and carrying more reports confirming Ritter's spying admissions and US underhandedness. In the process, the press administered a blow to the credibility of UNSCOM and an unusually subdued Richard Butler. However, the resurrected twin-reliance on the opposition and the CIA prompted the *International Herald Tribune* of 24 November to declare that US plans for Iraq 'had little chance of success', and later it described US policy as 'erratic'.

Saddam's government, encouraged by signs of American loss of direction and France's and Russia's qualified support for ending the sanctions, refused to lift the ban on UNSCOM. US and British warnings to Iraq 'to obey the will of the international community' sounded hollow and became shrill. The international community, including the Arab countries which received many official visitors from the USA and Britain, the latest being American Secretary of Defense William Cohen, refused to back any attack on Iraq in response to the ban on UNSCOM. But the two powers refused to alter their position – they were more concerned with loss of face and fear of another Saddam victory than with sensible behaviour. Against a background of international protest, the US and British air forces attacked Iraq relentlessly between 17 and 20 December. Operation Desert Fox, the codename for the attack, had no specific purpose in mind except to punish Saddam. Nor, as in attacking Serbia, did the air forces and the politicians behind them make a point of avoiding civilian targets. On 18 December an oil refinery in Basra was hit and damaged severely and more than a dozen civilians were killed. It did not matter; nearly a year later the promised report regarding this and the ensuing civilian casualties was still pending. Moreover, Clinton administration spokesmen, including General Anthony Zinni, head of Centcom, the military command of US forces in the Middle East, spoke of attacking Iraqi troops in their barracks and claimed that a number of Saddam's friends had been killed in these. Not a single name was mentioned.

After Operation Desert Fox and the claims that it had met its vague objectives, the US and British position escalated yet again. The vague equation used for punishing Saddam became more inexplicable; it no longer needed justification. Mounting daily air attacks against an array of Iraqi targets was added to opposition and CIA efforts. Saddam had declared that the no-fly zones imposed on Iraq were illegal because they were not included in UN resolutions and were in violation of international law. But the Americans and British refused to consider the legal merits of this objection and their planes roamed the Iraqi skies at will looking for targets of opportunity. The aircraft were supposedly defending themselves against Saddam's interference in the no-fly areas, despite the degradation of his air defence system and the weakness of his air force. The random attacks covered the north, south and centre of Iraq, resulting in civilian casualties and damage to oil pumping stations. Failure to pump oil denied Iraq the money it needed to buy food and medicine. Except for Kuwait and Israel, no one supports this on-going savagery. Though the attacks hurt what remains of Saddam's air defences, they undoubtedly do more damage to the welfare of the Iraqi people without contributing to the destabilizing of Saddam's regime.

The total bankruptcy of the US policy of relying on the Iraqi opposition, an incompetent CIA and air strikes was exposed in January 1999. Frank Riccardone, an expert on Iraq in the State Department, warned against arming the Iraqi opposition to undertake efforts to topple Saddam.[11] This was an attempt to stop Congress from attempting to arm some parties within the Iraqi opposition, to avoid being dragged into an unplanned adventure which might produce another Bay of Pigs, the abortive invasion of Cuba by US-supported exiles in 1961. This warning came after a visit to London in late November 1998 by special envoy to the Middle East, Martin Indyck, who met with Iraqi opposition leaders, once again advised them to unite and offered to support them as a group under the leadership of former Iraqi Foreign Minister Adnan Pachachi. The patrician, gentlemanly Pachachi, totally opposed to Saddam but harbouring serious misgivings about American policy, turned Indyck down. However disappointing Pachachi's rebuff, the fact that the Iraqi opposition remains without permanent leadership after years of confrontation with Saddam tells a much bigger story. In fact, it could be said that the Clinton administration spends more time trying to unite the anti-Saddam Iraqis than it devotes to overthrowing Saddam.

Riccardone's warning was seconded by British Minister of State for Foreign Affairs Derek Fatchett on 26 February 1999. Because Senators Lott, Helms and others persisted in their calls to provide more substantial help to the Iraqi opposition, Riccardone's original warning was given military content through the support of

General Anthony Zinni. He was more blunt, accusing the Iraqi opposition of incompetence and making clear that he opposed their proposals to create militias.[12] Rightly, he suggested that such a move would lead to an expanded conflict requiring armed intervention on the ground for which the USA was not prepared.

Amazingly the Kuwaitis, fearing that congressional enthusiasm for toppling Saddam might produce plans which succeeded before something sensible was found to replace him, warned against igniting a civil war in Iraq which would affect the whole region.[13] The Kuwait statement confirmed that, except for the United States and Britain, the whole world viewed punishing the Iraqi people through hitting Saddam's army and destroying Iraq's infrastructure as counterproductive and dangerous. However, the *Observer* of 28 March reported that Britain had begun tilting towards a change in this unproductive policy. While expressing doubts about the effectiveness of using the Iraqi opposition, Britain was turning in favour of another expansion of the oil-for-food programme.

This latest change of British policy aside, the preoccupation and reliance on indiscriminate punitive measures has never affected Saddam's control of Iraq and it made many of its suffering people blame the outside world for their misery and back him. Moreover, the exclusive dependence on his lack of cooperation with UNSCOM to punish and weaken him automatically gives him a free hand in other important areas. Perhaps nothing demonstrates this better than the killing, in all likelihood by Saddam's security people, on 27 February 1999 of the venerable Shia Imam Mohammed Sadiq Al Sadr and his two sons. It coincided with more reports of the execution of generals and colonels, bureaucrats and ordinary people, and unconfirmed stories of more Iraqi Army plots against Saddam. To the USA and Britain, maintaining a phoney no-fly zone was more important than capitalizing on this wave of unrest.

It was the Iraqi opposition which made much of the happenings inside Iraq. But, as usual, the opposition exaggerated the situation and raised unrealistic hopes without being able to help the anti-Saddam forces within their country. Furthermore, in trying to use the incidents to generate greater American and British support for themselves, the opposition forgot that human rights conditions within Iraq have never been a primary issue to the two countries leading the fight against Saddam. The opposition's inflated statements substituted noise for action, adding to their record of making foolish predictions regarding Saddam's impending demise. They confirmed that they were ineffectual, deserving of General Zinni's criticism and worthy of the *Economist*'s description of them as 'laughable'.[14] Meanwhile, there was no signs that the CIA's ability to undermine Saddam is any better than it was nine years ago.

In 1996 I used the following words to describe Saddam Hussein:

> He is the man who started a nine-year-war against Iran, used chemical weapons against the Kurds of his country, developed biological weapons capable of killing most of the people of the Middle East, threatened, then invaded Kuwait and started the Gulf War and came close to making an atomic bomb. Meanwhile, within his country, Saddam executed people at random, imprisoned and tortured thousands of others, placed all power in the hands of his family and relations and allowed them to steal, rape and murder scores of innocents.[15]

This biography extends my original condemnation while qualifying it.

The qualifications do not affect Saddam's criminal standing but they take into consideration the complicity of other countries in his regional adventures and their overlooking of the nightmare of his internal governance. Whatever attributes young Saddam had as a thinking thug who wanted to catapult his country into the twentieth century, they do not excuse any of the horrors his family and regime inflicted on the people of Iraq. (We are back to Stalin.) Despite that, and as has undoubtedly become obvious to the reader, the United States, Britain and other countries who armed and supported him then found no way to punish him without causing suffering to the Iraqi people also deserve condemnation.

The reasons for focusing on the roles of America and Britain have been made plain, in particular their lack of moral standards and the subsequent attempt to ignore their complicity through an arrogant disregard for the opinions and laws of the rest of the world. America's and Britain's contribution to Saddam's weapons of mass destruction was greater than that of France and the USSR. Now there is no USSR to stand up to them, France cannot stop them without solid European backing which it does not have, the

Arabs need them for protection mostly against their own people, and the rest of the world dare not offend them. America and Britain are dizzy with success, the practitioners of John Wayne diplomacy of 'do what I tell you or else'. Even the United Nations is captive to their intransigence, and they have arrogated to themselves the right to veto all UN personnel who disagree with them. They did force Butros Butros Ghali out of office. The amoral poacher has turned into an insensitive gamekeeper.

This sweeping judgement, and the anger and disappointment which produce it and accompany it, is made by a writer who is a naturalized and loyal American. The reasons for it are best demonstrated through examining the particulars of the Iraqi situation as it exists at the time of writing. To me, all that nine years of directionless confrontation with Saddam have produced is misery for the people of Iraq, the potential for destabilizing the Middle East further, and an American-British insistence on turning the clock back and acting as arbiters of the fate of Iraq and the rest of the region in the manner of the victorious powers in 1917.

Saddam is lucky in having his Iraqi, Arab and Western enemies. They have contributed to his survival as much as his security apparatus has, and they subordinate the welfare of the Iraqi people to their plans the way Saddam subordinates them to his plans for survival. The indiscriminate sanctions against Iraq have destroyed the infrastructure of the country and contributed to the strengthening of its central government. Saddam is the only patron known to the Iraqi people who remain in their country, and the atmosphere of constant crisis is exactly what he needs to maintain this position. America's commitment to an undemocratic Iraq reduces its efforts to topple Saddam to an attempt to spread its hegemony over the Middle East through sponsoring dictatorships. Most of the Iraqi opposition groups have no popular following, and a few of them are run by questionable characters with criminal records. Other oppositionists were Saddam's partners in crime until they learned how to make money out of siding with America, as in the case of one of Saddam's chief publicists who received money to publish a newspaper and start up a satellite television station. The exaggeration of Western and Iraqi opposition claims against Saddam – everything from his mother being a whore to predicting uprisings which never take place and rewriting the history of the draining of the marshes – has backfired and helped him.

Regionally, America's and Britain's Arab allies are dictators; except for the scale of their misdeeds, they are Saddam's criminal equivalents. Egypt, the Palestinian Authority, Saudi Arabia, Kuwait, Jordan and the rest of the Gulf states are not run by democrats and none of their leaders has a clean human rights slate. Because these countries are run by discredited pro-West regimes, the words and deeds of their leaders are not respected and have no influence on the Iraqi situation or the average Arab's perception of Saddam. For example, the Saudis too deny their Shias equal rights and members of this sect cannot join the Saudi Army or police force. Nor are Mubarak's claims that 98 per cent of Egyptians vote for him in presidential election likely to elicit anything but public derision. Arafat, though a latecomer to the scene, has one of the most dismal human rights records in the Arab world. This is not to speak of the arms- and drugs-smuggling activities of members of the late King Hussein's family. US dependence on allies such as these, like its dependence on the more reprehensible elements among the Iraqi opposition, cancels what is left of its moral position.

Furthermore, to my knowledge there has not been a single Western plan to overthrow Saddam which is thorough enough and sensible enough to stand a chance of success without producing incalculable consequences with which the Iraqi and Arab advocates of Saddam's removal could not cope. This covers all plans by Iraqi opposition groups with Washington connections, CIA attempts, combined opposition–CIA efforts, three-cornered Iraq opposition–CIA–Arab schemes or anything involving all these groups. The people who are really capable of overthrowing Saddam, serving Iraqi army officers and the Shia opposition, have not been helped or encouraged in any way. Perhaps it is because a weak Saddam is preferable to a strong colonel and the religious programme of the Shias is not acceptable to professional opposition leaders promoting themselves, the Arabs or the CIA. The ambivalence in US policy and the inevitable appearance of another dictatorship is underpinned by a desire to have a weak, controllable Iraq.

Lastly, the Iraqi people have not been offered incentives to rise against Saddam and America suffers from a credibility gap. Memories of what happened during the *intifada* run deep. People are afraid of being betrayed again, and nothing that has happened since the *intifada* has gone towards restoring faith in America. The United States has not told the Iraqi people that overthrowing Saddam would lead to the lifting of sanctions, the cancellation of the $586 billion debt[16] or support for democracy. Looking further back, nothing has been done to counter or even attempt to justify past witness: to erase the memory of disenfranchising the Shias; to undo the damage caused by IPC which denied Iraq its place as a major oil producer; to explain the killing of the only popular king in the country's history; to justify the overthrow of Kassem's populist regime and the use of Ba'ath Party thugs to kill thousands of educated Iraqis; to explain the encouragement given Iraq to conduct a nine-year war against Iran; or to explain the backing of Kuwait to undermine Iraq by pumping more oil, lowering its price and so hit at the ordinary Iraqi people. All these and many more crimes inflicted upon them are part of the Iraqis' national memory. What America and Britain are doing at present confirms the substantiated historical claim made by many Iraqis that their country, the only Arab state with the potential to move into the modern world, was and is the object of Western prejudice which preceded and supersedes opposition to the person of Saddam. Looked at through this historical perspective, Saddam, thug, thief and murderer though he may be, is a link in a long chain of events which has as its object the denial of a regional and international position to Iraq.

I will expand this condemnation by summarizing the status of the Iraqi opposition with special emphasis on the two groups that matter. There are over eighty groups divided within themselves, and no two of them can agree on a political programme to save their country. Despite the presence of talented individuals, the majority of these groups are not viable or effective and are given to bargaining away the future of a country over which they have no control. Most of them are no more than small groupings whose only aim is to become rich through receiving funds from the USA, Kuwait and Saudi Arabia. Even when they have some followers, dependence on rich sponsors, along with connections to Israel and Iran, vitiate their effectiveness. In addition, the United States has never been completely honest with them, has used them selectively and conveniently and has switched its support from one group to another for the most ridiculous of reasons. On occasions, they have backed the Iraqi Accord because it pretended to have a plan to

replace Saddam; on others, they have supported Dr Ahmad Chalabi and the INC because he is urbane and speaks impeccable
English (and they have been dismissive of more serious groups
simply because their members do not speak English well). Moreover, Saddam has proved himself a more astute operator than his
regime's opponents and his agents have managed to infiltrate their
ranks.[17] This put him a step head and enabled him to make fools of
them.

The two groups with popular followings, the Kurdish PUK and
KDP, and the Shia Dawa, do not work with the rest and only in a
qualified manner with the United States. The Kurds' demands for
autonomy have been attained and they do not want to repeat past
mistakes or endanger their achievements by allying themselves with
outside powers against their central government, even one headed
by Saddam. The immediate problem for the Kurds is not Saddam
Hussein. With or without him there is little chance of undoing their
present autonomy; this fact, which is ignored, should instead be
celebrated. The problem for the Iraqi Kurds is to stop their
constant internal feuding over who should lead them. In the words
of the veteran Kurdish leader Dr Mahmoud Othman:

> The Kurdish situation will become much better if Kurdish leaders
> [Barzani and Talabani] stop worrying about lining their pockets
> and wanting to achieve supremacy at the expense of each other.
> The rising level of education is solving the Kurdish problem, both
> Kurds and Arabs know that they have to live together. Even
> Saddam knows this, though we do not want him because he is a
> dangerous criminal and we want a democracy which gives what
> we have achieved permanent legal status. The problems are two:
> who is going to be the sole Kurdish leader, followed by getting rid
> of Saddam because he is a dictator who does not believe in the
> type of system needed by all Iraqis to live in peace.[18]

This is a superior piece of judgement. The Kurdish problem, except
for the endless and often bloody competition between Talabani
and Barzani, is pretty well settled. In addition to acceptance of the
Kurds' legitimate rights by every Iraqi I have interviewed, the
discovery of huge reserves of oil in central and southern Iraq
has reduced the importance of Kirkuk, the issue which stood in
the way of implementing many of the agreements between the Iraqi

central government and the Kurds in the past. Instead of emphasizing the disappearing enmity between Arabs and Kurds which is used to justify continued interference in Iraqi affairs, the USA and Britain would do well to force Talabani and Barzani into settling their leadership disputes. Because all Iraqi Kurds now accept the principle of autonomy and are no longer calling for an independent Kurdistan, that problem has been settled.[19] Were the Kurds to be left alone and not be used as pawns, they would readily reach an agreement with Iraq's central government that outlasts the Saddams of this world regardless of their powers of survival.

The problem of the Shia Dawa Party and SCIRI is different, perhaps bigger. Despite occasional flirtations and transitory co-operation agreements, these related parties are not acceptable to the United States, Britain, Kuwait and Saudi Arabia, the latter two because their populations include disenfranchised Shia minorities. Bereft of outside friends and a base inside Iraq, the Dawa depends on Iran and cooperates with SCIRI and Sayyed Mohammed Bakr Al Hakim. This association casts a shadow over the Dawa which it must find a way of dispelling by making an unequivocal policy statement regarding its undivided loyalty to Iraq. Failure to do that weakens an otherwise strong Shia case which began with British denial of their rights after the First World War. Instead of being shunned because of their Iranian connection, SCIRI and Dawa should be encouraged to distance themselves from Iran through being accepted unconditionally, even if that means the Shias end up in government. An Iraq governed by Iraqi Shias is no different form a Mexico governed by Mexicans.

Having covered the special situations of the two opposition groups who command street-level loyalty, I am forced to admit that their problems weaken them significantly as opponents of Saddam. Once again, we are left with nothing but professional oppositionists. And nothing demonstrates the ineffectiveness of these groups better than an unsound story carried by the *Sunday Times* of 15 February 1998. It reported that Saddam's opponents, minus the Kurds, SCIRI and Dawa, were forming a government in exile, listed twenty-nine cabinet members and gave the names of the would-be office holders. This was a self-serving piece of propaganda by opposition members who took the *Sunday Times* for a ride. To me, it is the most dramatic example of the difference between the realities of the opposition's situation and their empty dreams. The story made Saddam's opponents look stupid because some of the so-called members of the provisional cabinet had not been consulted, no headquarters for the government in exile had been chosen, the real opposition groups were excluded and the source was a journalist in the pay of Saudi Arabia. It provided ammunition for the Iraqi diehards who prefer Saddam to his opponents.

The weakness of the opposition is matched by the weakness of the argument for maintaining the sanctions and continuing, in the crude words of British Prime Minister Tony Blair, 'to keep Saddam in his cage'. (He refrains from describing Yugoslav leader Slobodan Milosevic in the same way.) Most of Saddam's weapons of mass destruction have been destroyed (from various sources I have counted 150 Scud missiles, 691 chemical weapons, 28,000 chemical munitions, 19,000 litres of botulinum toxin and 8000 litres of concentrated anthrax, and 32 establishments involved in making chemical and biological weapons, weapons-grade uranium, other chemical and biological agents, superguns and so on). The knowledgeable Professor Fred Halliday of the London School of Economics states that UNSCOM 'is getting close, 95 per cent of [Saddam's] arms are gone'.[20] On 7 March 1998, the *Independent* newspaper carried a story by Patrick Cockburn and Charles Glass which cited a statement by the US Ambassador to Kuwait, Jim Lorocco, to Americans residing in that country. Lorocco told them not to worry about gas masks to protect themselves against the possibility of an Iraqi gas attack because Saddam's warheads were ineffective. Little more than a month later, on 21 April, the *International Herald Tribune* reported that the IAEA was ready to declare that Iraq was free from atomic weapons and the potential to make them. According to the story, the US viewed the prospect of this declaration with undisguised alarm. In fact, there was nothing new in this – Secretary of Defense Richard Cheney told the world immediately after the Gulf War that Saddam 'was out of the nuclear business'.[21] Even without this evidence there is a case for dissolving UNSCOM, or at least for replacing it with something that works. Inspectors were not needed to enforce compliance with the various disarmament agreements between the West and USSR – sophisticated verification methods are available to do the job. A new verification programme aimed at keeping Saddam in check without the abrasive statements of

Richard Butler and the super-macho attitude of Scott Ritter can be devised.

The combination of a divided, unacceptable and feuding opposition with a maintenance of sanctions which is not totally justified and which punishes the Iraqi people and helps Saddam stay in power is made worse by the behaviour and standing of the country which is leading the fight against the Iraqi dictator. The French journalist–diplomat Eric Rouleau, an expert on Iraq, speaks of the United States having no credibility in the Middle East.[22] Former Assistant Secretary of State Richard Murphy, admits that he is not privy to US official thinking but expresses fear that present US policy might lead to the partition of Iraq, probably unintentionally.[23] Turkish Prime Minster Bulent Ecevit is blunter and laments the absence of a coherent US policy after so many years of confrontation.[24] The late King Hussein of Jordan was adamant that 'Saddam won't be brought down from outside'.[25] And to backtrack, how could the wisdom of the United States be trusted by people like the Kurdish leader Latif Rashid[26] and the Iraqi academic Laith Kuba when the two remember the refusal of the American adminstration to talk to them about the Kurdish situation in the aftermath of the Halabja atrocity? This is not to forget that, except for Christopher Drogoul of Banca Nazionale del Lavoro, no American citizen has been punished for helping Saddam attain mastery of weapons of mass destruction or following the disclosures of Saddamgate, the series of confused revelations which demonstrate a pattern of corporate and governmental support for Saddam over a dozen years. Neither George Bush, among the major contributors to Saddam's prominence, nor the peripherally involved Saïd Aburish have paid the price of their mistakes. In Britain, the Scott Inquiry into the arms to Iraq scandal did not even ask the right questions, and the people involved in arming Saddam legally and otherwise were absolved.[27]

In March 1999 a meeting of Arab League Foreign Ministers, made up of representatives of pro-US countries, as it were, opposed the US and British bombing of Iraq in a statement which reflected fatigue with the whole issue. France, the Russian Federation, China and many other countries, articulating the growing pressure to stop the USA and Britain from maintaining the sanctions and pursuing punitive policies, had made similar statements. Perhaps the clearest sign that the US attitude towards Iraq still follows an undeclared policy which differs from its day-to-day illogical behaviour is demonstrated by comparing the April 1999 bombing of Serbia with what happened to Iraq during the Gulf War. Special care was taken not to bomb civilian targets or sewage and water purification plants. To repeat, the condemnation of Slobodan Milosevic does not equal that of Saddam. Because of the racial content of Western thinking, the massacre at Mittlah Ridge is unlikely to be repeated in Yugoslavia. Smaller incidents against unarmed Serbian civilians have generated greater press and public concern.

I am in agreement with Bulent Ecevit. It is time for the USA and Britain – there is no longer a coalition of thirty-two countries or consensus within the Security Council – to agree to an immediate lifting of the sanctions. This would represent nothing more than an attempt to separate the Iraqi people from Saddam, and it would give them an incentive to punish him for his crimes against them. What is needed is a policy for Iraq which transcends the traditional US and British lack of support for democracy and allows the Iraqi people to decide their own fate. Instead of behaving in a manner that makes Saddam look successful, which he has not been, the USA and Britain need to admit that they have failed. America must cease trying to impose its hegemony on Iraq and to control it the way it controls and manipulates the rest of the Middle East. Iraq does need a Barazan Tikriti to replace his brother Saddam. America must accept that a country of 20 million people, possessing enormous natural resources and impressive human assets, deserves its place in the sun. Above all, it should stop supporting Saddam by making him and Iraq one and the same, and look beyond that to a free and democratic Iraq. America's and Britain's help is needed to remove Saddam, but his removal should not be dependent on finding an American-made Iraqi leader to replace him, and both countries should commit themselves to not trying to manipulate the fate of Iraq after that.

This can be done, and like all important moves it should start with small steps. The first step is a sensible approach to getting rid of Saddam. This should be aimed at detaching the small circle which represents the backbone of Saddam's regime – the Army, security and his family and tribe, perhaps even outside tribes which back him – from Saddam the person. A general amnesty must be offered to members of the Iraqi armed forces capable of overthrowing Saddam, the people who now back him for fear of punishment by the professional opposition and by America and Britain. Perhaps a reward or an overt or covert offer of help should be made to Iraqi officers capable of toppling him, the military men who comprise the military-security inner core of the country which still exists. Overall, this means that Saddam's departure will not lead to civil war or mass executions or punishment, and only very few criminals would be affected by it. Realistically, the prospect of democracy flourishing overnight does not exist, but even a new dictator would have to respond to the needs of the Iraqi people in a more humane way — and without outside interference, democracy could follow.

A warning must be issued to Turkey and Iran and other neighbours of Iraq capable of upsetting the balance of politics in the country not to undermine indigenous efforts to displace Saddam or to determine who should follow him. In other words, not only should America and Britain leave the nature of any future government to the Iraqi people, but they should prevail on others to behave in a similar fashion. The interests of the Iraqi people must be addressed, and promises to cancel the unrealistic debt and other punitive measures against them must be made. The Iraqis must be given a chance to compensate for the $115 billion their country lost through sanctions[28] and to rebuild their country. The Iraqi national feeling and the unity of the country must be made an aim of the countries capable of influencing events within Iraq, and support for splinter groups such as Turkey's help to Barzani and his KDP must stop. Support for many suspect opposition leaders must also be stopped. Perhaps an open, friendly approach should be made to Saddam's relations in power, not only to pry them loose from his hold but to fuel his paranoia. Above all, the USA and Britain must make an open and total commitment to democracy, even if only a limited form of it at the beginning. Altogether, these measures would convince the Iraqi people that a substitute for Saddam is available, and a better one at that, and that the USA and Britain are not out to destroy their country.

This is not a complete plan because detailing one is not the function of a writer. But unless something similar, or more methodical and focused, is done, then Saddam will haunt us for the foreseeable future. This is a plea for a policy that would ensure his removal. Not only is his repression of the Iraqi people continuing, but he has already stated, 'I don't want to see any of you run away when I invade Kuwait [again]'.[29] Nor would he be reluctant to use non-conventional weapons, such as he may still possess, if pushed into a corner. I do not dwell on his evil nature because I assume that what he stands for, without exaggeration, is enough to condemn him.

Nowadays, Saddam has meals prepared in every palace to hide his movements while Iraqi children starve; he cuts huge birthday cakes on television at a time when most Iraqis have not seen sugar for months. More and more doubles have appeared with Kavlar-lined hats to elude assassins. He gives his children greater freedom to redefine and expand man's endless cruelty to fellow man, and he is becoming a hero to a new generation of Arabs who despise the West exactly because of their treatment of Iraq. The man doing all this has refined and extended the torture methods used by Nazi Germany and Stalin's Soviet Union and created the most brutal police state of modern times. Unless America and Britain allow the Iraqi people enough room to remove him, Saddam will hand them a memorable defeat. Even if he is overthrown through assassination or an act of God, the starving of Iraqi children and support for incompetent would-be replacements must end. Creating a client state in Iraq, which is what America and Britain are pursuing without admitting it, would leave us with a Middle East problem that would haunt us for far longer than the Arab–Israeli conflict. Unless sensible behaviour reasserts itself in the immediate future, what America and Britain are doing reduces them to Saddam's criminal equivalents and partners.

This book is dedicated to the suffering children of Iraq.
I kiss the hems of your garments in humble reverence.
I weep for you every night.

Notes

CHAPTER 1: CRUEL ANCESTRY

1. Philip Hitti, *History of the Arabs*, p. 207
2. Geoff Simons, *Iraq from Sumer to Saddam*, p. 171
3. Cited in Jonathan C. Randall, *After Such Knowledge What Forgiveness?* p. 207
4. John Bulloch and Harvey Morris, *Saddam's War*, p. 59
5. Berch Berberoglu, *Power and Stability in the Middle East*, p. 31
6. Derek Hopwood et al., *Iraq, Power and Society*, p. 2
7. Malik Mufti, *Sovereign Creations*, p. 23
8. Christine Moss Helms, *Iraq: Eastern Flank of the Arab World*, p. 3
9. Abbas Kelidar, *The Integration of Modern Iraq*, p. 70
10. Hanna Batatu, *The Old Social Classes and Revolutionary Movements of Iraq*, p. 179
11. Batntu, p. 326.
12. Rhagid Solh, *Britain's Two Wars with Iraq*, p. 42
13. Dr Ali Al Wardi, *A Study in Iraqi Society*, p. 339
14. Solh, p. 50
15. W. H. F. Winstone, *Gertrude Bell*, p. 215

CHAPTER 2: THE SHADOW OF AL ZUHOUR PALACE

1. Dr Hamid Al Bayati, *The Bloody History of Saddam Al Tikriti*, p. 25
2. Wafic Samarai, *The Destruction of the Eastern Gate*, p. 354
3. Al Bayati, p. 23
4. Interview, London, July 1998
5. Interview with a former official of the Iraqi government
6. Interview, London, June 1998
7. Amir Iskandar, *Saddam Hussein, the Fighter, the Thinker and the Man*, p. 20
8. Mu'in Nunu, *The Ba'ath State and Islamization of Aflaq*, p. 302
9. Efraim Karsh and Inari Rautsi, *Saddam Hussein, a Political Biography*, p. 10
10. Iskandar, p. 393
11. Iskandar, p. 11

12. Karsh and Rautsi, p. 9
13. *Sunday Times*, 12 February 1998
14. Iskandar, p. 21
15. Iskandar, p. 22
16. Hassan Alawi, *The Borrowed State*, p. 105
17. Fuad Matar in *Saddam Hussein, the Personal and Political Story*, p. 45, bases his claim on Saddam's own words and says he was ten. Judith Miller and Laurie Mylroie in *Saddam and the Crisis in the Gulf*, p. 28, state that he was a child of eight.
18. Matar, p. 45
19. Nunu, p. 302
20. Interview on non-attribution basis, London, June 1998
21. William L. Cleveland, *A History of the Modern Middle East*, p. 363
22. Interview, Hassan Omar Al Ali, London, July 1998
23. Iskandar, p. 29
24. Matar, p. 292
25. Hanna Batatu, *The Old Social Classes and the Revolutionary Movements of Iraq*, p. 267
26. Liona Lukitz, *Iraq, the Search for National Identity*, p. 25
27. Dr Mohammed Zubeidi, *King Ghazi and His Aides*, p. 103
28. Zubeidi, p. 133
29. Batatu, p. 343
30. F.O. 22 July 1936, PRO FO 371/20017/E.3984
31. Dr Lutfi Farraj, *King Ghazi*, p. 166
32. Zubeidi, p. 135
33. Interview, Nuha Al Radi, London, September 1998
34. Saïd K. Aburish, *A Brutal Friendship, the West and the Arab Elite*, pp. 121–2, gives considerable details to support the suspicion that Ghazi was killed
35. Batatu, p. 343
36. Batatu, p. 30
37. Cleveland, p. 199
38. Batatu, p. 324
39. Batatu, p. 102
40. Nunu, p. 302
41. Mohammed Heikal, *Illusions of Triumph*, p. 95
42. Geoff Simons, *Iraq from Sumer to Saddam*, p. 272
43. Matar, p. 45
44. Elie Kedouri, *The Politics of the Middle East*, p. 199

CHAPTER 3: A GUN FOR HIRE

1. Dame Freya Stark, cited in Jonathan C. Randall's, *After Such Knowledge What Forgiveness?*, p. 207
2. Interview, Tamara Daghastani, daughter of monarchist General Ghazi Daghastani, London, April 1996
3. Daghastani
4. Raghid Solh, *Britain's Two Wars with Iraq*, p. 160 (Arabic)
5. Amir Iskandar, *Saddam Hussein, the Fighter, the thinker and the Man*, p. 35
6. From the author's notebook, September 1958

7. Interviews, Hani Fkaiki and Abdel Sattar Douri, September 1995; interviews with the rest, April 1998

8. Interview, CIA agent James Russell Barracks, January 1959. Author's notebook

9. Interview with former Jordanian Prime Minister Wasfi Tel, who showed me documents proving his point. Author's notebook

10. Ahmad Fawzi, *The Life, Trial and Death of Abdel Salam Aref*, p. 29

11. Fuad Matar, *Saddam Hussein, the Personal and Political Story*, p. 46

12. Hani Fkaiki, *Dens of Defeat*, p. 142; interview with the author, August 1995

13. Hanna Batatu, *The Old Social Classes and the Revolutionary Movements of Iraq*, p. 866

14. Author Larry Collins, then a UPI correspondent, a photographer by the name of Paul Davis and myself were the only people to get that close to Mosul – after a 300-mile taxi ride

15. Fkaiki, p. 139

16. Matar, p. 46

17. Abdel Amir Mua'la, *The Long Days*, p. 17

18. Dr Hamid Al Bayati, *The Bloody History of Saddam Al Tikriti*, p. 32

19. Mua'la, pp. 74 and 77

20. Young and I travelled to Baghdad twice. My involvement with Iraq during this period will be detailed later

21. Mua'la, pp. 25–6

22. Interview, Dr Tahseen Mua'la, London, August 1998

23. Mua'la, p. 109

24. Fkaiki, pp. 142 and 148

25. Fkaiki, p. 153 and interviews

26. Interview, former Nasser aide Abdel Majid Farid, London, April 1998

27. Efraim Karsh and Inari Rautsi, *Saddam Hussein, a Political Biography*, p. 18

28. Iskandar, p. 75

29. Humphrey Trevelyan, *The Middle East in Revolution*, p. 166

30. Al Bayati, pp. 58–9

31. Iskandar, p. 79; Karsh and Rautsi, p. 21

32. Cited in Ismael Aref, *Secrets of the 14 July Revolution and the Establishment of the Iraqi Republic*, p. 285

33. Al Bayati, p. 63

34. Mu'in Nunu, *The Ba'ath State and Islamization of Aflaq*, p. 30

35. Geoff Simons, *Iraq from Sumer to Saddam*, p. 274

36. Mua'la, p. 110

37. John Bulloch and Harvey Morris, *Saddam's War*, p. 54; Hassan Al Said, *Guards of the West, the Ba'ath and the International Game*, p. 353

38. Saïd K. Aburish, *A Brutal Friendship, the West and the Arab Estate*, p. 137

39. Yahya Sadawski, *Guns or Butter*, p. 52

40. Malik Mufti, an assistant professor at Tufts University, Boston, documented this in an unpublished paper called 'Renewed Unionism'

41. Aburish, p. 139

42. Interviews, Fkaiki. Fkaiki was there when Kassem was tried in the television station. Later his bullet-riddled body was shown to the people to end his supporters' resistance

43. Aburish, p. 139

44. The source which revealed McHale's name is another former *Time* correspon-

dent. The sources for the rest of the material are Iraqi exiles who spoke on condition of anonymity

45. Dr Hamid Al Bayati, *The Coup of 8 February 1963 in Iraq*, p. 163
46. Robert Kaplan, *The Arabists*, p. 173
47. Dr Ghassan Al Attiyah, *Al Quds Al Arabi*, London, 14 February 1996
48. Interviews, Fkaiki
49. Fkaiki, p. 298
50. Interview, Dr Ahmad Chalabi, London, August 1996
51. Iskandar, p. 87
52. Iskandar, p. 74
53. Simons, p. 275
54. Mua'la, p. 216
55. Ismael Aref, *Secrets of the 14 July Revolution and the Establishment of the Iraqi Republic*, p. 310
56. Fkaiki, p. 325; Al Bayati, p. 82
57. Marion Farouk- and Peter Sluglett, *Iraq since 1958, from Revolution to Dictatorship*, pp. 93–4
58. Iskandar, p. 91
59. Iskandar, p. 96; Bulloch and Morris, p. 41
60. Iskandar, p. 97
61. Matar, p. 52; Simons, p. 276
62. Interviews, Hassan Omar Al Ali, London, July and August 1998

CHAPTER 4: PLAYING STALIN TO BAKR'S LENIN

1. Majid Khaddouri, *Republican Iraq*, p. 179
2. David McDowall, *A Modern History of the Kurds*, p. 315
3. Interview, Dr Mahmoud Othman, London, May 1998. Dr Othman was Barzani's chief negotiator with central government for almost thirty years
4. Interview, Nasser aide Abdel Majid Farid, London, June 1998
5. Jonathan C. Randall, *After Such Knowledge What Forgiveness?*, p. 13
6. Hassan Alawi, *Iraqi Shias and the National State in Iraq*, p. 12
7. Interview, Dr Tareq Shafiq, a recognized international authority
8. Dr Abdallah Ismael, *Iraqi Oil Negotiations, 1952–1968*, p. 103
9. Dr Abdel Amir Al Anbari, 'An Inquiry into the Problem of the Law of Petroleum Concession Agreements in the Middle East', Ph.D. thesis at Harvard
10. Interview, Dr Adnan Pachachi, London, October 1998
11. Hassan Al Said, *Guards of the West, the Ba'ath and the International Game*, p. 277
12. Interview, Ahmad Chalabi, London, August 1995
13. Pachachi
14. Al Said, p. 350
15. Marion Farouk- and Peter Sluglett, *Iraq since 1958, from Revolution to Dictatorship*, p. 113
16. Interview on non-attribution basis, with a former Iraqi government official, London
17. Cited in Al Said, p. 352
18. Interview, Sa'ad Saleh Jaber, London, November 1998
19. Interview, Hassan Omar Al Ali, London, September 1998
20. Al Ali

21. Slugletts, p. 112
22. Efraim Karsh and Inari Rautsi, *Saddam Hussein, A Political Biography*, pp. 41–5
23. Interview on non-attribution basis with a former Iraqi government minister, London
24. Cited in Al Said, p. 325; Mu'in Nunu, *The Ba'ath State and Islamization of Aflaq*, p. 308
25. Interview, Abu Saïd Aburish, Seattle, November 1997
26. Off-the-record interview with a former Ba'athist official of the Ministry of Planning
27. Slugletts, p. 128
28. Hanna Batatu, *The Old Social Classes and the Revolutionary Movements of Iraq*, p. 110
29. Kanan Makiya, *Republic of Fear*, p. 39
30. Slugletts, p. 120
31. Hassan Omar Al Ali
32. Dr Fadhil Barak, *Mustapha Barzani, the Legend and the Truth*, p. 192
33. Interviews, Dr Mahmoud Othman, London, May, June and July 1998
34. Christine Moss Helms, *Iraq: Eastern Flank of the Arab World*, p. 30
35. Darieh Al Awni, *Arabs and Kurds, Conflict or Amity*, p. 87
36. Interviews, Dr Sahib Al Hakim, London, May–October 1998
37. Patrick Seale, *Abu Nidal, the World's Most Wanted Terrorist*, p. 29
38. Seale, p. 79
39. Batatu, p. 1093
40. Sa'ad Saleh Jaber
41. Interview, Dr Fuad Ma'sum, London, September 1998
42. Slugletts, p. 138
43. Haim Berger, *The Social Origins of the Modern Middle East*, p. 173
44. Interview, Kamran Karadaghi, May 1998
45. Fuad Matar, *Saddam Hussein, the Personal and Political Story*, p. 296
46. Amir Iskandar, *Saddam Hussein, the Fighter, the Thinker and the Man*, p. 144
47. Fouad Ajami, *The Arab Predicament*, p. 12
48. Batatu, p. 836
49. Karsh and Rautsi, pp. 39–40; Geoff Simons, *Iraq from Sumer to Saddam*, p. 280
50. Malik Mufti, *Sovereign Creations*, p. 198
51. Michael C. Hudson, *Arab Politics and the Search for Legitimacy*, p. 5

CHAPTER 5: SEEKING HEAVEN

1. Interview with Shaikhally's first cousin who wishes not to be identifed
2. Efraim Karsh and Inari Rautsi, *Saddam Hussein, a Political Biography*, p. 74.
3. Interview, Dr Ahmad Chalabi, London, August 1998
4. Interview, Dr Sahib Al Hakim, London, September 1998
5. Saddam said this during a private interview in 1982 to a Palestinian who was acting as a messenger between him and the US government. The record of this strange meeting will be detailed later
6. Adil Hussein, *Iraq, the Eternal Fire, the Nationalization of Iraqi Oil in Perspective*, p. 132
7. Fuad Matar, *Saddam Hussein, the Personal and Political Story*, p. 198
8. Hussein, p. 146

9. Matar, p. 297
10. Walter Laqueur, *The Struggle for the Middle East*, p. 132
11. Interviews, Sabah Mukhtar, London, June–September 1998
12. Hussein, p. 166
13. Majid Khaddouri, *Independent Iraq*, p. 64; Hanna Batatu, *The Old Social Classes and the Revolutionary Movements of Iraq*, p. 1094
14. Geoff Simons, *Iraq from Sumer to Saddam*, p. 281
15. Simons, p. 281
16. Daniel Yeargin, *The Prize*, p. 614
17. Berch Berberoglu, *Power and Stability in the Middle East*, p. 33
18. The request came to me from Dr Ramzi Dalloul, chairman of ARM
19. Interviews, Kamran Karadaghi, London, June–September 1998
20. Christine Moss Helms, *Iraq: Eastern Flank of the Arab World*, p. 121 confirms this
21. Helms. While I was aware of the project, Ms Helms is responsible for the figure
22. Hanna Batatu, *The Old Social Classes and the Revolutionary Movements of Iraq* p. 1095. Again, while the general facts were known to me, Batatu provides the supporting statistics
23. Interviews, Dr Heidar Abbas, London, June–September 1998
24. Helms, p. 34
25. Telephone interviews and correspondence with Michael Hamers, London, May– November 1998
26. Batatu, p. 1095
27. Alan Richards and John Waterbury, *A Political Economy of the Middle East*, p. 154
28. Matar, p. 316; Richards and Waterbury, p. 153
29. Abdel Hussein Sha'aban, *The Ideological Struggle in International Relations*, p. 196
30. Matar, pp. 228–9
31. Matar, p. 230
32. Interview, Dia Al Falaki, London, August 1998
33. Kanan Makiya, *Republic of Fear*, p. 88
34. Makiya, p. 90
35. Matar, p. 203
36. Derek Hopwood et al., *Iraq, Power and Society*, p. 220
37. Patrick Seale, *Abu Nidal, the World's Most Wanted Terrorist*, p. 95
38. Yezid Sayyigh, *Armed Struggle and the Search for State*, p. 435
39. Amatzia Baram and Barry Rubin, *Iraq's Road to War*, p. 152
40. Amir Iskandar, *Saddam Hussein, the Fighter, the Thinker and the Man*, p. 328
41. Iskandar, p. 339
42. Helms, p. 115
43. Hopwood et al., p. 259
44. Interviews, Ahmad Allawi, London, June–October 1998
45. Abdel Hussein Sha'aban, *Storm on the Land of the Sun*, p. 23
46. Cited in Sha'aban, *Storm*, p. 214
47. Matar, p. 298, 318
48. Sha'aban, *Storm*, pp. 215–16
49. Recollections of Lebanese journalist Suleiman Firzli. Interviews, London, June and July 1998

50. Marion Farouk- and Peter Slugett, *Iraq since 1958, from Revolution to Dictatorship*, p. 165
51. Makiya, p. 316; Slugletts, p. 198
52. Makiya, p. 316
53. Interviews, Dr Sahib Al Hakim, London, July–October 1988
54. Karsh and Rautsi, p. 186
55. Helms, p. 79
56. Hopwood et al., p. 19
57. Richards and Waterbury, p. 201
58. Slugletts, p. 163
59. Dr Sahib Al Hakim
60. Liona Lukitz, *Iraq, the Search for National Identity*, p. 155

CHAPTER 6: MARCHING TO HALABJA

1. Interviews with Iraqi officials Ghazi Al Ayyash and Sa'ad Bazzaz; Saïd K. Aburish, *A Brutal Friendship, the West and the Arab Elite*, p. 91
2. Kenneth R. Timmermann, *The Death Lobby, How the West Armed Iraq*, p. 45
3. Interview, Dr Ahmad Chalabi, London, September 1998
4. Dr Abbas Nazrawi, *The Iraqi Economy*, p. 129
5. Off-the-record interview, former member of the Iraqi cabinet, September 1998
6. Geoff Simons, *Iraq from Sumer to Saddam*, p. 319; off-the-record interview, former scientist in Iraq, August 1998
7. *Observer*, 3 March 1984
8. I am in possession of the document with Pfaulder markings on it
9. Observer, 3 March 1984
10. Timmermann, p. 55–6
11. Simons, p. 319
12. Saïd K. Aburish, *Pay-off: Wheeling and Dealing in the Arab World*, pp. 122–5
13. Mark Phythian, *Arming Iraq*, p. 15
14. Amir Iskandar, *Saddam Hussein, the Fighter, the Thinker and the Man*, pp. 225–6 (it is unclear whether this was said to the author or lifted from Saddam's writings)
15. Fuad Matar, *Saddam Hussein, the Personal and Political Story*, p. 297
16. Amatzia Baram and Barry Rubin, *Iraq's Road to War*, p. 256
17. This account is based on the recollections of a CIA agent who, over five years, unsuccessfully tried to entice me to cooperate with the agency
18. The same source as n. 17
19. Victor Ostrovsky and Claire Hoy, *By Way of Deception*, p. 3

CHAPTER 7: FROM PLANNING TO PLOTTING

1. Marion Farouk- and Peter Slugett, *Iraq since 1958, from Revolution to Dictatorship*, p. 230
2. Interview, Iraqi economist and political observer Rifa'at Sheikhally, London, June 1998
3. Faleh Abdel Jabbar, *Iraq, the State, Civil Society and Democratic Development*, p. 81
4. Interviews, Faleh Abdel Jabbar, London, June–October 1998

5. David Lesch (ed.), *The Middle East and the United States, a Historical and Political Reassessment*, p. 325
6. Efraim Karsh and Inari Rautsi, *Saddam Hussein, a Political Biography*, p. 105
7. Moshe Ma'oz, *Asad, Sphynx of Syria*, p. 147
8. Wafic Samarai, *The Destruction of the Eastern Gate*, p. 41
9. Interviews, Hassan Omar Al Ali, London, July–October 1998
10. Daniel Yeargin, *The Prize*, p. 709
11. Derek Hopwood et al., *Iraq, Power and Society*, p. 289
12. Interview, Dr Ahmad Chalabi, London, August 1998
13. Off-the-record interviews with Iraqi and Jordanian politicians and with a former CIA operative in Jordan
14. Mu'in Nunu, *The Ba'ath State and Islamization of Aflaq*, p. 367
15. Dilip Hiro, *Inside the Middle East*, p. 146
16. Slugletts, p. 209
17. Interviews, Ahmed Chalabi, Hassan Omar Al Ali et al., 1998
18. Ali Mu'min, *Years of Amber, the Way of the Islamic Movement*, p. 180
19. Malik Mufti, *Sovereign Creations*, p. 216
20. Patrick Seale, *Abu Nidal, the World's Most Wanted Terrorist*, p. 218
21. Slugletts, p. 211
22. Kenneth R. Timmermann, *The Death Lobby, How the West Armed Iraq*, p. 101
23. John Bulloch and Harvey Morris, *Saddam's War*, p. 29
24. Jan Goodwin, *The Price of Honour, Muslim Women Lift the Veil*, p. 240
25. Hassan Alawi, *The Borrowed State*, p. 90
26. Interviews, Dr Tahseen Mua'la, London, June–September 1998
27. Interview, Dr Mahmoud Othman, London, October 1998
28. Amir Iskandar, *Saddam Hussein, the Fighter, the Thinker and the Man*, p. 400
29. Fuad Matar, *Saddam Hussein, the Personal and Political Story*, p. 307
30. Heather Deegan, *The Middle East and Problems of Democracy*, p. 77
31. Christine Moss Helms, *Iraq: Eastern Flank of the Arab World*, p. 106
32. Yahya recorded his recollections of the career which was forced on him in *I Was the President's Son*
33. Slugletts, p. 220
34. Helms, p. 123
35. Dilip Hiro, *From Desert Shield to Desert Storm*, p. 145
36. Abdel Hamid Al Abbassi, *Black Pages of Ba'athist Iraq*, p. 21
37. Abbassi, p. 30
38. Mu'min, p. 196
39. Abbassi, pp. 28, 152
40. Abbassi, p. 29
41. Nicola Firzli et al., *The Iraq–Iran Conflict*, p. 21
42. Iskandar, p. 400
43. Mu'min, p. 185
44. Cited in Slugletts, p. 205
45. Interviews, Hani Fkaiki, London, October 1995
46. Timmermann, p. 112
47. Amatzia Baram and Barry Rubin, *Iraq's Road to War*, p. 256
48. Chalabi
49. John Bulloch and Harvey Morris, *The Gulf War*, p. 47
50. Interview, former member of the Jordanian cabinet, London, August 1998

51. Dr Ghazi Al Gosaibi, *The Gulf Crisis*, p. 28
52. Sa'ad Bazzaz, *The Gulf War and the One After*, p. 138
53. Abdel Hussein Sha'aban, *Storm in the Land of the Sun*, p. 58

CHAPTER 8: AN AIMLESS WAR

1. Marion Farouk- and Peter Sluglett, *Iraq since 1958, from Revolution to Dictatorship*, p. 199. This statement was repeated by Saddam on several occasions after Khomeini assumed power in Iran
2. Nicola Firzli et al., *The Iraq–Iran Conflict*, p. 115
3. Cited in Ephraim Karsh and Inari Rautsi, *Saddam Hussein, a Political Biography*, p. 148
4. Daniel Yeargin, *The Prize*, p. 713
5. Firzli et al., p. 127
6. Wafic Samarai, *The Destruction of the Eastern Gate*, p. 49. Samarai reiterated this in an interview with me
7. Christine Moss Helms, *Iraq: Eastern Flank of the Arab World*, p. 17
8. Mark Phythian, *Arming Iraq*, p. xxiii
9. Hussein Al Shami, *The Iraqi Crisis, the View from Within*, p. 81
10. Derek Hopwood et al., *Iraq, Power and Society*, p. 93
11. Hopwood et al., p. 91
12. Interview, Ahmad Allawi, London, September 1998
13. Farhang Rajaee (ed.), *The Iran–Iraq War, The Politics of Aggression*, p. 47
14. Fuad Matar, *Saddam Hussein, the Personal and Political Story*, p. 306
15. Firzli et al., p. 133
16. Cited in Karsh and Rautsi, p. 151
17. Phythian, p. 19
18. Andrew and Leslie Cockburn, *Dangerous Liaison, the Secret Story of US–Israeli Relations*, p. 268
19. Helms, p. 176
20. Phythian, p. 20
21. Samuel M. Katz, *Soldiers Spies*, p. 283
22. Mohammed Heikal, *Illusions of Triumph*, p. 115
23. Dilip Hiro, *Inside the Middle East*, pp. 352–3
24. John K. Cooley, *Payback: America's Long War in the Middle East*, p. 131
25. Saïd K. Aburish, *The Rise, Corruption and Coming Fall of the House of Saud*, p. 139
26. Abbas Nazrawi, *The Iraqi Economy*, p. 111
27. Samarai, p. 61
28. Rajaee (ed.), p. 43
29. Sahib Hakim, *Human Rights in Iraq*, p. 125
30. Hakim, p. 56
31. Interview on non-attribution basis with a former member of the security forces, London, August 1998. I can attest to this: in 1982 I visited Barazan in a makeshift office which looked as if it had been prepared for the occasion
32. Hakim, p. 126
33. Interview, Hakim, London, August 1998.
34. Alan Friedman, *Spider's Web. Bush, Saddam, Thatcher and the Decade of Deceit*, pp. 8–9

35. Interview, Hassan Omar Al Ali. London, November 1998. He was Iraq's Ambassador to the UN and Sajida's host during her trip.
36. Friedman, pp. 9–13
37. Kenneth R. Timmermann, *The Death Lobby, How the West Armed Iraq*, p. 153
38. Robert B. Satloff, *The Politics of Change in the Middle East*, p. 8
39. Satloff, p. 87
40. Amatzia Baram and Barry Rubin, *Iraq's Road to War*, p. 257
41. Friedman, p. 19
42. Joel Bainsman, *Crimes of a President*, p. 113
43. Interview on non-attribution basis, private CIA contact, August 1996
44. Baram and Rubin, p. 153; Timmermann, p. 159
45. Yeargin, p. 713
46. Interviews, General Wafic Samarai, former head of Iraqi military intelligence; Dr Heidar Abbas of Dawa; Ahmad Allawi of the Iraqi National Congress, all London, August 1998
47. Timmermann, p. 149
48. Timmermann, p. 157

CHAPTER 9: ILLUSIONS OF ALLIANCE

1. The Cockburn story appeared in the *Independent* in 1994 and he remembers it, as do others. Unfortunately, neither the *Independent*'s library nor the Colindale Newspaper Library can locate it
2. Farhang Rajaee (ed.), *The Iran-Iraq War, the Politics of Aggression*, pp. 34–7. The various reports were gathered together by the Centre for the Documents of the Imposed War in Tehran. Moreover, the UN began investigating this in early 1983 and issued its report confirming the use of chemical weapons in 1984 (SC 16433/March 26, 1984)
3. Marion Farouk- and Peter Sluglett, *Iraq since 1958, from Revolution to Dictatorship*, p. 265
4. Christine Moss Helms, *Iraq: Eastern Flank of the Arab World*, p. 183
5. Amatzia Baram and Barry Rubin, *Iraq's Road to War*, p. 125
6. Efraim Karsh and Inari Rautsi, *Saddam Hussein, a Political Biography*, p. 81
7. Bruce W. Jentleson, *With Friends Like these, Reagan, Bush and Saddam*, p. 48
8. Sa'ad Bazzaz, *The Gulf War and the One After*, addendum in my possession
9. Slugletts, p. 261
10. Kenneth R. Timmermann, *The Death Lobby, How the West Armed Iraq*, p. 290
11. Baram and Rubin, p. 109
12. Wafic Samarai, *The Destruction of the Eastern Gate*, p. 153
13. Middle East Watch, *International Report on Human Rights in Iraq*, p. 33
14. Mark Phythian, *Arming Iraq*, pp. 25–6
15. Samarai, *Destruction*, p. 153
16. Interview on non-attribution basis with a former Iraqi general, August 1998
17. Wafic Samarai, *The Road to Hell, Truths about Bad Times in Iraq*, p. 107
18. Samarai, *Hell*, p. 112
19. Samarai, *Hell*, p. 136
20. Malik Mufti, *Sovereign Creations*, p. 194
21. Faleh Abdel Jabbar, *Iraq, the State, Civil Society and Democratic Development*, p. 72

22. Samarai, *Destruction*, p. 134
23. Interviews, Ahmad Allawi, London, summer 1998
24. Samarai, *Destruction*, p. 34
25. Interview, Dr Heidar Abbas, London, August 1998
26. Samarai, *Destruction*, p. 48
27. Interview, Ghanim Jawad (Abul Huda), London, July 1998. A former member of the Iraq Communist Party, he has compiled a staggering record of Saddam's security and torture methods
28. Jawad
29. Conversation with Sa'ad Bazzaz, 1994. He was head of the Establishment of Television and Cinema and very close to the Tikriti regime
30. Interview, Ahmad Allawi, London, summer 1998. As a former classmate of both boys, Allawi stayed in touch with this situation
31. Hassan Alawi. *The Borrowed State*, p. 106
32. Interview, Hassan Omar Al Ali, London, September 1998
33. Several sources, all on non-attribution basis.
34. Karsh and Rautsi, p. 182
35. Samarai, *Destruction*, p. 198
36. Raghid Solh, *Britain's Two Wars with Iraq*, p. 312
37. David McDowall, *A Modern History of the Kurds*, p. 350
38. David McDowall, *The Kurds, A Nation Denied*, p. 105
39. McDowall, *Kurds*, p. 114
40. McDowall, *Modern History*, p. 352
41. Phythian, p. 74
42. Private source; Alan Friedman, *Spider's Web. Bush, Saddam, Thatcher and the Decade of Deceit*, p. 131
43. Jentleson, pp. 62–3
44. Pythian, p. 44; Timmermann, pp. 117–220, 312–70, 420–50
45. Phythian, p. 79
46. Timmermann, p. 378
47. Timmermann, p. 141; Phythian, p. 197
48. Conversation with John K. Cooley, who witnessed this while representing the correspondents' pool, London, 1994
49. Ritchie Ovendale, *The Middle East since 1914*, p. 147
50. Samarai, *Destruction*, p. 42
51. Bazzaz, *The Gulf War and the One After*, notes.
52. Jentleson, p. 58
53. Jentleson, p. 59; Geoff Simons, *Iraq from Sumer to Saddam*, p. 322
54. Rajaee (ed.), p. 107
55. Ghazi Al Ghosaibi, *The Gulf War*, p. 10
56. David W. Lesch (ed.), *The Middle East and the United States, a Historical and Political Reassessment*, p. 327
57. Friedman, p. 42
58. Lesch (ed.), p. 341
59. Karsh and Rautsi, p. 122; *The Iraqi File*, 17 May 1993; conversations with John Cooley, London, 1994
60. McDowall, *Kurds*, p. 108
61. McDowall, *Modern History*, p. 360
62. Saïd K. Aburish, *A Brutal Friendship, the West and the Arab Elite*, pp. 106–7

63. Karsh and Rautsi, p. 90
64. John Pilger, *Hidden Agendas*, p. 126
65. Interview, Gwynn Roberts, London, 1996
66. Abbas Nazrawi, *The Iraqi Economy*, p. 123

CHAPTER 10: THE FRIEND–FOE GAME

1. Mohammed Heikal, *Illusions of Triumph*, p. 81
2. Raghid Solh, *Britain's Two Wars with Iraq*, p. 11
3. Andrew Gowers and Tony Walker, *Behind the Myth. Yasser Arafat and the Palestinian Revolution*, p. 419
4. Yezid Sayyigh, *Armed Struggle and the Search for State*, p. 40
5. Sayyigh, p. 640
6. Dilip Hiro, *From Desert Shield to Desert Storm*, p. 56
7. Geoff Simons, *Iraq from Sumer to Saddam*, p. 335
8. Hiro, p. 55
9. Simons, p. 334
10. Abbas Nazrawi, *The Iraqi Economy*, p. 133
11. Nasrawi, p. 145
12. Nasrawi, p. 127
13. Pierre Salinger and Eric Laurent, *The Gulf War Dossier*, p. 8
14. Darieh Al Awni, *Arabs and Kurds, Conflict or Amity*, p. 107
15. Kanan Makiya, *Republic of Fear*, p. 317
16. James A. Bill and Robert Spongborg, *Politics in the Middle East*, p. 43
17. Hiro, p. 62; John Bullock and Harvey Morris, *Saddam's War*, p. 87
18. Interview, Ahmad Allawi, London, August 1998
19. Nazrawi, pp. 146 and 127
20. Sayyigh, p. 221
21. *Secrets of Iraqi Armament since 1968*, p. 68 (the book was written by a group of Iraqi writers who chose to remain anonymous)
22. Interview, Dr Ahmad Chalabi, London, September 1998.
23. Kenneth R. Timmermann, *The Death Lobby, How the West Armed Iraq*, p. 437; Bulloch and Morris, p. 47
24. Interview, Hassan Omar Al Ali, London, August 1998
25. Nazrawi, p. 147
26. Nazrawi, p. 147
27. Kanan Makiya, *Cruelty and Silence*, pp. 208–9
28. Interview, Faleh Abdel Jabbar, London, August 1998
29. Ahmad Allawi
30. Makiya, *Cruelty*, p. 268
31. Efraim Karsh and Inari Rautsi, *Saddam Hussein, a Political Biography*, p. 182
32. Off-the-record interview with a former Iraqi diplomat
33. Timmermann, p. 408
34. Salinger and Laurent, p. 11
35. Timmermann, p. 423
36. Sa'ad Bazzaz, *The Gulf War and the One After*, p. 137
37. Private CIA source
38. Bruce W. Jentleson, *With Friends Like these, Reagan, Bush and Saddam*, pp. 100–19

39. Heikal, p. 224
40. Alan Friedman, *Spider's Web. Bush, Saddam, Thatcher and the Decade of Deceit*, pp. 134–5
41. Heikal, p. 223
42. Off-the-record interview with a former Iraqi diplomat
43. Karsh and Rautsi, p. 207
44. Salinger and Laurent, p. 13
45. Off-the-record interview with a former Iraqi diplomat
46. Heikal, p. 171
47. Salinger and Laurent, pp. 13–15; Heikal, p. 156
48. Interview, Richard Murphy, New York, May 1998
49. Hiro cites Henderson, p. 67; Rupert Allason, *Sunday Times*, 16 March 1990
50. Conversation with Iraqi cultural attaché Nael Hassan, London, March 1990
51. Off-the-record interview with former Iraqi ambassador to a European country, London, September 1998
52. Amatzia Baram and Barry Rubin, *Iraq's Road to War*, pp. 12–13
53. Timmermann, p. 481
54. Milton Viorst, *Sandcastles, the Arabs in Search of the Modern World*, pp. 278–9
55. Saïd K. Aburish, *The Rise, Corruption and Coming Fall of the House of Saud*, p. 171, based on conversations with an Iraqi intelligence officer
56. Bazzaz, pp. 49–50
57. Salinger and Laurent, p. 48
58. Nazrawi, p. 153
59. Salinger and Laurent, p. 48
60. Baram and Rubin, p. 23
61. Ghazi Al Gosaibi, *The Gulf Crisis*, p. 24. The author confirms that Saddam made this statement without mentioning that it followed the restricted meeting
62. Baram and Rubin, p. 16
63. Baram and Rubin, p. 14
64. Hiro, p. 429
65. Aburish, p. 175; Viorst, p. 279
66. Viorst, pp. 176–7. The book presents a remarkable piece of investigative journalism on the subject
67. Bazzaz, pp. 65–8
68. Aburish, p. 174; Baram and Rubin, p. 17
69. Salinger and Laurent, p. 64
70. Salinger and Laurent, p. 66
71. Baram and Rubin, p. 20; Bulloch and Morris, p. 10
72. Salinger and Laurent, p. 98
73. John K. Cooley, *Payback: America's Long War in the Middle East*, p. 187
74. Hiro, p. 103
75. Heikal, pp. 246–7

CHAPTER 11: AN ABUNDANCE OF PRIDE, A SHORTAGE OF INTELLECT

1. Sa'ad Bazzaz, *The Ashes of War*, pp. 245–7
2. Pierre Salinger and Eric Laurent, *The Gulf War Dossier*, pp. 140–3; John K. Cooley, *Payback: America's Long War in the Middle East*, p. 195; Dilip Hiro, *From Desert Shield to Desert Storm*, p. 198

3. Victoria Brittain (ed.), *The Gulf Between Us*, p. 160
4. Salinger and Laurent, p. 155
5. Hiro, p. 117
6. Sa'ad Bazzaz, *The Gulf War and the One After*, p. 103; Saïd K. Aburish, *The Rise, Corruption and Coming Fall of the House of Saud*, p. 176; Mohammed Heikal, *Illusions of Triumph*, p. 264
7. Heikal, pp. 358–65
8. Brittain (ed.), p. 89; Heikal, p. 277
9. Hiro, p. 125; Heikal, p. 296
10. Aburish, p. 178
11. Heikal, p. 290
12. Phyllis Bennis and Michel Moushabeck, *Beyond the Storm*, p. 365
13. Salinger and Laurent, p. 205; Cooley, p. 201; Heikal, p. 290; off-the-record interview with an Egyptian diplomat, London, November 1998
14. Heikal, p. 321; Viorst in *Sandcastles*, p. 310, suggests that Bush's attitude towards Saddam led to the failure of the Arab efforts
15. John Bulloch and Harvey Morris, *Saddam's War*, p. 169
16. US News and World Report, *Triumph without Victory*, p. 181
17. Hiro, pp. 170, 259, 398, 414, 446; *Time* magazine, 20 August 1990; Geoff Simons, *Iraq from Sumer to Saddam*, p. 385
18. Salinger and Laurent, p. 246
19. *Triumph without Victory*, p. 94
20. Hiro, p. 312
21. Muhammad-Mahmoud Muhammadou, *Iraq, State Building and Regime Security, the Second Gulf War*, p. 146
22. *Sunday Times*, 3 February 1991
23. Bazzaz, *The Ashes of War*, p. 328
24. Muhammadou, p. 130
25. Hiro, p. 366
26. Muhammadou, p. 144
27. *Triumph without Victory*, p. 145 (this report reflected a CIA analysis of the situation which was dismissed by President Bush)
28. Abbas Nazrawi, *The Iraqi Economy*, p. 160; Simons, p. 11
29. Heikal, p. 13
30. Bob Woodward, *The Commanders*, p. 349
31. James Adams, *Trading in Death*, p. xiv
32. Simons, pp. 5, 12
33. Hiro, pp. 345, 353
34. Brittain (ed.), p. 53
35. Hiro, pp. 353, 319
36. Heikal, p. 400; Michael Parenti, *Against Empire*, p. 119
37. Bennis and Moushabeck, p. 372
38. Off-the-record interview with a former Iraqi Foreign Ministry official
39. Bazzaz, *The Gulf War*, pp. 433–4
40. Bennis and Moushabeck, p. 372
41. Bazzaz, *The Gulf War*, p. 444
42. Heikal, p. 7
43. Simons, pp. 10–11
44. After-the-fact report by Michael Evans, *The Times*, 23 March 1991

45. Hiro, pp. 387, 391
46. John Pilger, *New Statesman*, 8 March 1991
47. *Triumph without Victory*, p. 349
48. Ramsey Clark et al., *War Crimes, a Report on US War Crimes against Iraq*, p. 90
49. John Pilger, *Hidden Agendas*, pp. 49–50
50. Heikal, p. 404
51. Hiro, p. 361
52. Bennis and Moushabeck, p. 372
53. Dr Sahib Al Hakim, *Endless Torment, the 1991 Uprising and Aftermath*, p. 150
54. Brian MacArthur, *Dispatches from the Gulf War*, p. 361; Abdel Hussein Sha'aban, *Storm on the Land of the Sun*, p. 98; Heikal, p. 413
55. Pilger, p. 51
56. Fran Hezeltine, *Iraq since the Gulf War, the Prospects for Democracy*, p. 179
57. Najib Mustapha Mahdi Al Salhi, *The Earthquake, What Happened in Iraq after the Withdrawal from Kuwait*, p. 106
58. Kanan Makiya, *Cruelty and Silence*, p. 63
59. Walid Al Hilli, *Iraq, the Present and Prospects for the Future*, p. 187
60. Interview, Abu Tareq, London, August 1998
61. Hussein Al Shami, *The Iraq Crisis, the View from Within*, p. 98; Sha'aban, p. 155
62. Hakim, p. 159
63. Bennis and Moushabeck, p. 373
64. Al Shami, p. 97
65. Wafic Samarai, *The Destruction of the Eastern Gate*, p. 417
66. Interview, Dr Ahmad Chalabi, London, August 1998
67. Kanan Makiya, *Republic of Fear*, p. xx
68. Hakim, pp. 134, 200
69. Al Salhi, p. 148; Hiro, p. 402
70. Hezeltine, p. 190
71. Sha'aban, p. 99
72. Al Salhi, pp. 174, 369
73. Kanan Makiya, *Cruelty and Silence*, p. 79
74. Hiro, p. 404
75. Hezeltine, p. 135
76. Hakim, p. 217
77. Ritchie Ovendale, *The Middle East since 1914*, p. 161
78. Bennis and Moushabeck, p. 373

CHAPTER 12: PRINCIPALITY OF STONES

1. Off-the-record interview with a French government official of ambasadorial rank, Paris, June 1998
2. The chronological order of events is derived from valuable tables in Tim Trevan, *Saddam's Secrets, the Hunt for Iraqi's Hidden Weapons*; Phyllis Bennis and Michel Moushabeck, *Beyond the Storm*; Dilip Hiro, *From Desert Shield to Desert Storm*; and Ritchie Ovendale, *The Middle East since 1914*
3. Interview, Kurdish leader Dr Mahmoud Othman, August 1998
4. Interview, Iraqi academic Faleh Abdel Jabbar, September 1998
5. Private intelligence source

6. Interview on non-attribution basis with one of the public relations people there to promote the meeting for the world's press

7. Private intelligence source

8. Confirmed to me by Jabbar, London, December 1998

9. Interview, George Galloway, MP, January 1999. A radio interviewer told Galloway that he should not worry about the prospect of Iraq's dismemberment because Britain was capable of putting it together again

10. Interview, Tim Llewellyn, London, September 1998. Llewellyn spent a considerable amount of time researching this and interviewed many of the British companies which had been involved in it

11. Llewellyn, interview with Iraqi barrister Sabah Muhktar, also an authority on the subject, London, September 1998; interview, Michael Hamers of JMJ contractors

12. Geoff Simons, *The Scourging of Iraq*, p. 52

13. Maggie O'Kane, *Guardian*, 7 March 1998

14. Interview, Dr Heidar Abbas, London, October 1998

15. Robert B. Satloff, *The Politics of Change in the Middle East*, p. 35

16. Interview, Faleh Abdel Jabbar, London, November 1998

17. Najib Mustapha Mahdi Al Salhi, *The Earthquake, What Happened in Iraq after the Withdrawal from Kuwait*, p. 39

18. Private source: some of the Palestinians involved in this are known to me

19. Private source

20. Interview, Abul Huda (Ghanim Jawad), the eminent Iraqi opposition member, London, September 1998

21. John Simpson, *Observer*, 28 August 1991

22. Interview, Dr Hassan Omar Al Ali, London, September 1998

23. O'Kane, *Guardian*

24. The document was put together by the able Dr Sahib Al Hakim, who runs the Iraqi Human Rights Group which he personally sponsors (with difficulty)

25. Interview, Dr Ahmad Chalabi, London, September 1998

26. Interviews, Dr Latif Rashid and Dr Fuad Ma'asum, London, August and September 1998

27. Interview, Dr Amneh Murad, September 1994; interview, Dr Tareq Shafiq, September 1998

28. The *Independent*, 21 March 1991

29. Interview, Nuha Al Radi, London, September 1998

30. *New Yorker*, 1 November 1993

31. *New Yorker*, 1 November 1993

32. Simons, p. 52

33. Nuha Al Radi

34. Kanan Makiya, *Republic of Fear*, p. ix

35. Simons, p. 23

36. *Hansard*, 23 February 1993

37. Interview, Iraqi Ambassador to UNESCO, Dr Abdel Amir Anbari: Paris, June 1998

38. Simons, p. 54

39. Kenneth R. Timmermann, *Sunday Times*, 2 October 1994

40. Simons, p. 95

41. Wafic Samarai, *The Destruction of the Eastern Gate*, p. 449

42. Samarai, pp. 449–55, implicates the Americans. INC's Ahmad Allawi, himself

a brave participant in the fighting, says that the Americans were indeed informed but no help was expected and that Kurdish infighting doomed the campaign

43. Private source
44. Amatzia Baram, *Towards Crisis; Saddam Hussein's Strategy for Survival*, p. 9
45. Private Source
46. Baram, p. 13
47. Iraqi News Agency, 7 May 1996
48. Trevan, p. 411
49. This statement, which he uttered on several occasions, was confirmed by the *Sunday Times* of 25 January 1998, though he had said this before
50. Simons, p. 243
51. Simons, p. 81
52. Interview with a former French Foreign Minister who stated, 'What is happening is genocide, there is no other word for it', July 1998
53. Al Anbari
54. Abbas Nazrawi, *The Iraqi Economy*, p. 194
55. Abdul Hussein, Sha'aban, *Storm on the Land of the Sun*, p. 169

CHAPTER 13: NO EXIT?

1. *International Herald Tribune*, 28 January 1998
2. *Sunday Times*, 18 January 1998, claimed the Iraqis used anthrax and camel fox. The story was given to me by members of the Iraqi opposition before the *Sunday Times* received it. I refused to use it; there was no evidence to support the allegation
3. Andrew and Leslie Cockburn, *Out of the Ashes, the Resurrection of Saddam Hussein*, p. 274
4. Off-the-record interview with a member of the UN Secretariat, New York, April 1998
5. *Al Quds Al Arabi*, London, 4 August 1998
6. *Al Quds Al Arabi*, London, 29 September 1998
7. *International Herald Tribune*, 13 July 1998
8. *International Herald Tribune*, 20 October 1998
9. I interviewed seven of the people at the Washington meetings
10. *Al Quds Al Arabi*, 4 November 1998
11. *Al Quds Al Arabi*, 13 January 1999
12. *Al Quds Al Arabi*, 12 March 1999
13. *Al Quds Al Arabi*, 13 March 1999, published a statement to this effect by Saud Nasser Al Sabah of the Kuwaiti royal family
14. *Economist*, 2 January 1999
15. Saïd K. Aburish, *A Brutal Friendship, the West and the Arab Elite*, p. 54
16. Nazrawi, Abbas, *The Iraqi Economy*, p. 196
17. Three interviews with Dr Mahmoud Othman, June–November 1998
18. Cockburns, p. 226
19. Interview, Dr Latif Rashid of the PUK, London, September 1998
20. Lecture at Institute of International Affairs, Chatham House, London, December 1998
21. Cockburns, p. 32

22. Correspondence, March 1999
23. Interview, Richard Murphy, New York, June 1998
24. *International Herald Tribune*, 13 January 1999
25. *Al Quds Al Arabi*, 31 May 1998
26. Cockburns, p. 50
27. John Pilger, *Hidden Agendas*, p. 128
28. *International Herald Tribune*, 27 April 1998
29. Sa'ad Bazzaz, *The Ashes of War*, p. 271

Bibliography and Sources

Al Abbassi, Abdel Hamid, *Black Pages of Ba'athist Iraq*, London, 1988 (Arabic)

Abdel Jabbar, Faleh, *Iraq, the State, Civil Society and Democratic Development*, Cairo, 1995

Aburish, Saïd K., *A Brutal Friendship, the West and the Arab Elite*, London, 1977

Aburish, Saïd K., *Pay-Off: Wheeling and Dealing in the Arab World*, London, 1986

Aburish, Saïd K., *The Rise, Corruption and Coming Fall of the House of Saud*, London, 1994

Adams, James, *Trading in Death*, London, 1997

Ajami, Fouad, *The Arab Predicament*, Cambridge, 1992

Alawi, Hassan, *Walls of Mud*, London, 1993 (Arabic)

Alawi, Hassan, *The Borrowed State*, London, 1993 (Arabic)

Alawi, Hassan, *Iraqi Shias and the National State in Iraq*, London, 1990

Ali, Mohammed Kassem, *Iraq under Kassem*, Baghdad, 1967 (Arabic)

Al Anbari, Dr Abdel Amir, 'An Inquiry into the Problem of the Law of Petroleum Concession Agreement in the Middle East', unpublished Ph.D. thesis, Harvard University

Anon, *Secrets of Iraqi Armament since 1968*, London, 1993

Aref, Ismael, *Secrets of the 14 July Revolution and the Establishment of the Iraqi Republic*, London, 1986 (Arabic)

Al Attiyah, Dr Ghassan, *The Emergence of the Iraqi State, 1908–21*, London, 1988

Al Awni, Darieh, *Arabs and Kurds, Conflict or Amity*, Cairo, 1993 (Arabic)

Bainsman, Joel, *Crimes of a President*, New York, 1992

Barak, Dr Fadhil, *Mustapha Barzani, the Legend and the Truth*, Baghdad, 1989 (Arabic)

Baram, Amatzia, *Towards Crisis: Saddam Hussein's Strategy for Survival*, Washington Institute for Near East Policy, Washington DC, 1998

Baram, Amatzia and Barry Rubin, *Iraq's Road to War*, New York, 1993

Batatu, Hanna, *The Old Social Classes and the Revolutionary Movements of Iraq*, Princeton, 1978

Al Bayati, Dr Hamid, *The Coup of 8 February 1963 in Iraq*, London, 1966 (Arabic)

Bazzaz, Sa'ad, *The Gulf War and the One After*, Beirut, 1995 (Arabic)

Bazzaz, Sa'ad, *The Ashes of War*, Amman, 1995 (Arabic)

Bazzaz, Sa'ad, *The Kurds in the Iraqi Question*, Amman, 1996 (Arabic)

Be'er, Eliezer, *Arab Army Officers in Arab Politics and Society*, London, 1970

Bennis, Phyllis and Michel Moushabeck, *Beyond the Storm*, Edinburgh, 1992

Berberoglu, Berch, *Power and Stability in the Middle East*, London, 1989

Berger, Haim, *The Social Origins of the Middle East*, Boulder, Colorado, 1984

Bill, James A. and Robert Spongborg, *Politics in the Middle East*, London, 1994

Brittain, Victoria (ed.), *The Gulf Between Us*, London, 1991

Bulloch, John and Harvey Morris, *Saddam's War*, London, 1991

Bullock, Alan, *Hitler and Stalin, Parallel Lives*, London, 1991

Chomsky, Noam, *World Orders, Old and New*, London, 1994

Chomsky, Noam, *Power and Prospects*, London, 1996

Clark, Ramsay et al., *War Crimes, A Report on US War Crimes against Iraq*, Washington DC, 1992

Cleveland, William L., *The Making of an Arab Nationalist*, London, 1971

Cleveland, William L., *A History of the Modern Middle East*, Boulder, Colorado, 1994

Cockburn, Andrew and Leslie, *Dangerous Liaison, the Secret Story of US–Israeli Relations*, London, 1992

Cockburn, Andrew and Leslie, *Out of the Ashes, the Resurrection of Saddam Hussein*, New York, 1999

Cooley, John K., *Payback: America's Long War in the Middle East*, London, 1992

Corm, George, *Fragmentation of the Middle East*, London, 1992

Deagan, Heather, *The Middle East and Problems of Democracy*, London, 1983

Farraj, Dr Lutfi, *King Ghazi*, Baghdad, 1987

Fawzi, Ahmad, *The Life, Trial and Death of Abdel Salam Aref*, Baghdad, 1989 (Arabic)

Finer, S. E., *The Man on Horseback*, London, 1962

Firzli, Nicola et al., *The Iraq–Iran Conflict*, Paris, 1981

Fkaiki, Hani, *Dens of Defeat*, London, 1993 (Arabic)

Foster, Henry, *The Making of Modern Iraq*, London, 1936

Friedman, Alan, *Spider's Web. Bush, Saddam, Thatcher and the Decade of Deceit*, London, 1993

Gereges, Fawaz, *The Superpowers and the Middle East, 1955–1967*, New York, 1994

Goodwin, Jan, *The Price of Honour, Muslim Women Lift the Veil*, London, 1995

Al Gosaibi, Ghazi, *The Gulf Crisis*, London, 1993

Gowers, Andrew and Tony Walker, *Behind the Myth. Yasser Arafat and the Palestinian Revolution*, London, 1991

Al Hakim, Dr Sahib, *Human Rights in Iraq* (an extended version of the Middle East Watch Report with footnotes), London, 1992 (Arabic)

Hamdi, Dr Walid M. S., *The Nationalist Movement in Iraq, 1939–1941*, London, 1985

Hezeltine, Fran, *Iraq since the Gulf War, the Prospects for Democracy*, London, 1994

Heikal, Mohammed, *Illusions of Triumph*, London, 1996

Helms, Christine Moss, *Iraq: Eastern Flank of the Arab World*, London, 1984

Al Hilli, Walid, *Iraq, the Present and Prospects for the Future*, Beirut, 1992 (Arabic)

Hiro, Dilip, *Inside the Middle East*, London, 1982

Hiro, Dilip, *From Desert Shield to Desert Storm*, London, 1992

Hitti, Philip, *History of the Arabs*, London, 1956

Hopwood, Derek et al., *Iraq, Power and Society*, London, 1993

Hourani, Albert, *A History of the Arab People*, London, 1991

Hudson, Michael C., *Arab Politics and the Search for Legitimacy*, London, 1981

Hussein, Adil, *Iraq, the Eternal Fire, the Nationalization of Iraq, Oil in Perspective*, London, 1991 (Arabic)

Iskandar, Amir, *Saddam Hussein, the Fighter, the Thinker and the Man*, Paris, 1980

Ismael, Abdallah, *Iraq's Oil Negotiations, 1952–1968*, London, 1989 (Arabic)

Ja'afar, Asgar Ali Mohammed, *I Was Saddam's Prisoner*, London, 1984

Al Ja'afari, Mohammed Hamdi, *The End of Kasr Al Rihab*, Beirut, 1991 (Arabic)

Jentleson, Bruce W., *With Friends Like These, Reagan, Bush and Saddam*, New York, 1992

Kaplan, Robert, *The Arabists*, New York, 1993

Karsh, Efraim and Inari Rautsi, *Saddam Hussein, a Political Biography*, London, 1991

Katz, Samuel M., *Soldiers Spies*, San Fransisco, 1992

Kedouri, Elie, *The Politics of the Middle East*, Oxford, 1992

Kelidar, Abbas, *The Integration of Modern Iraq*, London 1979

Khaddouri, Majid, *Republican Iraq*, London, 1969

Khaddouri, Majid, *Independent Iraq*, Oxford, 1960

Kent, Marion, *Oil and Empire*, London, 1976

Khayssoun, Ali, *The Tanks of Ramadan*, London, 1988 (Arabic)

Kishtaimny, Khalid, *Social and Political Affairs in Iraq*, London, 1989 (Arabic)

Lacqueur, Walter, *The Struggle for the Middle East*, London, 1969

Lacqueur, Walter, *Stalin, the Glasnost Revelations*, New York, 1990

Lesch, David W. (ed.), *The Middle East and the United States, a Historical and Political Reassessment*, Boulder, Colorado, 1986

Luciani, Giacomo, *The Oil Companies and the Arab World*, London, 1984

Lukitz, Liona, *Iraq, the Search for National Identity*, London, 1995

MacArthur, Brian, *Dispatches from the Gulf War*, London, 1991

McDowall, David, *The Kurds, A Nation Denied*, London, 1992

McDowall, David, *A Modern History of the Kurds*, London, 1997

Mackey, Sandra, *The Saudis*, New York, 1990

Makiya, Kanan, *Republic of Fear*, Berkeley, 1989

Makiya, Kanan, *Cruelty and Silence*, London, 1993

Ma'oz, Moshe, *Asad, Sphynx of Syria*, London, 1988

Mattar, Fuad, *Saddam Hussein, the Personal and Political Story*, Beirut, 1980

Matar, Selim, *The Wounded Self*, Beirut, 1997

Middle East Watch, *International Report on Human Rights in Iraq*, New York, 1991

Miller, Judith and Laurie Mylroie, *Saddam Hussein and the Crisis in the Gulf*, New York, 1990

Morris, James, *The Hashemite Kings*, London, 1959

Mua'la Abdel Amir, *The Long Days*, Baghdad, n.d. (Arabic)

Mufti, Malik, *Sovereign Creations*, Cornell, 1996

Mu'min, Ali, *Years of Amber, The Way of the Islamic Movement*, London, 1993

Muhammadou, Muhammad-Mamoud, *Iraq, the Second Gulf War, State Building and Regime Security*, London, 1998

Naffisi, Abdallah Fah, *The Role of the Shia in the Political Evolution of Iraq*, Beirut, 1973 (Arabic)

Nazrawi, Abbas, *The Iraqi Economy*, Beirut, 1995

Nunu, Mu'in, *The Ba'ath State and Islamization of Aflaq*, Cairo, 1994 (Arabic)

Ostrovsky, Victor and Claire Hoy, *By Way of Deception*, New York, 1992

Ovendale, Ritchie, *The Middle East since 1914*, London, 1998

Ozrie, Abdel Karim, *The Problem of Governance in Iraq*, London, 1991 (Arabic)

Parenti, Michael, *Against Empire*, San Francisco, 1995

Phythian, Mark, *Arming Iraq*, Boston, 1997

Pilger, John, *Hidden Agendas*, London, 1998

Pipes, Daniel, *The Long Shadow, Culture and Politics in the Middle East*, New York, 1989

Pipes, Daniel, *Greater Syria, the History of an Ambition*, London, 1990

Al Radi, Nuha, *Baghdad Diaries*, London, 1998

Radzinsky, Edward, *Stalin*, London, 1996

Rajaee, Farhang (ed.), *The Iran–Iraq War, the Politics of Aggression*, Florida, 1993

Randall, Jonathan C., *After Such Knowledge What Forgiveness?* New York, 1997

Richards, Alan and John Waterburg, *A Political Economy of the Middle East*, Boulder, Colorado, 1990

Rumeihi, Mohammed, *Beyond Oil*, London, 1983

Sadawski, Yahya, *Guns or Butter*, Washington DC, 1993

Al Said, Hassam, *Guards of the West, the Ba'ath and the International Game*, Beirut, 1992

Al Salhi, Najib, Mustapha Mahdi, *The Earthquake, What Happened in Iraq after the Withdrawal from Kuwait*, London, 1998 (Arabic)

Salinger, Pierre and Eric Laurent, *The Gulf War Dossier*, London 1992

Salman, Rala, *On the Way*, Beirut, 1992 (Arabic)

Samarai, Wafic, *The Destruction of the Eastern Gate*, Kuwait, 1997 (Arabic)

Samarai, Wafic, *The Road to Hell. Truths about Bad Times in Iraq*, Kuwait, 1999 (Arabic)

Satloff, Robert B., *The Politics of Change in the Middle East*, Boulder, Colorado, 1993

Sayyigh, Yezid, *Armed Struggle and the Seaerch for State*, Oxford, 1997

Seale, Patrick, *Abu Nidal, the World's Most Wanted Terrorist*, London, 1992

Searight, Sarah, *The British in the Middle East*, London, 1979

Sha'aban, Abdel Hussein, *The Ideological Struggle in International Relations*, Latakia, Syria, 1985

Sha'aban, Abdel Hussein, *Storm of the Land of the Sun*, London, 1994 (Arabic)

Al Shami, Hussein, *The Iraqi Crisis, the View from Within*

Shlaim, Avi, *War and Peace in the Middle East*, London, 1995

Simons, Geoff, *Iraq from Sumer to Saddam*, London, 1996

Simons, Geoff, *The Scourging of Iraq*, London, 1998

Sluglett, Marion Farouk- and Peter, *Iraq since 1958, from Revolution to Dictatorship*, London, 1989

Solh, Raghid, *Britain's Two Wars with Iraq*, London, 1994 (Arabic)

Taylor, Philip M., *War and the Media*, Manchester, 1992

Tikriti, Barazan, *Assassination Attempts on President Saddam Hussein*, Baghdad, 1982

Timmermann, Kenneth R., *The Death Lobby, How the West Armed Iraq*, London, 1994

Trevan, Tim, *Saddam's Secrets, the Hunt for Iraqi Hidden Weapons*, London, 1999

Trevelyan, Humphrey, *The Middle East in Revolution*, London, 1970

US News and World Report, *Triumph without Victory*, New York, 1992

Viorst, Milton, *Sandcastles, the Arabs in Search of the Modern World*, London, 1994

Al Wardi, Dr Ali, *Social Aspects of Modern Iraqi Social History*, 5 vols, Baghdad, 1972 (Arabic)

Al Wardi, Dr Ali, *A Study in Iraqi Society*, Tehran, n.a.

Winstone, H. V. F., *Gertrude Bell*, London, 1978

Woodward, Bob, *The Commanders*, New York, 1991

Yahya, Latif, *I Was the President's Son*, Austria, 1994

Yeargin, Daniel, *The Prize*, London, 1991

Zubeidi, Dr Mohammed, *King Ghazi and His Aides*, Surbiton, Surrey, 1989

INTERVIEWS

Abbas, Dr Heidar: London, May and June–October 1998

Abdallah, Colonel Mohammed Radi: London, May 1998

Abdel Jabbar, Faleh: June 1998

Aburish, Abu Saïd: Seattle, November 1997

Abu Sherif, Bassam: London, September 1991

Abu Tareq (*nom de guerre* of former Iraqi army officer): London, August 1998

Akins, James A.: Washington DC, June 1994

Alawi, Abdel Amir: London, June 1994

Al Ali, Hassan Omar: London, July–November 1998

Ali, Sami Farraj: London, November 1998

Allawi, Ahmad: London, June–October 1998
Anbari, Dr Abdel Amir: Paris, May and June 1998
Attiyah, Dr Ghassan: London, July 1998
Attwan, Abdel Barry: London, June 1994 and August 1998
Al Ayyash, Ghazi, London, 1982
Barracks, James Russell: January 1959
Bazzaz, Sa'ad: on telephone, Amman, May 1994
Brelis, Dean: London, 1983
Caisseron, Jean-Claude: Paris, June 1998
Chalabi, Dr Ahmad: August 1995 and July–September 1998
Cheysson, Claude: Paris, June 1998
Critchfield, James: Washington DC, June 1994
Daghastani, Tamara: London, May and June 1994, June 1998
Douri, Abdel Sattar: June 1994
Al Falaki, Dia: London, August and September 1998
Farid, Abdel Majid: April and June 1998
Fawzi, Naji: London, October 1998
Firzli, Nicola: on telephone, Paris, August 1998
Firzli, Suleiman: London, May–July 1998
Fkaiki, Hani: London, June, August and October 1994 and 1995
Galloway, George, MP: London, July 1998
Gart, Murray: correspondence, July 1998
Al Hakim, Dr Sahib: London, July–October 1998
Hamers, Michael: on telephone and in correspondence, May–November
    1998
Hassan, Nael: London, March 1990
Jaber, Sa'ad Saleh: London, September and November 1998
Jawad, Ghanim (Abul Huda): London, June–September 1998
Karadaghi, Kamran: London, May and June–September 1998
Khoei, Sayyed Yusuf: London, June 1998
Kubbah, Dr Leith: London, September 1998
Llewellyn, Tim: London, July–September 1998
Mackey, Peg: London, September 1998
Mua'la, Dr Tahseen: London, June–September 1998
Ma'asum, Dr Fuad: London, September 1998
Mufti, Malik: correspondence, June 1994
Mukhtar, Sabah: London, June–September 1998
Murad, Dr Amneh: September 1994
Murphy, Richard: New York, April–June 1998
Mylroie, Laurie: Washington DC, June 1994
Othman, Dr Mahmoud: London, May–November 1998

Al Ozrie, Abdel Karim: June 1994
Pachachi, Dr Adnan: London, September and October 1998
Al Radi, Nuha: London, September 1998
Rashid, Dr Latif: London, July–September 1998
Roberts, Gwynn: London, 1996
Rouleau, Eric: Paris, June 1998
Samarai, Wafic: August 1998
Sha'aban, Dr Abdel Hussein: London, June and July 1998
Shafiq, Dr Tareq: London, August–October 1998
Sheikhally, Rifa'at: London, June 1998
Shukri, Dr Subhi: London, June 1998
Solh, Dr Raghid: London, June 1998
Styran, David: London, July 1998
Tawil, Anice: London, June and July 1998
Tel, Wasfi, Author's notebook, 1950
Wasfi, Dr Fawzi: London, October 1998

A number of people requested that their names be withheld. They include thirty-four Iraqis of various professions and political persuasions, a member of the Jordanian cabinet, three former CIA agents, a member of Yasser Arafat's staff, two Arab ambassadors in London, two British diplomats, two former members of the French cabinet and an official of the French Foreign Ministry.

PUBLICATIONS AND NEWS ORGANISATIONS

Al Quds Al Arabi, Baghdad television, BBC, CNN, *The Economist*, Energy Intelligence Group, *Guardian, Hansard, Independent, International Herald Tribune, Iraqi File*, Kurdish television, *Newsday, Newsweek, New Statesman, New Yorker, New York Times, Sourakia, Sunday Times, Time, The Times, Village Voice, Washington Post*

Index

A NOTE ON THE AUTHOR

Said K. Aburish was born in the biblical village of
Bethany near Jerusalem in 1935. He attended
university in the united States and subsequently became
a correspondent for Radio Free Europe and the *Daily
Mail*, and a consultant to two Arab governments.
He is now a journalist and author living in
London. His books include *Children of Bethany*; *The
Rise, Corruption and Coming Fall of the House
of Saud*; and *Arafat: From Defender to Dictator*.